MW01093436

# Approaches to Inclusive English Classrooms

MIX
Paper from
responsible sources
FSC
www.fsc.org
FSC® C014540

## PARENTS' AND TEACHERS' GUIDES

*Series Editor:* Colin Baker, *Bangor University, UK*

This series provides immediate advice and practical help on topics where parents and teachers frequently seek answers. Each book is written by one or more experts in a style that is highly readable, non-technical and comprehensive. No prior knowledge is assumed: a thorough understanding of a topic is promised after reading the appropriate book.

Full details of all the books in this series and of all our other publications can be found on http://www.multilingual-matters.com, or by writing to Multilingual Matters, St Nicholas House, 31-34 High Street, Bristol BS1 2AW, UK.

PARENTS' AND TEACHERS' GUIDES: 21

# Approaches to Inclusive English Classrooms

## A Teacher's Handbook for Content-Based Instruction

Kate Mastruserio Reynolds

MULTILINGUAL MATTERS
Bristol • Buffalo • Toronto

**Library of Congress Cataloging in Publication Data**
A catalog record for this book is available from the Library of Congress.
Reynolds, Kate Mastruserio.
Approaches to Inclusive English Classroom: A Teacher's Handbook for Content-based Instruction/
Kate Mastruserio Reynolds.
Parents' and Teachers' Guides
Includes bibliographical references and index.
1. English language—Study and teaching—Foreign speakers. 2. Inclusive education. 3. Language
arts—Correlation with content subjects. 4. Interdisciplinary approach in education. I. Title.
PE1128.A2R47295 2015
428.0071–dc23 2014044417

**British Library Cataloguing in Publication Data**
A catalogue entry for this book is available from the British Library.

ISBN-13: 978-1-78309-333-5 (hbk)
ISBN-13: 978-1-78309-332-8 (pbk)

**Multilingual Matters**
UK: St Nicholas House, 31-34 High Street, Bristol BS1 2AW, UK.
USA: UTP, 2250 Military Road, Tonawanda, NY 14150, USA.
Canada: UTP, 5201 Dufferin Street, North York, Ontario M3H 5T8, Canada.

Website: www.multilingual-matters.com
Twitter: Multi_Ling_Mat
Facebook: https://www.facebook.com/multilingualmatters
Blog: www.channelviewpublications.wordpress.com

Copyright © 2015 Kate Mastruserio Reynolds.

All rights reserved. No part of this work may be reproduced in any form or by any means without
permission in writing from the publisher.

The policy of Multilingual Matters/Channel View Publications is to use papers that are natural,
renewable and recyclable products, made from wood grown in sustainable forests. In the manufacturing
process of our books, and to further support our policy, preference is given to printers that have FSC
and PEFC Chain of Custody certification. The FSC and/or PEFC logos will appear on those books
where full certification has been granted to the printer concerned.

Typeset by Deanta Global Publishing Services Limited.
Printed and bound in Great Britain by Short Run Press Ltd.

*To Maddy,*
*Mighty girls can achieve anything they set their minds to...*

# Contents

# Acknowledgements

This book endeavour, creative, constructive and circuitous, would never have been accomplished without the at-home support, flexibility and space provided by Madeline Ryan Reynolds, Tym Hanson, Brandon Casey, Fadi Suleiman, Neal Sipress, Gina Erickson, Kara Shore, Melinda Daubitz, Patrick Reynolds and countless others. On the school front, I am grateful to Qatar University and the Foundation Programmes, and the University of Wisconsin–Eau Claire for the academic freedom, resourceful librarians and scheduling flexibility. I owe profound gratitude to Kate Nolin-Smith and Aram de Koven, who developed the glossary, edited the references and commented on initial chapters, respectively. Thank you to all my colleagues, whose work I shared in this tome; I am fortunate to stand on the shoulders of giants. Finally, I am indebted to Tommi Grover and Eli Hinkel, who took a chance on one of the new kids in TESOL town.

# Introduction

| **Chapter Aims and Topics** |
| --- |
| • Introduce the goals of this textbook. |
| • Convey the textbook's audiences. |
| • Provide an overview of the textbook. |

There is an art and science to teaching (Marzano, 2007). It is not a simple set of steps one takes without thought nor is there only one way to teach. No robot can replace a teacher. To oversimplify the complexities of teaching, particularly teaching English to speakers of other languages, is a disservice to all the language learners and to the excellent teachers who give so much to their students daily. Likewise, to reduce the myriad influences, pressures and constraints in any given K-16 educational environment reveals a lack of insight, competence and compassion. When the instruction of various subjects, or content areas, is simultaneously taught along with the learners' second or other language as it is when English learners (ELs) are included into general education classes, educators must understand the complexities of the subject area, second language acquisition and language.

Compassion and fairness are the dual impetuses for this text. This text is for the language learners in K-12 public schools who are born in homes in Danbury, CT, where Albanian is the native and first language spoken, or in Minneapolis, MN, or Columbus, OH, where learners begin their lives speaking Somali. It is for the Karen people who arrive via planes fresh from the refugee camps of northern Thailand having fled their homes in Myanmar and who may be unfamiliar with schooling and running water. It is for the migrant farmers' Spanish- or Quechan-speaking children who have lived in countless locations in the US and Mexico following the harvest and finding themselves in yet another rural school.

This text is also for the K-12 ESL teachers in California, New York and Colorado who endeavour to teach everything the ELs need from study skills to addition, biology and Shakespeare. It is for the English as a second language (ESL) teachers who 'float' without a room from noisy school library to hallway to the back of a classroom or two or three schools in one day. This text is for those ESL teachers, like my dear friend Lynn Emmons, who advocated tirelessly without success for better programming and more time with language learners.

It is for pre-service teachers so that they have a research-based text that shows them what does and what does not work. It is my hope that this text will demonstrate for them that there is more than one way to include ELs into their courses; we should not replicate the same model or approach everywhere out of convenience or tradition.

This text is for ESL coordinators, like Kristen Gundry and Jane Rich, who work within the shifting sands of educational expectations with limited resources and intense demands, yet they still manage to teach colleagues and administrators about the nature of language acquisition/learning and the inclusion of ELs while also teaching their own students and frequently mentoring student teachers. It is for these coordinators so that they may improve the quality of service provided.

It is also for the general educators who strive to be excellent teachers for all learners. This text serves school and district administrators who, with good intent, simply want to know how to serve the language learners and format their programming, but have limited time to become specialists. I hope this text will assist in better-informed decisions.

Knowing which programme models and approaches for EL inclusion to utilise in a district or school is not easy. Dahlman and Hoffman (2009: 22) concur, '…making initial decisions about which ESL program model to adopt, or how to improve an existing program is a complex undertaking'. Furthermore, I recognise that programme models and approaches are never as clear-cut or perfect as they appear in teacher education textbooks. This text will nonetheless endeavour to describe and critique them in order to provide tools and information for all those currently working with ELs and for those who will do so in the future. For each model and approach to EL inclusion discussed herein, all the available research evidence will be provided to highlight the effectiveness of the programme for ELs' language acquisition and learning.

And finally, this text is for my teacher educator colleagues and friends who have spent so much energy raising awareness of ELs' linguistic and academic needs and rights and have prepared thousands of general educators to include ELs. Li and Protacio (2010: 355) stated, 'Though sufficient attention has been drawn to ELLs' achievement crisis, little guidance or effort in research has been offered to address effective professional development practices to help teachers meet the varied and challenging academic, cultural and linguistic needs of ELLs…'. I hope this text will further our teacher education dialogues and enable us to make headway in the universal recognition of the need for general educator preparation for EL inclusion in the K-12.

This text is not exclusively for an educational audience in the United States. As English for academic purposes and content-based instruction make further inroads into contexts that have been previously more language-oriented in instruction, this text may provide a basis for creating programmes based on the particular needs of the local environment. It will also allow educators in other world English contexts, such as Australia, to compare models and approaches and share results.

This book will share with teacher educators, public school administrators, politicians and other stakeholders the various models and approaches for preparing mainstream teachers (i.e. general educators) to include ELLs in their content classrooms. This text is divided into two sections. The first section provides an overview and arguments for and against content and language integration and the inclusion of ELs into general education classrooms. Chapter 1 will outline the brief history of training efforts for mainstream teachers in ELL inclusion, describe the benefits, drawbacks and challenges of EL inclusion, and provide a rationale for the importance for mainstream teachers to meet the needs of ELLs in their classrooms (i.e. No Child Left Behind Act [NCLB], increased immigration/changing public school demographics, as well as enhancing their skills in differentiation of instruction and diversifying their classrooms). Chapter 2 will provide a foundation for general educators to understand how language is the medium for all content knowledge. Chapter 3 will describe a framework based on research-aligned teacher education standards, such as teaching English to speakers of other languages (TESOL) International, the National Council of Accreditation of Teacher Education/Council for the Accreditation of Teacher Preparation (NCATE/CAEP) and state standards. The framework presented to analyse approaches and models of content-based instruction for EL inclusion will serve as a basis for the evaluation through the remainder of the text in order to comparatively assess each model and approach.

Section 2 details several approaches and models to content-based instruction for EL inclusion taking a critical approach to each. These chapters will describe and evaluate EL inclusion teacher preparation models and approaches ranging from the name-branded models, TESOL-initiated research-based models, such as Sheltered Instruction Observation Protocol (SIOP) in Chapter 4 and Cognitive Academic Language Learning Approach (CALLA) in Chapter 5, to those initiated in other disciplines, such as Response to Intervention (RtI) in Chapter 6, and finally to those that were developed based on need, for various learner populations, with a specific focus, such as Specifically Designed Academic Instruction in English (SDAIE) in Chapter 7, the Center for Research in English Development and Education (CREDE) and Expediting Comprehension for ELLs (ExC-ELL) in Chapter 8 and Content-Based Language Learning through Technology (CoBaLLT) and Content and Language Integrated Learning (CLIL) in Chapter 9. The quality of each model and approach will be (1) weighed based on a research-supported evaluative framework designed for this text and (2) described with its strengths and weaknesses outlined. Additionally, explanations will be provided of how to implement the model accompanied by the key principles that the model brings to the field. The evaluation will be further evidenced by scholarly research on the models focusing on learner outcomes (i.e. both the mainstream teachers' ability to enhance content-area instruction for ELLs and the ELLs performance resulting from the modified instruction), *if the research exists*. Suggestions for the implementation of the model or approach in general education contexts as well as additional resources will be provided for further investigation. The culminating chapter (Chapter 10) will comparatively evaluate each model, share information about implementation and the laws relevant to EL instruction.

It is my hope that this text will help illuminate the art and science of serving ELs' needs, show that we should not reduce these complexities to a series of band-aid solutions or formulaic steps in order to reach the general education audience, and guide districts and teacher educators to make more informed decisions on EL inclusion programming.

## Chapter Summary

- The goals of this text are to
  - support K-12 general education and ESL teachers;
  - share and critique models of teacher preparation to include ELs effectively into general education classes;
  - convey the complexity of the challenge facing ELs, teachers and educational systems;
  - describe and critique approaches to teacher education for EL inclusion.

- This textbook's audiences are K-12 general education and ESL teachers, pre-service teacher education students, teacher educators, school district administrators, instructional coaches and professional development experts.

# Section 1

# Orientations to English Language Inclusion

In this section, educators will find a balanced analysis of the pros and cons of inclusive schooling of English learners. Readers will investigate the history of inclusive education, the rationale for why inclusive schooling is beneficial for English learners and their native English-speaking peers as well as a thoughtful description of the challenges of creating a productive inclusive environment for English learners. This section also includes a discussion of the role of language in teaching, introducing an alternative perspective on the importance of language in general education classes. Finally, this section introduces a framework of the knowledge, skills and dispositions (i.e. attitudes or orientations) that general educators need in order to be effective in English learner (EL) inclusion.

# 1 Why Must I Do This? The Drawbacks, Benefits and Challenges with EL Inclusion and the Impetus for General Educator Preparation in EL Inclusion

| Chapter Aims and Topics |
| --- |
| • Discuss the history and rationale for English learner (EL) inclusion and general educator preparation. |
| • Describe EL inclusion. |
| • Detail the benefits of EL inclusion. |
| • Reveal the impact of changes to demographics and the educational landscape on teachers' instruction and preparation. |
| • Depict the current preparation of general educators to include ELs into their courses. |
| • Deliberate the rationale for the inclusion of ELs into general education courses. |
| • Highlight educators' concerns regarding EL inclusion. |
| • Delineate the challenges to teacher preparation for EL inclusion. |

## History and Rationale for General Educator Preparation in EL Inclusion

Efforts to provide children with the least restrictive learning environment have been labelled the 'inclusion movement' and are realised by including all learners into the general education classroom despite their unique needs (e.g. special needs or English language learner [ELL]). The inclusion movement is an outgrowth of the civil rights movement of social equity and desegregation, making all public school classrooms accessible to minority populations of individuals of colour, individuals with special needs (i.e. physical, emotional, behavioural and cognitive differences) and individuals from linguistically diverse home environments. Most people think of the 1960s as the peak of civil rights work and influential educational law suits, such as *Lau vs. Nichols* (1974) in the US, but such laws did not come into effect until the 1970s. A sea change occurred during that time to permanently alter the educational landscape and laws were implemented to address issues of equality based on race, gender, class and ablism

(Education for All Handicapped Children Act, 1975; Individuals with Disabilities Education Act, 1997; the Lau Remedies, 1975; the Equal Opportunities Act, 1974) (Platt *et al.*, 2003). Advances in EL inclusion accompanied the inclusion movement of learners with special needs (Westby *et al.*, 1994). According to Reeves (2006: 132), the inclusion movement and 'universal access' gained popular acceptance also due to the standards and accountability movements of the 1990s. Philosophically, then, equal access for all learners by providing the least restrictive academic environment possible became the norm.

The resulting open access differentiates the US public school policy, and several other Western countries' school policy, from public schools in many other countries of the world. In many countries, such as Peru and Ukraine, students who do not speak the majority language are frequently excluded from educational opportunities or they must learn the language of instruction independently prior to accessing the educational system. Imagine if you and your family were sent to work in Peru, but your children were not allowed to attend school since they did not speak Spanish at all or not enough to participate actively in schooling.

> Consider these statistics and consider how these laws in combination with changing American demographics have impacted the K-12 schools today.
>
> - In 2004, 62.9% of all K-12 schools in the US had ELs (National Center for Education Statistics [NCES], 2002).
> - 'In 2007, an estimated 11 million elementary and secondary students, or 21 percent of all such students, spoke a language other than English at home' (Aud *et al.*, 2010).
> - For the 2007–2008 academic year, the number of children enrolled in K-12 increased by 8.5% overall while the number of ELs increased by 53% (National Clearinghouse for English Language Acquisition [NCELA], 2010).
> - The trend of increased EL enrolments in schools has been sustained over the last two decades; likewise, projections have indicated that this trend will continue into the next several decades (Fry, 2008), changing the demographic 'face' of our public schools.
> - The NCELA 2008–2009 data reported that approximately 5,346,673 ELs enrolled in grades pre-k to 12 in the US (NCELA, retrieved 18 June 2012).

The US has experienced dramatically increased enrolments of ELs in the last 20 years. Along with these increased enrolments, there has been a shift in the location and diversity of EL enrolments. No longer are ELs and their families living only on the coasts and in the south-west or Florida (NCELA, 2010). Ramirez (2007: 47) noted, 'Most of them [ELs] are in border states in the Southwest, but the fastest growth recently has been in the Carolinas, Kentucky, Indiana, and Tennessee. They are seeking more opportunities (i.e., pull-factors, such as jobs, affordable housing, and community attitudes) and migrating into areas that have not seen much in the way of immigration for decades. Furthermore, in Fairfax County, Virginia, public "schools serve 21,000 students who speak more than 140 languages"'. When working with current populations of ELs, teachers must be mindful of the diversity of home languages and cultures. For example, many educators think that EL educators work with Spanish speakers from Mexico. In reality, ELs come from all over Latin America, Asia, the Middle East and Eastern Europe. There is even more complexity in these descriptions too. For example, the 'Mexican' child may have been born in the US and might not be highly proficient in Spanish or his/her native Quechan. It is important that teachers working with ELs have positive attitudes and dispositions about working with learners from the world over.

Various educational systems, teachers, aids, reading specialists and administrators are being asked to include more diverse learners in areas where the systems are new to these changes. In differing states, political debates continually make headlines over immigration policy or access to public schools based on residency status. With all these changes, educators are expected to stretch their skills and dispositions in new directions.

## What does EL Inclusion Look Like?

There are several realisations of inclusive classrooms, including 'full inclusion' in which the language learner is present in the general education class for the entire day with or without the assistance of a trained general educator, English as a second language (ESL) educator or paraprofessional (Harper & de Jong, 2004; Turnbull *et al.*, 1995). When the learner is placed in a general education class with no support either in the class from an ESL-trained general educator or ESL/bilingual support staff or from pull-out tutorials, the realisation is called 'sink or swim'. ELs without any language clarity or language learning assistance will tune out, shut down and fail or they will seek to overcome the language barrier and thrive.

Imagine coming to a new country with your family. Everything is new, exciting and scary. You go to school and are placed in a classroom with children who do not speak your language. Your teacher cannot even communicate with you. In class, the teacher explains things, but you do not understand a word. You are given a paper to work on, but you cannot figure out what to do with it and you do not have the words or concepts to complete the assignment. What would you do in this environment day after day?

When an EL is fully included into the general education class with support for the majority of the day, it is considered full inclusion (aka push-in). In a general education class of this type, the general educator may be the sole teacher, might co-teach with an ESL teacher or have the support of an ESL teacher or bilingual education assistant. In the co-teaching situation, both the general educator and the ESL teacher might collaboratively plan with each one teaching a segment of the content or the ESL teacher might have no planning or instructional role other than support and clarification. Support in this instance might entail explaining the concept in easier language, defining, giving examples and teaching enabling concepts or skills, among other supports.

In a full inclusion environment, the roles of the content teacher and support personnel are adjustable. Imagine a scenario in which the content expert and the language expert have the opportunity to plan their lessons with each facilitating part of the lesson to all the learners. Now, compare that to the scenario of the content expert solely planning and delivering content information. And finally, compare those two scenarios to one in which the content expert plans and delivers the material without collaboration, but has the benefit of an ESL teacher or bilingual aide to help explain, clarify and/ or elaborate for the ELs during the lesson.

Another realisation is 'partial inclusion' in which the learner is placed into the general education class for part of the day and withdrawn during a class or two. Learners can be pulled out for one-on-one work with an ESL teacher or for an ESL-specific lesson with a small group. During these individual pull-out sessions, ELs are supposed to be taught language and subject matter concepts. However, one-on-one sessions often turn into tutoring, because the learner(s) are behind in their academic work. In individual pull-out sessions, ESL teachers try to provide the concepts and skills that the learners need in order to be successful when they return to the general education class. For example, the learner might be learning how to write simple declarative sentences in the present tense or to read and understand a history textbook description by identifying key adjectives and using word attack strategies to figure out the new words.

When there are several or many ELs who are at the same grade level and who need similar second language concepts, they are often removed from the general education class and grouped together for formal instruction. This realisation of a pull-out session is a sheltered content class with all the ELs learning the same content topic for a course period (Reeves, 2006). For example, all fifth-grade ELs might be scheduled to attend one class of history that has been modified to teach them the history and the language in a more approachable way.

Another approach to providing ELs with the language support they need is programmes in which they spend no time or limited time in the general education course. ELs might have similar schedules to their native-speaking peers, but in classes of only ELs. The standards and the content are roughly the same, but ELs would be taught language-specific information along with the academic content. In these programmes, it is considered good practice to integrate ELs into the specialty courses (e.g. art, music and physical education) with their peers in order to decrease the social marginalisation of ELs, facilitate friendships and language with native-speaking peers and bolster the self-esteem of ELs. Stand-alone, sheltered content classes (Echevarria & Graves, 2011) are not typically considered inclusive if the focus is on core content subjects, such as math, science, social studies/history or English language arts/literature, because they exclusively serve ELLs. These classes provide a 'shelter' from the general education classes by specifically adapting language and content instruction for ELs. Sheltered content classes are usual in areas with high numbers of language learners (i.e. high incidence areas. Unfortunately, providing a shelter also has negatives, such as social marginalisation and stigmatisation of those learning the language. Inclusion into the specialty courses does not always accomplish the aforementioned goals; oftentimes, there is no social bridge for the ELs in those environments. See Chapter 10 for more information on each programme design.

Although sheltered content classes have their merits, the drawbacks are equally as important. Proponents of inclusion (against sheltered content stand-alone classes) note the marginalisation and isolation of ELs from their grade-level peers and fret about the possible loss of academic content when language is a joint focus of the class time.

---

**Three Important Concepts in Second Language Acquisition**

**Comprehensible input:** All language that an ELL can hear, see and understand is *input*. But not all input is understandable; some information that we hear is not understood by us. *Comprehensible input*, then, is the incoming information to the language learner that is understood, because the incoming information has been modified to make it understandable. For example, a teacher could say, 'Measure the perimeter of the rhombus. Blacken the bubble on your scantron'. To an EL, this might be completely incomprehensible because it relies on understanding the command form (i.e. measure), the mathematic terms (i.e. perimeter and rhombus) and the academic assessment culture of using scantron forms for an answer key. A comprehensible way to explain the same concept would involve explaining what a scantron is and how to mark the answers on it while demonstrating with an example and using approachable language such as 'Find the correct measurement of the perimeter, the outside of the shape. The shape is a rhombus, like a rectangle. It has numbers on each side. Add up the sides to find the perimeter. Once you have the perimeter, find the correct answer in the choices (e.g. A, B, C or D). On the scantron, find the number of the problem, find the correct answer, then using your pencil shade or colour in the right circle/bubble'. Often, comprehensible input requires a lot more words, synonyms, examples and elaboration.

**Social language:** *Social language* is a description of language that is used daily in personal conversations to establish, develop and maintain relationships. Social language is the language used when two sisters talk on the phone catching up about their lives, when old friends meet after a long time or when a customer makes small talk with the grocery store clerk or the bank teller. Some examples of social language are, speaker one, 'Hey, it's been such a long time since I've seen you. How are you? What's been going on?' Speaker two, 'Oh my goodness! I can't believe it's you. I'm so glad we ran into each other. I'm fine. Good in fact. The family's growing. We have a new one on the way'.

**Academic language:** Academic language is the language of schooling and the typical jargon-laden language used in various subjects. Academic language is the terms and definitions typical of a subject area, such as rhombus, perimeter, proof and isosceles triangle. It is also the typical patterns of the language used often in the subject. For example, a proof is based on logical and if/then sentences. 'Statement: If $x \mid y=z$, then $x \mid y$ or $x \mid z$'. In history, patterns include basic descriptions of times and locations in the past, so they typically host past tense verbs, a rich array of descriptive adjectives as well as temporal-specific terms, such as feudal or serf.

A blend of social and academic language is employed throughout the course of a day at school depending on when, where and who is speaking for what purpose. If the purpose is to determine the cafeteria menu and the speakers are kids in the lunch line, then social language is being used. If the purpose is to convey how legends help us understand maps while in geography class and the speaker is the teacher, academic language will be employed.

## What Benefits does Inclusion Afford ELs?

ELs benefit in terms of academic and second language learning and socialisation when they are included effectively in the mainstream, general education classroom. First, if ELs are included successfully into the general education classroom, they have access to the grade-level content material provided by a content expert, the general education teacher (Fearon, 2008; Reeves, 2006). When the general education teacher is cognisant of creating rich linguistic and interactive experiences for the learners, they can provide a model for language use and an abundant source of comprehensible input in social and academic language (Cummins, 1979, 1980, 1992) and negotiated language with the learners.

Second, ELs are integrated into the classroom learning so they collaborate with grade-level peers (Chen, 2009; Duke & Mabbott, 2001; Nordmeyer, 2008; Nordmeyer & Barduhn, 2010). This collaboration can offer even more linguistic input in social and academic language (Cummins, 1979, 1980, 1992) and allow students to develop friendships. When collaborating on learning activities, all students would then encounter realistic diverse environments similar to what they will experience in their work and lives outside the classroom. The hope is that this interaction with peers will increase opportunities for cross-cultural understandings among students, develop social relationships and reduce the marginalisation of non-native English speakers.

Chamot (2009) shared three other benefits to ELs when they learn content and language simultaneously. She indicated that when learners study language through content topics and instruction, they acquire new content information that keeps them on track with grade-level expectations. Students are also learning academic language (Cummins, 1979, 1980, 1992) in context, so they can, '...practice the language functions and skills needed to understand discuss, and read and write about the concepts developed' (Cummins, 1979: 20). ELs tend to be more motivated to learn content as opposed to studying grammar and vocabulary in abstract and disconnected ways. They learn how the language is used in academic settings, so they are motivated to engage with the material.

Society benefits when ELs are properly served in our schools. Not only are we preparing all learners to participate in our diverse society as adults, we are overcoming fears and prejudices and creating a healthier society in the process (Hurtado, 2001; McClain, 2008). We are helping communities by educating bilingual learners to fill business, service and educational roles in our communities that help us maintain a national competitive edge. All societies need innovators and critical and creative thinkers to envision the next technological revolution, such as the internet. We do not know from where this new vision will come; when we reach out and invest in our diverse learners, we are expanding our future possibilities. If we exclude them, underserve them, we are short-circuiting the possibilities for future innovations.

We also empower learners to succeed in life so as to be productive members of our communities. ELs tend to be at higher risks of dropping out and/or performing poorly in school and on standardised tests than other students (August & Hakuta, 1997; Crawford, 2004; Gándara & Baca, 2008). Studies show that ELs drop out at dramatically higher rates than other groups due to overwhelming educational challenges such as literacy and interrupted schooling, and personal obstacles such as poverty (Bennici & Strang, 1995; Echevarria *et al.*, 2006; Fry, 2008; New York Immigration Coalition, 2008; Snow & Biancarosa, 2003). Echevarria *et al.* (2006) summarised research on dropout rates.

> A recent study of high school attrition in Texas (Johnson, 2004) showed that 49% of Hispanic students who were ninth graders in 2000–2001 left high school before graduation, compared with only 22% of White students. Another study of districts in the South showed similar discrepancies between Hispanic dropout rates and White dropout rates. (Wainer, 2004: 196)

Findings by the NCES (2004) indicated that language minority students (aka ELs) who spoke English with difficulty dropped out at a rate of 51% and ELs who 'spoke English' with some proficiency dropped out at a rate of 31% in comparison with those who spoke English as 'native speakers' who dropped out at a rate of 10%. In the NCES report for 2012, researchers found that Hispanics who were foreign born dropped out at 31% while the native-born Hispanics' dropout rate was 10%, which yielded an average of 16%.

To illustrate the achievement gap based on different literacy backgrounds, a child, Milagros, in elementary school who is learning to read in her second language without first language literacy (i.e. being able to read and/or write in her native language) is challenged to develop her second reading decoding, comprehension and inference abilities without the oral language background to assist in meaning making. A native English-speaking peer, Kara, who has years of oral language experience in her background can link the sounds, expressions and vocabulary to her reading attempts. At the dinner table, Kara has heard, 'Pass me the salt and pepper, please'. When she reads the word 'salt', the collocation 'and pepper' is one of the options that her schema accesses, so when she sees the words, she is not only prepared to read 'and pepper', but she already knows them as the items that people put on their food. In contrast, Milagros grapples with the phonemes of /salt/ individually decoding them, without the background knowledge of Kara. The sounds have no meaning without direct instruction; '*Salt* is a white crystal that we use to flavour our food and we need to live'. Sadly, many educators see second language learning and the inclusion of ELs into courses as a literacy issue similar to that of native-English speakers, but it clearly is not (August & Shanahan, 2006).

Now, consider Milagros and Kara after years of schooling. Milagros has not had the meaningful connections and direct instruction she has needed and has slipped incrementally behind Kara month after month. As the content material has increased in difficulty, so has Milagros' lack of comprehension and frustration. She would naturally become turned off school if she were spending endless hours in classes that moved on without her understanding. When she had the chance, she might decide that her family needs another income to help out. So why not babysit neighbourhood kids full time? She will make wages below the poverty level. She may work under the table, not paying taxes. She may not have a house, dental care or a retirement fund. Who knows what Milagros could have contributed intellectually to her community? Who knows what kinds of health needs she will have as she ages? How will she live later in life as a senior? Once she has her own family, what if she decides that she needs more money and seeks less savoury sources of income? When we effectively teach learners like Milagros, we include them into our communities and develop productive members.

The successful inclusion of ELs into the general education classroom when educators collaborate has also been shown to create learning environments conducive to success for all the students (Duke & Mabbott, 2001). One reason for this success is the enhanced and concerted co-planning of lessons (Brice *et al.*, 2006), which helps educators who have specific areas of expertise based on their teacher preparation that oftentimes exclude the knowledge of second language acquisition. Brice *et al.* (2006) state, '... students in ELL classrooms, speech and language or special education classrooms, and general education classrooms all benefit from more lesson planning and co-planning with other school professionals'. Another reason is the depth of content learning and time spent, as noted earlier. According to Simons (2008), 'Inclusion can ease the burden of lesson planning for the teachers. Sharing ideas with each other while creating content and language objectives and activities can solidify lessons (Coltrane, 2002)'.

## How are these Changes Affecting Teachers' Instruction and Preparation?

The shifts in cultural, social, political, economic and philosophical perspectives over the last 40 years have nearly cemented the practice of inclusion of ELs into the general education (aka mainstream or regular education) classroom (Harper *et al.*, 2007; Platt *et al.*, 2003).

Economic changes over the last decade and consistent decreases in educational funding on all levels, from the federal government to states and local districts (Arroyo, 2005), have rapidly increased the trend of inclusion. Nationwide, districts have been scrambling over drastically reduced funding (Evers, 2013), cutting corners, consolidating or eliminating programmes and laying off personnel (Christie, 2012; Owen, 2012; Shinonhara, 2012; Tagami, 2012).

Education policy changes started holding all school personnel accountable for second language learners' progress under the requirements of the No Child Left Behind Act (2001) (NCLB) for adequate yearly progress (AYP) in language and content.

> According to the NCLB,
>
> The purposes of this part are...to help ensure that children who are limited English proficient, including immigrant children and youth, attain *English proficiency*, develop high levels of academic attainment in English, and *meet the same challenging State academic content and student academic achievement standards as all children* are expected to meet (English Language Acquisition, Language Enhancement, and Academic Achievement Act, SEC. 3101). (Italics inserted)

Teachers not only need to teach their academic content and demonstrate progress, but also show notable progress on annual language proficiency assessments as well. And they need to do this in all four language skills (i.e. speaking, listening, reading and writing).

Under Title III of the ESEA, states are required to provide for an annual assessment of English language proficiency (ELP) in the *domains of reading, writing, listening, and speaking* for all Title III-served English Learners in grades K-12. (Edfacts/consolidated state performance, 2009–2010) (Italics inserted)

Due to these circumstances, educators feel that they cannot debate the inclusion of ELs, instead educators are striving to find the most effective programmatic formats and strategies possible to bring about second language acquisition and content learning simultaneously so as to meet AYP indicators expected of the No Child Left Behind Act (2001).

## How Are Teachers Prepared for EL Inclusion?

Many general educators seek guidance and affirmation that they are in fact doing what is best for ELs. They indicate that second language acquisition theory and principles and best practices for EL inclusion were not part of their teacher preparation and they do not feel comfortable with their knowledge base when working with ELs. In study after study, teachers have stressed their lack of preparation and comfort with EL inclusion. For example,

- 'Given the current demographic shifts in the U.S. population, it is likely that all teachers at some point in their careers will encounter students who do not yet have sufficient proficiency in English to fully access academic content in traditional classrooms. Many teachers do not have preparation to provide high-quality instruction to this population of students' (Ballantyne *et al.*, 2008).

- Batt (2008) indicated that 39% of teachers surveyed reported that 'not all' general educators working with ELs are qualified (in terms of any preparation) to do so; while 29% of teachers felt that one of their greatest challenges was their colleagues' lack of knowledge/skills to work productively with ELs.

These context changes and a plethora of research noting the majority of general educators' lack of training (Batt, 2008; Gándara & Baca, 2008; Gándara et al., 2005; Gutiérrez et al., 2000; Li & Protacio, 2010; National Center for Education Statistics, 2002) and feelings of unpreparedness for teaching ELs (Ballantyne et al., 2008; Migliacci & Verplaetse, 2008; Reeves, 2006; Verplaetse, 1998) caused educational entities, such as the US Department of Education's Office of English Language Acquisition (OELA), state educational agencies, educational support agencies, school districts and teacher preparation programmes to adopt a wide array of teacher preparation efforts. These efforts were funded partially based on need; districts with higher numbers of ELs received more funding and consequently more training in terms of expectations for performance and training frequency and duration. Therefore, many general educators in areas with fewer ELs still have not had the preparation to work with ELs. For more information on pre-service and in-service general education teacher preparation efforts, see Chapter 10.

## Why Prepare General Educators to Include ELs?

Teachers have tremendous pressures upon them to meet all their learners' unique needs. Their time and attention are being spread thin with constant ongoing formative assessment, modifications for diverse learners with a wide range of diagnosed and undiagnosed special needs, as well as learners who lack the basic foundations of food or shelter and those who need constant attention. In this context, we ask every teacher to teach writing and literacy to all our diverse learners.

Why would we ask them for another significant adaptation? It is because general educators have most language learners the majority of the day (Berube, 2000; Harper & de Jong, 2004). A March 2002 report from the American Association of Colleges of Teacher Education, Committee on Multicultural Education highlighted the issue of teacher preparation for EL inclusion.

Although most [culturally and linguistically diverse] CLD students spend the majority of their school day in grade-level classrooms, most teachers in these classrooms have little or no training in the differential learning and development needs of these students. Of the total number of public school teachers across the nation, only 12 percent of teachers who have CLD students in their classrooms have had eight or more hours of professional development specific to the needs of this student population (NCES, 2002). Consequently, few teachers are prepared to provide instruction specifically designed to meet the linguistic, cognitive, academic, and emotional development needs of these students. (American Association of Colleges of Teacher Education, 2002: 3)

Even schools with ESL staff place language learners with a higher level of language proficiency into the mainstream, or general education classes. *Mainstreaming* is a term used to describe the placement of language learners into the general education classroom, not an ESL classroom.

---

**Proficiency and proficiency levels:** *Proficiency* in another language is a person's ability to communicate a message. In the field of second language acquisition, the term *fluency* used to be employed to describe when a person could effectively communicate in another language. Over the years, through research and observation, professionals arrived at the understanding that learning another language is a long journey. This journey is a continuum from first language to second language through stages such as beginner, intermediate and advanced. This continuum is referred to as a second language learner's proficiency level, or ability, at a point on the journey.

Interestingly, experts understand that a language learner's journey to native speaker of another language is flawed. The destination is 'native speaker'. The reality is that the target of native speaker is an unrealistic destination. Even highly proficient second language speakers retain their native language accent, syntax, expressions and/or prosody even when they are extremely effective at communicating in their second language. For example, when one listens to Antonio Banderas speak English, his English language comes easily. He is able to express himself without hesitation or errors that could cause the listener to misunderstand. He is highly proficient and maintains some aspects of his native language in his accent and prosody (i.e. intonation, word and sentence stress and rhythm). Contemporary scholars do not promote the goal of 'native speaker' for second language learners; rather, they promote high levels of proficiency as the target.

*Proficiency level* can be measured on a scale. There are several proficiency scales known in the field. The first and most commonly employed was created by the American Council on the Teaching of Foreign Languages (ACTFL) and ranges from low to high using the terms *novice, beginner, intermediate, advanced* and *distinguished*. The ACTFL's scale also uses low, mid and high degrees within each level, so that a language learner's proficiency can be placed on the scale as low intermediate or advanced high. Recently, another scale has emerged from World Class Instructional Design (WIDA), which has become common throughout the US as more than 35 states use the WIDA proficiency scale, or indicators, and the WIDA model test to assess language learners' annual language learning to show AYP for NCLB reporting. The WIDA proficiency scale, which will be described more in Chapter 2, has seven proficiency levels from low at Level 1 to highly proficient at Level 6. Level 7 is a native speaker. (For more information about WIDA, see www.wida.us.)

---

In Wisconsin, the lowest proficiency levels (WIDA ones and twos) receive the most ESL support, while the intermediate levels (WIDA three) and up are mainstreamed. Some learners at the intermediate level may have some pull-out academic or language support, but that varies considerably by numbers and ESL teachers' caseloads. Smaller and/or rural school districts may have no licensed ESL staff, but a bilingual paraprofessional may follow the language learner into the mainstream class to provide linguistic support. Larger and/or more urban school districts are likely to have ESL staff and sheltered content or language classes for ELs with lower language proficiency.

Given that the ELs, even in excellent circumstances, are in the mainstream the majority of the day, is that enough time for language learning? Language learning is a long-term process. Cummins (1979, 1980a, 1980b, 1992) found that social language takes between 1 and 3 years to acquire if learners have access to ample interaction opportunities. Academic language takes between 5 and 7 years with effective instruction, but may take up to 10 years if the language learner has experienced limited or interrupted learning or is illiterate in his/her native language. This means that learners cannot acquire enough language in intensive, short duration programmes that they need for academic survival, let alone success. And that the general educator will bear part of the language acquisition responsibility along with the ESL staff and the learners themselves.

Traditionally, pre-service teacher preparation has focused on the acquisition of content information with few courses on methods of instruction, assessment or curriculum design (National Research Council, 2010). To illustrate this, consider the number of content courses required of teachers in comparison with methods courses in the data from Table 10.11. Teacher preparation programmes have traditionally not expected awareness of second language acquisition principles or language patterns.

Effectively including ELs into the general education class requires modifications to *all aspects* of instruction and assessment. Most critically, it requires teachers to change the ways that they speak and listen to students. In teacher-centred classrooms of the past, teachers presented new information and engaged students in the 'I-R-E' question/ answer sequence (Cazden, 1988, 2001). Using the IRE exchange sequence, the teacher initiated (I) a display question (i.e. a question for the student to display his/her knowledge) to gauge learners' comprehension, a student would respond (R) to the question and the teacher would evaluate (E) whether the response was correct or incorrect. For example,

**Teacher**:     Who can tell me what homophones are?
**One student**:   Homophones are two words that sound alike but have different meanings and spellings.
**Teacher**:     Good. Now, we are going to talk about groups of homophones.

This interactional sequence does not confirm the students' understanding, only that one can recite the definition. When this interaction sequence is the only discussion taking place in a teacher-centred environment, it is considered non-conducive to learning.

Cazden's (1988, 2001) research discussed the quality of the interaction when this IRE exchange sequence was the classroom standard. Cazden (2001) found this interaction to be superficial and unhelpful to the learning process. Currently, teachers are encouraged to engage in instructional conversation with their learners by generating questions that require thinking and 'fewer known-answer questions' to guide learn-ers to construct their own knowledge (Echevarria & Graves, 2011: 124). Instructional conversation allows learners to co-construct knowledge with their teachers and peers (Goldenberg, 1992–1993; Tharp & Gallimore, 1988; Vygotsky, 1978; Wertsch, 1991).

These are just a few differences in approaches to instruction that warrant the modi-fication of how teachers are oriented to and engage in teaching. If schools of education, districts and teacher educators do not change the ways in which teachers are prepared, they will be unable to include ELs effectively.

## General Educators' Concerns about Inclusion of ELs: Inclusion Drawbacks

General educators new to the inclusion of ELs and unfamiliar with ELs' unique needs tend to fear a 'dumbing down' (i.e. watering down) of the curriculum/content material (Adams & Jones, 2006; Wassell *et al.*, 2010) and/or a slowing down of content delivery/ instruction (O'Brien, 2009). The concerns are that ELs cannot learn content with 'lim-ited English' (Dove & Honingsfeld, 2010) or will require more attention, interaction and support so that the teacher will not be able to deliver lectures or content fast enough to keep pace with their department or district curriculum plans. This issue is one of cover-age versus depth of content. Good instruction of ELs does not connote a watering down of the objectives or content; rather, it means spending time on vocabulary and language comprehension then teaching in more depth with discovery learning and interaction. The instruction quite possibly proceeds a bit slower (O'Brien, 2009), but the learning is more connected and lasting. Discovery learning and interaction opportunities in the classroom *do* require more time. Teachers cited time as one of the greatest challenges to inclusion in Batt (2008) and Platt *et al.* (2003).

Time constraints are exacerbated by the pressures of testing and meeting the US Department of Education's and states' annual measurable achievement objectives (AMAOs) and AYP targets required by the No Child Left Behind Act (2001) (Callahan *et al.*, 2010). General educators tend to observe that when they change how they are organising and implementing learning and assessment that all learners, not just ELs, learn and demonstrate their learning better. However, traditional testing formats used in many standardised tests do not always measure the deeper learning in constructivist classrooms.

General educators fear also that 'regular' students will become bored by the slower progress through the curriculum (Batt, 2008; Menken, 2006; Stasz & Stecher, 2000; Valli & Buese, 2007). In actuality, native English-speaking students tend to learn the material better and in more depth when the curriculum is modified for ELs. The con-cerns about ELs slowing down the class and frustrating other learners have not emerged from the research literature, but collaboration and in-depth instruction have been shown to improve all learners' performances (McBride, 2007).

A legitimate concern shared by general educators and administrators is whether the EL is appropriately taught in general education classes. In Platt *et al.* (2003), the complexity of English language proficiency and academic background were concerns for general educators and administrators about the effectiveness of EL inclusion, because the knowledge of ESL specialists has traditionally fallen outside the general education teacher preparation and in-service professional developments. (For more information about the drawbacks of EL inclusion, see Simons [2008].)

In spite of knowledge about and beliefs in equal educational access, many educators believe that ELs should have native-like proficiency prior to inclusion in the general education classroom (Batt, 2008; Reeves, 2004; Simons, 2008). Ever present in reports from K-12 ESL colleagues is the sentiment they perceive from general educators, 'Send them [ELs] down the hall to the ESL teacher to fix them' [sic]. Reeves (2004) brought this perspective to life,

> ...the teachers saw that students [ELs] were eligible for equality of educational opportunity only after gaining full English proficiency. Despite their varying levels of comfort with this reality, all three teachers continued to instruct, assess, and grade ELLs in ways that assumed English proficiency to encourage English proficiency and, in turn, put ELLs on the English-only pathway to educational opportunity. (Reeves, 2004: 60)

If teachers do not modify their instruction from teacher-centred, lecture format to active and linguistically interactive hands-on learning, the situation is essentially one in which the learner is drowning in information that is presented too fast without modification and lacking in opportunities to negotiate meaning, in other words to figure out and make sense of new information through discussion (Echevarria & Graves, 2011; Echevarria *et al.*, 2004; Short, 1993, 1994, 2002; Short & Echevarria, 1999). Reeves (2006: 2) described the transmission model of instruction as 'an exclusionary learning climate for ELLs, particularly for those with low levels of English proficiency'.

Another drawback of EL inclusion results mainly from the general educators' dispositions and abilities. The inclusion scenario hinges on the degree to which general education teachers understand the learner's culture(s), language and other needs, how well they create a welcoming, inclusive and culturally pluralist environment, how they modify their planning, instruction, ways of speaking and listening, materials and assessments. A challenge for the unprepared general educator is that EL inclusion can be implemented unsuccessfully; they lack the knowledge and skills to create effective multicultural learning environments and differentiated instruction (Harper & Platt, 1998; Reeves, 2004).

Part of this problem is multifaceted. First, the general educators do not see the medium of the language used in instruction (Diaz-Rico & Weed, 2002; Gibbons, 2002). Second, they do not understand, value or relate to the learner's home culture. And often they teach too far above or below the learner's level of linguistic comprehension and/or academics. When these patterns exist, the situation is ineffective. Importantly, most of the onus for inclusion rests on the shoulders of general educators (but not all) and whether or not they feel that the EL belongs in their class (Walker *et al.*, 2004; Yoon, 2008).

If teachers do not work at integrating the EL into the classroom, the learners are frequently relegated to the periphery or are without a 'safe haven' (Nordmeyer, 2008; Nordmeyer & Barduhn, 2010; Platt *et al.*, 2003). Learners can be physically on the margins of classroom activity or grouped with other second language learners, special needs students or a paraprofessional.

> For example, an in-service general educator was studying to obtain her master's in teaching English to speakers of other languages (TESOL) through a grant in order to better include ELs in her classes. She was an excellent student, positively disposed towards ELs and motivated to change her practices. About two-thirds through the programme, the educator invited me in to observe her classes and give feedback on the effectiveness of her efforts. Her class was very good in the lesson preparation, delivery, materials and linguistic modifications, everything except one key variable. All the ELs were grouped at the far back of the classroom together and noticeably distant from their peers for the whole lesson. When I brought her attention to this small, but significant problem, she gasped in dismay. She saw it then for the first time and immediately corrected the situation. The little details of inclusion matter a great deal.

Peers may or may not reach out to non-native English speakers and the EL might be more isolated without those to whom he/she can relate. Barkley (2010: 25) explained that this sense of belonging is necessary for learners to feel comfortable engaging in the classroom. Harper and Platt (1998) bring to life the lack of belonging:

> Frequently these students [ELs] are intimated in mainstream classroom settings and are reluctant to draw attention to themselves. Teachers who are insensitive to their needs or who are unable to continuously monitor their comprehension due to large class size and other concerns may simply overlook them. (Harper & Platt, 1998: 31)

Finally, most educators, general and ESL, are not prepared to collaborate with paraprofessionals/translators, specialists and administrators (Batt, 2008). Models, such as pull-out, push-in or co-teaching in inclusion environments, take trust, organisation and time among other features (Theoharis & O'Toole, 2011); three commodities that are not always present. One key factor in inclusion is also the administration's support and understanding of the dynamics of successful EL inclusion (Batt, 2008; Theoharis & Theoharis, 2008). If an administrator understands the time constraints, scheduling, co-planning and assessment, the educators might be afforded the same hour for prep time daily at a minimum. According to Theoharis and Theoharis (2008: 231), 'Many administrators do not have sufficient knowledge of educational diversity (e.g., special education, ELL) and are not prepared to create and sustain inclusive service delivery systems'. Without the leadership and concerted effort on the part of the administration, teachers are not empowered to collaborate effectively.

## Challenges to Teacher Preparation for EL Inclusion

There are numerous systemic and dispositional obstacles to including ELs into general education classes; the most important obstacle is lack of teacher preparedness. Thirty-three states do not have a coursework, hours of training or licensure requirement for EL inclusion (Ballantyne *et al.*, 2008). This situation poses the first challenge. If states do not have some form of preparation requirement, pre- and in-service teachers are left to their own devices to gather this information. Without a requirement at the state level, teacher education programmes are loath to add more courses or to *infuse* EL inclusion preparation by modifying their existing preparation frameworks, because there are already complex requirements and expectations placed upon their preparation programmes (see Chapter 10). For example, most states require, as they should, pre-service teachers to take coursework in teaching learners with cognitive, behavioural and physical special needs. However, only a handful of states require training for EL inclusion or ESL instruction.

Second, many teacher education programmes require a high number of credits to earn a bachelor's degree so that teachers spend four or more years being trained in their primary content area (National Research Council, 2010). Consider the stresses placed upon teacher education programmes in the current economic climate in which stakeholders want all university students to graduate in four years. Thus, there is little instructional room or time in university teacher preparation programmes to include coursework on EL inclusion for pre-service general educators. Thus, programmes do not always include the competencies necessary for effective inclusion on their own volition.

Third, without preparation in pre-service teacher training programmes, school districts and state departments of public instruction must take on this role without the funding or leverage to ensure compliance or change of instructional practices at the local level. Districts must decide how to reach out to the general educators and engage them with EL inclusion preparation while balancing other professional development funding priorities, such as data analysis or technology training. Without specific federal or state funding for these initiatives, districts must make difficult choices. When districts see stark needs (e.g. markedly low standardised test scores or 'a failing school' status) or have designated funding, they are trying to connect with the target audience of general educators. A common issue seen by countless consultants and TESOL teacher educators hired as a consultant/presenter/trainer by a school district is when the district offers an optional workshop oriented to general educators on 'ESL students' only to have the ESL teachers and paraprofessionals attend. Often ESL teacher educators find themselves preaching to the choir. When the general education teachers are required to come, on the other hand, consultants/presenter/trainers encounter a different attitude altogether.

Fourth, many general educators simply do not view themselves as language teachers. Instead, they view themselves as content expert teachers (Elfers *et al.*, 2009). The literature describes this role and dispositional issue as one aspect of the 'buy-in' necessary on the part of teachers. Not having studied language, they do not know or understand the subject of teaching language, let alone the unique needs of the ELL in terms of second language acquisition (Adger *et al.*, 2002; Murray & Christian, 2011a, 2011b; Wong-Fillmore & Snow, 2002). They do not view themselves as language teachers, so they reject the content-based instruction (CBI), the integration of academic content information with language learning skills, information presented to them necessary for effective inclusion. Frequently, the general educators reduce the information down to 'just good teaching' (Adams & Jones, 2006; Nordmeyer, 2008; Reeves, 2006), because the techniques, materials, etc. *appear* similar (August & Shanahan, 2006). Or they will rebel with 'we just don't have the time for this'. These people typically reject and dismiss completely the new information out of hand.

Fifth, if there are no dispositional or orientation issues on the part of the general educator that predispose them against inclusion efforts or preparation, some still struggle with foundational teaching skills, such as lesson design or materials use, the presentation of new materials, not to mention the challenges of differentiated instruction for various language proficiency levels (Reynolds & Gable, 2007). Reynolds and Gable (2007) observed over 200 general educators teaching content to mixed classes of native and non-native English speakers in a high-incidence, southern urban instructional setting. In a small percentage of these observations, the teachers understood the principles and practices of CBI, wanted to be able to achieve the integration of content and language into the courses, saw the need for this with their ELs and the benefits for native English-speaking students, but failed to accomplish the objectives of CBI due to weak teaching skills, like classroom management and lesson planning. These findings were supported by those of August and Shanahan (2006).

In the Reynolds and Gable (2007) study, various interactive workshops were held to prepare the district's general educators; however, only a small percentage of the involved teachers understood the material presented and were able to effectively implement CBI in their classrooms. In one high school English class, the teacher taught a combination of literary analysis (e.g. symbols and symbolism in literature), the vocabulary, background information and the reading skills necessary to comprehend the texts. However, this situation was more an exception to the rule.

The vast majority of the teachers basically did not comprehend the linguistic and second language acquisition information or could not envision how to implement instructional modifications beneficial to ELs. So, they would seize upon and employ only one strategy, such as writing new vocabulary words on the board, and feel they were doing enough. Two differences exist between typical ESL and general education teachers. One difference is that ESL teachers must employ a high frequency of differing strategies (i.e. more than one strategy per class). The second difference is that ESL teachers utilise a wider variety of strategies (i.e. building background knowledge; pre-teaching key vocabulary; explicitly teaching vocabulary with visuals, gestures and demonstrations; and practicing the vocabulary in oral and written language in close-ended exercises, open-ended communicative activities and tasks) (Reynolds *et al.*, 2014).

Why do ESL teachers do this differently? Because they *have to* for meaning's sake. If they did not, they would have a group of ELs staring blankly at them and would be unable to accomplish even the most basic of objectives. Every novice ESL/English as a foreign language (EFL) teacher has had the experience of overestimating the comprehension or knowledge of his/her students, and the shock of being in front of a confused class without any way to proceed. This situation occurs because the teacher did not adequately analyse the enabling skills needed to comprehend the information or did not provide the variety of information and practice necessary for learners to scaffold the learning, make connections and construct meanings.

## Conclusion

The drawbacks, concerns, challenges and obstacles of inclusion are superseded by the real needs of ELs and the moral imperative (Adams & Jones, 2006) of effectively teaching them. With some effort and change on the part of teacher preparation entities, many of the existing challenges and obstacles can be overcome. The question remains, what is the best way to prepare general educators to create effective inclusive climates for their ELs?

| Chapter Summary |
| --- |
| • The inclusion movement has a long history tied to equity and access for all students. |
| • Demographic changes are sweeping the US, to which educators and systems must be responsive. |
| • Three types of EL inclusion models exist: full inclusion, partial inclusion and sheltered content. |
| • ELs benefit from inclusion through access to<br>  • academic subject matter from the academic specialist;<br>  • reduction of the achievement gap if coursework is modified to allow the development of their second language;<br>  • opportunities for socialisation with peers;<br>  • authentic academic language in context. |
| • Educational policies hold all K-12 educators, schools and districts responsible for the academic learning and language development of ELs. |
| • General educators feel underprepared to include ELs into their courses; in fact, most have not received any preparation. |
| • Concerns of general educators when including ELs are: 'watering down' of the curriculum, slowing down of the curriculum, time constraints, boredom of native speakers and whether the general education classroom is the proper environment for EL instruction in the first place. |

## Activities and Discussions

(1)  How do general educators and ESL teachers teach similarly and differently? Using the graphic organiser, compare and contrast practices. Hint: You might need to define and describe the environments first. Consider the material, the class arrangement, the regular classroom rituals and expectations, the roles and responsibilities of the teacher and learners, the class size, etc.

| Criteria | General Educators | ESL Educators |
|---|---|---|
| Subject matter | | |
| Class arrangement | | |
| Classroom rituals | | |
| Materials | | |
| Expectations | | |
| Roles (T & S) | | |
| Responsibilites (T & S) | | |
| Class size | | |

(2)  Debate the pros and cons of EL inclusion.

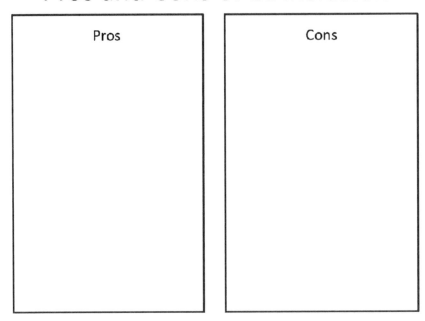

# Pros and Cons of EL inclusion

| Pros | Cons |
|---|---|
| | |

(3)  Interview a pre-service teacher and/or an in-service educator about his/her EL instructional preparation and inclusion. Use these questions as a guide:

- How were you prepared to work with ELs in your university teacher preparation programme (or other)?
- Have you received any school district professional development to work with ELs? If so, what topics and practices did it include? Were these topics and practices helpful or not? Why?
- Do you work with ELs? How many? What languages do they speak? Does their language ability in English pose any educational barriers? What do you see as their comprehension of the subject material in relation to their native-speaking peers? How do you differentiate instruction for them?

(4)  How would you go about creating an EL inclusive general education classroom? Where would you start? What would you modify to prepare for them? How has the information in this chapter changed your view of EL inclusion?

(5)  What does content and language integration look like? Take one subject matter topic and outline what language learners would need to understand and make sense of the material. What is different from the native-speaking student?

# 2 I Just Want to Teach Math! Language is a Foundation for all Content Areas

| **Chapter Aims and Topics** |
| --- |
| • Discuss the reasons for difficulties creating language objectives. |
| • Debate the importance of content knowledge and language. |
| • Illuminate the language structures in academic subjects and multiple discourses theory. |
| • Depict the current status of the teaching of language forms. |
| • Share ways of modifying speech. |
| • Describe how understanding linguistic systems helps general educators. |
| • Examine which language forms to teach and how to teach them. |

## Language is the Centre of All Learning

Language is an ever-present and reliable tool for the vast majority of us. So common is language that for many individuals, it is barely noticed. We DO notice it and in a big way when we lack communication abilities, such as when we are learning an additional language. I still recall with horror, when learning French, times that I had to stand up and give a presentation in the language. Never confident in public speaking, trying to pull it off in French was incredibly intimidating. Even when we have our talking points in hand and we have studied the topic and know it, our second language skills can still fail us. We can literally be without words. It is at those times when we realise that language is the centre of learning, because it is our means to communicate any idea or concept. It is at those times that we see the central role that language plays in all learning. Bunch (2013: 299) concurs, 'Language has long been understood to play a central role—perhaps *the* central role—in teaching and learning'.

General educators due to their teacher preparation and interests have not necessarily had this epiphany. Often in workshops for general educators on English learner (EL) inclusion, studies report, 'high school teachers who teach content area subjects are "resistant" to attending trainings because they think the trainings will not be helpful to them as they do not teach "language"' (Perez-Selles, 2011: 18). This perspective reveals blindness to their use of language in their classrooms.

# Creating Language Objectives for ELs

General educators need to write content and language objectives in order to effectively include ELs into their classes. Writing language objectives is a significant challenge for many general educators. The reason for the difficulty is that general educators do not consider language as an object of study and therefore cannot see the language of their discipline. One pre-service teacher who participated in an inclusion workshop explained it in these words, 'I learned the basic idea between thought and language. I never viewed language as a means of transferring ideas and information'. In other words, they see the language as a means of communication only, not an area of study. When all the students in a given classroom are native speakers, the means of communication is not a problematic language barrier. When some students in a general education class are non-natives, the manner in which the language is used becomes crucial. Although general educators employ the language as a medium through which to share the academic concepts, they do not see the patterns they typically employ to communicate. The language of their academic discipline is invisible to them.

The vast majority of general educators have no university requirements to take an additional language or to study linguistics. Pre-service teachers typically must take (1) general electives in humanities, math, natural and social sciences and English literature and composition (for native speakers of English); (2) major coursework in their chosen discipline to prepare them to teach; and (3) education courses, which tend to include foundations of education (i.e. history of education, philosophy of education, educational laws and policies and diversity training), instructional design and delivery, and assessment courses. Without a linguistics lens on the discourse patterns of the subject, they can only use the language.

# 'Content is King'?

Content is considered by many to be the most important element in general education teacher preparation. The reason for this belief is that the general educator, for good reason, should be knowledgeable at a high level of expertise in his/her domain. With the amount of knowledge available today and the need to demonstrate expertise not only in the classroom but also on standardised tests, pre-service teachers must undertake roughly 60 academic credits to learn the complexities of their domain. This emphasis on the content knowledge has traditionally left little curricular space for teacher education courses. Coupled with the lack of respect for the study of education and limited time to complete a four-year academic degree, the content knowledge has been advantaged over the study of how to teach and the language of the academic discipline.

The National Council for Accreditation of Teacher Education (NCATE)/Council of Accreditation of Education Programs (CAEP), the leading teacher education programme accreditation organisation in the US, has thorough standards for teacher education, which start with academic content and pedagogical content knowledge (http://www.ncate.org/Standards/NCATEUnitStandards/UnitStandardsinEffect2008/tabid/476/Default.aspx#stnd1). In the NCATE standards, the expectation that general educators understand the linguistic structures of their academic domain is not present. In this case, linguistic structures or patterns are the common or typical ways that speakers and writers convey information in their specific academic domain. As was mentioned in Chapter 1, historians employ descriptions in the past tense using richly descriptive adjectives to illuminate social stratification or living conditions, for example. Scientists utilise the present tense for descriptions of objects in nature and descriptive adjectives of size, colour, shape and texture.

# Invisible Language Structures of Disciplines

As a result of this preparation, when asked to design language objectives to include ELs into general education classes, teachers tend to seize upon the content vocabulary of the discipline. For instance, if an Earth Science class is studying plate tectonics, the typical content vocabulary, i.e. the words highlighted in the textbook, would include: fault, earthquake, volcano, vent, lithosphere, seafloor spreading, subduction, crust, plate, plate tectonics, strike-slip fault, seismology, seismologist, seismograph, Pangaea, focus, magna, outer core, seismic waves, mantle, etc. These words are the academic vocabulary of the discipline, and they would need to be taught to all the students; however, ELs would also need to understand all the other words and phrases in textbooks, handouts, teacher-made PowerPoint slides, videos and the teacher's oral explanations as well.

Consider the words outside of the academic vocabulary italicised in this passage on plate tectonics in this example:

The surface of the Earth is covered in water and land. The inner core of the Earth is intensely hot liquid rock that gives off heat and radiation. This layer is called the *asthenosphere*. The top layer of land, the *lithosphere*, is comprised of plates, called tectonic plates, which float on the surface of molten rock. The lithosphere is roughly 100 km (62 mi) thick. When there is a break between layers of the Earth's crust, the molten rock spews forth in the form of *lava* or *magma* from volcanoes. This process creates new land; for instance in Hawaii, where volcanoes continuously erupt with lava that cools into new land.

The *tectonic plates* that float on the lithosphere move slowly around the planet and collide with each other, like bumper cars. When the continents and plates move it is called *continental drift*. Together, the movement of these plates is called the *theory of plate tectonics*. It is hypothesized that these plates once were one large plate, called *Pangaea*, which split apart to make the 7 tectonic plates we have today. The seven plates are Antarctica, Australia, Eurasian, North America, Pacific (the Pacific Ocean area), and South America. There are also several minor plates: Arabian, Caribbean, Indian and Scotia plates.

The plates float on the surface of the Earth's crust and move slowly in different directions, like the cereal in the milk in your bowl. The plates run into each other, pull apart and rub against each other. For example, the Indian minor plate is slowly pushing north-east at 5 centimetres (2.0 in) per year against the Eurasian plate, which is forcing the Himalayan mountains skyward. The places where two places interact with each other are called, *plate boundaries*, and have different names depending on how they interact. When plates move apart, the area is called a *divergent zone*. When plates are moving together, they are called a *convergence zone*. When they are rubbing up against each other, they are called a *transformation zone*. Sometimes two plates run into each other and one plate is forced downward toward the Earth's center, it is called a *subduction zone*. When the plate is forced downward and gets closer to the Earth's molten core, it begins to melt. Depending on whether the plate slides against or is forced downward, a different effect occurs, either an earthquake or volcano respectively.

Aside from the italicised words, which may be explicitly taught, the other information in the passage could present comprehension challenges to ELs depending on their level of proficiency. In this passage, there is other content knowledge (e.g. the seven continents [FYI, some countries in South America teach that there are only six continents, so this could be cultural as well]), cultural knowledge (e.g. bumper cars) and metaphorical and simile information (e.g. 'the cereal in the milk in your bowl').

The patterns present include:
- Three possessive forms: 'theory of plate tectonics', Earth's and your.
- Verbs and tenses: present, present continuous, regular and irregular verbs, phrasal verbs.
- Sentence constructions: simple (subject, verb, object [SVO]) declarative sentences, compound object sentences, sentences with dependent, adverbial and relative clauses.
- Embedded definitions: 'The top layer of land, the *lithosphere*, is comprised of plates, called tectonic plates…'.
- Adjectives describing nouns and a series of adjectives: 'several minor *plates*'.
- Exemplification – providing an example.
- Adverbs of frequency (e.g. sometimes) and relation (e.g. depending on, in relationship to).
- Parallel constructions. (When all items are treated as the same number. For example, the sentence with plates, cars, they are all treated as plurals. We do not say plates, car_, they.)
- Pronouns: referential (e.g. it, they) and collective (e.g. they).
- Subject/verb agreement.
- Conjunctions: but, and.
- Pluralisation.

Each academic topic has its own vocabulary and its own ways of expressing the important ideas in the discipline that are unique to the nature of the specific discipline. See Chapter 5 on discourse analysis for more details.

## Multiple Discourses Theory

In the 1990s, James Paul Gee and the New London Group proposed a theory, called multiple discourses theory (Cazden *et al.*, 1996), to describe how individuals become literate in various disciplines. Gee (1992; http://www.ed.psu.edu/englishpds/Articles/CriticalLiteracy/What%20is%20Literacy.htm) explained that individuals learn new information in a field by apprenticing in the discourse of the field, or *enculturating* in the field. For example, if you wanted to be a pilot, you would take classes, read books, talk to instructors, take test flights, conduct flight simulations and log flight hours including talking to the air traffic controllers, taking off, negotiating weather patterns and landing. All of these activities would involve the use of speaking, listening, reading and writing as well as learning new field-related jargon (or academic vocabulary). With the coaching of a trained professional pilot, you would start with the basics: learn the terms, procedures and *thinking of a pilot*. Eventually, you would begin to express the ideas and thoughts of a pilot and see weather patterns and planes differently than a layperson.

Gee explained that individuals apprentice in all the academic disciplines in school in much the same manner. We acquire the language of the discipline by reading, listening, speaking and writing about the discipline. The specific linguistic codes, the forms and patterns common in the discipline, are acquired in this way without a great deal of analysis. Learners eventually appropriate them for their own uses, much like a child will mimic phrases that their parent typically says.

Moreover, it is not simply the academic vocabulary that the learners are acquiring, it is the meanings behind the words, the communicative competencies (i.e. linguistic, discourse, sociocultural, strategic and organisational/actional) as well as the ways a person in the discipline typically expresses the ideas.

## Communicative Competencies

To be highly proficient in a language, a learner must learn more than vocabulary and grammar to construct sentences. According to Canale and Swain (1980, 1981, 1983), to be proficient in a language a learner needs to have linguistic, discourse, sociocultural and strategic competencies. Celce-Murcia *et al.* (1995) amended these to include organisational/actional. Linguistic competence is the ability to construct grammatically and syntactically correct sentences. Discourse competence is the ability to create longer written and spoken passages that are cohesive and coherent. Sociocultural competence is the knowledge of which words and phrases to use when and with whom. For example, it is knowing that it is not acceptable to address a respected community leader as 'dude' or 'honey'. Strategic competence is the ability to avoid communication breakdowns and repair conversations that are in danger of silence. An example is when you are on the phone with your best friend and find yourself at the place in the conversation when you cannot remember what the topic originally was and you say, 'Well, anyway...' and start a new topic. Finally, organisational/actional competence is the understanding of usual sequences in talk or writing, so participants know whose turn it is to talk and what one typically or formulaically says or writes in a given encounter. See Chapter 4 for more on communicative competencies.

Imagine what news anchors typically say in presenting the news. They describe the events as 'stories', which has significance because it means that the information is based on what others tell them, not first-hand knowledge. They use the phrases 'alleged thief' or 'suspected arsonist' to show that a person is accused of a crime, but not necessarily guilty. They say, 'This just in on the case of.... Witnesses claim...' and 'Breaking news in the case of the missing Colorado hiker'. These patterns are above the word level and are employed formulaically by newscasters in presenting their work; they learned these expressions by apprenticing in the news industry.

## Diagramming Sentences is Passé

Long gone are the days of diagramming sentences (i.e. identifying parts of speech and mapping them hierarchically on charts) in order to understand how sentences are constructed (Figure 2.1).

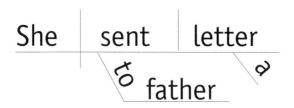

**Figure 2.1** Example: She sent a letter to her father

Linguistics has developed considerably in the last 40 years, particularly with the advent of functional linguistics and discourse analysis. Functional linguistics and discourse analysis are important tools for all educators to better understand the patterns of oral and written language.

Functional linguistics is 'an approach to understanding grammar that focuses on how language works to achieve a variety of different functional and communicative purposes' (Locke, 2005: ix). Functional linguists investigate which choices speakers and writers make different contexts. As Locke (2005: xi) explained, 'grammar is viewed as a resource for creating meaning in spoken and written language. This is very different from the view of grammar as a set of rules, rules that are to be applied even when they seem arbitrary'. In other words, the emphasis of functional linguistics is to understand *how language is used* by people every day instead of how it *should be used*. With this emphasis comes a reconsideration of the 'grammar rules'; in their place, functional linguists seek patterns of language in use (i.e. linguistic patterns). Discourse analysis is a tool used to understand the language patterns in use. Research methods in discourse analysis employ sampling passages of spoken and/or written language and analysing the patterns present in the language.

General educators would benefit from understandings of linguistics in terms of how individuals use language and for what purposes. One particularly useful approach to teaching the structures, or rules, of English has been suggested Diane Larsen-Freeman, which she named 'grammaring' (2003). The grammaring approach to language suggests that teachers can present the *form*'s structure, the *meaning* of the form and how it is *used* by speakers in various contexts. For example, if one were teaching the phrasal verb 'to set out' (form), it has several meanings depending on its context of use. In social language, if one said, 'he sets out his clothes for work', the form is third-person singular pronoun + regular present tense phrasal verb + possessive + noun. The meaning is he laid them out in preparation. The use is to describe his habitual activities. If the context were academic, there are two forms:

- She set out to explore. Form: third-person singular pronoun + regular past tense phrasal verb + infinitive. Meaning: beginning an expedition. Use: describing the beginning of an expedition in the past tense in spoken or written form.
- They set out the work plans. Form: third-person plural pronoun + regular present tense phrasal verb + article + compound noun. Meaning: outlining one's ideas or plans. Use: describing the design of the plans for others in spoken or written form.

The use of 'to set out' would depend on the context as well, what the speaker or writer is trying to accomplish. Often, there is overlap among the areas, but ELs need all three facets of the information in order to be able to understand how to form the phrase, what it means and when and how to use it. If only the form were the focus, a teacher would only need to explain that the verb 'to set out' is conjugated like other regular verbs.

Other changes to the teaching of language resulting from functional linguistics and discourse analysis are the focus on meaningful communication and the contextualised instruction of patterns (aka rules). In other words, the teacher provides a context or background for the identification and application of grammatical rules. *Meaningful communication* emphasises the use of language to express one's own meanings. Social meanings are easier in most cases to glimpse the purpose and need. One needs food, so one learns food vocabulary and the phrases, 'I'm hungry. May I have some…'. Academic meanings are a bit more difficult for learners to see their own need to communicate. Many academic tasks are presented as busywork tasks in which the learners see nothing of interest or inspiration. Finding an academic topic to stimulate a learner's interest is challenging for all teachers. When one does strike upon the topic that a learner wishes to invest, the learner would need to be able to read and listen for comprehension to gather information, and speak and write to share his/her knowledge and understanding on the topic. Finding ways to make the process meaningful, so that learners desire to participate in the process and learn the patterns that the discipline typically employs to communicate these meanings is vital. The linguistic structures and patterns can then be taught to learners to aid in their comprehension for their own purposes as opposed to learning for learning's sake.

---

**Meaningful Learning:** This process happened with my daughter in second grade. She became inspired to learn about manatees by her teacher who told the children they would each be able to choose one animal to research and write a book about. She chose manatees from the texts provided by the teacher and available for research. The teacher taught them how to find key information and make notes. With the teacher's support, the class then read the books repeatedly and took notes on the important parts. The teacher then presented them with an example book and instructed the children about the format of the book: title page, description

*(Continued)*

of the animal, habitat, food, predators and what they liked about the animal. My daughter wrote her book and drew accompanying pictures. As she worked on this, she came home and told me that she was researching manatees. She mentioned what she liked about them and told me what she had learned. It was important to her that she was learning about something she really liked. This was a meaningful, communicative, academic task in action. When she finished the book, and after they were shared in class, she brought it home and read it to me several times. She also read it to anyone who visited; she was so proud. Through this process, she revisited the language patterns numerous times and appropriated the discourse (i.e. habitat and predators) into her speech.

This example also shows how we can teach linguistic patterns in context as opposed to in isolation. Typical patterns that would be present in these kinds of texts would be items such as 'The [animal's] natural habitat is...' and 'The animals that could hurt the [animal] are.... These are called predators'. Sharing these typical linguistic patterns for expressing meanings/ideas and indicating how the form is constructed, what it means when it is used and how it is used will allow the learners to appropriate (i.e. adopt) the forms and enable them to utilise them in the future. If the forms were taught in isolation, the learners would not be able to see how or when to use them or why. Furthermore, they would not be meaningful to the learners and thus easily forgotten.

## Understanding Language Systems Helps

Linguistic knowledge and awareness would improve general educators' overall instruction for all learners. It would prevent instructors from seeing local errors (i.e. errors that do not confuse the meaning) as flagrant issues in writing, for example. It would allow them to focus on global errors (i.e. errors that obscure meaning) and better expression of ideas. It would assist teachers to analyse patterns so that they fathom possible issues and pitfalls in learners' comprehension and to support learners in contextualising and comparing patterns they observe. Bateson (1979) discusses the need for all learners to identify patterns in the world around them (i.e. musical, environmental, mathematical, social or linguistic) in order to enable them to contextualise, compare, learn independently and make sense of new information on their own.

I remember the boredom of analyzing sentences and the boredom later, at Cambridge, of learning comparative anatomy. Both subjects, as taught, were torturously unreal. We could have been told something about the pattern which connects: that all communication necessitates context, that without context, there is no meaning, and that contexts confer meaning because there is classification of contexts. The teacher *could* have argued that growth and differentiation must be controlled by

communication. The shapes of animals and plants are transform[ation]s of messages. Language is itself a form of communication. The structure of the input must
somehow be reflected as structure in the output. Anatomy *must* contain an ana-
logue of grammar because all anatomy is a transform[ation] of message material,
which must be contextually shaped. And finally, *contextual* shaping is only another
term for *grammar*. (Batteson, 1979: 17) [sic]

Understanding language patterns would raise educators' awareness of their own
language use and enable them to modify their linguistic delivery (the ways the teacher
speaks) of new material to learners to improve communication and comprehension
(Echevarria & Graves, 2003).

One key technique in developing an EL inclusive classroom is modifying the ways
the teacher speaks through simple adjustments that offer access points for language
learners. For example, pausing frequently and appropriately will give learners milli-
seconds of think time to process the incoming information. Pausing after phrases or
short sentences (i.e. thought groups), not after each word, is most appropriate. It is not
advisable to distort the rhythm of the language and sound like a robot (see Figure 2.2
for other linguistic modifications).

- **Modify your speech**

  - Enunciate clearly
  - Direct learners' attention to key ideas and vocabulary through intonation or writ-
    ing on blackboard
  - Face the students
  - Increase (5-7 seconds) wait time to process language and to think
  - Keep oral presentations short
  - Limit use of idioms, slang, and colloquial expressions; if they are important to the
    content or very common, use them and explain them
  - Include instructional conversations into presentation of new materials (See
    Chapter 4)
  - Paraphrase/rephrase statements and learners' statements often
  - Model tasks and appropriate language use for the tasks
  - Repeat in a variety of ways (recycle, connect, and extend)-Say the same
    things in different ways to convey meaning—do not worry about repeating
    yourself
  - Use simple sentences, such as subject-verb-object (SVO) sentence formats.
  - Provide new or difficult words orally, in written form and with a visual (see Figure 2.3).

**Figure 2.2** Ways to linguistically modify speech

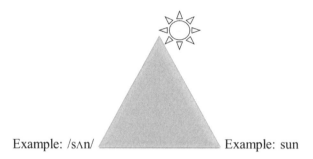

Example: /sʌn/                                          Example: sun

**Figure 2.3** Oral, written and visual information needed to understand new vocabulary

Understanding language patterns would allow for better guidance of learners in expressing their content understandings and meanings when reading and writing across the curriculum. Finally, this understanding would enhance the communication of formats (e.g. customary written forms, such as a science laboratory report), rhetorical modes (e.g. narratives, description, exposition and argumentation) and genres (e.g. fables, mystery, historical fiction, legend, biography, essay and narrative) in various content areas. Since each academic field has its own patterns of discourse, the discourse-level writing expectations would vary. For example, in science writing, individuals would need to be able to observe and write detailed descriptions of observations, they would need to write processes and sequential information in cause/effect situations in science report formats.

## What Aspects of Language to Teach?

When evaluating all the language patterns that are present in the classroom environment, the spoken language of the teacher, peers, videos, audiobooks and the written language in textbooks, in directions, in workbooks and on worksheets, instructors can quickly become overwhelmed with the amount of language that one could possibly teach to ELs. The challenge for all teachers is to choose appropriately and make informed choices. *You cannot teach everything, so choose the most important, comprehensible, useful or relevant academic language*! Focus on what content is essential or critical for learners to know and understand and what they need to be able to use. **Critical content!! Essential content first**. It is advisable to start a new concept with the most important, overarching parts of the concept. Once the students have understood the essential content, details can be added to flesh out the concept. Some non-essential details may need to be skipped or wait until later.

When choosing what academic language to teach, instructors will also want to consider:

- The learners' proficiency level(s). What do the learners at an intermediate level need in comparison to an advanced level?

- Bloom's Taxonomy skills (Bloom, 1956) that would be relevant or inherent to the content topic (e.g. comparing, justifying, evaluating, describing).
- The functions of language (e.g. giving advice, arguing/debating, reaching consensus, agreeing/disagreeing) that would be pertinent to the content topic.
- The enabling skills necessary to complete academic tasks and determine if the students have the academic language to complete them; if not, teach them the language or sentence frames to perform the tasks.

---

A sentence frame is also known as a sentence starter. Teachers provide learners with the sentence frame to complete, which guides the learners to acquire the format and academic language. Some sentence frames examples are:

- (Science) From my observations of _____, I noticed that _____ occurred after _____ (hours/days/weeks).
- (Literature) In the biography of _____, I learned that he/she experienced _____ challenges and overcame them by _____.
- (Math) The square root of _____ is _____. I determined this by _____.

---

In order to figure out which academic language structures to teach, instructors can also observe and record the language used in content classrooms, analyse the language used in content textbooks, select authentic language tasks; have students use a variety of language skills and tools (i.e. speaking, listening, reading, writing, grammar, vocabulary and pronunciation) to learn about content topics, or allow students options in selecting academic language to learn and practice.

## Presenting New Linguistic Information

It is crucial to note that in no way is this text advocating for the teaching of grammar for entire class periods, nor to the exclusion of content instruction; rather, the idea is to encourage the blending and highlighting of content and language discussions, so that learners can view the structures and patterns of language in the content. To enable language learners to acquire academic language, one approach is to teach a focus on form(s) (Doughty & Williams, 1998). Teachers can develop language objectives that would be taught in brief discovery activities (i.e. inductively) or in 'mini-grammar workshops'. Influenced by functional linguistics, educators should consider more than simply sentence-level grammar and include into language objectives patterns of discourse, such as narrative, sequential, descriptive, cause and effect, exemplification and comparison. Again, the patterns to be taught are determined by the proficiency level of the learners and the patterns present in the subject area spoken and written language.

When approaching a deductive presentation of new grammatical/structural forms, a four-step process is recommended:

(1) Presenting the form, meaning and use with contextualised examples.
(2) Using discovery activities, so learners can analyse the patterns.
(3) Providing practice close-ended exercises (e.g. matching, fill in the blank and transformation drills), so that learners have structured exercises to understand how the form works.
(4) Affording open-ended communicative activities and tasks, such as information gap, spot-the-difference, ranking and problem-solving tasks, and projects, such as creating a poster, designing and presenting a new product or fashioning a brochure with the highlights of a location/historical period.

It is important to have a variety of different iterations of the material. In other words, it is helpful to recycle the form in different ways, review the concept when necessary and retry with various activities and tasks.

The sequence of this four-step process may vary depending on deductive presentation versus inductive presentation. The four-step process is deductive, giving information first, then discovery/analysis and controlled and less-controlled practice. If the process were inductive, Step 2 would be first and accompanied by guiding analysis questions and prompts from the teacher. Step 1 would come next as a facilitated conversation. Finally, Steps 3 and 4 would be implemented to the degree necessary based on the initial steps. Some of the exercises may or may not be necessary if the learners and instructor engage deeply in the initial inductive steps.

Other recommended guidelines for teaching structural forms are:

- Provide clear grammatical explanations.
  - Study the form.
  - Think about how you will explain it.
  - Develop models and examples.
  - Script what you will say in user-friendly language (i.e. write out your explanation to ensure clarity).
  - Present the information orally and with written support using a document camera or PowerPoint presentation.
- Vary the presentation format.
  - Utilise differing participation formats: teacher-fronted, student-centred, pair work, small-group and group work.
  - Employ *inductive* and *deductive* approaches to the presentation of the grammatical points at different times. Some forms are better taught in one way versus the other. Also, learners who employ field-dependent learning styles (those who need to see the whole context or field) are more successful with inductive presentation; whereas those who utilise field-independent learning styles (those who do not need the whole context, but can isolate a specific item from the whole context and focus on it) are more successful with deductive presentations. (For more information on field in/dependence, see Maghsudi's article http://bibliotecavirtualut.suagm.edu/Glossa2/Journal/dec2007/Linguality%20in%20Third%20Language%20Acquisition.pdf.)

- Vary fluency and accuracy activities – employing a variety of activities depending upon the goal of developing language fluency (so the language becomes more automatic and less hesitant) or accuracy (so the language is correct) is suggested. It is recommended that when a learner is at lower proficiency levels or has just been introduced to a new grammatical form or pattern that fluency activities are utilised to build the learner's ease of use and confidence with the form. Later, once the form comes more easily to the learner, it is important to ensure that the learner is using it correctly. If a teacher emphasises only correctness from the outset, learners tend to shut down and not take risks; therefore, practice with subtle guidance is vital for learners.
  - Fluency – informal conversations, role plays, tasks, games.
  - Accuracy – exercises, writing formal reports, error analysis activities.

## Conclusion

Language is the medium of sharing any information. Without language, no learning can occur. Language is the central element of all learning in all subject areas. Therefore, language awareness on the part of general educators is key to communicating any academic concept.

With language awareness, the general educator can thoughtfully use EL-friendly language in the classroom to communicate essential content concepts and patterns typically employed in the content area.

Ways of presenting new information and providing language focus were shared along with other considerations, such as accuracy and fluency choices, when teaching language learners.

---

### Chapter Summary

- General educators should learn about the language of their discipline in order to convey information more effectively to learners and create intertwined content and language objectives.
- Multiple discourses theory reveals that each academic domain has varied and patterned ways of communicating. Being literate in the academic discipline is also being able to communicate like field specialists and understand the ways that they communicate.
- The academic discourse of a class is both oral and written; the discourse patterns appear in texts, videos, handouts and teacher talk.
- Teachers can modify their oral communication to facilitate ELs' comprehension.
- Teachers need to analyse their academic discourse for patterns to teach learners and present the language structures in clear, interactive and developmental ways.

## Activities and Discussions

(1) Debate the following statement: 'General educators should be trained in the language of their content area even if it means taking one less content course in their major'.

(2) Discussion: Should language forms be taught in academic content classes? If so, what are the best ways to do so? If not, why not?

(3) Conduct a discourse analysis of a content textbook. Choose an appropriate content textbook you use or could use in a general education class. Select one chapter randomly.

   (a) Select and list five content vocabulary words.
   (b) Identify and list 15 other vocabulary words that could challenge ELs. Are there any patterns within the vocabulary? Are there any categories that emerge?
   (c) Isolate figurative and colloquial language or slang and write the examples.
   (d) Ascertain the discourse formats in the chapter. Are the paragraphs explanatory, narrative, descriptive, sequential, compare/contrast? Select an example to share.
   (e) Evaluate the length and types of sentences. What are the most common and least common sentence patterns? List examples.
   (f) Identify the most common tense(s) present in the chapter. Provide examples.
   (g) Identify if these parts of speech are present and, if so, write examples. If not, why not?

      (i) Adjectives:
      (ii) Adverbs:
      (iii) Intensifiers:
      (iv) Negatives:
      (v) Comparatives:
      (vi) Superlatives:
      (vii) Determiners:
      (viii) Auxiliary verbs:

   Write your summary on the board to share with the class. Compare and contrast the various content areas' patterns of grammar.

(4) Present one concept from an instructional unit to teach in class. You will present it to a peer and attempt to use some of the linguistic modification strategies presented in this chapter.

   **Step 1:** Choose an important concept from a unit to work on. Example: civil rights movement, Mayan decorations on temples, fossil formation, rainforest habitats, adding fractions, plot, the business cycle or allusions.
   **Step 2:** Review a couple of strategies you would like to use in your presentation of new materials.
   **Step 3:** Imagine, plan, preview *what* you want to say and *how* you will say it. Write a script of EXACTLY what you intend to say when you present it.

**Step 4:** Practice with a colleague. Give and receive feedback on the clarity and success of your goals.

**Step 5:** Present to the whole group.

(5) From the list of grammar points, please choose one and script (or write everything you would say) to present this grammar point using the grammaring (i.e. form, meaning, use) approach to a class who has never seen it. Remember to write example sentences. List all the activities you would do when teaching this grammar point.

- Copula (to be)
- Subject-verb agreement
- Phrase structure
- Adjectives (physical, personality characteristics, etc.)
- Demonstrative adjectives (i.e. this, that, these, those)
- Comparatives and superlatives
- Negation
- Imperatives
- Wh- questions
- Articles
- Possessives
- Passive voice
- Prepositions
- Conjunctions
- Adverbs
- Conditional
- One tense (choose from present, past, future, past perfect, simple past, future perfect, future perfect, simple future, progressive)
- Direct objects or indirect objects

# 3 A Framework for General Educator Development in EL Instruction

| Chapter Aims and Topics |
|---|
| • Share information about language proficiency levels. |
| • Describe how field-specific terminology will be used: <br>    • Content-based instruction (CBI). <br>    • English learner (EL) inclusion. <br>    • Strategies for EL inclusion: affective, curricular modifications, materials modifications, instructional delivery and linguistic modification strategies. <br>    • Concepts to help illustrate the types of models and instructional patterns to be evaluated. |
| • Outline what general educators need to know to create EL inclusive environments. |
| • Discuss the skills and knowledge EL inclusive teachers need to have to be effective with ELs. |
| • Identify an evaluative framework for analysing CBI models. |

## Language Proficiency Levels

As mentioned in Chapter 2, language proficiency is a range of skills/abilities in a second language. *Proficiency* is a learner's ability, which can be measured by proficiency level, to communicate messages through speaking or writing and to understand/interpret incoming messages through listening and reading. Any given language learner will have differing abilities in the four skills (i.e. speaking, listening, reading and writing). Some learners are better at oral communication for reasons including an auditory processing strength or more oral language exposure. Other learners are stronger in written communication due to the slower speed of processing required in writing and reading, or a tendency towards introversion or a preference for independent learning. In determining a learner's proficiency level, one must be cognisant of the individual learner's strengths and weaknesses.

Often, test scores are reported by aggregating (i.e. compiling and averaging) the four language skills, which oversimplifies the true abilities of the learners. One needs to be aware that a learner's ability to converse with ease does not mean that the learner is strong in literacy. In the past, this assumption has misguided many a professional and layperson.

There are several well-known and widely implemented proficiency guidelines in the field of second/foreign languages. The first of its kind is the American

Council on the Teaching of Foreign Languages (ACTFL) proficiency indicators (www.actfl.org) which were first developed by foreign language teachers in the US to measure learners' second language speaking ability. The ACTFL employs a scale ranging from novice (beginner) and intermediate to advanced and superior to describe learners' abilities. These guidelines start with the lowest proficiency of novice (i.e. beginner) and move through intermediate, advanced and superior, which is the highest. The ACTFL also has guidelines for the receptive skills of reading and listening. Educators in the field still use these general terms to estimate the proficiency range of a student. The ACTFL has also developed writing proficiency guidelines.

> The novice range begins with absolute basics and grows quickly dependent upon exposure to (i.e. comprehensible input) and practice with using the language. The absolute beginner may struggle to conjugate a noun and a verb together. Absolute beginners can be a bit misleading, because they can use some extremely common, formulaic expressions, such as the greeting sequence, 'Hi. How are you? I'm fine. And you?'. Language learners in English at the novice level can eventually construct a simple sentence in the present tense about personal topics or concepts related to the here and now. The novice's repertoire also contains common sets of vocabulary (known in teaching English to speakers of other languages [TESOL] as notions or notional sets): colours, numbers, weather, seasons and/or clothing. As the language learner's proficiency grows, more and more vocabulary words, expressions and grammatical forms will be acquired and learned. Gradually, various verb tenses will be developed.
>
> The intermediate level of proficiency has low, mid and high levels through which learners tend to progress more slowly than the novice level. The information becomes more sophisticated in that it is more complex using more rare words and expressions. Verb tenses become more complex and the ability to change verb tense for different purposes is a necessary skill. For example, telling a story about a past occurrence and what you would do differently ('When I was 6, I thought I wanted to be a firefighter until I discovered that you had to take an exam and study really hard. If I had to do it over again, I would have made different choices'.). The amount of communication increases too. Sentences get longer and more complex with compound sentences or relative clause constructions ('I wanted to become an engineer or an astronaut, but I wasn't good at math, which changed all my plans'.). Accurate control over grammatical forms becomes increasingly important. At the intermediate level, learners can communicate about topics outside of their personal sphere, such as pollution or politics.
>
> The advanced level is increasingly global and more complex. Longer sentences with more complex grammatical forms are employed. Longer, sustained, spoken monologues or talks and/or written discourse in different genres are produced and understood through reading and listening. The language includes fewer inaccuracies and the learner employs an increasingly wide range of ways to express the same
>
> *(Continued)*

ideas. He/she can appropriately modify the language used according to his/her audience. At the advanced level, the learner can easily accomplish the vast majority of everyday tasks with few linguistic challenges or communication breakdowns. Only rare expressions, vocabulary, topics or specialised academic or technical language pose challenges for the advanced proficiency level.

The distinguished level of proficiency can participate fully in social, professional and academic spheres with ease and confidence. Individuals at this level still might encounter new expressions or vocabulary, but they would be uncommon, and the individual has mastered strategies for learning new information in the moment. The advanced proficiency level can use the language without difficulty almost all of the time.

In the field of TESOL, three organisations' proficiency guidelines have become the standard depending on where one teaches in the world: the Council of Europe's Common European Framework (CEFR) (http://www.coe.int/t/dg4/linguistic/Cadre1_en.asp), TESOL International Association (http://www.tesol.org/advance-the-field/standards/prek-12-english-language-proficiency-standards) and World-Class Instructional Design and Assessment (WIDA) (www.wida.us). The CEFR will be addressed in Chapter 9, because it informs the Content and Language Integrated Learning (CLIL) model. Because the WIDA proficiency guidelines, known as performance definitions, guide more than 35 US states' EL education and have informed the most recent version of the TESOL proficiency standards, this text will reference WIDA's performance definitions from 2007. The WIDA 2012 performance definitions are essentially the same as the 2007, but are articulated in a much more complex manner than is necessary for this text.

In the range of proficiency for WIDA's 2007 iteration, there are six levels ranging from a low of 1=entering, upward to the highest level of 6=reaching. (See Table 3.1 for a description of each level.) The aggregate scores of speaking, listening, reading and writing are identified annually on a standardised proficiency test of academic English in states requiring the WIDA Assessing Comprehension and Communication in English State-to-State (ACCESS) model test.

## Getting on the Same Page: Terminology

In order to be able to compare differing ways of preparing general educators to include ELs effectively into their classes, we need to reach some understanding over terms. First, general educators, mainstream and subject or content-area teachers are synonyms and will be employed interchangeably. Content teachers can be licensed in core content areas: language arts/English, mathematics, sciences and social studies/history or in 'special' subjects such as foreign languages, art, music and physical education. Terms used to refer to English as a second language specialists are ESL or EL teachers; these specialists hold a state-license in ESL. Classroom assistants or bilingual paraprofessionals may also support the language learners in general education classes, but they do not have specific teacher preparation in ESL or bilingual education.

**Table 3.1** WIDA proficiency indicators

At the given level of English language proficiency, ELLs will process, understand, produce or use:

| 6 – Reaching | • specialized or technical language reflective of the content areas at grade level<br>• a variety of sentence lengths of varying linguistic complexity in extended oral or written discourse as required by the specified grade level<br>• oral or written communication in English comparable to English-proficient peers |
|---|---|
| 5 – Bridging | • specialized or technical language of the content areas<br>• a variety of sentence lengths of varying linguistic complexity in extended oral or written discourse, including stories, essays or reports<br>• oral or written language approaching comparability to that of English-proficient peers when presented with grade level material |
| 4 – Expanding | • specific and some technical language of the content areas<br>• a variety of sentence lengths of varying linguistic complexity in oral discourse or multiple, related sentences or paragraphs<br>• oral or written language with minimal phonological, syntactic or semantic errors that do not impede the overall meaning of the communication when presented with oral or written connected discourse with sensory, graphic or interactive support |
| 3 – Developing | • general and some specific language of the content areas<br>• expanded sentences in oral interaction or written paragraphs<br>• oral or written language with phonological, syntactic or semantic errors that do not impede the communication, but retain much of its meaning, when presented with oral or written, narrative or expository descriptions with sensory, graphic or interactive support |
| 2 – Beginning | • general language related to the content areas<br>• phrases or short sentences<br>• oral or written language with phonological, syntactic, or semantic errors that often impede the meaning of the communication when presented with one- to multiple-step commands, directions, questions, or a series of statements with sensory, graphic or interactive support |
| 1 – Entering | • pictorial or graphic representation of the language of the content areas<br>• words, phrases or chunks of language when presented with one-step commands, directions, WII-, choice or yes/no questions, or statements with sensory, graphic or interactive support<br>• oral language with phonological, syntactic, or semantic errors that often impede meaning when presented with basic oral commands, direct questions, or simple statements with sensory, graphic or interactive support |

*Source*: WIDA 2007 Proficiency Guidelines visual image and the three types of supports with permission of WIDA Consortium.

*CBI*, or content-based language learning, is the thoughtful integration of academic concepts and skills with language knowledge (i.e. grammar and vocabulary) and skills (i.e. speaking, listening, reading and writing) development. The term stems from the principle that any topic, social or academic, can be a means through which one can learn/acquire another language.

*EL inclusion* is a language-rich immersion environment in general education classes in which an assortment of diverse strategies is employed to make the academic content concepts and skills clearer, comprehensible and more easily understood and retained. Importantly, the academic content and language are dual focuses, so that both are balanced to create meanings and understandings. Effective EL inclusion emphasises the language patterns present and needed in the academic subject and provides scaffolded support for language learners that facilitates second language acquisition (SLA) and learning. In this sense, scaffolded supports are any tool or strategy to make learning the concept apparent and more straightforward. For example, using visuals, vocabulary instruction with associated word banks, stem sentences and graphic organisers to assist in the reading of a textbook passage.

Four other categories of strategies, rooted in SLA research, principles and effective practices, are equally as vital in the EL inclusive class. *Affective strategies* are those strategies that create an emotionally safe learning environment. A large body of research has shown that high anxiety and stress when learning another language actually decrease the language learner's ability to focus on and use the language (Krashen, 1979, 1981, 1982); the *affective filter* is the term used to describe the emotional blockages that occur when a learner is experiencing high anxiety. In the EL inclusive class, ELs need a low-risk, face-saving and constructive environment where they can practice the language without fear of embarrassment, harsh criticism and/or social ostracisation. Examples of affective strategies are touching base with the EL one-on-one prior to calling on the learner in front of the class, allowing the learner think time and creating a supportive environment in the class so that other learners do not criticise or ridicule the learner about his/her language use.

*Curricular modification strategies* refer to those strategies employed by the teacher when planning for content and language teaching. Beginning with the grade-level academic standards, the general educator and/or ESL teacher create learning outcome objectives for both the academic content and the language needed. When the content standards are the starting point, and educators engage in backward design, an analysis is made of what content concepts, skills and language (i.e. vocabulary, sentence frames, expressions, and discourse patterns) are needed for mastery by the learners at the end of instruction (see Figure 3.1). In other words, the educator compares the grade-level standards against the final assessments, learners' language proficiency levels and needs, and academic and linguistic information presented in the texts and other materials to determine the content and language objectives for the unit.

When planning, curricular modification strategies are choices made about the content, what is essential, and language, what is needed and where the learners are in their proficiency. Other curricular strategies are when to teach which concepts, how to integrate the four language skills (i.e. speaking, listening, reading and writing), how to assess both conceptual and language learning, etc.

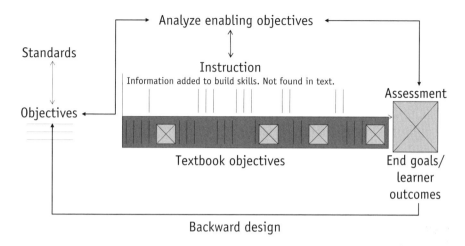

**Figure 3.1** Relationship between standards, objectives, assessments and materials

The third category of strategies is *materials modification/development/acquisition*. This group of strategies describes the creation of materials or the alteration of existing materials that are needed to support learning. Many materials and resources made for native speakers assume language and cultural knowledge not necessarily shared by the EL. For example, if a math story problem is situated at a circus and it asks the learners to determine the cost of snow cones for four friends at $1.50 each, the learners may or may not have any experience of a circus or snow cones. Therefore, teachers need to analyse and alter the materials so that they are intelligible, comprehensible and culturally appropriate. Teachers might also need to develop materials that utilise the content information and allow for language practice or create tools, such as word banks or illustrated glossaries. They also might need to acquire materials to support language learning of the content area, such as supplemental readers on the topic for silent reading or visuals to illuminate a concept. All these materials strategies would be considered during the planning stages, but implemented with instruction.

*Instructional strategies* are ways that educators can make academic content and language more accessible during the delivery of new material/direct teaching. Some instructional strategies might be planned into the lesson plan (e.g. small group work or pre-teaching vocabulary), but many are on-the-spot modifications when the educator notices learners' lack of comprehension. Some examples of instructional strategies employed in delivery are acting out the meaning of a word or drawing a visual. Another instructional delivery strategy set is related to how the teacher speaks. In Chapter 2, it was mentioned that teachers alter the ways they question and interact with the learners. This is an instructional delivery strategy related to how the educator speaks. This subcategory of instructional strategies is known as *linguistic modifications* and includes the use of comprehension checks, paraphrasing and recasting (i.e. restating) learners' errors into accurate grammatical forms.

Each of these categories of strategies is vital in the creation of an effective EL inclusive environment. These strategies will be referred to in the evaluative framework at the end of this chapter, as well as in upcoming chapters on the models. Additionally, further examples and details of how to use the strategies will be illustrated.

Other terms and concepts that provide a foundation for understanding are the ways we discuss the types of programmes and activities in the classroom. For the purposes of this text, a *model*, referred as 'expert-created, pre-packaged, stepwise objectives and instruction' is a particularly dicey term. In this text, models and frameworks will be considered synonymous for any type of comprehensive programme with specific tenets or guidelines, which are being promoted in the field for content-based language instruction (CBI).

*Approaches* will be employed to describe programmes for teacher preparation. Brown's (2007b) definitions will be adapted for our use:

- *Methodology* – The study of pedagogical practices in general (including theoretical underpinnings and related research). Whatever considerations are involved in 'how to teach' are methodological.
- *Method* – A general set of classroom procedures for accomplishing linguistic objectives. Methods tend to be concerned with (1) teacher and student roles and behaviours and (2) such features as linguistic and subject matter objectives, sequencing and materials. They are almost always thought of as being broadly applicable to a variety of audiences and contexts.
- *Technique* – Any of a wide variety of devices used in the language classroom for realising lesson objectives. Techniques tend to span over classes and can be used with differing topics to achieve varying goals. Example: cooperative learning.

Instead of employing Brown's definition of *activities* – any task, exercise or other action designed to allow learners to practice a language skill, strategy, etc. – this text will delineate activities into three categories following Nunan's (2004) definitions: exercises, communicative activities and tasks. *Exercises* are typically close-ended work used to practice grammatical or lexical forms that have only one or a very small set of correct answers. Imagine, for example, a worksheet with fill in the blank, multiple choice or conjugation exercises. *Communicative activities* are open-ended speaking/listening/reading/writing activities in which a learner has freedom to answer in any way he/she sees fit. 'They are similar to language exercises in that they provide *manipulative practice of a restricted set of language items*. They resemble pedagogical tasks in that they have an element of communication' (Nunan, 2004: 24). There are endless possibilities for correct answers. For example, a ranking activity in which the learners choose their own priorities on a given set of items, such as most prestigious jobs, and share their lists with other learners with the end goal of reaching a consensus on how the general public views these jobs.

Willis and Willis (2001: 173) viewed *tasks* as 'a classroom undertaking where the target language is used by the learner for a communicative purpose (goal) in order to achieve an outcome'. Whereas Nunan (2001: 4) indicated that 'a pedagogical task is a piece of classroom work that involves learners in comprehending, manipulating, producing or interacting in the TL [target language] while their attention is *focused on mobilising their grammatical knowledge in order to express meaning in which the intention is to convey meaning rather than manipulate form* [emphasis added]. The task should also have a sense of completeness, being able to stand alone as a communicative act in its own right with a beginning, middle and end'. Tasks have intellectual and linguistic activity inherent to them. An example of a task is the creation of a class newsletter of school events or a bilingual brochure for the local art museum. The task *must* have

- an identifiable goal or outcome;
- a series of steps that language learners must take;
- an exchange of information and sharing ideas/meanings;
- the processing of language to communicate a real message, not just to manipulate grammar forms.

  The task *may* have

- a real-life activity/something you do regularly;
- a product as an outcome.

For example, a ranking task is something we do every day. We rank priorities, favourite books or DVDs. The product of a ranking task is the ranked list of the items rated according to most to least important, most to least romantic or most to least funny. The grammatical form(s) used is the superlative, adjectives, comparatives and statements expressing opinions. The steps taken would be to read the list, consider personal thoughts on the items to be ranked, outline a personal list, compare with a partner or group and synthesise a group list taking all members' opinions into consideration. The outcome is that an individual, pair or small group share their personal opinions to develop the list. Some examples of academic tasks and products associated with tasks are listed in Table 3.2.

## A Theoretical Framework for Evaluation

In order to guide the analysis of the models and approaches described in this text, this chapter will outline a theoretical framework upon which the analysis will be based. Drawing from TESOL/National Council for Accreditation of Teacher Education (NCATE) standards for P-12 Teacher Education Programmes (2009) and seminal, research-based sources, including Chamot (2009), Echevarria and Short (2003, 2005), Echevarria *et al.* (2004), Li and Protacio (2010), Lucas and Villegas (2011), Murray and

**Table 3.2** Examples of task-based products

| | |
|---|---|
| Measure the area of your bedroom for new carpet. Find the cost and type of carpet. Tell a caregiver how you did it, how much carpet is necessary and what colour you would like. | Research a recent development in archaeology and create an advertisement highlighting what is happening, where and why it is important. |
| Interview a medical researcher to learn about what he/she researches and its importance. | Study the lives and habitat of a horseshoe crab and create a poster explaining it. |
| Debate the righteousness of the actions of the central characters of a novel or play. | Read about an art style and write a critique of an art show in that style. |
| Create a presentation describing all the ways that humans have and are currently exploring the world around them. | Investigate a problem in the world today and write a proposal to the UN offering a solution. |
| Construct your own math story problem using fractions and tell it to a peer. | Find and map all active tectonic plates and describe the results of their activity in your assigned region of the world. |
| Listen to a radio broadcast of a current world issue and make a short video describing it to the class. | Describe and illustrate the carbon cycle and hypothesise its long-term impact on human life in a short story. |

Christison (2011a, 2011b), Short (1993, 1994, 2002), Snow and Brinton (1997) and Téllez and Waxman (2006), a framework was developed and will be employed to compare and contrast various models and approaches (see Table 3.3) to content-based ESL instruction in general education classes.

Echevarria and Short (2003, 2005), Echevarria *et al.* (2004) and Short (1993, 1994, 2002) espoused a CBI methodology that integrated content and language objectives into grade-level, mainstream lessons. Their criteria for quality EL instruction in sheltered content classes and in general education classes via the Sheltered Instruction Observation Protocol (SIOP) model were (1) the implementation of various affective, instructional materials development and curricular strategies to make course content meaningful to the English language learner; (2) the integration of four skills + (i.e. speaking, listening, reading, writing, grammar, pronunciation and vocabulary) instruction into content courses through interactive, authentic and hands-on ESL techniques; (3) the utilisation of linguistic modifications to make auditory and visual input for ELs more comprehensible; (4) an awareness of social and academic language (Cummins, 1979, 1992, 1996); furthermore, they advocated for scaffolding of instruction and communication (through instructional conversation); (5) a high level of interaction in classes on the content material; and (6) continued assessment of learner progress.

Snow and Brinton's (1997) seminal edited volume contributed the following recommendations for quality instruction of content material for ELs: (1) thematic-based approaches (Stoller & Grabe, 1997); (2) advocacy for ELs (Wilcox Peterson, 1997) and collaboration among general educator and ESL professionals (Teemant *et al.*, 1997); and (3) fair assessment of ELs' content knowledge (Cushing Weigle & Jensen, 1997; Turner, 1997).

Chamot (2009) called for teachers who instruct ELs in grade-level content material to employ three types of objectives (i.e. content, language and learning strategies objectives); hands-on engagement in cognitively challenging, academic tasks; and direct instruction of the linguistic aspects of academic texts. The learning strategies suggested by Chamot are both general learning strategies, such as note-taking (Reimer, 2008), and language learning strategies, such as looking for context clues (Oxford, 1990).

Lucas and Villegas (2011) furthered the work of previous scholars by adding dispositional/orientation considerations, such as an awareness or 'consciousness' of the sociolinguistic, sociopolitical and sociocultural issues of language use and education. They brought to the discussion of what 'linguistically responsive teachers' need is a strong emphasis on the value of linguistic diversity and learners' home cultures and languages. They advocated for general educators to learn about the home lives, cultures, experiences and proficiencies of their learners. Finally, like other scholars, they argued persuasively for the need for general educators to understand the key principles of SLA/learning (i.e. social and academic language; comprehensible input; social interaction; transfer of knowledge and skills from the first to the second language; and anxiety/affective considerations).

Like Wong-Fillmore and Snow (2002) and Schleppegrell (2004), Murray and Christison (2011) suggested that general educators have a firm understanding of oral and written forms of the English language.

- Wong-Fillmore and Snow (2002: 3) suggested the following foundational knowledge of language for teachers '…teachers should know about language in terms of questions they should be able to answer and relate to their classroom practice'. In terms of oral language, teachers should be able to answer questions, such as:
- What are the basic units of language?
- What's regular and what isn't [sic]?
- How is the lexicon acquired and structured?
- Are vernacular/dialects different from 'bad English' and if so, how?
- What is academic English?
- Why has the acquisition of English by non-English-speaking children not been more universally successful? (Wong-Fillmore & Snow, 2002: 3)

As for written language, Wong-Fillmore and Snow (2002) recommended

- Why is English spelling so complicated?
- Why do some children have more trouble than others in developing early reading skills?
- Why do students have trouble with structuring narrative and expository writings?

- How should one judge the quality and correctness of a piece of writing?
- What makes a sentence or a text easy or difficult to understand? (Wong-Fillmore & Snow, 2002: 3)

Murray and Christison's two volumes (2011a, 2011b) synthesised a broad expanse of information on what English language teachers (not general educators) need to know, which share many of the ideas related to language knowledge presented by Wong-Fillmore and Snow (2002), Adger *et al.* (2002) and Bartles (2005). To Wong-Fillmore and Snow's outline, I selected several key linguistic needs from Murray and Christison's first volume: types of sentences (i.e. declarative, interrogative, imperative and exclamatory), sentence construction and the sound system (i.e. phonological system) of English.

Téllez and Waxman (2006) culled lists of the NCATE/TESOL (TESOL, 2003) and the National Board for Teachers' Professional Standards (NBPTS) professional standards for EL teachers that included many previously noted criteria for quality EL instruction. The NBPTS added to the emerging set of criteria: (1) knowledge of subject matter; (2) meaningful learning; (3) multiple paths to knowledge; (4) supportive, diverse instructional resources; and (5) reflective practice (as cited in Téllez & Waxman, 2006: 8–9).

The last aspect of quality teaching added to this evaluative framework is the ability of teachers to make informed choices (Brown, 2007b) based on solid SLA principles and best practices in content and language instruction for the particular context with its unique variables (Kumaravadivelu, 2001). This is a vital component as it allows educators to be responsive to the immediate needs and strengths of learners in their classroom at the specific school location.

Although this review of recommendations and suggested criteria for quality preparation of EL teachers, general educators and content-area teachers seems daunting, the recommendations have been synthesised into a usable evaluative framework for this book (Table 3.3).

# The Qualities of Successful Professional Development Programmes

This chapter so far has addressed what information general educators should ideally learn in order to be prepared to include ELs into their content classes. Li and Protacio (2010) drew from a large body of research to develop four 'essential elements' that should guide the design of professional development experiences for teachers. The criteria they outline are

1. The content of the professional development must focus on specific classroom strategies;

**Table 3.3** Evaluative framework for teacher preparation models, approaches and initiatives in EL inclusion

---

*I. Knowledge*

When preparing teachers to include ELs into their content courses and to work with linguistically and culturally diverse groups of ELLs, they should have *knowledge* of the following areas:

- The structures and features of the English language.
  - The distinctions between oral and written language.
  - The basic units of language, such as parts of speech, types of sentences and the sound system of English.
  - The construction of differing discourse units from the sentence level to a variety of social and academic genres and formats.
  - The irregularities of English.
  - The pragmatic/sociocultural dimensions of language (e.g. voice, audience) and how language varies accordingly.
  - An appropriate target for language acquisition/learning is real language use; 'standard' English is a myth.
- The key principles of second language acquisition/learning (Ellis, 2008).
  - Instruction needs to include:
    - A balance predominantly on meaning but also on forms.
    - An understanding of individual differences in learners.
    - Environmental modifications to reduce anxiety and affective issues.
    - Extensive comprehensible input.
    - Interaction with peers and instructors on the academic topics.
    - Opportunities for learners to develop both 'a rich repertoire of formulaic expressions and a rule-based competence'.
    - Opportunities for spontaneous as well as controlled production.
    - Output opportunities.
    - Social and academic language (Cummins, 1979, 1992).
    - Transfer of knowledge and skills from the first to the second language.
- An understanding of ELLs' proficiency levels and their abilities and challenges at those levels.
- The laws pertinent to ELs' instruction in the particular context.
- The resources available to learn about ELs' educational backgrounds, first languages and cultures.
- A sociolinguistic consciousness (Lucas & Villegas, 2011).
  - Understanding of the relationships between language, culture and identity.
  - Awareness of the sociopolitical context of language use and language education, particularly in the specific context.
- The subject matter; knowledge of one core content area or specialty area.

*(Continued)*

**Table 3.3** (Continued)

*II. Performance*

When preparing teachers to include ELs into their content courses and to work with linguistically and culturally diverse groups of ELLs, they should have *abilities and skills* in the following areas:

Curricular and Instructional Planning

- Planning with assessments as clear targets (e.g. backward design; Wiggins & McTighe, 2005).
- Creating content, language and learning strategy objectives.
- Pre-teaching and/or integrating necessary skills, such as process writing, note-taking, etc. into the curriculum.
- Integrating speaking, listening, reading, writing, grammar, vocabulary and pronunciation instruction and practice into lessons.
- Developing units with clear connections through a thematic focus.
- Modifying, developing and locating materials for linguistic accessibility of lessons.
- Analysing the linguistic features of oral and written discourse so as to be able to bridge the gap between ELs and a wide variety of genres, subject areas, academic discourse communities and texts.
- Addressing multiple ESL proficiency levels in the same class by planning for differentiated instruction.
- Making informed choices (Brown, 2007b) based on solid second language acquisition (SLA) principles and best practices in content and language instruction for the particular context with its unique variables (Kumaravadivelu, 2001).

Instructional Delivery

- Creating comfortable learning environments and classroom communities with low anxiety.
- Identifying learners' background knowledge and building upon it.
- Making informed choices about instruction and employing a wide variety and frequency of approaches, techniques and resources depending on learners' needs.
- Explicitly teaching new vocabulary and language needed for oral (speaking and listening) and written (reading and writing) engagement with the academic content using supports and tools for meaning making.
- Creating meaningful, academically focused, engaging, interactive and experiential lessons and tasks that include ELs in activities (Migliacci & Verplaetse, 2008).
- Directly teaching new academic information in small portions or 'chunks' with practice and interaction opportunities.
- Modifying the delivery of speech to heighten learners' comprehension (i.e. making linguistic modifications) or modifying the complexity or quantity of written material to make it more accessible.
- Scaffolding instruction using a variety of supports, such as graphic organisers, visuals, modelling, sentence frames, etc.
- Providing cognitively challenging materials to ELs that are linguistically accessible.

Assessment

- Offering learners a variety of ways to demonstrate their knowledge of the content or language. For example, using performance and alternative assessment (see task and product examples above).
- Providing suitable and judiciously chosen accommodations for ELs during academic assessments. Accommodations are state-mandated supports for learners during standardised assessments, such as providing increased time for the test, breaks, dictionaries and/or trans-lators for directions.
- Measuring learners' content knowledge and language ability separately.
- Providing ongoing feedback on content knowledge and language ability that is constructive and regular.
- Assessing learners' progress in language learning according to proficiency indicators.
- Modifying text and teacher-made assessments to support ELs. For example, using visuals and models in directions.

*III. Orientations/Dispositions*

When preparing teachers to include ELs into their content courses and to work with linguistically and culturally diverse groups of ELLs, they should have *awareness of, value for and appreciation of* the following areas:

- Value for linguistic and cultural diversity.
- Inclination to advocate for the linguistic and programmatic needs of ELLs.
- Willingness to collaborate with language specialists, content teachers, administrators, parents, etc. to provide high-quality instruction for ELs and to create EL-friendly schools and communities.
- Hold high expectations for ELs and all learners.
- Inclination to provide assessments that level the playing field for ELs so that they may demonstrate their knowledge in a variety of ways.
- Value for reflective instructional processes.
- Willingness to develop positive home/school connections with ELs' parents.
- Willingness to treat cultures respectfully and to eliminate stereotyping of peoples and cultures.

2. The structure of professional development must engage teachers in active learning;
3. [The] collaboration is key in professional development; and
4. [The] professional development must be sustained. (Li & Protacio, 2010: 356)

The design of various content-based instruction (CBI) models in the following chapters will be evaluated with these essential criteria in mind in order to determine whether they provide the range of knowledge, performance skills and orientations essential for the creation of EL inclusive environments. Also, the upcoming models have been applied as professional development 'packages' for in-service and pre-service educators.

## Conclusion

Information in this chapter provides a foundation for understanding some of the variables that guide teachers' choices when working with ELs. The proficiency level(s) of the learners in the class steer teachers to adjust their material and instructional delivery to the learners' level of comprehension. Content-based language instruction classes, whether sheltered content or general education, integrate the subject matter concepts and skills with language learning objectives based on learners' proficiency level abilities and needs.

In CBI, a variety of strategies are employed to make the incoming information more comprehensible to the second language learner: affective strategies, curricular planning modifications, materials modification, development and acquisition, instructional strategies and linguistic modifications. These strategies are part of the knowledge and performance skills needed by educators to create EL inclusive content classes. Other terms and definitions to aid in describing EL inclusive models were defined.

An evaluative framework was presented through which we will analyse the upcoming models to determine to what degree they provide the knowledge, performance and orientations necessary for general educators.

---

### Chapter Summary

- ELs' abilities in speaking, listening, reading and writing can be placed on a proficiency scale that describes their performance or comprehension, which can aid general educators in gearing their instruction to the learners.
- Terminology to be employed in this text was defined.
  - CBI.
  - EL inclusion.
  - Concepts to help illustrate the types of models and instructional patterns to be evaluated.
- CBI is teaching both the academic subject material along with an emphasis on the language needed for comprehensibility and use in academic communication.
- EL inclusion environments are general education classes that have been modified to make them accessible and safe for ELs.
- An outline of strategies essential in the creation of EL inclusive environments was described. The strategies mentioned for EL inclusion were affective, curricular modifications, materials modifications, instructional delivery and linguistic modification strategies.

- An evaluative framework for analysing CBI models was presented for comparing models used to teach general educators about EL inclusion.
- The rationale and research underpinning the evaluative framework was expounded.

## Activities and Discussions

(1) Discuss with a peer the terminology presented in this chapter. Which terms do you use similarly and differently? Are there any terms that would cause confusion in discussions?

(2) Rank your second language ability on the WIDA proficiency scale. Create a class survey to compile your peers' level of second language proficiency and the language they have studied. Why do you feel that your second language proficiency level is the level you identified? How do you think you could improve it? Share your thoughts with a partner.

(3) Find a second language speaker's video on the internet of roughly two minutes and rate the speaker's second language proficiency on the ACTFL or WIDA proficiency scale.

(4) Discuss the evaluative framework. Are there any areas missing? Are there any areas duplicated? Based on your knowledge, what would you change about it and why?

(5) Create a graphic organiser to represent a visual of the evaluative framework. Share with your peers.

# Section 2

# Models of English Language Inclusion

In this section, readers will be introduced to eight preparation models that have been proposed to guide general educators in English learner inclusion. From the guidelines articulated by the Center for Research on Education, Diversity and Excellent (CREDE) to the comprehensive models of training for English learner inclusion, such as Sheltered Instruction Observation Protocol (SIOP), Cognitive Academic Language Learning Approach (CALLA), Response to Intervention (RtI) and *Specially Designed Academic Instruction in English* (SDAIE), and those for content-based instruction in foreign language contexts, programmes to help general educators to work productively and thoughtfully with English learners will be presented. Each model will be presented with elaborations on the key elements that the model introduced to the field accompanied by practical ideas and examples. Critical analysis of each model and guidelines are outlined so that readers can weigh the advantages and disadvantages of each programme. The final chapter weighs the models against each other and offers insights into which model is most appropriate for varying educational contexts.

# 4 Models: Sheltered Instruction Observation Protocol Model

| **Chapter Aims and Topics** |
|---|
| • Present the history and development of the Sheltered Instruction Observation Protocol (SIOP; pronounced sigh-op) model. |
| • Describe the key features of the SIOP model. |
| • Present the communicative competencies principle for language objectives. |
| • Discuss the language objectives format and instruction by proficiency level. |
| • Consider the role of vocabulary in language objectives. |
| • Analyse interaction and oral discourse patterns. |
| • Provide tips for facilitating conversation, in particular instructional conversation. |
| • Offer materials supports to enhance learners' understanding. |
| • Describe lesson delivery, strategies and assessment in the SIOP model. |
| • Analyse the SIOP model for strengths and weaknesses against the evaluative framework. |
| • Describe the optimal context and suggestions for the implementation of the SIOP model. |

## Introduction

In the mid-1990s, one instructional model combining subject matter instruction with language development emerged (Short, 1993, 1994; Short & Echevarria, 1999). This model, the SIOP model, has become widely recognised as a sound programme model for teaching both content and language in sheltered content environments. *Sheltered content* is a class for English learners (ELs) only that strives to support the language development of the ELs while teaching the grade-level academic content. It is currently the most widely known and implemented model of content-based English language instruction in the US.

The SIOP model began to be developed through a collaboration between the Center for Research on Education, Diversity & Excellence (CREDE) and the Center for Applied Linguistics (CAL) in which researchers sought to identify characteristics of instruction that were the most productive and effective for diverse and at-risk learners, including ELLs. Many instructors at the time did not agree on specific strategies that comprise an effective sheltered lesson. Researchers Jana Echevarria, Mary Ellen Vogt and Deborah

Short collaborated with expert practicing teachers and conducted a thorough review of the second language acquisition theoretical and practice-oriented literature to identify the essential aspects of effective instruction in sheltered content lessons. From this collaboration, a model of effective instruction emerged, known as the SIOP, which they used to observe teachers. These observations helped improve the model through years of pilot testing (http://www.cal.org/siop/about/history.html). Through a series of research studies, the SIOP model was validated, which means that it has been shown through research to be a valid tool for the observation of sheltered content instruction (Echevarria & Short, 2003, 2005; Echevarria *et al.*, 2004; Short, 1993, 1994, 2002; Short & Echevarria, 1999).

## Description of the Model

Echevarria, Vogt and Short identified eight categories of strategies, which they crafted into a rubric for observation. These strategies present a comprehensive array of performance attributes that teachers need to inform their instruction. Since the SIOP was originally utilised as an observation tool, it has a scale of zero to four for each of the eight categories spanning preparation, instruction and assessment practices.

The eight components are (see Figure 4.1):

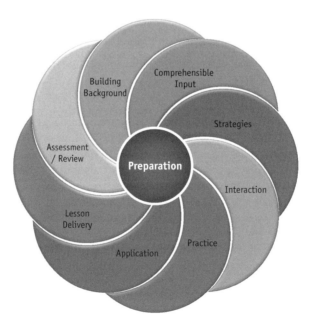

**Figure 4.1** SIOP model components

(1) **Preparation**: pre-planning to integrate curriculum and lessons with both content and language as well as differentiating objectives for multiple proficiency levels.

(2) **Building Background:** connecting to and developing learners' cultural, conceptual and linguistic background knowledge.

(3) **Comprehensible Input:** providing information to the learners and modelling academic language that has been modified to enhance comprehensibility.

(4) **Strategies:** employing instructional strategies to enhance learning.

(5) **Interaction:** designing interactional opportunities within the classroom on content and language objectives to allow for second language acquisition to take place.

(6) **Practice/Application:** including exercises, communicative activities and tasks to allow learners to practice content and language concepts and skills using hands-on materials.

(7) **Lesson Delivery:** gearing the pacing of lessons and learners' engagement/time on task in the appropriate amount to allow for content and language learning.

(8) **Review/Assessment:** building in multiple opportunities for revisiting content and language concepts and providing ongoing, constructive feedback to learners on their achievement on objectives.

(Adapted from Using the SIOP Model @ 2002. Center for Applied Linguistics.)

Observers evaluated the preparation, instruction and assessment practices of teachers in sheltered content courses to determine the degree to which they were employing supportive instructional planning, delivery and assessment practices.

(1) Preparation

The 'preparation' category describes the curricular and lesson planning organised by teachers that are necessary for serving ELLs' academic and linguistic needs. All of these strategies are considered during the planning of the curriculum and individual lessons.

The first set of items deals with the construction of content and language objectives appropriate for learners' ages and educational backgrounds. Both types of objectives should be analysed and weighed based on the needs of the learners. The *content objectives* should be grade-level academic objectives (i.e. academic concepts and procedures to be learned) usually based upon the academic standards of the country, state and/or field. In cases of interrupted schooling (i.e. when learners have experienced significant changes to their learning such as those of refugees or migrant farmers' children who are in multiple schools per year), the teacher would also consider the *enabling skills* needed by the learner. For example, if the primary objective were multiplying fractions, the teacher would need to consider the learners' background experiences with the concepts of fractions, multiplication and understandings of addition and subtraction of fractions. Enabling skills are any skill a learner would need to accomplish a given task.

Enabling skills can be conceptual and/or linguistic. If students are asked to do a discussion task in which they need to share their predictions on a science experiment using the sentence frame, 'I think that ___ will happen, because....', the linguistic enabling skills needed to be able to participate include: giving opinions, using future tense, using 'because' as a conjunction to offer a reason or justification for the opinion, creating a compound sentence, employing subject/verb agreement for starters.

Educators recommend that content objectives should be written as learning outcome objectives. *Learning outcome objectives* focus on what the learner needs to be able to know or do at the conclusion of the instruction. They are not focused on what the teacher will say or do or on the activities of the lesson. Student outcome objectives are usually written using the format, 'Students will be able to...' and focus on what the students will learn in the lesson (see Table 4.1).

Content objectives can be analysed by a teacher when preparing a lesson to identify the linguistic aspects of the academic concept. Teachers of ELs would consider the language expectations of the content objectives as well as the linguistic demands of the activities the learners would engage in during the lesson. This analysis is one path to determining language objectives. *Language objectives* are the specific concepts, forms and competencies the language learners need to learn or acquire to develop their language proficiency. Since language proficiency is composed of both competence and performance, the learners would need to understand concepts as well as be able to use the linguistic concepts in interaction. Linguistic competence is the knowledge of a linguistic concept, such as the construction of the simple regular past tense using –ed endings; whereas performance is the ability to write a description of a past event using the –ed forms.

One pillar of the SIOP model is Cummins' (1979, 1980a, 1980b, 1992) research on social and academic language. The distinction that Cummins' proposed was between

**Table 4.1** The differences between objectives and learning outcome objectives

| Concept | Teacher- or activity-focused objective examples | Learner outcome focused objectives |
|---|---|---|
| Multiplying fractions | • Explain the process of multiplying fractions diagonally across. • Students will do a worksheet on multiplying fractions. | Students will be able to multiply fractions by using the technique of multiplying diagonally across the fractions. |
| Feudal period in Europe | • Describe to students the mutually dependent relationship between the feudal lord and peasant farmers. • Students will read and discuss a description of the relationship between the feudal lord and peasant farmers on page X. | Students will be able to describe orally and in writing the mutually dependent relationship of the feudal lord and peasant farmers. |

the language people use socially, to develop interpersonal relationships and accomplish personal transactions and language for academic purposes. What might one say socially to friends and acquaintances on a given day? Casual greetings, requests, giving advice and telling stories or anecdotes. For example, children in the school cafeteria are likely to say, 'Can I have some pizza?' or 'I don't like grapefruit juice'. According to Cummins' research, it takes between 1 and 3 years to acquire social language. This makes sense because social language is frequently highly formulaic, uses repeated patterns, is present daily and does not become much harder or more nuanced.

Academic language refers to the types of vocabulary and sentence formats that are typical in classrooms. The following example of academic language has been intentionally chosen to highlight how complex and difficult academic language can appear to the uninitiated. Also, it is perplexing to see academic language and its patterns until we are in the learners' shoes facing complex language.

> Poststructuralism, then, tends to take a very different view on issues such as science, objectivity, and truth, categories that remain relatively unproblematic for structuralism. Poststructuralism also takes far more seriously the potential of a superstructuralist stance (which structuralism rarely engaged with seriously) by making the cultural and ideological, or rather the discursive, as not merely a secondary by-product of material relations, or even as relatively autonomous, but rather as primary. (Pennycook, 2001: 106)

Reread this passage again with an eye towards just the sentence structures. What kinds of sentence formats are present? There are two sentences with dependent clauses (e.g. 'tends to take a very different view on issues such as science, objectivity, and truth' and 'which structuralism rarely engaged with seriously') embedded in each one, which makes the sentences longer and cognitively more challenging. A series of ideas are also listed in the middle of the first sentence (e.g. science, objectivity and truth). Vocabulary that could be difficult include terms such as post-structuralism, superstructuralist, structuralism and discursive. Other vocabulary that are not field jargon, but which could cause a language learner difficulty, even at the advanced proficiency levels, include stance, autonomous, objectivity and relatively.

Academic language takes between 5 and 7 years to acquire according to Cummins, but may take up to 10 years if the learner has experienced interrupted learning or has no literacy development in his/her background. The reasons for this are that academic language is not explicitly taught, formats of the language can be specific to the academic domain and are only acquired in the classroom or while reading academic texts.

When determining language objectives, educators should also consider the *communicative competencies* needed to be proficient in another language. The communicative competencies outlined by Canale and Swain (1980, 1981, 1983) are linguistic, discourse, sociocultural and strategic. Celce-Murcia *et al.* (1995) amended these to include organisational/actional (see Table 4.2).

**Table 4.2** Communicative competencies

| Competencies | Examples |
|---|---|
| *Linguistic (sentence-level) competence*<br>• The bits and pieces<br>• Syntax, grammar, lexicon, semantics, phonology<br><br>Article + noun + past tense irregular verb + adverb + preposition + article + adjective + compound noun= | • The dog ran rapidly to the red fire hydrant.<br>I like to swim. [pronoun, verb present tense, preposition/infinitive]<br>Statement citing preference.<br>• Colourless green ideas. *Semantics*. |
| *Discourse (global-level) competence*<br>• How all the pieces fit together to form a comprehensive whole.<br>• Transitional knowledge: topic shifts/ changes, transitions in discourse shown by discourse markers, and cohesion. | My argument breaks down into three categories. First, there were numerous assassins, because one man could not fire 15 shots in 30 seconds without an automatic rifle. Second, bullets approached the president from several angles as was shown in the autopsy. Third, witnesses saw smoke and heard sounds from the grassy knoll. |
| *Sociocultural competence*<br>• Extralinguistic knowledge: register, role relationships, showing respect or power, distance/closeness, friendships/alliances, etc. | • **Speaker A:** Hala, my friend, is going to apply for the position here. I hope she gets it.<br>• **Speaker B:** Well, we will see what her *qualifications* are and if she *looks good* on paper. There are *no* guarantees. |
| *Strategic competence*<br>• Communication strategies employed during breakdowns in communication or to redirect misdirected talk in an appropriate manner. | • **Speaker A:** Can we go to the grocery store? I need to pick up a kumquat.<br>• **Speaker B:** Huh? A kumquat?<br>• **Speaker A:** You know, a tiny orange-like fruit. I need it for a recipe. |
| *Organisational/actional competence*<br>• Rhetorical organisation: typical patterns, turn-taking, act sequences (e.g. greetings, requests, apologies, closings).<br><br>• Rhetorical organisation for academics would be the types of linguistic activities associated with Bloom's Taxonomy, for example. | Social Language:<br>• **Speaker A:** Hey, Gina. How are ya?<br>• **Speaker B:** Hi ya, Tym. Fine. 'n you?<br>• **Speaker A:** We really need to catch up. I'll call ya.<br>• **Speaker B:** Look forward to it. See ya.<br>• **Speaker A:** Take care!<br>Academic Language, Compare/Contrast:<br>• **Speaker A:** What did the feudal lord do to protect the peasant farmers? And what did the peasants do in turn for the lord?<br>• **Speaker B:** The feudal lord was responsible for the physical protection of the farmers and their lands from outside raiders or thieves whereas the farmers were responsible to tithe (pay taxes) and to serve in armies when under attack. |

A teacher would want to analyse the learners' linguistic needs against the communicative competencies and the linguistic expectations of the in-class interaction and learning outcomes. English language learners in middle school learning about the feudal period would need different linguistic concepts at different proficiency levels. These needs would differ on an individual basis. Learners who are at the World-Class Instructional Design and Assessment (WIDA) assessing comprehension and communication in English state-to-state (ACCESS) model proficiency Levels 1–5 would have different needs in each competency, for example:

- Level 1 proficiency might need linguistic concepts of simple declarative sentences in the present tense and the appropriate social and/or academic vocabulary (e.g. The lord protects farmers. Farmers pay taxes).
- Level 2 proficiency might need linguistic concepts of past tense regular –ed verb forms; common transition words (e.g. and, but, or) and the appropriate social and/ or academic vocabulary (e.g. The lord protected the peasants, but the farmers needed to pay taxes. Farmers served in the army).
- Level 3 proficiency might need linguistic concepts of past tense irregular verb forms, compound sentences, complex transition words/phrases (e.g. whereas, while, at the same time) and the appropriate social and/or academic vocabulary (e.g. The feudal lord protected the peasants, while the peasant farmers paid taxes and served in the army).
- Levels 4 and 5 proficiency would need more detail and elaboration on the concepts. They can add additional detail, examples and opinions on the academic concepts. They can compare and contrast various facets of the concepts (e.g. The feudal lord had the responsibility to protect the peasant farmers, maintain laws and civil order and serve as judge in conflicts; whereas the peasant farmers were tenants who cared for the land and animals. From the farms, the peasants gave to the lord payments of produce, like wheat or eggs, or livestock, like chickens or pig, which were their taxes. When the feudal area was threatened, the peasants would serve in the feudal lord's army).

For the learning outcome objectives about the feudal period, one would consider the language needed to describe and possibly to compare and contrast the feudal lord's and the peasant farmers' responsibilities and benefits in this system as well as the linguistic forms needed to be able speak, listen, read and write about this topic. One approach to this task is to identify which forms and formats are present in the oral or written texts. In the foregoing written example, one can see the sentence format (aka sentence starter or stem sentence), 'The lord had the responsibility to_____; whereas the farmers had the responsibility to_____'. Sentence starters are one instructional strategy teachers could share with the ELs, which teachers would want to pre-think during lesson preparation.

In the preparation of a SIOP lesson, therefore, understandings of linguistic needs, expectations, learners' proficiency-level abilities and the communicative competencies are crucial for teachers to organise effective lessons. The SIOP model emphasises the clarity of defined content and language objectives targeted towards the academic and linguistic needs of the learners. SIOP trainers advocate explicitly sharing these content and language objectives with ELLs in previews of lessons.

In certain situations, like working with children who have experienced interrupted or no prior academic learning or those ELs who also have officially identified special education needs, teachers implementing the SIOP model would need to adapt the academic content by choosing the critical concepts needed by the learners and emphasising them in all parts of the lesson from the presentation of new material to interactive, practice activities and formative/summative assessment.

Once a SIOP teacher had constructed solid content and language objectives for the lesson, the teacher would want to develop meaningful activities that integrate lesson concepts (e.g. surveys, letter writing, simulations, constructing models, ranking, values clarification, information gap tasks and other communicative tasks; see Klippel [1998] or Ur [1995] for excellent examples of communicative activities and tasks) with language practice opportunities for the four skills (e.g. speaking, listening, reading and writing). The teacher would consider developing activities and tasks in which the learners could interact with each other, the texts and materials, technology and the teacher that are meaningful and motivating for them. For example, the math teacher wishing to teach measurements and shapes might have learners design a birdhouse or a dress. The learners could collaborate in the design by discussing and drawing out the dimensions, measuring the parts and then constructing the item. Throughout the process, learners would share their understandings, practice social and academic language and develop their understandings of the concept.

The lesson is now emerging in its content and language objectives, procedures in terms of activities and tasks, the only item missing is the presentation of new material. The SIOP model does not include guidance on the presentation of new concepts, but does discuss the supplementary materials a teacher would need to include. According to the SIOP model, supplementary materials would be used often to make the concept clear and meaningful. So a plethora of visuals, graphs, models and demonstrations are needed so that learners can connect the new content vocabulary to the written and oral forms of the word.

Although the SIOP model does not include guidance on how to present new materials, new material can be presented by the teacher in either a deductive or inductive manner. Deductive presentations of new material are formatted with the rule or concept being introduced and explained by the teacher followed by practice activities. An inductive presentation of new materials starts with an activity or task that learners can reasonably do based on logic and/or general world knowledge (that they have). Learners might be given a file of images and a written text sample and asked to analyse the information, describe the problem and propose solutions. Supports for language learners in the files could include sentence starters, word bank definitions of some terms and/or an audio track of the written passage. (Teachers would differentiate this task by proficiency levels and support the lower proficiency levels in person as needed.)

If a teacher were teaching on the suffragette movement, the file could include photos of only men voting, women protesting and marching, letters between suffragettes expressing their frustration and strategising, as well as written descriptions of the issue by women who were not allowed to vote. Then, the teacher could facilitate a discussion about the situation with prompts such as, 'What is the problem? How did you know? What would you suggest to resolve or fix the problem? What solutions could you offer?'. The teacher could ask the students to employ sentence starters, 'A good solution we had was….' or 'I think that a solution would have been…'. From this starting point, the teacher could then review the written text sample with the learners and ask them to identify a key linguistic form, such as adjectives to express frustration or modal verbs. When the learners engage in discovery learning on linguistic concepts and forms in text followed by authentic practice, they are likely to retain the information longer.

According to Using the SIOP Model (Short, 2002), the various components of lesson preparation combine to integrate the language and concepts into long-term learning in both areas. Content specialists bring content knowledge, curricular understandings, instructional and assessment methods from their field to the instruction of ELs in inclusive classes. While language specialists bring the ability to identify language structures and skills inherent to the content, knowledge of language learning processes and curricular options, methods of teaching and assessing the acquisition of additional languages. When these professionals synthesise their knowledge and abilities, an integrated approach to the instruction and assessment of ELs emerges. This integrated approach features exercising various methods for both content and language teaching, creating materials that combine the content concepts and academic language, connecting subject matter information to language skill use and assessing both language and content learning.

## (2) Background Building

The second component of the SIOP model is background building, which consists of making connections between the learners' background knowledge, past and new learning and highlighting key vocabulary. This component is focused on how the teacher constructs explicit connections either conceptual or linguistic so that the learners can make direct links to their past experiences in life and learning. For example, if a teacher is teaching a nutrition lesson about the Healthy Eating Plate, and asks students to share which fruits they would like to eat, it might be a good idea to give examples of fruits from the learners' past experience. If learners came from South East Asia, fruits would differ considerably from North America. So the teacher might connect the concept by showing a rambutin or dragon fruit as examples for the students instead of a cranberry, which is indigenous to North America and might be unknown to the learners. Connections to past learning using the Healthy Eating Plate concept might be to refer to the types of grains raised by farms that the class had recently learned about and how those grains are made into food.

The third part of background building is highlighting key vocabulary, which is a rather large topic that includes which words to teach and how to teach them. In the preparation phase of SIOP, the teacher would identify both the content vocabulary as well as the language vocabulary that the students would need.

According to Bernier (1997), there are three types of vocabulary: content terms, language terms and language masking content terms. Content terms are those that teachers would normally identify with the content and that would appear in bold or in a glossary. Content terms are regularly employed in presentations of new material and in textbook readings. These are the vocabulary that teachers generally 'see' and associate with explicit teaching. Examples of content terms from Bernier's (1997: 96–97) work are '"regular" history terms or historical jargon, archaic language (e.g., flappers, yeoman, draft animals, dowry), non-history terms or terms borrowed from other fields (e.g., overproduction, recession, cattle prod), obscure acronyms (e.g., FBI, CIA, WPA, GOP, V-J Day), and non-English vocabulary (e.g., elite, suffrage, bourgeoisie, laissez-faire)'.

The second type of vocabulary that Bernier identified is words that are not part of the content, but which would present a barrier to ELs' comprehension. These vocabulary include metaphors, colloquial language, class-based constructions (i.e. terms known by certain socio-economic statuses but not others), cultural idioms and literary allusions. These are the words that are generally overlooked by general educators or are considered common knowledge. Common academic terms and phrases are also part of this category, because teachers do not always notice the learners' unfamiliarity with these terms or phrases.

The third type of vocabulary noted by Bernier is language that masks content. This type of vocabulary, '...includes the fluid boundaries between the two previous categories. Terms appropriated by teachers and scholars that hide content due to variant or multiple meanings (e.g., class, high, right), unfamiliar metaphors (8-hour day/24-hour day) and oxymorons (military intelligence, arms race, American foreign policy)' (Bernier, 1997: 97). When teachers evaluate texts against these categories, they tend to become overwhelmed with the number of words that are obstacles for ELs' comprehension.

The teacher would want to make critical choices of which vocabulary to highlight. One strategy to help with these tough choices is to consider high- and low-frequency vocabulary. High-frequency vocabulary words are those words that English speakers use often. The most frequent words in English are: the, to, and, he, a, I, you, it, of. Lower-frequency vocabulary words are those that are rarer, including: attic, tearful, tailgate, hydraulically, unsparing and embryogenesis (http://www.wordfrequency. info/sample.asp#simple). Teachers in elementary schools are also familiar with high-frequency vocabulary, but call them sight words or Dolch words (Dolch, 1936). Dolch words are common vocabulary needed by emerging English readers to know by sight. (See Appendix B for an original list of Dolch words.)

Extending the concept of high- and low-frequency vocabulary, teachers can esti-mate roughly whether the vocabulary word is more or less common, if the word is vital for the academic content area or if the word will be needed in other courses and/or in the future; if the answers to these questions are no or not likely, it would be a word that I recommend skipping, providing a simpler synonym or a direct trans-lation in the native language. Otherwise, one would need to teach the word explic-itly (see Figure 4.2).

Stahl's (2005) and Folse's (2006) research on vocabulary instruction presents important tips on teaching vocabulary. Stahl found that learners needed at least 12 exposures to a new vocabulary word to remember it. Folse recommends that teachers should teach a small core of vocabulary words and conduct a series of quick exer-cises (i.e. fill in the blank, multiple choice, sentence completion as well as open-ended activities) to cause students to recall the word from their long-term memory several times within a 2- to 3-day period. He found that the learners retained the vocabulary term longer when they had to access it often in a short space of time. In teaching a content lesson, this would mean that the teacher would need to teach the vocabu-lary words using visuals, real objects, synonyms, etc. and then provide numerous different exercises, activities and tasks. All these opportunities to practice would be

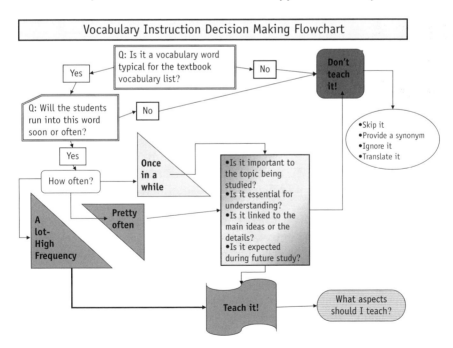

**Figure 4.2** Vocabulary instruction decision-making flowchart

interwoven with speaking, listening, reading and writing on the academic topic to cause the learners to recall the concept.

(3) Comprehensible Input

The third component of the SIOP model is comprehensible input, which means that information that is incoming to the learners is clear, intelligible and makes sense to them. This component has also become known in the field as linguistic modifications and supports.

---

**Suggested Linguistic Modifications**

- Ask questions often and include all students equally.
- Avoid using only directives (e.g. open your books to page…).
- Ask questions that are open-ended and that require higher-order thinking to engage the learners cognitively.
- Create opportunities for meaningful verbal interaction with genuine interest on the part of the teacher and learners.
- Create real comprehension check opportunities and activities to measure the learner's degree of understanding.
- Enhance opportunities for various groupings (i.e. participant structures).
- Provide EL students with more simultaneous written, oral and visual information.
- Allow for longer wait time for EL student responses.
- Create opportunities for EL kids to produce extended discourse (i.e. longer turns talking and writing, not just sentences).
- Try to engage the learner one-on-one prior to whole classroom interaction to ensure that he/she is ready.

---

Comprehensible input is a concept introduced by Krashen (1979, 1980, 1981). According to Krashen, comprehensible input is oral and/or written information that a learner can perceive and is understandable. If the incoming information were formed using complex grammar or unfamiliar forms or vocabulary, it would not be comprehensible to the language learner. On the other hand, if the learner can understand most of the incoming oral and/or written information, because most of the grammar, vocabulary, sentence formats/complexity or other forms are known to the learner, it is accessible and comprehensible. Krashen termed this concept $i+1$ to demonstrate that the input needs to be relative to the learner's proficiency level. For language acquisition to occur, the input also cannot be too easy or too hard. The term $i+1$ means that the incoming language is just above the learner's current level of comprehension (i.e. most language is understood, but one new form may be present) so the learner can figure out the new information. New terms or grammar need to be present as well in order for the student to continue to develop his/her language.

In the SIOP model, researchers recognised the need for the teachers' speech to be appropriate for the students' proficiency level. They advocate a slightly slower rate of speech, clear enunciation and the use of sentence structures appropriate to the learners' proficiency level. Comprehensible input would also include which vocabulary words are used by the teacher (and text) and whether they are comprehensible to the learner.

The SIOP researchers included the Vygotskian concept of Instructional Conversation (Vygotsky, 1986; Wertsch, 1985) into the model. Vygotsky found that individuals (i.e. novices) learned new information when they interacted using instructional conversation with an expert (someone who happens to know more about a given topic). Anyone can play any role as a novice when she/he is learning something new and outside of his/her experiences. Anyone can be an expert if he/she has information, even just a small bit of information, that another person does not have. Students can be the experts to the teacher on information the teacher has not experienced before.

The key to learning, according to Vygotsky, is the communication, the verbal and/or written information that is shared between individuals or groups in a way that takes into account the learners' background knowledge. The interaction should be meaningful and dialogic, meaning based on a back and forth of communication between individuals. If, for example, you were teaching a child how to cook an egg, you would show how to crack the egg and say, 'Crack the egg on the side, like this. You have to hit it pretty hard to make it crack, but not too hard to shatter it'. The child might respond, 'Okay. So, I do it like this [demonstration]. But not too hard, right?' and you might reply, 'Right. Forcefully, but not too hard. Try it'.

This interaction causes the learners to move from their actual level of development (starting point) to their personal potential or proximal level of development (individual's potential in terms of the end point). This is called the Zone of Proximal Development (ZPD).

If a learner was learning about types of maps, the teacher would identify where the learner's knowledge of maps began. For this example, the teacher determines through the past curriculum and reviewing with the students that the learners had seen and interacted with road maps and physical maps (i.e. those including mountains, rivers and other physical features) and knew how to use legends and directional features (i.e. compass rose). That is the learners' actual level or starting point in the ZPD. The end point, or proximal level, that they can personally achieve at their age and cognitive level (i.e. potential) is to differentiate kinds of maps and understand the differences among political maps, economic or resource maps, climate maps and thematic maps. Typological maps might be too hard at this stage/age. The teacher would orally present different kinds of maps, showing each of them visually and labelling them (in writing, too). The teacher would engage the learners through discussion in identifying what features are prominent on each map. Then the teacher could ask learners to complete a task in teams using various maps located at stations (stations are centres set up in a classroom with materials and activities/tasks for learners to complete. They work in small groups or individually and circulate around each station). Afterwards, the teacher would facilitate conversations with the learners to debrief them from their tasks and end the lesson by prompting learners to share their understandings of the uses and features that distinguish each type of map. Through the sharing of knowledge in the direct instruction, the interactive dialogues between teacher and students and students in small groups as well as the debriefing discussions, learners would arrive at their proximal level, or potential level, of knowledge of types of maps.

According to the SIOP model, information becomes more comprehensible to ELLs when teachers employ instructional conversation into their lessons, whether in the presentation of new vocabulary or in discussions. The SIOP model was influenced by the previous research of Cazden on interaction patterns in more traditional, teacher-centred classes. Cazden (2001) found a pattern of questioning that she called the initiation-response-evaluation/initiation-response-feedback (IRE/IRF) sequence, which she found to be superficial and unhelpful to the learning process. The IRE/IRF sequence starts with the teacher initiating (I) a display question or known-answer question to gauge learners' comprehension. A student responds (R) to the question. The teacher evaluates (E) whether the response was correct or incorrect. For example, T: What is the colour of the sky? S: Blue. T: Good. So....

Instructional conversation is one technique for interacting with learners beyond the IRE/IRF pattern. *Instructional conversation* is comprised of several features that connect the topic to learners' knowledge through explanations, questioning and authentic interaction between the teacher and learners.

| *Instructional conversation features* | *Examples* |
| --- | --- |
| (1) Thematic focus: In an instructional conversation, one theme is the topic of the conversation. Tangents are avoided unless they are teachable moments somewhat related to the topic. | Topic: global warming |
| (2) Activation and use of background knowledge and relevant schema | **Teacher (T):** So, class, what have you heard about global warming?<br>**Student 1:** I heard the earth is getting hotter.<br>**Student 2:** I heard it's getting hotter and the weather is crazier. But why did we have such a cold winter, if it's getting hotter?<br>**Student 3:** I heard it's getting warmer, because the polar bears now don't have a place to live and the ice is melting.<br>**T:** Okay. With a partner, I would like you to list in 3 minutes everything you have heard about global warming.<br>The teacher then writes all the small groups comments on a list at the board. |

| | |
|---|---|
| (3) Direct teaching: Direct teaching/instruction is when the teacher explicitly explains a new concept. Resources and tools would be employed to aid learners' comprehension. | **T**: Great. This is a good start. We know that the earth is getting hotter, ice caps and glaciers are melting, the weather is getting more extreme, in other words there is more intense heat and cold. Now, do you know why? I'm going to tell you. Be sure to pay attention, because I will ask you to write down what you understand afterwards. Ready?<br><br>    Well, scientists started recording the temperatures for places all over the world over 100 years ago. In some places, like China, the temperature has been recorded for much longer. When they had all these data, information, they realised that there were patterns and that the temperatures were rising, increasing, getting warmer. See this chart with rising temperatures in Maine. [Teacher shows chart.] See how the temperatures start here and are at this now [pointing]. When scientists realised this, they started conducting experiments, such as measuring the carbon dioxide ($CO_2$) released in the air from cars, factories and even cows. And they learned that humans have had a big impact on the temperatures rising, because of industry, use of electricity and resources (burning fossil fuels like coal, oil and wood), burning of garbage and other things. The theory of global warming states that the increased amount of carbon dioxide released into the environment builds up in the atmosphere where it is trapped. See in this visual how the carbon dioxide is trapped? The sun beats down on the atmosphere heating up the $CO_2$ gas like a magnifying glass. The more $CO_2$ gas and sunlight, the hotter it gets, like a greenhouse, where plants are grown. So, the ice at the polar caps (north and south pole) has melted more and more. Let's look at this cool website to see how the ice is melting over the years (http://climatekids.nasa.gov/time-machine/).<br><br>    Okay, class, now, I would like you to write your thoughts on a piece of paper showing me what you understood about why global warming is occurring. |
| (4) Promotion of more complex language and expression | **T**: Why do you think the carbon dioxide is trapped in the atmosphere?<br>*or*<br>How do you think we could reduce the amount of carbon dioxide released into the air? |
| (5) Elicitation of bases for statements or positions (e.g. how? why?) | **Student 4**: I think the carbon dioxide is trapped, because there is a bubble of air around the world.<br>**Student 5**: I think it is trapped, because it has nowhere to go. |

| (6) Fewer 'known-answer' questions | The teacher would avoid questions such as 'Who can tell me why the planet is warming?' after the direct teaching. Rather, the teacher would ask students to summarise their ideas and then ask them more complex questions as in (5). |
|---|---|
| (7) Being responsive to student contributions (teachable moment) | When Student 4 says, 'I think the carbon dioxide is trapped, because there is a bubble of air around the world', the teacher would respond to this contribution by affirming it, 'You are right! There are three layers of air around the earth called the troposphere, which is closest to the earth, the stratosphere, in the middle, and the mesosphere, which is sort of a bubble around the earth. These layers keep the air around the earth, so it doesn't just float off into space. If these layers didn't keep the air here, then we couldn't breathe or live. So, Student 5, you are right, too, it doesn't have any place to go'. |
| (8) Connected discourse | The connection of the discourse can be seen in the previous passages. Ideas build off of each other, students are responded to when they contribute, etc. |
| (9) A challenging but non-threatening atmosphere | The teacher asks the learners to think about the topic, but does not do it in an aggressive or domineering manner. |
| (10) General participation, including self-selected turns | Students are free to take turns and are encouraged to share their thoughts at the appropriate time. All students are asked to participate at various stages. All comments are welcomed and integrated into the instructional conversation. |

Teachers construct their presentations (i.e. direct teaching) and discussions thematically, asking open-ended questions and helping learners' to make connections with their words and references to background experiences. They encourage all learners to participate and create a classroom environment where all the learners feel safe. They do this by providing linguistic supports and helping learners save face, when necessary. For example, the teacher might recast a student's contribution to clarify and guide their thinking on the concept. Teachers follow up and respond authentically to the students' contributions as well. They extend the learning by asking how and why questions, which encourage both complex language constructions and critical thinking. The use of instructional conversation significantly alters the discourse of the classroom to allow learners to practice with the new academic language.

Teachers might want to consider techniques to facilitate discussion. Taking instructional conversation techniques as a foundation, the tips listed in Table 4.3 aid the facilitation of conversations (see Table 4.3).

Other aspects of this component of the SIOP model are the teacher's clarity of explanations of academic tasks and the use of a variety of techniques to elucidate new information. In practice, this means that teachers should pre-think or even script their explanations of tasks so that they keep directions understandable and

**Table 4.3** Guidelines for facilitating conversations

*Some suggestions to help in the facilitation of conversations are:*

Develop shared guidelines for the conversation (e.g. appropriacy, relevancy, respect and participation)

Make sure the participants have insights on the topic to share (from life experiences, readings, etc.)

Be comfortable with silence

Ask open-end questions
- Focal questions followed by guiding questions
- Probing questions that break down the bigger question into smaller parts to mine all aspects/to visit all angles
- Leading questions (i.e. asking questions to offer hints or guide thinking)
- Clarifying and confirming questions (e.g. 'What I am hearing is…. Is that what you mean?')

Encourage through your questions
- Evidence to support ideas/opinions
- Specificity
- Connections

Build on individual contributions

Manage pacing through
- Providing time limits
- Reminding students of time remaining
- Looking for natural conversational lulls and pauses

Play devil's advocate – asking questions from an opposing perspective

Reopen the conversation to the whole group after engaging directly with one student

Repeat and rephrase the overarching/focal question to keep the learners focused

Be careful about taking on the 'expert' role too fast or too often; allow the learners to take it on by not always offering the answer quickly

Redirect thinking or misunderstandings

Recast learners' contributions both for second language acquisition and for other students' comprehension

Provide time for students to think through ideas and test them out in small groups

Consider suitable wait time

Deal with random comments appropriately
- Provide feedback
  - Judgements?
  - Vary praise
  - Being non-committal
  - Receive the comments (e.g. 'I hear what you are saying')
  - Redirect
  - Reposition the statement or question

Work with students taking a 'wrong' stance
- Avoid confrontation
- Avoid the topic, if it is off target
- Provide evidence for both positions

Build in time for reflection, summation and timeouts for participants and you

Take the groups' temperature and check comprehension of objectives unambiguous. They can also clarify by reviewing oral and written instructions with the learners in a stepwise manner.

The use of a variety of techniques to clarify new information provides assorted scaffolds, such as demonstrations, modelling of language and academic concepts, visuals, hands-on activities, gestures and body language, to allow access to the new concepts and connects to the earlier discussion of the presentation of new material, instructional conversation and facilitating conversations. A teacher would want to consider how best to explain new information in ways that are concrete for learners. The coupling of the demonstration with the oral and/or written explanation would provide new content information along with the necessary academic language. Table 4.4 lists supports that WIDA suggests.

## (4) Strategies

The fourth component of the SIOP model describes strategies used by learners and teachers. An important distinction arises at this juncture in the discussion of this SIOP component. Communication and learning strategies are employed by ELs to aid their acquisition of the new language. Instructional strategies are utilised by the teacher and are associated with this component of the SIOP model. Those strategies associated with learners are more closely identified with the Cognitive Academic Language Learning Approach (CALLA) model in Chapter 5.

Teachers employ a variety of instructional strategies in lessons to scaffold information and question learners. Some of the instructional strategies advanced by SIOP trainers are English as a second language (ESL) tasks and activities, such as ranking, jazz chants, total physical response (TPR) and values clarification. Think alouds are another strategy mentioned in this component. Think alouds are when a teacher demonstrates to learners how to read a text by reading a sample out loud. This strategy differs from a teacher read aloud, because the teacher is also supposed to orally articulate the complex questions and processes that she/he thinks during the reading. For example, an excerpt from Aesop's fable, Belling the Cat, follows.

**Table 4.4** Supplementary resources suggested by WIDA

| Sensory Supports | Graphic Supports | Interactive Supports |
|---|---|---|
| • Real-life objects (realia) | • Charts | • In pairs or partners |
| • Manipulatives | • Graphic organizers | • In triads or small groups |
| • Pictures & Photographs | • Tables | • In a whole group |
| • Illustrations, diagrams & drawings | • Graphs | • Using cooperative group structures |
| • Magazines & newspapers | • Timelines | • With the Internet (Websites) or software programs |
| • Physical activities | • Number lines | • In the native language (L1) |
| • Videos & Films | | • With mentors |
| • Broadcasts | | |
| • Models & figures | | |

(WIDA Standards, 2007)

When reading this fable aloud, the teacher would pause, momentarily put the book down to signify that she/he is working outside of the text and gesture that she/he is thinking. Then the teacher would share his/her inner thoughts. In the following excerpt, the teacher's inner thoughts are shown in brackets.

> Belling the Cat (**Teacher**: I wonder what 'belling' means. I've never heard the word bell used to talk about an action.) Long ago (**T**: How long? Hm?), the mice (**T**: Which mice? Where?) had a general council (**T**: Mice talk? They have a council, like a meeting?) to consider what measures (**T**: Oh, measures like actions or steps) they could take to outwit their common enemy, the Cat. Some said this and some said that (**T**: I wish I knew what some of them said. I'd like to hear their ideas); but at last a young mouse (**T**: Cool! A young hero) got up and said he had a proposal to make, which he thought would meet the case (**T**: Oh, solve the problem). 'You will all agree,' said he, 'that our chief danger (**T**: Biggest danger) consists in the sly and treacherous manner (**T**: Cats do stalk their prey) in which the enemy (**T**: The cat) approaches us. Now, if we could receive some signal of her approach, we could easily escape from her (**T**: Like a fire alarm!). I venture (**T**: A fancy word for suggest), therefore, to propose that a small bell be procured (**T**: Procured is another word for found), and attached by a ribbon round the neck of the Cat (**T**: LOL. How are they going to put a ribbon around the cat's neck?). By this means we should always know when she was about, and could easily retire (**T**: Retire means hide) while she was in the neighbourhood'. (**T**: The British spelling of neighborhood). This proposal (**T**: Idea) met with general applause (**T**: Clapping), until an old mouse (**T**: A wise mouse?) got up and said: 'That is all very well, but who is to bell the Cat?' (**T**: Hahaha, bell the cat means to put the bell on the cat!) The mice looked at one another and nobody spoke (**T**: I would not want to do that if I was a mouse. I mean how could they even DO that. They are so small.) Then the old mouse said, 'It is easy to propose impossible remedies.' (**T**: It is easy to make up solutions that are impossible.)

Although the SIOP creators note these types of instructional strategies in training workshops, they also overlap instructional strategies with scaffolds to increase comprehensible input. The comprehensible input strategies have been noted in that category.

## (5) Interaction

Many researchers, teachers and a large body of research combine to advocate that the role of interaction is a vital part of acquiring a new language. In the SIOP model, interaction, the fifth component, is delineated in terms of frequency of interactional opportunities, grouping configurations, wait time for students' responses and clarification in the first language (L1). According to Long (1981), learners must have opportunities to produce input and output. It is the process of participating in interaction on numerous topics, on a regular basis and with differing interlocutors (i.e. conversation participants) that allows learners to acquire the new language. In other words, in Hatch's (1978) words, 'We learn language by *doing* language'.

Therefore, employing the SIOP model in the classroom, teachers would desire to include speaking, listening, reading and writing activities in which the learners could share their content knowledge and use their academic language. Interaction may be synchronous or asynchronous and occur inside or outside of the classroom between students (native and non-native peers), students and teachers, students and written texts, podcasts and videos, and interactive, content-focused tasks or games are crucial to instill interaction into the content classroom.

## (6) Practice/Application

The next component describes the types of practice and application activities that teachers provide the learners so that they can better understand the content concepts as well as the accompanying academic language. In the SIOP model, teachers are encouraged to include interactive activities with hands-on materials and/or manipulatives in order to make the concepts more meaningful and real to learners and cause them to use the academic language. An expectation on the part of SIOP proponents is to integrate all language skills into lesson activities (i.e. speaking, listening, reading and writing).

The SIOP model originators encourage trainers to infuse ESL techniques, such as jazz chants, learning games, values clarification among others, into content classes. These techniques allow for linguistic practice and engagement of the learners. At one training session, a team I participated with was charged to develop a jazz chant on the weather. A 'jazz chant is a rhythmic expression of spoken English' (http://jazzchants. net/what-is-a-jazz-chant) and resembles raps, songs and poems. I created one with my sixth-grade ELs to teach different climate zones, semi-arid, arid, humid subtropical, tropical, humid continental, subarctic.

Learning games include a huge array of possibilities, such as bingo, matching, 20 questions, charades and Pictionary. You can search on the internet the key words of the content topic with (1) a classroom exercise (i.e. matching, fill in the blank, cloze activity, ordering, sorting, categorising, labelling); (2) games (e.g. jeopardy, catch phrase, I spy, risk, battleship, Wheel of Fortune, Family Feud or Password); or (3) a task (e.g. information gap, values clarification/opinion gap, reasoning gap, ranking, problem solving, role play, simulation, brainstorming). Key words can be used in combination to identify games in a content area, such as global warming + bingo, continent or geography + 'information gap activity', role play + American civil war, charades games + Harry Potter, colonial America + simulation. Importantly, use quotes to only find the type of item you desire, 'information gap activity', or you will not return the items you hope. Also, searching by grade/age level, or classroom, will help narrow your search. The key point is to use the language of the content area and what is needed by the learners to develop their proficiency. For more language games, see http://edition.tefl.net/ideas/games/15-classroom-language-games/; http://www.eslkidstuff.com/Gamescontents.htm#.U1ErRvm1ZPQ; http://iteslj. org/c/games.html.

A values clarification task is when participants share their opinions on a topic; for example, if one was teaching about the ethics of industrialists/robber barons and philanthropy, you could have students discuss if they were extremely wealthy, would they want to give their money to charities to build parks, schools, libraries and art museums. Another illustration of a values clarification would be the ethics of the US dropping the atomic bomb on Japan in World War II.

## (7)  Lesson Delivery

The lesson is delivered in ways that clearly link to both the content and language objectives. Teachers manage the class environment and lesson delivery so that pacing is appropriate to learners' proficiency levels and learners are engaged 90–100% of the class period. Pacing a lesson and engaging learners are tricky. One has to create stimulating lessons with interactive tasks while weighing learners' comprehension. One needs to 'cover' the content, but not to the exclusion of learners' understandings. Simultaneously, one should not proceed too slowly or risk losing students' interest. In inclusive classes with native speakers of English, teachers would need to balance comprehensibility and pacing, so as to keep learners' engaged.

## (8)  Review/Assessment

Teachers review with the students all the key content and language concepts at the conclusion of the lesson. They provide formative, ongoing feedback to learners on their language, content and work output. Teachers employ comprehension checks of lesson objectives. Teachers might want to consider meaningful checks of learners' comprehension in discussions as many non-native speakers will say they understand when they do not in order to save face.

Based on observations of hundreds of content teachers in a southern large urban school district, Dale Gable and I found that two categories of comprehension checks were being used (Reynolds & Gable, 2007). Which category of comprehension checks in Table 4.5 do you think is the most likely to reveal insights into the learners' understandings of a subject? Why?

The assessment/review component of the SIOP model is not developed as fully as other model components. Since this is a large body of knowledge, additional reading on both language assessment and content/language assessment is recommended. For reading on the appropriate assessment of language and content, see Valdez-Pierce's (2003) *Assessing English Language Learners*, Brown's (2004) *Language Assessment*, Madsen's (1983) *Techniques in Testing*, O'Malley and

**Table 4.5** Comprehension check questions

| Column A | Column B |
| --- | --- |
| • Right? | • Could you tell me what you mean? |
| • Okay? | • Could you tell me more about that? |
| • You know? | • What do you think about that? |
| • Does that make sense? | • What is your opinion? Perspective? Take on that? |
| • You got it? | • What is your understanding of this? |
| • Does everyone understand? | • Can you put that in your own words? |
| • Is that clear? | • Can you retell me the story? |
| • Any questions? | • Have you done something similar? |
| • Do you understand? | • How does that relate? |
| • Yes or no? | • Where have you seen or done this? |
| • Agree or disagree? | • Have you experienced this? |
| • Right or wrong? | • Have you witnessed this in real life? |
| • Is it _____ (this) or _____ (that)? | • If this was you, how would it look/feel? |

Valdez-Pierce's (1996) *Authentic Assessment for English Language Learners: Practical Approaches for Teachers* and/or Hughes' (1989) *Testing for Language Teachers*. For issues related to high-stakes, standardised tests for ELs, see Coltrane's (2002) ELLs and high-stakes assessments: A review of the issues (http://www.cal.org/resources/digest/0207coltrane.html, http://www.cal.org/content/download/1531/16148/file/EnglishLanguageLearnersAndHighStakesTests.pdf).

# Strengths

One strength of the SIOP model is its solid research (Echevarria & Short, 2003, 2005; Echevarria *et al.*, 2004; Short, 1993, 1994, 2002; Short & Echevarria, 1999) and practical base. One can clearly see the links to research and theories in applied linguistics, such as Cummins' (1979, 1980a, 1980b, 1992, 1996) social and academic language distinction, Krashen's (1979, 1980, 1981, 1982, 1985a, 1985b) comprehensible input, Vyogotsky's (1986) ZPD and instructional conversation, Cazden's (2001) classroom interaction research and Long's (1981) interaction model.

The SIOP's *observation protocol* has been shown to be a reliable and valid tool to distinguish between sheltered instruction and non-sheltered instruction (Guarino *et al.*, 2001). Their study explained that 'The SIOP is a 30-item instrument scored on a 1 (no evidence) to 7 (clearly evident) Likert-type scale. The three subscales are Preparation, Instruction, and Review/Evaluation. The protocol was administered to four experienced teachers on Sheltered Instruction (SI) from three major universities in the southwest. These teachers observed six video recordings of teachers engaged in SI. Three of the videos were deemed by specialists to be highly representative of the tenets of SI while the other three were not. Reliability, assessed by Cronbach's alpha, achieved an acceptable level of .90 or higher … All three subscales [the SIOP Model] reliably discriminated sheltered instruction from non-sheltered instruction' (Guarino *et al.*, 2001: 1; http://www.csulb.edu/~jechev/SIOP%20Article%20Guarino.pdf).

The SIOP model of content-based instruction alone, not the observation protocol, has been supported by numerous other studies (http://www.siopinstitute.net/research. html). This is a clear distinction that is worth noting.

On the whole, research conducted outside the auspices of the SIOP team have yielded positive results overall. For example, McBride (2007) surveyed teachers instructed in SIOP and discovered that most employed EL engagement strategies taught to them after the training. Her research did not include the ELs' learning outcomes resulting from SIOP training. Likewise, Ray (2011) conducted a self-report study of teacher perceptions investigating the training and implementation of SIOP and found that 'Teachers reported a high degree of implementing SIOP strategies. They perceived the strategies improved student learning in most cases. There was no statistically significant relationship found between the degree of SIOP implementation and perceptions of the effectiveness of SIOP'. In this study, there were no objective quantitative or qualitative measures that directly assessed the implementation quality or quality of strategies, nor were the ELs' learning outcomes analysed.

## Strengths that May Also be Weaknesses

Another strength that can be a weakness is the comprehensive or wide-ranging nature of the model. Once a general educator is prepared in the model, the planning time necessary to implement the instructional, linguistic and materials modifications makes it unmanageable and thus anachronistic (unusable or makes itself a fossil). Teachers generally complain about the complexity of the model and the feeling of being unable to include all the strategies/modifications into their instruction. Responding to this issue, the Fort Worth Independent School District, with whom I have consulted, modified the SIOP model. They reduced the number of strategies/modifications to what they considered a core of essentials. In this context, this adaptation of the SIOP model may have been due to the number of licensed teachers in Texas, who obtained their teaching licenses not through a university teacher education programme but by taking a standardised test.

The model includes best practices in general education as well as those necessary for second language acquisition. The model offers sound, concrete, practical suggestions for general educators to employ. Unfortunately, the generality of the strategies (e.g. cooperative learning and graphic organisers) and the lack of direct explanation and connection to second language acquisition cause many educators to claim that the strategies are 'just good teaching', which minimises the implementation efforts. For example, cooperative learning allows for interaction among students which creates a plethora of input and output opportunities for learners. If a teacher only employs cooperative groupings, of course the teacher would say that that is just good teaching. Furthermore, if the task provided to the cooperative groups is close ended (meaning there is only one correct answer), lacks critical thinking or a means to engage both orally and in written form, the cooperative group would not communicate enough to generate enough linguistic input and output to aid second language acquisition.

## Weaknesses

From my analysis using the evaluative framework (Table 4.6), the weaknesses of the SIOP model tend to be in the curricular planning against assessments (i.e. backward design) and explicit information about language/content assessment, creation of teacher-made tests, testing accommodations, appropriate EL proficiency assessments, providing ongoing feedback on content and language learning.

**Table 4.6** Evaluative framework for teacher preparation models, approaches and initiatives in EL inclusion

| I. Knowledge | SIOP model |
|---|---|
| When preparing teachers to include ELs into their content courses and to work with linguistically and culturally diverse groups of ELLs, they should have *knowledge* of the following areas: | |
| • The structures and features of the English language.<br>• The distinctions between oral and written language.<br>• The basic units of language, such as parts of speech, types of sentences and the sound system of English.<br>• The construction of differing discourse units from the sentence level to a variety of social and academic genres and formats.<br>• The irregularities of English.<br>• The pragmatic/sociocultural dimensions of language (e.g. voice, audience) and how language varies accordingly.<br>• An appropriate target for language acquisition/learning is real language use; 'standard' English is a myth. | Not explicitly taught in the model. This information is generally viewed as knowledge teachers already possess. |

| | |
|---|---|
| • The key principles of second language acquisition/ learning (Ellis, 2008).<br>• Instruction needs to include:<br>• A balance predominantly on meaning but also on forms.<br>• An understanding of individual differences in learners.<br>• Environmental modifications to reduce anxiety and affective issues.<br>• Extensive comprehensible input.<br>• Interaction with peers and instructors on the academic topics. | The SIOP model does a good job on this category including most foundational second language acquisition (SLA) aspects except: meaning/form balance, spontaneous/controlled production and transfer.<br><br>Although the SIOP model does not provide specific guidance on individual differences and anxiety reduction, these concepts permeate the model. |
| • Opportunities for learners to develop both 'a rich repertoire of formulaic expressions and a rule-based competence'.<br>• Opportunities for spontaneous as well as controlled production.<br>• Output opportunities.<br>• Social and academic language.<br>• Transfer of knowledge and skills from the first to the second language. | |
| • An understanding of ELLs' proficiency levels and their abilities and challenges at those levels. | This information is not explicitly taught; familiarity with the information is expected. |
| • The laws pertinent to ELs' instruction in the particular context. | Not present |
| • The resources available to learn about ELs' educational backgrounds, first languages and cultures. | Not present |
| • A sociolinguistic consciousness (Lucas & Villegas, 2011).<br>• Understanding of the relationships between language, culture and identity.<br>• Awareness of the sociopolitical context of language use and language education, particularly in the specific context. | Not explicitly taught in the model. This information is generally viewed as prerequisite knowledge for teachers. |
| • The subject matter; knowledge of one core content area or specialty area. | Not explicitly taught in the model. This information is generally viewed as knowledge teachers already possess. |

(Continued)

**Table 4.6** (Continued)

| II. *Performance* | |
|---|---|
| When preparing teachers to include ELs into their content courses and to work with linguistically and culturally diverse groups of ELLs, they should have *abilities and skills* in the following areas: | |
| Curricular and Instructional Planning | |
| • Planning with assessments as clear targets (e.g. backward design [Wiggins & McTighe, 2005]). | Not present |
| • Creating content, language and learning strategy objectives. | A strength of this model is the content and language objectives. Learning strategies are mentioned, but they are not objectives. |
| • Pre-teaching and/or integrating necessary skills, such as process writing, note-taking, etc. into the curriculum. | Not present |
| • Integrating speaking, listening, reading, writing, grammar, vocabulary and pronunciation instruction and practice into lessons. | A strength of the model is the overt inclusion of these items with the exception of pronunciation. |
| • Developing units with clear connections through a thematic focus. | A strength |
| • Modifying, developing, locating materials for linguistic accessibility of lessons. | A strength |
| • Analysing the linguistic features of oral and written discourse so as to be able to bridge the gap between ELs and a wide variety of genres, subject areas, academic discourse communities and texts. | Not overtly mentioned in the model |
| • Addressing multiple ESL proficiency levels in the same class by planning for differentiated instruction. | It is discussed in the model, but how to differentiate is not taught. |
| • Making informed choices (Brown, 2007b) based on solid SLA principles and best practices in content and language instruction for the particular context with its unique variables (Kumaravadivelu, 2001). | Unique context features and informed choices based on the context do not seem to factor heavily into the SIOP. |
| Instructional Delivery | |
| • Creating comfortable learning environments and classroom communities with low anxiety. | Expected in implementation |
| • Identifying learners' background knowledge and building upon it. | A strength |

| | |
|---|---|
| • Making informed choices about instruction and employing a wide variety and frequency of approaches, techniques and resources depending on learners' needs. | A strength |
| • Explicitly teaching new vocabulary and language needed for oral (speaking and listening) and written (reading and writing) engagement with the academic content using supports and tools for meaning making. | A strength |
| • Creating meaningful, academically focused, engaging, interactive and experiential lessons and tasks that include ELs in activities (Migliacci & Verplaetse, 2008). | A strength |
| • Directly teaching new academic information in small portions or 'chunks' with practice and interaction opportunities. | Direct teaching is included, but not the chunking notion |
| • Modifying the delivery of speech to heighten learners' comprehension (i.e. making linguistic modifications) or modifying the complexity or quantity of written material to make it more accessible. | A strength |
| • Scaffolding instruction using a variety of supports, such as graphic organisers, visuals, modelling, sentence frames, etc. | A strength |
| • Providing cognitively challenging materials to ELs that are linguistically accessible. | A strength |
| Assessment | |
| • Offering learners a variety of ways to demonstrate their knowledge of the content or language. For example, using performance and alternative assessment (see task and product examples above). | Not discussed |
| • Providing suitable and judiciously chosen accommodations for ELs during academic assessments. Accommodations are state-mandated supports for learners during standardised assessments, such as providing increased time for the test, breaks, dictionaries and/or translators for directions. | Not discussed |
| • Measuring learners content knowledge and language ability separately. | Not discussed |
| • Providing ongoing feedback on content knowledge and language ability that is constructive and regular. | Not discussed with the exception of comprehension checks |

*(Continued)*

**Table 4.6** (Continued)

| | |
|---|---|
| • Assessing learners' progress in language learning according to proficiency indicators. | Not discussed |
| • Modifying text and teacher-made assessments to support English learners. For example, using visuals and models in directions. | Not discussed |
| *III. Orientations* | |
| When preparing teachers to include ELs into their content courses and to work with linguistically and culturally diverse groups of ELLs, they should have *awareness of, value for and appreciation of* the following areas: | |
| • Value for linguistic and cultural diversity. | Background expectation |
| • Inclination to advocate for the linguistic and programmatic needs of ELLs. | Not mentioned |
| • Willingness to collaborate with language specialists, content teachers, administrators, parents, etc. to provide high-quality instruction for ELs and to create EL-friendly schools and communities. | Not mentioned |
| • Hold high expectations for ELs and all learners. | A strength |
| • Inclination to provide assessments that level the playing field for ELs so that they may demonstrate their knowledge in a variety of ways. | Not mentioned |
| • Value for reflective instructional processes. | Not mentioned |
| • Willingness to develop positive home/school connections with ELs' parents. | Not mentioned |
| • Willingness to treat cultures respectfully and to eliminate stereotyping of peoples and cultures. | Although the SIOP model does not provide specifics, these concepts permeate the model. |

There is a grouping of assumptions or background expectations that could be more explicitly taught in the model. These assumptions or expectations include the linguistic knowledge of general educators (i.e. expectations that the teachers understand grammatical and discourse forms and can teach them explicitly); positive predispositions towards differing cultures and languages and preparation to understand race and diversity issues (i.e. white privilege, unconscious bias); and modifications/informed choices based on the unique features of the specific context. While my readings have shown that some of these concepts, like culturally congruent pedagogy, inform and undergird the model (Echevarria & Short, 1999), there is no specific preparation provided in the model.

According to Perez-Selles (2011), sheltered instruction training programmes, such as the SIOP model, cover only the tip of the iceberg in terms of the information that general educators need to include ELs effectively into their classes. Furthermore, the report recognises that the SIOP model was cutting edge when it was developed, but has since become outdated by more research in best practices of content-based instruction.

Other weaknesses of the SIOP model include too little information about language awareness and how to develop language objectives, L1 and cultural supports, and sociocultural awareness. Some methodological considerations are either too general or assumed, such as cooperative groupings, proficiency-level differentiation and materials development/modification (Table 4.6).

## Optimal Context for Implementation and Suggestions

The optimal context for the implementation of the SIOP model is in high-incidence districts (districts with higher numbers of ELs), but where one-way or two-way bilingual programmes cannot be developed (for more on bilingual programmes, see Chapter 10). Another vital component is that there is strong administrative support for the professional development of general educators, a predisposition for collaboration among educators as well as a developed peer-coaching infrastructure. A district ideal for implementing the SIOP model might look like Madison, WI, or Columbus, OH, districts with large numbers of ELs who speak a wide variety of first languages (i.e. heterogeneous populations): Asian (Asian Indian, Chinese, Filipino, Hmong, Japanese, Korean and Vietnamese); Native Hawaiian and Pacific Islanders; Hispanic (Cuban, Puerto Rican, Mexican and other Latino areas); Eastern European (Albanian, Russian, Lithuanian, Latvian, Polish and Ukrainian); and Middle Eastern (Saudi, Syrian, Iraqi and Somali). Due to the high numbers, all teachers in the district would need to include ELs effectively into their classes. Because of the diverse first languages or local politics and state mandates, bilingual education is not a productive option.

Suggestions for the implementation of this model are to develop an effective professional development action plan with the support of administration and teachers. Including teachers at all levels into the development of a plan is vital for teacher buy-in. If the plan comes exclusively from the administration or lead teachers, classroom teachers might feel an even heavier load and resist. If classroom teachers view it as a means to improve their overall teaching abilities, they are more likely to engage with the plan.

Once a district has 'buy-in' at all levels, the district would want to decide if it invites in SIOP trainers, which is an option with this model, or whether the district would want to do other general training for the whole staff. This general training can be problematic due to many factors; for example, teachers do not see themselves as language teachers and do not see the language of their fields. Another option is to identify within or train a core of lead teachers to work within schools as instructional coaches. This approach tends to yield better results. Sustaining the initiative is crucial to making the SIOP model workable.

## Activities and Discussions

(1) From one content standard, create a content objective and explain how you will assess the objective at the end of the unit. Evaluate the objective and assessment to determine what language the student would need to be able to employ to meet this content objective. This will be your language objective.

(2) Develop a presentation of new material for your content objective utilising a variety of scaffolds (i.e. visuals, demonstrations, simulations) and comprehensible input/linguistic modifications to make the information meaningful to the learners. Script your presentation by writing down exactly what you will say including the questions you will ask. Present this to a partner who will play the role of a language learner and provide feedback.

(3) Using your content and language objectives from activities (1) and (2), develop a series of interactive activities to integrate the four language skills that the students can participate in to develop their content and language. Share this outline with your peers.

(4) Choose a topic of common knowledge that is current in the world. Write down a series of questions that you can ask peers to facilitate a conversation on the topic. In facilitating a conversation, when should you tell the learners something as opposed to asking leading questions?

(5) Linguistic modification practice. Find a recipe to teach to your peers. Please prepare to present it and modify your output towards comprehensibility for your EL inclusive audience.

---

### Chapter Summary

- The SIOP model is comprised of eight components: Preparation, Background Building, Comprehensible Input, Instructional Strategies and Scaffolding, Interaction, Practice/Application, Lesson Delivery and Assessment/Review.

- Teachers should create learner outcome objectives for content and language that cover the range of learners' language needs to develop their communicative competencies.

- Language objectives can be differentiated by language proficiency level.

- New information may be presented to learners deductively or inductively, but clarity of information, its comprehensibility to the learners, is vital.

- Teachers need to consider more than just the content vocabulary and make critical choices as to what to explicitly teach.
- Connections to learners' background knowledge and funds of knowledge are a key learning strategy for ELs.
- Teachers need to envision different ways of interacting with learners, such as through instructional conversation and facilitated discussions.
- The SIOP model employs a wide variety of instructional strategies from exercises to activities to tasks for practice and application.
- The SIOP is a comprehensive model of content-based ESL instruction, but is not a perfect model due to the lack of detail in some areas (i.e. assessment), expected knowledge (i.e. language awareness, sociocultural awareness) and generalisations (i.e. cooperative learning).

# 5 Models: Cognitive Academic Language Learning Approach

| Chapter Aims and Topics |
|---|
| • Present the history and development of the Cognitive Academic Language Learning Approach (CALLA) model. |
| • Express key features of the CALLA model. |
| • Present the Language Experience Approach (LEA). |
| • Outline cognitive and schema theory as it relates to vocabulary. |
| • Contrast types of objectives from the CALLA perspective. |
| • Consider the instructional preparation and process in CALLA. |
| • Elucidate needs assessment design. |
| • Discuss discourse analysis in relation to content-based instruction. |
| • Describe lesson procedures and sequencing in CALLA. |
| • Offer task-based instruction and instructional strategies employed in CALLA. |
| • Depict the CALLA classroom environment. |
| • Outline materials, assessment and accommodations in CALLA. |

## Description of the CALLA Model

Anna Uhl Chamot and the late J. Michael O'Malley were the designers of the CALLA model, which infused content and language learning together in rigorous language learning environments. The CALLA model utilised the discourse features (i.e. patterns in the language) of academic texts to inform teachers' choices in language objectives. Since their initial collaboration, several research studies (Chamot, 1995, 2007; Chamot & O'Malley, 1986, 1987, 1989; Galland, 1995; Thomas, 1992) have been conducted on aspects of the CALLA model to identify 'the factors that can assist or impede second language acquisition' (Chamot, 2009: 3). The majority of the research supports for the CALLA model are related to classroom intervention studies on the instruction of learning strategies (Chamot, 2009).

The CALLA model is a framework originating during the late 1980s (Chamot, 2009; McGraner & Saenz, 2009; O'Malley & Chamot, 1994) that shares many roots and similarities with the Sheltered Instruction Observation Protocol (SIOP) model. In this chapter, similarities to the SIOP model will be briefly noted, but differences and items noteworthy for the CALLA model will be emphasised.

Foundational theories and research that influenced both the SIOP and the CALLA models' originators include Cummin's social and academic language distinction, Krashen's Comprehensible Input Hypothesis, Long's Interactional Theory and the cooperative learning approach (see Chapter 4).

Other theoretical and practical influences on the CALLA designers were (1) language skills integrated across the grade-level academic curriculum. An example is teaching writing and reading skills in science. One could ask learners to investigate an endangered species through English learner (EL) supportive reading instruction and then teach the writing process for the learners to express their understandings of the species' daily habits, habitat and plans to protect its environment. (2) The focus of oral language and learners' background experiences to aid in the development of literacy skills, such as the LEA.

## Language Experience Approach

The CALLA designers were also influenced by the LEA, which helps early literacy students of any age. The LEA is not so much an approach as it is a technique for developing writing, reading, grammar and connections to oral language skills.

I have employed the LEA technique in my English as a second language (ESL) content classes with some success in teaching origin tales and mystery genres. The technique is basically a co-writing activity guided by the teacher. The teacher would start the reading process by previewing a text, such as a Hmong origin tale of farming and hunting. The teacher would utilise pre-reading techniques of picture walks, predictions and vocabulary instruction, and then read the story through a teacher read aloud, guided reading, silent reading, choral reading or a combination thereof. After having read the story, the teacher would need to check the learners' comprehension of the main ideas, details and inferences through a series of oral and written activities or tasks. Once the teacher was confident that the students understood the tale, the teacher could then segue into the LEA for writing practice using the origin tale format. The teacher would outline the task, previewing with the students the process of creating their own origin tale using the model seen in the reading. The teacher would guide the learners through the process with a series of questions possibly starting with 'What is an artefact or an important part of human life that we want to focus on?' How about why we have pets or why we have art?' The class as a whole would discuss and vote on the topic. Once the topic was established, the teacher would continue to guide with questions to identify all parts of the tale, setting, characters, plot, climax and resolution. The students would be asked to discuss or write in small groups possible options for each of these parts, and then share them with the class. The teacher would guide the conversation so that everyone's ideas were considered fairly in a safe atmosphere. Finally, when the outline of the tale had been established, the teacher would guide the students to collectively write the story. Students would be guided to share their sentences to create the story while the teacher serves as the scribe at the board/document camera/overhead projector. The teacher would write exactly what the students say without any modifications. This is important because these are the learners' thoughts and voices, not the teacher's. When the story was complete, the students would be encouraged by the teacher to read the story aloud and make modifications (i.e. grammatical, conceptual and lexical) or to elaborate the story. The story would then need to be copied by the students and read again at home or in class.

## Cognitive Theory

Another influence on the CALLA model was (3) cognitive theory, which emphasised long-term memory/retention and three types of knowledge: declarative, procedural and metacognitive. *Declarative knowledge* is information we learn and can talk about. For example, reciting facts such as the steps in a scientific method or formula ($E=mc^2$). *Procedural knowledge* is knowing how to do something such as calculating a math problem. *Metacognitive knowledge* is the awareness of and ability to reflect on what you know. In other words, it is the ability to think about your understandings and thinking. For example, we would know about photosynthesis and be able to describe the process in plants (i.e. declarative knowledge). We might try to replicate it through an experiment (i.e. procedural knowledge) and think about our understandings of it (i.e. metacognitive knowledge) to revisit the process analytically.

Procedural knowledge differs from declarative because we apply the knowledge to doing something. For example, we learn how to read maps, and then we can use the knowledge of how to read a map to read a wide variety of different types of maps.

Metacognitive knowledge utilises the other two sets of knowledge in a controlled manner. You might reflect on the information you have about photosynthesis to utilise the higher-order thinking skill of analysis to think through how photosynthesis might occur differently in varying climates and light sources, such as in a hothouse in northern locations that experience extremely low light in the winter. These knowledge distinctions and the focus on cognition (i.e. thinking) by the learner are important aspects of the CALLA model that teachers are encouraged to consider in the CALLA model.

## Content, Language and Learning Strategy Objectives

When utilising the CALLA model in EL inclusion, these knowledge distinctions would inform the types of content and language objectives developed by the teacher. For instance, a teacher might evaluate that type of knowledge to directly teach the concept of the compass rose and cardinal directions (i.e. north, south, east, west), which is declarative. She/he might also teach how to utilise this information in reading a map, which is procedural. The ability to answer the question, 'How did you find the distance between your home town and Peru?' would be metacognitive. The language concepts that would be inherent in these content concepts would be the cardinal and ordinal directions (i.e. up, down, left, right, top, bottom, next to, above, below) as the

ELs would need to know those words to be able to give or interpret directions and the use of discourse markers (e.g. first, then, next, finally) to describe how one charted a route (i.e. <u>First</u>, I located my home town. <u>Second</u>, I located where Peru was on the map. <u>Third</u>, I drew a line south/southwest that connected my home town to Lima, Peru.).

This focus on cognition and types of knowledge had other effects throughout the CALLA model, one of which was the inclusion of learning strategy objectives. Like in the SIOP, CALLA teachers are expected to write content and language objectives. But in the CALLA model, teachers are also expected to write learning strategy objectives for their lessons.

*Learning strategies* are plans or procedures an individual uses to learn something new or solve a learning problem. Chamot and O'Malley (1994: 6) explain learning strategies as 'tricks [learners] used for various language learning activities'. A typical learning strategy for writing is to employ the process approach to writing, which is essentially a strategic plan for choosing and narrowing a writing topic, researching the topic, planning the format of the writing via outlines, for example, drafting, editing and revising. The process approach to writing is a strategic plan that breaks down the task into approachable pieces that help learners to improve their writing. Process writing was another of the practical influences on the designers of the CALLA model.

*Learning strategies* is a general term for a wide variety of 'tricks' that individuals employ to remember, learn and figure out new information. The concept can be further delineated to communication, conversation management strategies and language learning strategies that individuals use in communicating in a first or second language. Oxford (1990), O'Malley and Chamot (1990) and Kasper and Kellerman (1997) conducted research into which strategies are productive for language learners. Oxford's seminal text outlined the types of language learning strategies (i.e. memory, cognitive, compensation, social, affective and metacognitive) as well as application ideas and an assessment of learners' strategies, called the Strategic Inventory for Language Learners (SILL). Examples of the types of strategies that Oxford shares are:

- Memory: associating/elaborating, using imagery or physical response to make mental linkages (Oxford, 1990: 39).
- Cognitive: repeating, recombining, analysing expressions for the constituent parts (e.g. elements [plural noun] decomposed [past tense verb with a prefix] through this chemical reaction [compound noun in a prepositional phrase], summarising and paraphrasing (Oxford, 1990: 44) to strengthen one's thinking.
- Compensation: making informed guesses, using gestures, approximating the message, coining words and circumlocution (Oxford, 1990: 48) to aid when one forgets or does not know a word or how to communicate a message (e.g. word coinage. Could you please stop playing the what's-it game? What's-it game is a made up word, a coined word).
- Social: asking for help, clarifying, correcting during interactions with others; developing cultural understandings and cooperating with a variety of language speakers (Oxford, 1990: 145).

- Affective: relaxing, using music or laughter, taking wise risks, affirming oneself, writing a learning diary (Oxford, 1990: 141) to help reduce anxiety (e.g. self-affirmation. 'You did a good job. Don't worry about the tense blunder').
- Metacognitive: paying attention, organising information or learning, planning in advance for a language task, seeking practice opportunities, self-monitoring and self-evaluating (Oxford, 1990: 137). For example, I once rewrote all the common French verbs that I used regularly into a chart. In the process, I discovered that the only difference between the future and conditional forms was an unpronounced 's' (je mangerai and je mangerais). So, in oral communication they all sounded the same. The discovery facilitated my processing of messages and enhanced my speed of communication.

Kasper and Kellerman's (1997) text offers an informative taxonomy, which also provides examples within categories of strategies. Strategies to aid in achievement or to compensate for a lack of knowledge as well as those to reduce the message to make it more manageable within the language that the learner has control over. Knowing these strategies, teachers can make them explicit to ELs to enhance their communication skills. Many foreign language students bloom with the newly discovered strategy of circumlocution (i.e. talking around a word they do not know) when they are studying abroad.

Language learning strategies provide cognitive tools for learners to apply in differing situations, which allow them to extend their communicative abilities and move towards independence and autonomy in their language learning process (see Figure 5.1). For example, when you learn the strategy of circumlocution, you are in a position to be able to 'talk around' a vocabulary word you do not know. You might indicate where the item is, the park. What it looks like (size, shape, colour): the size

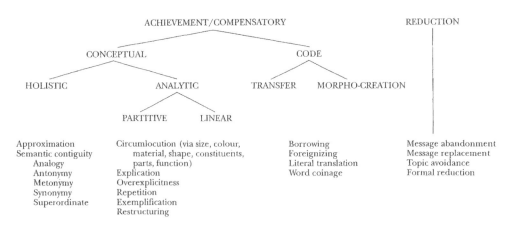

**Figure 5.1** Types of communication strategies by category
(Kasper & Kellerman, 1997: 20, with permission from Taylor & Francis)

of a small house, multicoloured, but frequently grey, red, blue, white and black. There are round shapes and flat stages connected by ladders. What function it has: children play on it. They climb on it. You find them in parks. Oh! It is a jungle gym. This strategic process allows you to acquire the needed vocabulary words of jungle gym and connect it to like knowledge in your memory. This similar knowledge is called a schema. Teachers could teach circumlocution in the stepwise manner that CALLA advocates. For instance,

(1)  Say, 'I can't think of the word. Uhhh'.
(2)  It's ___ (describe the colour, size, shape)
(3)  You can find it at the/in the ___ (name the place: park, library, mall, kitchen)
(4)  It does things like ___ (chop, heat water, make holes in paper)

## Schema Theory

*Schema*, or schemata, is theoretically how we mentally store information in meaningful clusters in our brains. Think of schema like a word web or the internet, vast connections of different concepts linked by our synaptic connections. If I were to say *fire hydrant*, what are all the associations that come to mind? Americans typically say: dog, red, next to the street, water, hoses, fire trucks, about 2 feet high. Individuals from other countries are mystified when the word 'dog' is mentioned. Why is that? In the US, in children's storybooks people see countless pictures of communities with someone walking a dog on a leash. The dog is typically pictured urinating on fire hydrants. These same images are not necessarily constantly present in children's books in other countries. In many countries, fire hydrants are not red. In some locations, fire hydrants do not exist. Or people do not walk their dogs on leashes past red fire hydrants. The list goes on. When you read fire hydrant, your schema, the collection of all the connected visuals, associations and background experiences, are accessed. Since schemata rely on past information and experiences, they are culturally bound and influenced. Schema theory is another tenet of the CALLA model's theoretical framework. Developing learners' schema for background knowledge (content) and vocabulary words (language) is just as important in CALLA as learning strategy instruction.

## Explicit Instruction of Learning Strategies

The CALLA model advocates the *explicit instruction* of learning strategies. The insertion of learning strategies that are congruent, in alignment with the curriculum (i.e. the content and language objectives in lessons), is an important task for EL inclusive teachers. Moreover, the CALLA model suggests that in the explicit instruction of learning or communication strategies, teachers should approach the instruction through preparation, presentation of the strategy, practice opportunities, evaluation of learners' abilities to utilise the strategy and expansion. O'Malley and Chamot (1989: 72) offered this instructional sequence for learning strategy instruction:

- *Preparation*: Develop students' awareness through a variety of activities.
- *Presentation*: Teach the strategy explicitly in a stepwise manner.
- *Practice*: Provide opportunities for practicing the strategy in varied contexts.
- *Evaluation*: Teach students to evaluate their own strategy use.
- *Expansion*: Encourage students to apply the strategies in other learning areas.

Through this process, learners would develop their autonomy.

The SIOP model, like the CALLA model, also advocates for the explicit instruction of learning strategies and suggests that the teacher analyses the strategy for the steps inherent in it, so as to be able to teach these steps to learners in the clearest and easiest manner (see Figure 5.2). For example, Echevarria and Graves (2007: 102) explain the steps of 'finding a main idea to 1) Read the paragraph, 2) Decide what the whole paragraph is about. 3) Test to make sure you have the best answer (the answer that tells what the whole paragraph is about). 4) Reread and start over if you are not sure. 5) If you are sure, write main idea down'.

## The CALLA Model's Preparation, Teaching Process and Materials

To implement the CALLA model, a teacher would start by assessing learners' background knowledge on the content and language objectives. The teacher would identify what each learner could know about the topic and each learner's strengths and needs in speaking, listening, reading and writing, grammar and vocabulary. From this needs analysis, the

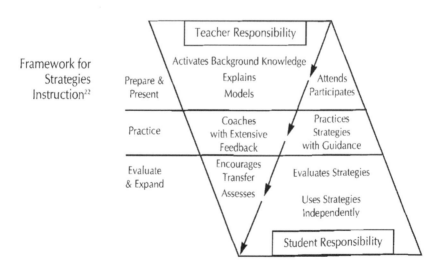

**Figure 5.2** Teacher's and students' roles in explicit strategy instruction
(O'Malley & Chamot, 1990: 66, with permission from Cambridge University Press)

teacher would map out reasonable content, language and learning strategy objectives for the lesson and identify which materials would be supportive of the learners' comprehension. In theory, all three types of objectives would overlap and enhance the others.

## Needs Assessment

Novice teachers often wonder where to begin their instruction with ELs. A best practice is to commence with research into the language skills and needs of the learners. In many foreign language programmes, students are pretested for placement using the information from learners' scores on any combination of speaking, listening, reading, writing, vocabulary and grammar assessments. This information is used to determine an approximate placement at proficiency levels close to needs of the learners.

In K-12 English for academic purposes programmes, this process is a bit more complex because most students arrive at differing times during the academic year, have widely different skills and needs, and placement tests do not occur at the beginning of the year. Needs assessments and diagnostic tools for teachers specific to the vastly different contexts and learners are difficult to obtain. In many cases, they simply do not exist. The teacher then takes on a researcher or detective role in order to determine where to begin instruction.

Teachers do though have some data upon which they can rely. For instance, in World-Class Instructional Design and Assessment (WIDA) consortium states, they may have the WIDA Assessing Comprehension and Communication in English State-to-State (ACCESS) composite score (i.e. one aggregate or compiled score of various language skills, such as speaking, listening, reading and writing) from the previous spring that provides a great deal of information as to the strengths and needs of the learners; this is especially true if the teachers also have the descriptive scores that breakdown the four skills strengths and needs. Teachers also tend to share brief written reports of learners' needs.

Often ELs arrive at a new school with literally no records. Surprisingly, there is no standardised school record format or process for records transfer that I have encountered. Teachers including ELs would wish to learn more about the particular child they instruct. Many teachers begin the academic year, or time with a newcomer student, by developing trust and personal rapport as well as diagnosing learners' needs by gently implementing a variety of activities to gather detailed information on their academics and language skills.

This needs assessment is another noteworthy aspect of the CALLA model. The model developers recommend that teachers' identify the learners' needs in the academic content by designing academic activities and tasks typical of the general education classroom to determine what linguistic aspects and skills need the most assistance. Academic placement, when limited information is known about the learners' academics and language skills, is by age with the hope that learners are at grade level. Importantly, even when the learner does not have grade-level academic preparation, ELs are not placed more than one grade level below their age. The rationale for this practice is that learners experience social and personal issues when they are placed with children below their age group.

When teachers work with a population of learners for a long period of time, some tendencies surface, but these are not universal. For example, the Hmong community in the Midwest US, who first arrived in the late 1970s, has a variety of linguistic needs depending on how much English is used in the home. If the family communicates predominantly in English in the home, the learners do not usually need social language development when they enter kindergarten. These children would need a literacy focus and oral academic language. If the family predominantly speaks Hmong in the home, the children would begin school with general needs in oral social language and literacy.

General tendencies and needs are more difficult for learners with interrupted schooling. Migrant farmers' children, who move with the family following harvests, have inconsistent academic and linguistic exposure. Therefore, it is vital that the teacher identifies the child's individual strengths and needs.

## Guidelines for Designing Needs Assessments

Needs assessments are comprised of background information or a home language survey, close-ended exercises and open-ended activities in the four skills. They are designed to gather enough information to roughly determine what the learner can do in the language. If the learner is a true novice (i.e. no second language abilities) or is unable to complete a task, the proctor would discontinue the needs assessment in order to avoid negative washback effects. (Washback effects are the positive or negative feelings and thoughts that learners have after an assessment. For instance, if a test is far too hard for the learner, the learner may feel that she/he is not smart or the teacher is unfair to make such a hard test. The resulting actions on the part of the learner may be to give up or get angry.) In order to reduce stress and anxiety and potential negative feedback, needs assessment activities and tasks might not even be described to the learners as a test. Learners are typically encouraged to do their best on it though, to show what they can do.

When gathering background information, teachers would develop a 'gut instinct' about the learner based on their interactions; this snapshot is an initial estimate of the learner's proficiency on the American Council on the Teaching of Foreign Languages scale (i.e. novice, intermediate, advanced, superior) to roughly gauge his/her proficiency from the outset and guide the design of the needs assessment. Teachers may wish to learn this background information: age of learner, grade level, native language(s), years studying English, past schooling and exposure/use of English/native language(s) in the home. This will give the teacher enough information to gauge the appropriacy of topics, reading passages and item formats (i.e. activity types).

When designing the assessments it is important to consider how the information should be used. The use of a needs assessment is not to compare learners' performance and rank them from high to low proficiency as educators did in the past when employing *norm-referencing* (i.e. comparing test scores and ranking the learners based on peer performance on the same test). Instead, needs assessments tend to be *criterion referenced*, meaning they are designed and scored against identified and scaled performance criteria. The scores for learners then show what the learner can do and still needs against these criteria. The individual learners' scores are not compared against other learners. The learners' performance strengths and weaknesses might be grouped for future instruction.

In designing item formats to be used in the needs assessment, teachers may desire to follow these guidelines:

(1)  Know your assessment targets. For each task, ask yourself, 'What do you hope to learn about the learners' proficiency with this task?' 'Will this task require the learner to produce what you need?'.
(2)  Choose age, grade-level topics that correspond to the individual(s) maturity. Avoiding topics that would be perceived as too young, condescending or culturally inappropriate is an important consideration.
(3)  Choose high-interest topics.
(4)  Include all four language skills (i.e. speaking, listening, reading and writing) plus tools (grammar, pronunciation and vocabulary) in the assessment. They do not have to be separate sections. The teacher can combine pronunciation with speaking. But avoid doing speaking and listening together, because the teacher will not be able to gather data on both simultaneously.
(5)  Write clear directions and questions in learner-friendly language according to the rough estimate of proficiency level.
(6)  Provide examples or models in the directions (see Figure 5.3).

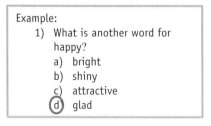

**Figure 5.3** Example in directions

(7)  Avoid the duplication of questions (unless you intend to conduct a split halves reliability test), but spread a wide net in terms of data collection. Try to keep the assessment simple without overdoing the questions or tasks as it will fatigue the learners and take too much time.
(8)  Determine sections of your needs assessment according to the information you need and the type of language skill.

(a)  Individual information section:

   (i)   Background information/questions.

   (ii)  Learning strategies.

   (iii)  Interest inventory.

(b)  Four skills assessment items.

(c)  Include an administrator/proctor section:

   (i)   Assessment objectives.

   (ii)  Listening transcript(s).

   (iii)  Answer keys.

   (iv)  Rubrics.

      (1)  Speaking.

      (2)  Writing.

   (v)   Include references/works cited for listening and reading passages, pictures/visuals, speaking and writing prompts, etc.

(9)  Tell the learner, in learner-friendly, non-threatening language, what the purpose of the task is. Indicate why you are collecting these data.

Importantly, needs assessments do not need to be proctored in one sitting. The activities and tasks can be spread over days, so that students are not overwhelmed or negatively stressed. A goal is to avoid negative washback. *Negative washback* is a term to describe the damaging feelings that learners experience towards an exam(s), teacher(s), learning in general or themselves as a result of a test. An example is when a learner fails a test that is inaccessible due to language barriers. The result is that the learner feels there is no need to study in the future because he/she will never succeed. When educators create inaccessible and impossible tests and assessments, it does nothing but discourage the learners.

Needs assessment activities and tasks can and should be presented to the learners in a manner that is both light and fun as well as focused on yielding accurate information in order to avoid negative washback. Experienced teachers use the first weeks of a term to learn about the students, establish rapport and explain routines and expectations, so this is a prime time to proctor parts of a needs assessment. If a learner arrives midterm, a paraprofessional could administer a needs assessment or parts of it could be completed while other children are busy with independent or small-group work.

Each of the four skills and content sections of the needs assessments needs to be considered individually. If a teacher needs to determine learners' academic content background, the teacher would need to design separate language and content assessments. It is advisable to determine past content knowledge in the native language, if possible; otherwise, the information will be compromised.

When gathering information about the learners' proficiency in the four skills, it is crucial to record the information systematically and keep accurate records. The teacher should identify ways to record the oral excerpt and play electronic recordings to increase reliability.

It is advisable to design a needs assessment comprised of activities/tasks that ask learners to perform a skill; this strategy allows for more direct testing of the four skills than indirect testing. For example, if you wish to understand the level of the learners' writing, you ask them to write a sentence, paragraph or essay (i.e. direct testing), as opposed to the traditional way of asking students to answer grammatical and vocabulary multiple-choice questions to infer the writing ability of the learner (i.e. indirect testing). There may also be an overlap of language skills, called integrative testing, which might alter the information the teachers have to make instructional and placement choices (see Figure 5.3). For instance, integrative testing is when speaking and listening are being assessed at one time as in an oral proficiency interview or when a learner needs to write about a reading passage.

It is also important to consider the scoring of the needs assessment. Having rubrics for speaking and writing with predetermined levels of performance allow for more objectivity in scoring and enable teachers to know whether the objectives have been met (Figure 5.4).

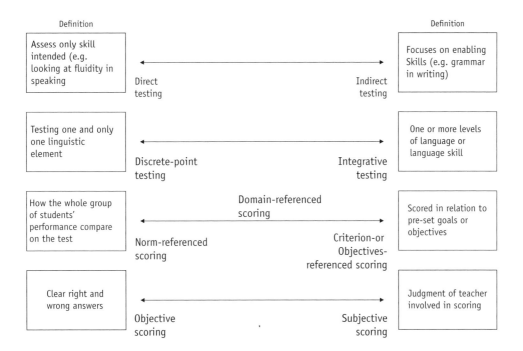

**Figure 5.4** Continuum of test types and scoring

# Needs Assessments: Listening and Reading Comprehension Sections

To measure listening and/or reading comprehension, teachers should choose item elicitations (i.e. listening passages) that are appropriate topics and a good length. Older, academic learners can handle a 4- to 5-minute listening passage; whereas younger and/or lower-proficiency learners can only handle 1–2 minutes. The listening passage should be recorded so the proctor does not need to read it and it is spoken seamlessly. Also, if you had more than one learner, all learners would need the exact same recording for reliability of the measure. Radio broadcasts from www.NPR.org have a variety of passages that would be effective for older students. Oral stories online or on Tumble books are good sources for listening comprehension passages for younger students.

Teachers may wish to consider the complexity and length of the reading passages chosen. The reading passage(s) may be chosen from grade-level or proficiency-level readers, and those slightly easier and harder reading passages in order to determine where the learner struggles with reading. In terms of passage length, older, academic learners could handle anywhere from a half page of single-spaced text; whereas, a middle school–aged learner or a lower-proficiency student could probably only handle one four- to five-sentence paragraph with a title.

Tools to help teachers identify how difficult a text might be for language learners are the Flesch–Kincaid formula that uses Microsoft Word text summaries to evaluate the number of words and the length of sentences, among other items, and the website Readability Score (http://readability-score.com).

The item response formats (i.e. item formats or activities) allow students to demonstrate their understandings of the listening or reading passage. A classic example of item formats usually experienced on tests is multiple choice, matching or fill-in-the-blank. Teachers should consider using some

(1)  Close-ended questions to:
  (a)  Ask some questions about the overall/overarching meaning(s) in the passage. These help the teacher perceive that the learner understands the main ideas.
  (b)  Ask some discrete-point questions about details in the passage.
  (c)  Facilitate grading, such as true/false, multiple choice, matching.

Examples:
  1)  What is "a story that tells where you were when a crime was committed"?
      a. breakthrough        b. crime        c. alibi

  **Directions:** Match the word to the definition by writing the letter next to the number
            Ex: 1) A hunch            a) A guess of feeling

  7)  ____ Plot            a) Reason for committing a crime
  8)  ____ Mystery         b) Creepy
  9)  ____ Motive          c) Parts of a story or movie
  10) ____ Mysterious      a) Unknown
  11) ____ Investigate     a) To detect or look

(2) Open-ended questions that ask learners to share their opinions, ideas and under-standings and to gather a sample of extended discourse. These help the teacher to see more full understandings.

Example:

2)    Please give me an example of an alibi

_____
_____
_____
_____

(3) Inferential questions because they require the learner to comprehend informa-tion from the passage in a holistic way. These are frequently harder questions for the learner as well, but are a high-level language skill that learners need for academics. This information will help teachers to differentiate the learners at higher-proficiency levels. In the example given below, the learners were asked an inference question, which was to figure out what crime occurred when listening to a passage.

(4) Drawing responses (for listening), which allow the teacher to see what the learner understands without the need to read, write or speak his/her responses. For example, a teacher might pre-record oral directions from the library to the classroom on a school map, give the learner the map with the room names on it, ask the student to listen to the directions, identify where the student is starting from and then draw the path directed on the recording. If the teacher chose to implement a drawing response, it is helpful to follow these guidelines:

(a)  Pre-record the listening passage.

(b)  Draw an exemplar in the directions, so learners can see a visual of what is expected.

(c)  Be sure to have all materials necessary on hand. For example, if you have col-ours mentioned, bring colour markers.

Example:

Directions: On your paper you have a room where a crime occurred. Listen to find out where the clues are and try to figure out what crime occurred. Draw the clues in the room where they were found. Remember, you are not graded on your drawing ability, but on placing the clues in the proper place.

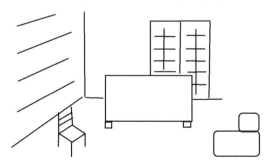

Pre-recorded listening passage: The room you see is a living room with two glass doors that open to a garden on the wall opposite from the door you entered. On your left-hand side is a row of book shelves filled with books from floor to ceiling. There is a chair on the left. Next to the chair is a broken glass, a clue. Draw a broken drinking glass. In front of you is a desk with a lamp, on the desk is another set of clues, file folders. Draw them on the desk. In front of the desk is a dead body facing down. There is a piece of paper in the victim's right hand. It's a clue. On your right-hand side is a couch or sofa. In front of the sofa is a knife. It is an important clue.

(5) Include transcripts and an answer key in the administrator's/proctor's section. The above transcript would need to be written and/or having the room's image with the items drawn on it in the answer key is recommended.

## Needs Assessments: Speaking Ability and Pronunciation Intelligibility Section(s)

When assessing learners' speaking, be very clear on what the assessment target is; it is advisable to write it down. For instance, within the skill of speaking, there are sub-skills, such as speaking fluidity, hesitations, pauses, pronunciation intelligibility, oral grammar, oral vocabulary and message clarity. In order to be more objective and systematic in scoring, teachers should employ a speaking rubric and align it with the assessment targets.

Teachers can ask a learner to tell the teacher more about himself/herself, talk about a hobby or tell a story. Commonly, teachers use modified oral proficiency interviews (MOPIs) to gauge speaking abilities. Questions in a MOPI are structured from novice to superior using these guidelines:

Novice          Intermediate                    Advanced              Superior

(a)  concrete topics to abstract topics;
(b)  personal topics to global topics;
(c)  topics that require short answer to those that require more lengthy answers (i.e. extended discourse).

For example, a set of questions might resemble:

(1)  Could you please tell me about your family?
(2)  What is your favourite school subject and why do you like it?
(3)  So, you've been studying about global warming in your earth science class. What are some of the ways that humans can help the environment?
(4)  What is your opinion of the debate on global warming? Do you think it is occurring or not? Why?

This structure allows the evaluator to determine where in the scale the learner begins to struggle to convey information. Then, the proctor would ask probing questions at that level to be confident in his/her evaluation.

Since the information in the speaking assessment needs to be analysed, it is almost impossible to do this while talking with the student. It is best to record the speaking and/or pronunciation sections, if at all possible. This eliminates the need for the teacher to be the sole recorder of data and allows the teacher time to analyse the data. It also allows the teacher to be more systematic and listen to the passage repeatedly. Even if the teacher does record the data, he/she should leave time between questions to take notes on thoughts, comments and observations.

## Needs Assessments: Writing Section

Assessing writing is very similar to assessing speaking in terms of identifying the assessment target, but the targets themselves are different. In writing, a teacher can assess: content/ideas, complexity of expression/argumentation, organisation, format, cohesion, written grammar (e.g. subject/verb agreement and tense), vocabulary appropriacy/complexity and/or mechanics (i.e. punctuation, spelling and capitalisation). The assessment targets for writing would be very different according to the grade level of the learner; in lower elementary school, targets might be letter writing, whereas in middle school, the target might be writing personal reflections in two or three paragraphs. Teachers would also wish to create or identify a writing rubric that aligns with the assessment targets. Finally, teachers would need to ensure that the learners knows what is expected in the writing. Make expectations clear in the directions. For example, 'Please use informal writing, but write complete sentences'.

## Needs Assessments: Assessing Grammar and Vocabulary

To accurately and holistically assess a learner's grammar, teachers would need to develop very detailed and comprehensive tests. A needs assessment is a rough assessment of learners' abilities, so identifying the minute details of grammar needs are a bit beyond the scope. There are simply too many grammatical concepts to be assessed to be included in a short needs assessment; teachers need to employ discretion in what grammatical forms to include. For needs assessments, I recommend teachers analyse the learners' speaking and writing production for strengths and needs in grammar. So you can save time and the learners' energy by integrating the tools (i.e. grammar, vocabulary and pronunciation) with the skills (i.e. speaking, listening, reading and writing). If a teacher chooses topics wisely in speaking and writing tasks, information can be gathered on a variety of tenses, parts of speech and sentence/paragraph construction and cohesion.

One item format (i.e. question type) that allows teachers to get a quick understanding of learners' grammar is cloze tests with or without a word bank. Cloze tests are written passages with an introductory sentence followed by the deletion of every fifth

> Dinosaurs lived millions of years ago all over the planet. There were many types _____ dinosaurs ranging from small _____ large, plant-eaters to meat _____ and those that walked _____ on two legs to _____ that walked on four _____. For many years scientists _____ that dinosaurs' skin was _____ color of modern day _____, such as lizards. This _____ was due in part _____ the fact that scientists _____ had fossil evidence that _____ not show the color _____ the skin. Now, many _____ believe that dinosaurs were _____ fact very colorful, because _____are the ancient ancestors _____ modern day birds.

**Figure 5.5** Cloze test example

or seventh word. The student would read the passage and enter the appropriate missing word and form it to the proper grammatical category. Cloze tests are known to be holistic due to the random deletion of the words, so they are thought to provide an overview of learners' grammatical proficiency. The CALLA (2009) suggests using cloze tests (Figure 5.5).

The same approach can be utilised in vocabulary assessment to see how large the learners' vocabulary is as well as the accuracy of use. Teachers will need to sample a broad range of vocabulary to see what the learner is familiar with (passive vocabulary) and the vocabulary the learner regularly uses (active vocabulary). Depending on the learner and the context, teachers should consider choosing vocabulary from these sets: survival, social and academic language and those that are high-frequency, common/formulaic expressions and less-common words. Other areas the teacher might need to consider are:

(1)   The meanings of prefixes, suffixes and root words.
(2)   Collocations, associations, synonyms, antonyms, etc.
(3)   Grade-level needs for academic vocabulary.
(4)   Slang, colloquial language, idioms.

The item formats that can be used are the identification of objects in pictures (e.g. those from picture dictionaries), close-ended matching, multiple choice, true/false and odd-man-out all with or without images.

The teacher would pool all the information together, evaluate it and analyse the patterns of error in order to determine what linguistic objectives to begin teaching.

## Discourse Analysis and Awareness

Another tenet of the CALLA model is an awareness of discourse (see Chapter 2) and teaching the linguistic patterns present in the academic subject. A teacher would analyse the linguistic demands of the material and consider the patterns of language inherent in the text or common in the classroom discourse for the specific topic. The CALLA (1994) text includes an informative chart of syntactic features of word problems. It illustrates the common features of word problems, such as comparatives, and the linguistic format for comparatives (i.e. greater/less than; as much as; as... as). If a teacher were teaching equalities/inequalities, the teacher should then also explicitly teach and highlight the oral and written ways in which speakers of English discuss equalities/inequalities. The discourse analysis of texts becomes a crucial skill for teachers implementing the CALLA model. An analysis of social studies texts adapted from O'Malley and Chamot (1994) reveals the following discourse features.

- Long, grammatically complex sentences with multiple embedded clauses are common. For example, 'Ghengis Khan was one of the most powerful leaders from the east. He divided his khanate into 3 parts for each of his sons. Batu, one of his sons, lead attacks on Slavic areas like Kievan Rus with warriors from his tribe, who were known as the Blue Horde' (O'Malley & Chamot, 1994: 259–260).
- The functions of language that commonly occur are explaining, informing, describing, analysing, comparing, contrasting, making judgements and arguing positions.
- Information is presented chronologically and as historical narratives.
- Cause and effect statements are frequent. A frequent use of 'Because…' as a sentence starter. For example, 'Because there were no large trees for lumber, people in the area developed other types of building materials, like adobe'.
- Various verb forms are used in the same paragraph. For example, 'I <u>found</u> Rome a city of bricks and <u>left</u> it a city of marble. Augustus <u>is supposed to have spoken</u> these words as he <u>lay dying</u>. He was Rome's first emperor, and <u>started</u> the first of its great building programs. He <u>claimed</u> that he <u>had had</u> over 80 temples rebuilt' (O'Malley & Chamot, 1994: 259–260).
- Subjunctive mood.
- Frequent use of pronouns *it* and *they* as referents to previously mentioned individuals.
- Vocabulary: abstract concepts (like peace, freedom, democracy, communism, ethnic cleansing), descriptive adjectives, etc.

This in-depth linguistic analysis is a unique feature of the CALLA model and a tool with which many general educators would be unfamiliar.

## Lesson Procedures and Sequencing

The sequence of instruction in CALLA follows the preparation, presentation, practice, evaluation and expansion pattern seen above.

---

**Preparation:** The teacher prepares the learners to be able to understand the incoming information.

**Presentation:** The teacher presents the new information.

**Practice:** The learners practice the language through activities and tasks about the content.

**Evaluation:** The teacher evaluates the learners on content and language.

**Expansion:** The learners do expansion activities to further their connections and understandings.

---

Teachers are encouraged to begin lessons by determining what the students already know about the topic and the related language. Then, they would pre-teach vocabulary and provide graphic organisers to aid comprehension. Next, they would wish to deliver new material in a workshop-type environment permeated with cooperative learning activities on the content topics. In CALLA lessons, content and language have equal time with learning strategies integrated within them. Teachers are expected to alternate between direct instruction and application activities in tasks, so the learners have adequate opportunities to interact on the topic.

The original CALLA text did little to explain delivery strategies for the presentation of new material or types of small-group activities. However, the second edition by Chamot (2009) made strides in the linguistic accessibility of information presented by the teacher, instructional strategies and assessment.

## Presentation of New Materials

The presentation of new material or concepts by the teacher, or 'direct instruction', needs to occur when students need information with which they have no prior experience. Direct instruction has been likened to 'lectures', but the concepts do not necessarily need to be delivered in a lecture manner.

The teacher conducts productive and engaging delivery of new information for ELs in interactive ways. If an English literature teacher chose to focus on the objective of foreshadowing (i.e. a warning, clue or signal of something that would happen in the future. For example, 'I knew from the first time she played with crayons that she was going to be an artist'), the teacher might need to explain the concept by discussing with the students what the term might mean. In order to avoid talking at the students, the teacher could develop a series of guiding questions to facilitate a conversation on the subject, serve as a scribe and use a semantic map (Figure 5.6) to help the learners visualise the word's meaning and role in literature. Figure 5.6 shows examples of what students might volunteer when brainstorming about the meaning of the word foreshadowing. What do you think the term *foreshadowing* means? What words make up this term? If this term explains a pattern present in literature, what do you think it might do in the work? How would one see it? A teacher might also demonstrate making shadows in order to aid students' understanding.

**Figure 5.6** Semantic map of foreshadowing

After initiating a conversation on this term, the teacher could present a passage of text heavy in foreshadowing, read it aloud and then highlight the phrases in the passage that show the concept. This is essentially a demonstration.

It would be a good interactive language task for learners to analyse different passages for foreshadowing language in small groups, which they could share with the rest of the class. The teacher could gauge the students' comprehension of the concept during the debriefing in a whole-class discussion.

The teacher might need to explain the concept more formally. If so, the teacher would want to pre-plan exactly what the essential knowledge is for this concept. In other words, what is the vital knowledge of the concept the teacher wants the student to understand, know and do. Equipped with these parameters, the teacher would want to prepare a presentation outlining the concept. In the case of foreshadowing, (1) 'foreshadowing is an action, observation or image given early in a story, which indicates subtly a plot development that will take place later, and prepares the reader for conflict' (Cascio, n.d., http://www.ehow.com/info_10027397_foreshadowing-story.html). (2) It is a technique used by writers to help readers predict what will be happening in the text. It is like fortune telling and psychic readings. (3) The use of foreshadowing deepens the writing, making it more interesting and detailed for the reader. (4) The use of foreshadowing can guide readers to guess the correct outcome, but it might intentionally mislead the reader as well.

The teacher could develop a PowerPoint with these four essential aspects enhanced by supporting visuals and well-chosen examples. The clarity of the language used in the PowerPoint is crucial. The teacher would want to analyse the language in the presentation to determine if it is accessible to the learner. I might choose images of fortune tellers/psychics or detectives for my PowerPoint. The images should be chosen to clarify the written language as well as being stimulating for the learners.

It is also imperative to keep the presentation short, to the point and interactive. Ways to do this are to focus on the succinct use of comprehensible language in the PowerPoint and teacher's oral explanation. At times, with ELs, more words do not actually mean more understanding (see Chapter 4 for linguistic modifications). The PowerPoint helps ensure that the teacher sticks to the point; however, the teacher would need to self-scrutinise while delivering the material in order not to prattle on, have too many asides or to veer off topic. The teacher can also ask critical thinking questions on the PowerPoint to keep the learners engaged and to check comprehension. **Repetition is crucial.**

Solid presentations of new materials for ELs:

- Gain the students' focused attention. They are alert. The presentation stimulates learners' interest.
- Include visual and auditory forms of the new material in order to allow multiple access points.
- Include frequent checks of learners' comprehension by the teacher.
- Connect to previously learned material by activating schema.
- Are memorable and trigger short-term memory with interesting presentation – original, dramatic, etc.

- Are presented in learner-friendly language that is clear and comprehensible. Teachers explain new terms and concepts and write them on the board to aid in comprehension.
- Emphasise the important concepts, provide examples and illustrations, but are focused.
- Are not too long and wordy or too short without elaboration.

# Task-Based Instruction and Instructional Strategies

Task-based instruction is one realisation of communicative language teaching with roots in the interactionist research of the early and mid-1980s. The CALLA model builds upon this solid research base by encouraging teachers to combine direct instruction of new material with task-based practice opportunities, so that learners have multiple opportunities to practice the academic language of the topic.

Tasks are not often included in textbooks. Even if they are not provided they should be included because they help students to process the language in a meaningful, personal and deep way; compel students to learn more new vocabulary; allow for creativity and different ways of thinking about language; provide contextualised four-skills practice; cause more authentic interaction among students; make the language more memorable; allow for the input, negotiation of meaning and output that learners need to acquire the language; forge the neural pathways to increase automaticity in language use; allow for higher-order thinking; and reinforce grammatical and phonological forms. They are *secretly structural.* They help learners practice the grammar in context.

According to Nunan's (2004) definitions, close-ended activities are language exercises, open-ended activities are communicative activities and tasks are communicative but have distinct characteristics that set them slightly apart. For example, open-ended activities are communicative because a learner has the freedom to answer in any way that he/she sees fit. 'They are similar to language exercises in that they provide <u>manipulative practice of a restricted set of language items</u>. They resemble pedagogical tasks in that they have an element of communication' (Nunan, 2004: 24). There are endless possibilities for correct answers.

Question and Answer:
- **Speaker A**: Do you have a dog?
- **Speaker B**: _____
  Possible answers:
- Yes, I have a dog.
- I have a Chihuahua.
- My family has three dogs.
- No, I don't have a dog.
- I don't like dogs.

Whereas tasks are communicative in nature, they have a distinct structure with a beginning, middle and end. There is a clear goal or outcome. They require a wide range of language knowledge. These can be lesson-based *little tasks* or unit-based *big tasks*, like projects. In language textbooks they frequently appear as extension activities. Some examples of tasks are:

- Preparing a brochure about indigenous cultures and artisanal crafts in your community.
- Write a will leaving your most prized possessions to your close friends and family.
- Values clarification tasks – What are your views on celebrity worship? Is it a good or bad thing for society?
- Discussions with an end goal – How do you think cyber-warfare affects international business and governments?
- Role plays – Student A is the reporter, Student B is the president. Design a series of questions and responses on current issues and conduct an interview. Record the answers and write a summary.

The sky is the limit when developing tasks, as almost any life task can be applied to the academic content; it is important though to keep the language focus in the forefront of the learners' and the teacher's minds, otherwise the task becomes the focus and the language is forgotten or overlooked. Rank ordering, categorising, sorting, role plays, problem solving, values clarification, planning an experiment or nature walk, making observations, measuring, explaining, justifying/defending a position and critiquing are all tasks that can be applied to academic content topics. I keep Bloom's Taxonomy next to my computer to help me develop academic tasks that are congruent with the content I teach. I have found ranking activities are easy and excellent for any list of items in a text. We could take a list of elements necessary to sustain life, for example, and ask students to discuss which ones are the most important for life and which ones the least. We could extend that discussion to have them consider what would happen if the least important element was not present for us (Table 5.1).

One important instructional strategy in content-based instruction that can be linked to tasks is 'Activity Before Content' (ABC). Throughout this chapter, the suggestion for the sequence of lessons was direct instruction followed by practice activities, which is essentially the deductive model of instruction. One presents a rule and then gives learners opportunities to practice the rule. Increasingly, educators have found that an inductive approach to a lesson is more memorable and engaging for learners. In the inductive approach, a teacher would ask the learners to do an activity or task (one they could reasonably do with the language and knowledge they have or resources provided), and then ask them what they learned or understood of the activity or task. The teacher would then connect the ideas to the content concepts through guiding questions or presentation of new material. This inductive approach can be labelled *activity before content*, and is a useful strategy to engage learners with the material. An example of ABC is to ask learners to analyse a variety of light bulbs that had been previously dissected and to try to figure out how the electricity passes from the outlet to the light fixture and bulb, and how it is transformed into light. The teacher's role is to help

**Table 5.1** Examples of tasks by chapter topic

| Proficiency Level | Chapters/Topics | Task Ideas |
|---|---|---|
| Beginner level (A1 Common European Framework [CEFR]) | (1) Names and occupations<br>(2) Relationships<br>(3) Directions and transportation<br>(4) People<br>(5) Events and times<br>(6) Clothes<br>(7) Home and work<br>(8) Activities<br>(9) Weather and ongoing activities<br>(10) Food<br>(11) Past events<br>(12) Appearance and health<br>(13) Abilities and requests<br>(14) Past, present and future plans | • Research and write your family tree<br>• Write a diary of 1 week in the life of a famous celebrity<br>• Design a fashion line and hold a fashion show<br>• Create a weather report for various mega-cities or your own weather channel<br>• Create your own restaurant and menu<br>• Write a goals statement for a scholarship or school admission |
| Beginner level (A2 Common European Framework [CEFR]) | (1) Getting acquainted<br>(2) Going out<br>(3) Talking about families<br>(4) Coping with technology<br>(5) Eating in, eating out<br>(6) Staying in shape<br>(7) Finding something to wear<br>(8) Getting away<br>(9) Taking transportation<br>(10) Shopping smart | • Create a Facebook profile<br>• Conduct speed dating<br>• Design a personal advertisement<br>• Host a radio programme on fitness<br>• Guide a tour group<br>• Write a brochure/travel website for your town<br>• Write a newspaper column on shopping on a budget |
| Intermediate level (B1 CEFR) | (1) Greetings and small talk<br>(2) Movies and entertainment<br>(3) Staying at hotels<br>(4) Cars and driving<br>(5) Personal care and appearance<br>(6) Eating well<br>(7) Psychology and personality<br>(8) Enjoying the arts<br>(9) Living with computers<br>(10) Ethics and values | • Host a dinner party<br>• Write a movie, arts and entertainment guide<br>• Report to the police a traffic accident you witnessed<br>• Write a magazine article about the people and lifestyles in your community<br>• Design an English tourist map<br>• Debate how much technology children should have access to |

| | | |
|---|---|---|
| Intermediate levels (B2 CEF) | (1) Cultural literacy<br>(2) Health matters<br>(3) Getting things done<br>(4) Life choices<br>(5) Holidays and traditions<br>(6) Disasters and emergencies<br>(7) Books and magazines<br>(8) Inventions and technology<br>(9) Controversial issues<br>(10) Enjoying the world | • Design an innovative technology and market it<br>• Create an emergency plan for your school<br>• Facilitate a teens' group on living independently<br>• Write a blog about your life, opinions and issues that are important to you<br>• Write a letter to a local leader you admire describing one social problem and offering a reasonable solution<br>• Redesign your education system so that students learn more and make this country stronger<br>• Make a poster of what people should teach their children<br>• Read and present on one historic natural disaster<br>• Create your own magazine<br>• Create your own app to sell on ITunes |
| Advanced level (C1 CEF) | (1) New perspectives<br>(2) Musical moods<br>(3) Money matters<br>(4) Looking good<br>(5) Community<br>(6) Animals<br>(7) Advertising and consumers<br>(8) Family trends<br>(9) History's mysteries<br>(10) Your free time | • Create a map of local/regional mysteries<br>• Choose a new technology, rate it and compare and contrast it to other technologies and consumer reports rating<br>• Write a pet care guide<br>• Listen to various pieces of music and describe the music, mood and how it makes you feel<br>• Create your own business plan<br>• Write a position paper to the editor about the world's population<br>• Create your own perfect world |

them understand how Edison made this discovery and how the light is transformed. Another example is to ask students to imagine and draw their perfect room, and then analyse how much it would cost to build this room by estimating the size and cost of lumber, drywall, carpet/tile, roofing and concrete. Then a teacher could help them to understand the math concepts needed in construction work.

## Materials Needed

CALLA texts are rife with examples of lessons and resource materials in the four core content areas (i.e. science, math, history and language arts), which provide holistic examples of lessons and materials on topics, such as a scientific method or the American colonies. Internet searches with a subject topic and CALLA or CALLA model keywords will yield examples. However, these are examples and are not intended to cover the immense range of activities/tasks, visuals, L1 readings, graphs, etc. needed by CALLA teachers. Therefore, teachers need to gather or develop skills to construct these materials.

The CALLA model (1994, 2009) advocated for the acquisition and creation of linguistically accessible materials by teachers and schools. The originators of the CALLA model recommended that teachers obtain resource materials in print and non-print forms (e.g. 'audio, visual, graphic, manipulative and concrete') (Chamot, 2009: 151). Typical resources are grade-level and slightly below grade-level fiction and non-fiction texts, picture dictionaries, audiobooks, fraction blocks and science kits (Chamot, 1994: 383). 'Additional materials include Spanish editions of mathematics textbooks, bilingual materials, Spanish encyclopedias, classroom science libraries of trade books, and science apparatus used for experiments and demonstrations' (Chamot, 1995: 383). I have found that letter tiles from Scrabble or Bananagrams and manipulatives from math are helpful, too.

## Assessment and Accommodations in CALLA

Assessment is an area of strength of the CALLA model. The model's originators emphasised the need for valid and systematic standardised assessments of ELs as well as practical learning-centred, teacher-friendly alternative assessments.

*Formative assessments* are assessments that are conducted throughout instruction to gauge the learners' acquisition of the key concepts or skills. They are ongoing and inform/guide the next steps an educator takes in instruction. Formative assessments differ from summative assessments in that *summative assessments* are the evaluations at the end of instruction to show overall learning. Summative assessments are not usually employed to provide guidance to the teacher about future instruction.

Alternative assessments are any type of assessment other than a traditional multiple-choice test. A range of assessments can be seen in Figure 5.7, a continuum to clarify the concept. They can be employed as formative or summative assessments as well, so they can yield important information to determine what the learners are able to do and what they continue to need.

One type of alternative assessment is a performance assessment in which learners are asked to enact some activity or language that will be assessed. For instance, a performance assessment in a language classroom is a role play. Role plays can be developed into performance assessments for the content classroom. For example, if a class was learning about the second US Continental Convention, students could be asked to study one historical figure's stance on state's rights. The students could then write a

**Figure 5.7** Continuum of traditional to alternative assessments

role play debating two sides of the argument and playing the roles of the key historical figures. The students' knowledge of the position and the language they used to express this position could be assessed.

In the CALLA model, teachers are encouraged to create performance assessment tasks to measure the content and language learning of the student. The process identified for the creation of performance assessment tasks is to identify the purpose of the assessment (i.e. target and objectives), the instructional outcomes the instrument will address and lastly to construct the instrument against teaching English to speakers of other languages (TESOL), WIDA and/or state performance standards. Teachers are encouraged to share the instrument format, rubrics and scoring with students in advance so students understand expectations (Chamot, 2009).

Perhaps because tasks and performance assessments require the same type of design and construction, the CALLA model does not detail how to construct performance assessments. A best practice in the field is to align instruction and assessment in terms of the types of activities and tasks students do during instruction with those they would perform during an assessment. Many classroom activities and tasks can be mirrored in the assessments.

The CALLA model also notes the types of test and test procedure accommodations that ELs are entitled to. These accommodations include assessment in the native language, modification of linguistic complexity, use of glossaries and/or dictionaries, oral directions and/or questions and extra assessment time (Chamot, 2009); although many states have parameters about accommodations that teachers would wish to examine.

## Type of Classroom Environment

One important distinction between the SIOP and CALLA models of content-based instruction is that the SIOP model was originally researched and tested in sheltered content classes (content classes taught by a trained ESL instructor geared towards a whole class of ELs) in high-incidence areas; whereas the CALLA model focuses on general education courses with native and non-native speakers as well as sheltered content classes. The reason this distinction is important is that the research on the SIOP model is applied to the general education class environment, but was conducted in classes with exclusively non-native speakers of English and teachers who had a background working with them. The CALLA model research was conducted in a high-incidence urban district environment with ELs in two classes. Chamot (1995) describes the programme:

> The focus of each program is on secondary EL students. About 450 students participate in the Mathematics program and 410 students in the Science program each year. The CALLA Mathematics program serves students who tested below fourth grade mathematics level in their native language at school entry, while the CALLA Science program serves all middle school beginning and intermediate level EL students and all high school intermediate level EL students. Thus, the CALLA Mathematics program is aimed at accelerating the progress of students whose mathematics background is below grade level, while the CALLA Science program includes a more heterogeneous mix of students, though most have limited previous study of science. (Chamot, 1995: 381)

The focus on the type of English learning contexts impacts the range of applicability. How widely in terms of classroom context can each of these models apply? The CALLA model (1994, 2009) does make efforts to explain how the model could be modified for use in general education classes, sheltered classes, pull-out ESL programmes (when a student or small group is withdrawn from the general education classroom for a period during the day). It also addresses other student populations, such as pre-literate students in elementary, middle and secondary level, those in need of compensatory assistance and those with special needs.

## Strengths

In my opinion, the greatest strengths of the CALLA model are that it is practical and comprehensive. The applied examples presented in the model of how teachers approach the content, language and learning strategy objectives for the four core content areas (history/social studies, math, science and language arts) with exemplar materials aid in making the instruction more approachable to novices. It is comprehensive; all four language skills and vocabulary are integrated into lessons through the content, language and learning strategy objectives. The CALLA model relies heavily on the research of learning strategies to aid learners' independent learning.

Another strength is the focus on connections to learners' background knowledge and pre-teaching new vocabulary prior to presentations of new material.

The CALLA model is also strong in holding high expectations for ELs and emphasising cognitively challenging material.

The addition of discourse analysis for teachers to glimpse the linguistic structures present in academic subjects is insightful and valuable. This is an area that teachers really need in order to understand the challenges of academic discourse.

The model has numerous tools (i.e. graphic organisers, checklists and questionnaires) for teachers to implement immediately in their instruction and assessment. For example, there are checklists for logging learning strategy instruction, for learners' self-assessment and for CALLA lesson objectives. There are also questionnaires for use with learners to determine their learning strategies. Like the SIOP, the CALLA model has an evaluation framework tool too.

The CALLA model's inclusion of task-based instruction is a strength as tasks have been shown by research to allow for input, negotiation of meaning and output (Doughty & Pica, 1986; Long, 1981, 1983; Pica & Doughty, 1985a, 1985b; Pica et al., 1986, 1987, 1993, 1996) as well as the acquisition of new vocabulary. The inclusion of tasks also enhances the engagement with the content, which makes the content accessible, if teachers are willing to create them. CALLA does little to instruct teachers in how to design tasks or materials, which can be a challenge for many teachers.

The CALLA model is strong in assessment: needs assessment, formative assessments and the interplay between planning objectives and assessments. However, the model provides only a few examples of formative assessment tasks and no guidance on how to construct a needs assessment. There is no discussion of summative assessments other than standardised testing.

## Strengths that May Also be Weaknesses

The key strengths of CALLA are its simplicity and its ease of comprehension by general educators. A weakness of the model is that it tends towards over-simplification, which results in the declaration by general educators that 'I already do that'. With the recently revised second edition of the CALLA text, it will be interesting to see if the weaknesses have been addressed.

In a brief survey of the research literature, several authors (Jurkovič, 2010; Reimer, 2008; Westbrook, 2009) conducted a variety of research projects on the learning strategies portion of the CALLA model using differing methodologies, but relying heavily on students' self-report to determine learning outcomes. Their findings were congruent with numerous other studies on language learning strategies, most notably the work of Oxford (1990), that direct instruction of learning strategies improved the performance of ELs.

Research on the comprehensive implementation of the CALLA model was conducted by Chamot (2007) who considered five differing evaluative studies on the CALLA model. The findings were based on different assessment measures and revealed 'substantial progress' by ELs on content knowledge, language and learning strategies objectives. The quantitative measurements showed significant educational effects of the methodology, which were sustained over time. Likewise, Riveria and Mazak (2010) directed a pre/post study that showed ELs self-report of improvement in speaking, listening, reading and writing using the CALLA model.

## Weaknesses

The weaknesses of the model involve many 'bigger picture' issues. For example, the CALLA model does not take a stance or treat sociolinguistic awareness, sociopolitical and diversity perspectives, value for linguistic and cultural variety or advocacy issues and needs in the field. Many of the orientations from the evaluative framework (Table 5.2) are not discussed in the model.

**Table 5.2** Evaluative framework for teacher preparation models, approaches and initiatives in EL inclusion

| I. Knowledge | CALLA model |
| --- | --- |
| When preparing teachers to include ELs into their content courses and to work with linguistically and culturally diverse groups of ELLs, they should have *knowledge* of the following areas: | |
| <ul><li>The structures and features of the English language.<ul><li>The distinctions between oral and written language.</li><li>The basic units of language, such as parts of speech, types of sentences and the sound system of English.</li><li>The construction of differing discourse units from the sentence level to a variety of social and academic genres and formats.</li><li>The irregularities of English.</li><li>The pragmatic/sociocultural dimensions of language (e.g. voice, audience) and how language varies accordingly.</li><li>An appropriate target for language acquisition/learning is real language use; 'standard' English is a myth.</li></ul></li></ul> | Due to the discourse analysis of the content topics, this is a strength of the CALLA model; however, the teacher would need to know the language as a subject well enough to be able to analyse the oral and written texts. The CALLA model does some instruction on linguistic forms by providing examples. |
| <ul><li>The key principles of second language acquisition (SLA)/learning (Ellis, 2008).<ul><li>Instruction needs to include:<ul><li>A balance predominantly on meaning but also on forms.</li><li>An understanding of individual differences in learners.</li><li>Environmental modifications to reduce anxiety and affective issues.</li><li>Extensive comprehensible input.</li><li>Interaction with peers and instructors on the academic topics.</li><li>Opportunities for learners to develop both 'a rich repertoire of formulaic expressions and a rule-based competence'.</li><li>Opportunities for spontaneous as well as controlled production.</li><li>Output opportunities.</li><li>Social and academic language.</li><li>Transfer of knowledge and skills from the first to the second language.</li></ul></li></ul></li></ul> | The CALLA model includes key principles of SLA, such as the need for interaction, academic and social language and cognition in language learning. The remainder of the principles mentioned by Ellis are not mentioned in the model. |

| | |
|---|---|
| • An understanding of ELLs' proficiency levels and their abilities and challenges at those levels. | There is no direct mention of proficiency levels and challenges at the levels, with the notable exception of low-literacy abilities. |
| • The laws pertinent to ELs' instruction in the particular context. | There is no mention of laws. |
| • The resources available to learn about ELs' educational backgrounds, first languages and cultures. | A strength of the model is that learners' educational background is connected to and their first language is supported whenever possible. Resources are not shared for learning about a variety of languages and cultures. |
| • A sociolinguistic consciousness (Lucas & Villegas, 2011)<br>  • Understanding of the relationships between language, culture and identity.<br>  • Awareness of the sociopolitical context of language use and language education, particularly in the specific context. | This is not a strength of the CALLA model. |
| • The subject matter; knowledge of one core content area or specialty area. | The subject matter is not explicitly taught in the CALLA model. It is an expectation that those who are being trained in CALLA are well versed in one core content area. |

*II. Performance*

When preparing teachers to include ELs into their content courses and to work with linguistically and culturally diverse groups of ELLs, they should have *abilities and skills* in the following areas:

| | |
|---|---|
| • Curricular and Instructional Planning | |
|   • Planning with assessments as clear targets (e.g. backward design [Wiggins& McTighe, 2005]). | Planning assessments with clear objectives is a strength of CALLA, but it is not directly linked to backward design. |

*(Continued)*

**Table 5.2** (Continued)

| | |
|---|---|
| • Creating content, language and learning strategy objectives. | A strength of this model is the content, language and learning strategy objectives. |
| • Pre-teaching and/or integrating necessary skills, such as process writing, note-taking, etc. into the curriculum. | This is a strength of the lesson format. |
| • Integrating speaking, listening, reading, writing, grammar, vocabulary and pronunciation instruction and practice into lessons. | A strength of the model is the overt inclusion of these items with the exception of grammar and pronunciation. |
| • Developing units with clear connections through a thematic focus. | This is not a focus of the CALLA model. |
| • Modifying, developing and locating materials for linguistic accessibility of lessons. | Although the CALLA model creators' noted teachers need to do this, they did not provide guidance on how. |
| • Analysing the linguistic features of oral and written discourse so as to be able to bridge the gap between ELs and a wide variety of genres, subject areas, academic discourse communities and texts. | This is a strength of the CALLA model. |
| • Addressing multiple ESL proficiency levels in the same class by planning for differentiated instruction. | Not mentioned |
| • Making informed choices (Brown, 2007b) based on solid second language acquisition (SLA) principles and best practices in content and language instruction for the particular context with its unique variables (Kumaravadivelu, 2001). | Unique context features and informed choices based on the context do seem to factor *implicitly* into CALLA. |
| • Instructional Delivery | |
| • Creating comfortable learning environments and classroom communities with low anxiety. | Expected in implementation, but not discussed. |
| • Identifying learners' background knowledge and building upon it. | A strength |
| • Making informed choices about instruction and employing a wide variety and frequency of approaches, techniques and resources depending on learners' needs. | This is a weakness of CALLA, as it is not explicitly addressed. |
| • Explicitly teaching new vocabulary and language needed for oral (speaking and listening) and written (reading and writing) engagement with the academic content using supports and tools for meaning making. | A strength |

| | |
|---|---|
| • Creating meaningful, academically focused, engaging, interactive and experiential lessons and tasks that include ELs in activities (Migliacci & Verplaetse, 2008). | A strength |
| • Directly teaching new academic information in small portions or 'chunks' with practice and interaction opportunities. | Direct teaching is included, but not the chunking notion. |
| • Modifying the delivery of speech to heighten learners' comprehension (i.e. making linguistic modifications) or modifying the complexity or quantity of written material to make it more accessible. | Mentioned, but not in detail. |
| • Scaffolding instruction using a variety of supports, such as graphic organisers, visuals, modelling, sentence frames, etc. | Scaffolding of this kind is mentioned in examples, but not as a strategy in the text. |
| • Providing cognitively challenging materials to ELs that are linguistically accessible. | A strength |
| • Assessment | |
| • Offering learners a variety of ways to demonstrate their knowledge of the content or language. For example, using performance and alternative assessment (see task and product examples above). | A strength in emphasising performance assessments. |
| • Providing suitable and judiciously chosen accommodations for ELs during academic assessments. Accommodations are state-mandated supports for learners during standardised assessments, such as providing increased time for the test, breaks, dictionaries and/or translators for directions. | A strength |
| • Measuring learners content knowledge and language ability separately. | A strength |
| • Providing ongoing feedback on content knowledge and language ability constructively and regularly. | Implied |
| • Assessing learners' progress in language learning according to proficiency indicators. | Not explicitly mentioned |
| • Modifying text and teacher-made assessments to support English learners. For example, using visuals and models in directions. | Not included |

*III. Orientations*

When preparing teachers to include ELs into their content courses and to work with linguistically and culturally diverse groups of ELLs, they should have *awareness of, value for and appreciation of* the following areas:

| | |
|---|---|
| • Value for linguistic and cultural diversity. | Background expectation |

*(Continued)*

**Table 5.2** (Continued)

| | |
|---|---|
| • Inclination to advocate for the linguistic and programmatic needs of ELLs. | Not mentioned in the second edition |
| • Willingness to collaborate with language specialists, content teachers, administrators, parents, etc. to provide high-quality instruction for ELs and to create EL-friendly schools and communities. | Not mentioned in the second edition |
| • Hold high expectations for ELs and all learners. | A strength |
| • Inclination to provide assessments that level the playing field for ELs so that they may demonstrate their knowledge in a variety of ways. | A strength |
| • Value for reflective instructional processes. | Reflective practices are infused within the model in the form of checklists teachers can employ to monitor their implementation of the model. |
| • Willingness to develop positive home/school connections with ELs' parents. | Not mentioned |
| • Willingness to treat cultures respectfully and to eliminate stereotyping of peoples and cultures. | Not mentioned |

One of the significant areas of discussion in TESOL is affective awareness and creating low-anxiety academic environments. This is an area that I am surprised is not treated in the CALLA model.

In terms of the planning and delivery of instruction, differentiation and proficiency levels are not discussed, which is an essential skill set when working in the general education classroom as there are many differing levels of language and content needs. Scaffolds are discussed in CALLA, but usually as materials support. They are not incorporated like other types of scaffolds necessary to construct meanings between languages. The variety and frequency of instructional strategies necessary to construct meaning are not discussed, so the content sample chapters tend to make the inclusion of ELs appear to be less complex than it is. Finally, the informed choices that teachers make about instruction for the specific content and variables does not factor into the CALLA model in a manner that would enlighten many who have no prior EL training.

# Optimal Context for Implementation and Suggestions

The optimal context for the implementation of the CALLA model is in general education classes taught by general educators with linguistic knowledge and/

or co-taught with an ESL specialist. Because the information present in the CALLA model is concrete and content focused, it appears more oriented towards the general education classroom where the language learners are at slightly higher levels of proficiency than in newcomer or sheltered content programmes.

The CALLA model could be implemented in low-incidence areas with few ELs spread throughout a district, if the general educator and ESL specialists could collaborate on curricular, lesson and assessment development and instructional delivery. An instructional coaching approach would also be an option with the CALLA model.

This model could be implemented in higher-incidence districts, but in those cases the language needs of the learners would need to be weighed. It would be best if this model was utilised as a transitional model to aid learners with intermediate and higher levels of proficiency to enter the general education classroom as it provides less support than the SIOP's sheltered content.

## Conclusion

This chapter outlined the ways in which the CALLA model espouses integrating content knowledge and skills along with language through the amalgamation of the four language skills into lessons with content and language objectives. CALLA also introduced the need for explicit learning strategies instruction to aid ELs. The lesson sequence of preparation, presentation, practice, expansion, and evaluation suggested in the CALLA model was described, accompanied by samples of activities, tasks and materials recommended for use in the model. The CALLA model includes information on needs and performance assessments and this chapter added to this information on how to develop needs assessments on the four language skills so that needs assessments can serve as formative assessment guides to instruction. An evaluation of the strengths and weaknesses of the CALLA model against the evaluative framework was presented.

## Activities and Discussions

(1) Write integrated content, language and learning strategy learner outcome objectives for one lesson. Use the objective format 'Students will be able to... (action verb)...'. Share them with the class and improve them collectively.

(2) Conduct a discourse analysis of one academic class. Observe, record and analyse a video of an academic class at the grade level you wish to teach. Watch and analyse the lesson for the linguistic structures employed repetitively as part of the discourse. For example, consider *patterns* in grammar, phonology, lexicon, pragmatics, semantics, functions and notions of language, formats of presentation (exposition, narrative, descriptive, etc.), the five communicative competencies and/or all the language skills (speaking, listening, reading, writing, grammar, pronunciation and vocabulary), etc. Example: the teacher repeatedly used the

expression 'by and large.' The teacher was telling stories of past war battles (narrative, past tense, sequence language, etc.). Consider the patterns that would be the biggest impact for ELs' comprehension if they were taught/learned prior to this lecture. In one page with two columns, *list* all of the linguistic structures used repetitively (with an example if necessary) that could be chosen as a subject of further language development. Choose one 'Big Impact' linguistic concept and outline a mini-workshop focused on improving ESL learners' understanding, performance and awareness of this concept (two-page maximum).

(3)  Plan an inductive lesson using the CALLA model (preparation, presentation, practice, evaluation, expansion) focused on discovering a linguistic pattern common in an academic text. Share with the class.

(4)  Ranking task: Which of the following goals are most important in your language classes? Individually, rank the goals from 1=most important to 5=least important. With a partner, discuss which ones you have ranked highest and lowest and WHY. As a team, make one list of ranked goals. Goals:

(1)  Students practice the language in speaking and writing.
(2)  Students understand the grammar rules.
(3)  Students do all the activities in the book.
(4)  Students use English only.
(5)  Students develop their confidence to use English.

(5)  Values clarification task: Which approach is more successful in helping EL students to acquire the language? Why? Focusing on grammar and accuracy during speaking and writing *or* practicing language without any explicit focus on grammar.

(6)  Problem-solving task: Situation: You have 12 high school and adult students in one of your English courses who have a lot of difficulty concentrating. Three students like to play around, make jokes, text and talk on their mobiles during class and try to avoid working on English. Four students will go along with the three playful students, but they will work if the others will let them. Two students are silent in classes and do not participate at all. The rest are hard-working students who wish to learn English for work or for getting into a good university.

- What do you do to solve this problem so that the hard-working students learn what they want, but you do not frustrate the playful ones? What do you do for the silent students?

## Chapter Summary

- The CALLA model has roots in literacy development and reading/writing across the curriculum as well as cognitive learning theory and schema theory.

- Content, language and learning strategy objectives are expected for each CALLA lesson and for a CALLA curriculum.

- Learning strategies are the tools that learners use to simplify academic tasks and improve their autonomous learning. Instructional strategies are the ways that teachers go about lesson delivery. Learning strategies should be taught explicitly and in a stepwise manner to learners.

- Needs assessments are important tools that help EL inclusive instructors know what the learners can do when they arrive at their class by providing valuable data on the four language skills.

- Lesson sequences in CALLA follow a preparation, presentation, practice, evaluation order. Presentations of new materials should be engaging and interactive and they should be brief so that learners can immediately practice what they have learned.

- Activities and tasks are interwoven into the lesson sequence to provide the practice opportunities with the language and content the learners need for SLA. Designing activities and tasks that are content based is a key skill of the EL inclusive educator.

- The CALLA model originators advocate the use of hands-on materials to engage learners, which may cause teachers to adapt, create or find many materials that are both the correct content at the proper proficiency levels.

- Assessments in CALLA engage learners in demonstrating their understandings of content through the academic language they learned in performance assessments.

# 6 Models: Response to Intervention

| **Chapter Aims and Topics** |
| --- |
| • Present the history and development of the Response to Intervention (RtI) model. |
| • Express key features of the RtI model. |
| • Describe the three tiers of RtI in terms of eligibility, instructional strategies and assessment. |
| • Cultural considerations in RtI. |
| • Affective awareness. |
| • Assessment issues in RtI. |
| • Guidelines for implementing RtI with English learners (ELs). |
| • Effectiveness of the RtI model for ELs. |

## Overview

The RtI model was developed in the field of special education to aid schools, general educators and special educators in improving the identification and speed of the instructional response to special education learners in need. RtI is a scaled approach to responding to learners' instructional and behavioural needs in a timely manner, so that learners do not need to fail in order to demonstrate their need for supplemental or specialised services. In the past, before children who were struggling with learning could be provided with services, assessments needed to show a discrepancy between their IQ and their academic achievement (Echevarria & Hasbrouck, 1999). The RtI process is now used as an alternative that speeds up academic support services for children who are struggling before they fall too far behind.

The RtI model was developed over 40 years in the field of special education (Barrett *et al.*, 2004; Esparza Brown & Sanford, 2011; Fuchs & Fuchs, 2006, 2007; Fuchs *et al.*, 2008; Howard, 2009; Rosa-Lugo *et al.*, 2010), but found its entrée into the general education classroom with the impetus from the Individuals with Disabilities Education Act (IDEA) (1997) and the Individuals with Disabilities Education Improvement Act (IDEIA) (2004). The IDEIA provides schools with the freedom to meet learners needs by '...no longer requir[ing them] to identify a severe discrepancy between academic achievement and intellectual ability to qualify a child with a specific learning disability for special education' (Buffum *et al.*, 2009: 18). The RtI model is said to alleviate some of the inherent issues in the field of special education including over-referrals to special education programmes, '...misdiagnoses of students' needs, delays in receiving assistance, infrequency of students exiting special education and use of inferior intervention programs' (Buffum *et al.*, 2009: 20). All of these issues are similar to those that ELs experience in the schools' English language programmes. There is also concern that ELs are over-represented in RtI programmes (Linan-Thompson, 2010).

The RtI model was originally designed for native speakers who grapple with learning academic content because of cognitive or learning disabilities or meeting behavioural expectations (Echevarria & Hasbrouck, 2009). It has subsequently been applied to serving ELs, which is the focus of this chapter.

## Description of the RtI Model

The RtI model uses three levels, or tiers, to classify the types of needs and appropriate responses to learners' needs. The first tier is the core curriculum level delivered with adequate and appropriate instructional modifications for all students. The RtI model notes that 80% of all learners will be served adequately at the first tier (Johnson *et al.*, 2006). The RtI model '…shifts the responsibility for helping all students become successful from the special education teachers and curriculum to the entire staff, including special *and* regular education teachers and curriculum' (Buffum *et al.*, 2009: 2). Therefore, the core curriculum for all the students in a whole-class learning situation (i.e. participant structures) with *differentiation* according to abilities and modifications for clarity and comprehensibility becomes the first stage of interventions. All students have access to high-quality instruction and support in the general education classroom when they struggle whether it is a challenge with math, dyslexia or second language learning. At this level, all students experience ongoing monitoring and formative assessments in order to have their needs identified in a timely manner. This ongoing monitoring and assessment creates a quick turnaround cycle of data-driven instructional response. In one school, educators are using weekly developmental reading assessments (*DRAs*) to determine which children need more intensive guided reading instruction in small groups (for more on the use of DRAs for ongoing formative instruction, see http://www.pasd.k12.pa.us/cms/lib02/pa01001354/centricity/domain/34/dra_summary.pdf). In comparison to older models of instruction where learners with special needs would be assessed on achievement measures at the end of a unit or term and only provided support after the appropriate paperwork (e.g. individual education plans [IEPs][1]) and approvals had been obtained, which could take a year to finalise and implement, RtI assessment and monitoring occur on a daily basis. Instantaneous, generalised interventions occur for all learners without the immediate need for IEPs. Learners with special needs continue to have IEPs to guide their instruction, but these are used at RtI Tiers 2 and 3. As for ELs, IEPs for second language learning are gaining traction in some districts and states, but they are not widely used or required.

# Response to Intervention Model, Tier 1

Tier 1 is the general education class with common modifications for most learners who are learning on grade level. The modifications made for ELs are habitually those needed to clarify terms, concepts or language expression in all four skills or to build background knowledge and connections. An EL who would receive Tier 1 supports is a language learner who is roughly on par with grade-level academics. This learner has language proficiency close to his/her peers, but might need more clarification on vocabulary outside of the academic terminology for the content. He/she might make grammatical or pronunciation mistakes in spontaneous communication, but the errors tend not to obscure the meaning too much. This EL may be literate in the first language(s) (L1) and/or have experienced academic instruction in his/her L1. This EL can read and write nearly as well as a grade-level peer, but makes atypical mistakes in word choice, formatting, mechanics (i.e. capitalisation, punctuation or spelling) and common expressions (i.e. colloquial expressions).

The way the RtI model works is to vary several aspects of instruction from group size to the frequency of support. Each tier of the RtI model modifies by these parameters '1) Size of instructional group, 2) Mastery requirements of content, 3) Frequency of progress monitoring, 4) Duration of the intervention (weeks), 5) Frequency with which the intervention support is delivered, 6) Instructor's skill or specialization level, 7) Focus of the content or skills' (Johnson *et al.*, 2006: 3.2). For instance, for Tier 1, these parameters would be adjusted accordingly (see Table 6.1).

**Table 6.1** Tier 1 parameters for RtI

| Parameters | Tier 1 Realisation |
|---|---|
| Size of instructional group | Whole class |
| Mastery requirements of content | Grade-level academic content objectives are expected. Common grade-level screening measures and classroom-based monitoring to ensure mastery of content. |
| Frequency of progress monitoring | Generally, school-wide screens occur three times annually. 'Recommendations on progress monitoring vary. In general, progress monitoring occurs at least once every three weeks, often as frequently as weekly, twice weekly, or even daily' (NRCLD, 2006: 3.4). |
| Duration of the intervention (weeks) | Students stay in their home classroom for the entirety of the academic year, unless they receive Tier 2 or Tier 3 services. Interventions are in class in the form of instructional delivery modifications. |
| Frequency with which the intervention is delivered | General educators would modify their instruction daily for all learners and instruction is based upon the grade-level curriculum. |
| Instructor's skill level | General educators must be 'highly qualified' according to NCLB (2001). |
| Focus of the content or skills | Grade-level academic expectations of content and skills apply at Tier 1. |

For ELs, general educators are expected to modify their instruction and employ a variety of instructional delivery strategies similar to those of the Sheltered Instruction Observation Protocol (SIOP) in order to serve their non-native English students. They are shown when to refer an EL to the English as a second language (ESL) resource teacher and when she/he needs to make modifications prior to referral.

The types of instructional modifications/strategies suggested for ELs (Collier, 2010; Sun *et al.*, 2010) at Tier 1 are:

- *Oral Language*: conversation management strategies (e.g. teaching students how to hold the speaking floor, elaborate a response, ask questions to gather more information, interrupt politely or take conversational turns when working in small groups); intercultural communication strategies (e.g. acknowledging differences, learning about others' cultural patterns and perspectives, avoiding stereotyping); interaction practice (e.g. activities that allow for learners to work collaboratively on tasks or projects); audiobooks.
- *Literacy*: early literacy measures; family literacy activities (e.g. family story night, read-along activities); phonological awareness; L1 or bilingual texts; letter naming fluency; alphabet knowledge; guided reading and writing activities; oral reading fluency; process writing; PARS (i.e. preview, ask questions, read, summarise); word attack strategies; comprehension strategies; experience writing.
- *Instructional*: modelling; application of grade-level benchmarks; bilingual aide; advance organisers; thematic instruction.
- *Other*: rest and relaxation strategies (i.e. using energisers, positive self-talk or stretching breaks); native or non-native buddies; language games, analogy (e.g. fish is to lake: monkey is to _____ [jungle]).

## Vignette of a Tier 1 General Education Class Session with Modifications for ELs and Learners Special Needs

The topic for the day is how to derive the key information from a math story problem and determine which arithmetic equation to use. In her planning, the classroom teacher has predetermined her learning outcome objectives for her various groups of learners. An example of a hypothetical set of content and language objectives is listed in Table 6.2. They are differentiated by the level of expectation (i.e. what the learner is expected to learn of the material) and the supports provided.

### Grade 3

**Differentiated Content and Language Objectives** (Written as learning outcomes=what do you expect your students to KNOW/be able to DO at the end of the unit that they did not know? These must be measurable. Note which supports will be offered.)

At the end of the instruction, students will be able to:

**Table 6.2** Differentiated content and language objectives for a general ecucation class with modifications for diverse learners

| Differentiated content objectives. *Cite each objective where the standard is being met, e.g. (Standard #) | WIDA 1–2s: novice/beginners | WIDA 3–4: low/mid intermediate | WIDA 5: high intermediate/low advanced | Struggling readers: native English speakers | Gifted | SPED-1: Learner with mild dyslexia, 1 with ADD and 1 with Asperger's* |
|---|---|---|---|---|---|---|
| Identify and derive the key information for a math story problem | Mastery of the Obj. Using a simplified text. With guidance, additional time and individual comprehension checks | Mastery of the Obj. independently and comprehension checks | Mastery of the Obj. independently and comprehension checks | Mastery of the Obj. Using a simplified text. With guidance and individual comprehension checks | Mastery of the Obj. independently with a more complex text | Mastery of the Obj. One learner with mild dyslexia with guidance and support; others with individual comprehension checks |
| Determine which arithmetic equation (+, −, ×, ÷) to use and write the equation to solve the problem | Mastery of the Obj. Using sentence frame provided. With guidance, additional time and individual comprehension checks | Mastery of the Obj. with individual comprehension checks | Mastery of the Obj. | Mastery of the Obj. with guidance and individual comprehension checks | Mastery of the Obj. | Mastery of the Obj. with individual comprehension checks |
| Solve the problem and connect the solution to the story | Mastery of the Obj. with comprehension checks | Mastery of the Obj. | Mastery of the Obj. | Mastery of the Obj. with comprehension checks | Mastery of the Obj. | Mastery of the Obj. with comprehension checks |

*Differentiated language objectives*

| | | | | | |
|---|---|---|---|---|---|
| Read story problem for comprehension and orally describe the problem | Mastery of the Obj. with guided reading of a simplified text | Mastery of the Obj. with additional time | Mastery of the Obj. | Mastery of the Obj. with guided reading | Mastery of the Obj. with a more complex reading | Mastery of the Obj. with guided reading for a learner with dyslexia |
| Scan for key information in a math story problem | Mastery of the Obj. with direct instruction of a simplified text | Mastery of the Obj. with direct instruction and additional time | Mastery of the Obj. with direct instruction | Mastery of the Obj. with direct instruction and guided reading | Mastery of the Obj. with a more complex reading | Mastery of the Obj. with direct instruction and guided reading for a learner with dyslexia |
| Identify and link important vocabulary used in the story problem to arithmetic concepts | Mastery of the Obj. with direct instruction of a simplified text | Mastery of the Obj. with direct instruction and additional time | Mastery of the Obj. | Mastery of the Obj. with direct instruction and guided reading | Mastery of the Obj. with a more complex reading | Mastery of the Obj. with direct instruction and guided reading for a learner with dyslexia |

*Other environmental and classroom management accommodations would need to be employed, but are not noted here due to space.

The teacher would then plan a lesson that integrates the direct instruction on the format of the math problem, understanding the story, using key vocabulary and linking it to the arithmetic operation, scanning for key information, identifying what is key information and what is extraneous, writing the equation and solving the problem.

The teacher might follow these procedures.

(1)   Introduce the topic and objectives of the lesson.
(2)   Conduct pre-reading activities using an example math story problem.
    (a)   Ask students to identify vocabulary words that are new or unusual.
    (b)   Discuss the vocabulary words with the class.
    (c)   Ask students when they have seen math story problems and what they think they are supposed to do to solve them.
    (d)   Clarify any misunderstandings related to the role of math story problems and what students should do with them.
(3)   Explain the format(s) of math story problems with the exemplar.
    (a)   Highlight identifying key vocabulary to connect it to the appropriate arithmetic operation.
    (b)   Explain that there are many ways to express the same arithmetic operation.
        (i)   Addition:
            (1)   How many do you need altogether?
            (2)   What is the total for the children?
            (3)   What is the sum of all the candies?
            (4)   There are three toy cars. Thirteen more toy cars are added. How many are there in total?
        (ii)   Subtraction:
            (1)   What is the difference between the groups?
            (2)   How many less does Juan have than Rodrigo?
            (3)   Nouf starts with 65 cookies. She gives 29 to Aiyisha. How many cookies does Nouf end with?
        (iii) Multiplication:
            (1)   What is the total of group A by group B?
            (2)   There are nine toys in each box. How many toys are in six boxes?
            (3)   Jihan has three boxes of candy. Each box holds four candies. How many candies does Jihan have?
        (iv)   Division:
            (1)   There are 50 rocks in Clarita's rock collection. If the rocks are organised into five groups, how big is each group?
            (2)   Darin is inviting 15 children to a party. He has 45 candies. How many candies will each child get?
            (3)   There are 18 children in the class and 54 milk boxes. If the milk boxes are divided equally among the children, how many does each child receive?

(4) Ask students to read a math story problem and identify key vocabulary. Employ small groups to offer guided practice to language learners, struggling readers and any learners with special needs. Circulate to gauge learners' comprehension of the story problem and their ability to read the story. Provide simplified readings with easier vocabulary to some groups and more complex readings to others. For gifted learners provide more complex readings and/or complex math; asking them to relate the story to a real-world problem will challenge them cognitively and keep them on task so that the teacher has more time to work with others.
(5) The teacher would gather the students back to the whole group to discuss the reading and solve the problem. The teacher would summarise the importance of understanding the story problem by reading for comprehension of key information.
(6) The teacher would explain, writing the equation from the information provided in the story problem. The teacher would ask the students what the next step would be (solving the problem), since presumably they know how to do this.
(7) The teacher would then present other math story problems and explain how to determine which arithmetic equation (+, −, ×, ÷) to use when there is more than one option.
(8) The teacher could give a matching task for individual or small-group practice in determining the operation. To debrief that task, the teacher would play a guessing game with the class.
(9) Next, the teacher would teach the skill of scanning for key information.
  (a) The teacher would explain that the problem should be read first to figure out which math operation is being asked.
  (b) Then, the teacher would explain how to scan a text for key information to complete the equation.
  (c) The teacher would ask students to practice this with the appropriate level of reading. Students could work in teams and write their equation and their process on a large sheet of blotter paper that they could post on the wall.
  (d) The teacher would ask learners' groups to share their work by explaining their process and the equation.
  (e) The teacher would guide learners to self-identify errors in the process or equations.

## Response to Intervention Model, Tier 2

Tier 2 is outside the general education class in small group or individual instruction. This may resemble an EL pull-out environment. An EL who would receive Tier 2 supports is a language learner who is struggling with some enabling concepts or skills needed to perform grade-level academics. This learner has language proficiency unlike his/her peers, because this learner struggles to communicate or is often incomprehensible. He/she makes numerous grammatical or pronunciation mistakes in spontaneous communication to the point that the errors tend to obscure the meaning much of the time. This EL gets confused and has difficulty following oral and written directions. This EL may not be literate in the first language(s) or experienced with academic instruction in his/her L1. This EL can read and write only basic simple sentences in academic language; the written language that the learner can produce is vague or lacking in complexity. Written academic texts would have numerous grammatical or mechanical errors or anomalies. The learner's reading of academic texts might be difficult and/or the learner does not comprehend some main ideas/concepts and struggles with most details.

*Enabling skills*, also known as academic enablers (DiPerna, 2006), are sets of knowledge or skills that help learners to accomplish a further, bigger activity. For example, to be able to add fractions, learners need to understand what a fraction represents and how to add. To be able to find a location on a map and provide directions, learners need to know to identify cardinal directions through the compass rose (i.e. north, south, east, west) as well as ordinal directions with right, left, straight, forward, give the directional information in command form, etc. For an EL, the enabling skills necessary to write an essay would include:

- Sentence-level language abilities: such as conjugating verbs in a variety of tenses, employing subject-verb-object (SVO) format for simple sentences, using varying sentence types and lengths, using adjectives, choosing appropriate vocabulary/nouns and verbs (i.e. word choice), etc.
- Discourse-level abilities: writing thesis statements, using appropriate formatting, developing argumentation, using transitions, etc.
- Sociocultural level: addressing the audience appropriately.

Once learners are beyond their first couple of years of schooling, they have already developed skills in literacy, math and studying that will be further built upon in other learning. If a learner has not acquired an important enabling skill, a Tier 2 intervention might be designed to provide the learner with this vital knowledge for application in future class learning.

Teachers can pre-empt possible problems when working with ELs by analysing and anticipating the enabling skills assumed in a particular academic task or concept. Some focus questions the teacher can ask himself/herself are:

- What must a student say to complete this task?
- What language must they know (grammar, vocabulary, pronunciation, etc.) to use the language to work within the group to complete the task?
- What background learning does this task expect learners to have to complete it?

The second tier of the RtI model is the critical juncture at which the needs of struggling learners have been identified and supplementary interventions occur. Tier 2 is the first line of aid for learners outside the general education course. At this level, learners with special needs have been identified as struggling with cognitive, learning or behavioural issues and having needs beyond those that would be served with basic instructional modifications in the general education classroom. ELs who are being served at Tier 2, on the other hand, need more than immersion instruction with some general linguistic support. Learners have not learned what is considered 'essential' information in the general education classroom, so they receive intensified, systematic interventions and more focused instruction in small groups or pull-out, one-on-one sessions with specialists. The RtI model performs with increasing time and intensity of instructional intervention based on the degree of learners' needs. Effective communication among staff is vital in the rapid response of this model. For example, a pull-out session for an EL to develop the skills he/she needs to read an academic text might focus on learning to read headers and subheaders, to have an advance organiser or to identify the main ideas, developing word attack strategies (e.g. sounding out the word, identifying word parts [prefix, root, suffix], flipping between short and long vowel sounds, stretching out the sounds, comparing parts of the word to other similar words, using picture clues, reading ahead and rereading) to figure out new words in context, note-taking strategies to aid in recall or pre-reading the chapter summary to help in identifying important concepts to be learned. The teacher might also teach the learner how to use a dictionary or a thesaurus. The teacher would engage the learner directly with a chapter from the general education classroom that the learner would be reading at the moment or in the future to demonstrate the strategies in context and then provide scaffolded practice for the learner to strengthen his/her abilities.

Many ELs at mid- to high-intermediate or advanced proficiency (WIDA Levels 4–6) can be appropriately and sufficiently served in their linguistic and academic needs at grade level by an instructor who is willing to modify for them. The modifications mentioned in many RtI resources do not elaborate on the types of modifications that general educators should be making in general (Table 6.3). As a common practice, ELs are automatically placed at Tier 2 in many schools because some schools are unsure of how to meet ELs needs in the general education classroom or because the learners simply need more intensive language development. If the former situation is the reason, this practice is a disservice to the learners. Due to issues of the social stigmatisation of exclusion and lack of access to academic content as well as the complex interplay of background, educational experience(s), L1 and culture variables, ELs should be included into the general education classroom first. Of course, Elizalde-Utnick (2008) found that even if the quality of instruction of ELs at Tier 1 was high and modifications were being made, ELs might continue to need Tier 2 services. This is particularly true when the academic and linguistic gap is wide.

Parallel to the assessment practices in special education, but congruent with the education of ELs, the quality and frequency of assessment measures should be taken into considerations in decisions about placement into Tier 2. For ELs, Tier 2 placement may lead to small-group, pull-out services or small classes of ELs depending

**Table 6.3** Tier 2 parameters for RtI

| Parameters | Tier 2 Realisation |
| --- | --- |
| Size of instructional group | Small groups of two to four learners. |
| Mastery requirements of content | Learners' specific needs are addressed by direct instruction, skill building and practice. |
| Frequency of progress monitoring | One to three times weekly are typically suggested. |
| Duration of the intervention (weeks) | Nine- to twelve-week duration for interventions; this may be repeated as necessary. |
| Frequency with which the intervention is delivered | Thirty to sixty sessions two to three times weekly depending on the degree of the learners' need. |
| Instructor's skill level | Instructors are specialists in the particular area of need with recurrent professional development. |
| Focus of the content or skills | Individual needs, whether literacy/reading (e.g. phonics, decoding, reading strategies or sight words), writing (e.g. formation of letters, word, sentence or conveying messages in text), math, problem solving, etc. are the focus of instruction. |

on the numbers of ELs in a grade, school and/or district. A great deal of concerted orchestration of staff and resources needs to be organised and coordinated.

The types of instructional modifications/strategies suggested for ELs at Tier 2 (Collier, 2010; Linan-Thompson, 2006; Sun *et al.*, 2010) are:

- *Oral Language*: discussions on how to deal with socially uncomfortable or uncertain situations; total physical response (TPR); sheltered role plays.
- *Literacy*: explicit instruction of literacy strategies; phonological awareness; word attack; fluency and comprehension strategies; word recognition; repeated connected text reading; encoding; letter–sound recognition. (For more on literacy development, see Chapter 8 on the ExC-ELL model.)
- *Instructional*: academic language instruction; interactive teaching.
- *Other*: vocabulary and concept knowledge development; practice in the four skills targeted towards the needs of the proficiency level; guided practice with planned interaction; cross-cultural counselling for families; multimedia information about local, regional and national culture, norms, interactional patterns, school, services and laws; peer tutoring; more intensive Tier 1 interventions.

## Total Physical Response

TPR is a technique originated by Asher (1969) to teach new languages through active learning and movement. The teacher creates an immersion in the target language, the students' new language, to engage the learners through commands similar to the game 'Simon Says'. The idea is that students learn the oral commands and associate a movement and/or object with the word/phrase (e.g. stand up, sit down and turn around). The teacher repeats nouns, verbs, adverbs or combinations of them, demonstrating a movement for learners to associate with the word or phrase. Commands, for example, may be touch your nose, eyes or ears or slowly run in place, quickly run in place, walk sleepily, etc. The teacher introduces the words and actions slowly at first and asks students to mimic the action (introduction phase). Then, the teacher slightly increases the speed and rearranges the order of commands (repetition stage). The teacher repeats the words until he/she believes students' have learned them. Then the teacher calls out the commands without demonstrating the action (comprehension check stage). It is at this time that the teacher can determine learners' comprehension and retention of the words and actions. The end stage is when the teacher asks individual students to lead the 'Simon Says' for the class (student leadership stage).

This technique can be applied to teaching some vocabulary or skills in content areas. For example, teachers could provide visuals of a cell's structure and employ the systematic stages (i.e. introduction, repetition, comprehension check and student leadership) while asking students to point to a part, such as the mitochondria or cell membrane. This technique can be employed with content area vocabulary (nouns and verbs) that is concrete, meaning it can be physically interacted with. Students can move, touch, bounce or point to the object. TPR is not applicable for abstract concepts and complex language.

# Vignette of a Tier 2 Small-Group, Pull-Out Session

The ESL specialist would gather ELs with similar needs, such as writing simple declarative sentences (e.g. This leaf comes from a maple tree.). The teacher would explain the word order of a declarative sentence (e.g. SVO). The teacher would give examples and practice activities, such as error analysis activities (i.e. activities that require learners to identify and fix errors in sample SVO sentences). The students would then be asked to create simple declarative sentences on knowledge they have and identify the SVO of each. For example, 'I ride the bus to school every day'. Subject=I, verb=ride, object=the bus. Or 'My favourite food is spaghetti'. Subject=favourite food, verb=is, object=spaghetti. Then, the teacher would ask them to discuss a science topic while the teacher serves as the scribe, writing their sentences on the board and modelling the SVO pattern in the written form. The students would be led to conduct a group analysis of the pattern of the model on the board. The students would then be asked to read the science topic (i.e. identifying types of trees by their leaf shapes) and underline the declarative sentences as well as the specific parts (i.e. SVO). The session might end with a short written activity in which the students share their understandings of the reading using the SVO pattern.

# Response to Intervention Model, Tier 3

Tier 3 is outside the general education class in small-group or individual instruction and has frequent, intensive sessions. In special education situations, this might mean one-on-one instruction most of the day. An EL who would receive Tier 3 supports may struggle with academic concepts or skills far below grade level. This learner has either no language proficiency or is so new to the language that the learner cannot communicate beyond basic needs or formulaic phrases (i.e. novice or WIDA 1 proficiency). The learner may frequently remain silent choosing not to interact (i.e. the Silent Period [Krashen, 1981]).

The third tier of the RtI model is the most intensive level of intervention, which is designed for those learners who have demonstrated more significant learning problems. They receive increasingly intense interventions focused on closing the achievement gap. At this tier, learners would have even more time with specialists in small-group or individual environments. Depending upon the number of tiers a district or school chooses, some may choose more than three tiers, special education interventions may or may not be at Tier 3.

The services and exit criteria in Tier 3 are designed against the needs of the student as identified in the learner's IEP. This individual focus allows for freedom of movement within the programme so that learners are not placed in dead-end programmes where they cannot leave. Learner progress is monitored closely. When students achieve their objectives in relation to the general education curriculum and IEP, they are free to return to Tier 1 or 2 services, as needed (Fuchs & Fuchs, 2006). There is a fluidity of movement between tiers so learners are not locked into any tier permanently so as to avoid tracking in dead-end programmes (Table 6.4).

Tier 3 for ELs may be either serving a combination of second language acquisition (SLA) and special education needs or it may be even more intensive English language acquisition (ELA) classes for newcomers or lower levels of proficiency (e.g. WIDA Levels 1 and 2). The ELA classes would be taught to a class of ELs by a licensed ESL instructor. These ELA courses could be either language-oriented or content-oriented language classes. ELs could have as few as 1 hour per day or as many as 7 hours per day of ELA instruction depending on the degree of need and financial and human resources.

Tier 3 for ELs with special education needs is a special situation indeed. To put the numbers in perspective, consider that the EL population is no different from the general student population in terms of numbers of special education and gifted students (Figure 6.1). ELs are unique in the fact that they are learning in two or more languages. In the general student population, roughly 10% have special education

**Table 6.4** Tier 3 parameters for RtI

| Parameter | Tier 3 Realisation |
|---|---|
| Size of instructional group | Individually or in small groups of two or three |
| Mastery requirements of content | At Tier 3, each learner has an individualised education plan (IEP) of learning goals against which mastery is determined with remediation in the specific area of need. Learners are taught compensatory strategies to aid their independent work. |
| Frequency of progress monitoring | Continuous |
| Duration of the intervention (weeks) | Longer than Tier 2 sessions. Typically one semester. |
| Frequency with which the intervention is delivered | Daily depending upon the learners' needs |
| Instructor's skill level | Special education instructors, ESL specialist and/or other specialist |
| Focus of the content or skills | Individually focused by the learner's IEP |

needs and another 10% have gifted aptitudes. The remaining 80% are 'regular' learners. The same percentages hold true for ELs as well. The proportion of learners with special education needs does not increase dramatically for ELs, although ELs are over-represented statistically in special education programmes. On the contrary,

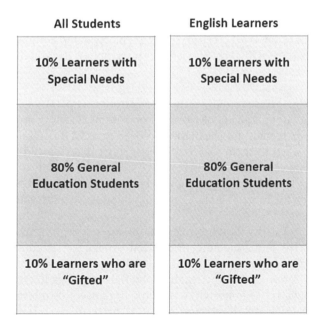

**Figure 6.1** Percentages of learners with special needs in the general and EL populations

many ELs do not receive gifted services even when they are gifted as many people assume they are not gifted simply because they are working through two or more languages.

Assessments of ELs should cover the range of cognitive, learning and academic ability sets and be conducted in their L1 in order to best serve the population. The assessments in the L1 show achievement and performance. Achievement tests conducted in the second language provide murky results at best, because there is no way to determine if the language barrier was the problem or if the learner could/couldn't do the academic task.

In the rare instance when an EL also has cognitive, learning or behavioural challenges, that learner is entitled to both ELA and special education services. In practice, I have often found that ELs with special education needs do not receive both sets of services because school personnel do not have the time, personnel feel that special education services trump ELA instruction or service opportunities have scheduling conflicts. There are few specialists with both ESL and special education preparation and training to address this overlap. One resource educator who attempts to bridge the gap is Catherine Collier. She has two helpful texts: *Curriculum Materials for the Bilingual Exceptional Child* (2003) and *Separating Difference from Disability* (2009).

Collier (2009) explains many of the challenges of language and culture in the assessment of ELs. A linguistic and cultural obstacle for an EL on an assessment can be seen in the following question:

> Lara is at the circus with two friends, Akiko and Olga. They are hungry. Corn dogs cost $3 each, popcorn is $2.50 each, sodas are $1 each and caramel apples are $1.50 each. The girls have $20 each. If each girl buys one of each item, how much will he/she have left?

English language learners, due to their background experiences, may not be able to conceptualise a circus, the money or the food items. Corn dogs are a particularly American food item. Soda is not the highest frequency word for colas. The words might appear completely alien to them and they may struggle just to read them. For example, are there dogs for sale?

In addition to Tiers 1 and 2 strategies, the types of instructional modifications/strategies suggested for ELs at Tier 3 (Collier, 2010; Sun *et al.*, 2010) are:

- *Oral Language*: oral discussions; role playing to solve problems; role playing to develop cognitive and academic interaction strategies; listening comprehension strategies; guided lectures.
- *Literacy*: visualisation; analysing reading materials; proofreading strategies.
- *Instructional*: advance organisers (i.e. graphic organisers or questioning that helps learners to identify organisational features, patterns or differences in a text); demonstrations; reciprocal questioning (i.e. students play the role of teacher by analysing a passage and developing a list of 'teacher questions' to ask the class

about the concept. The teacher then answers the questions or asks clarifying questions to encourage the learners to reconsider and reorganise their questions and understandings).

- *Other*: active and reflective processing (i.e. encouraging learners to process information with conscious effort and to reflect on their own mental processes. Teachers can do this by asking students to write down the steps they take to write a science lab report or to think about and make connections to their personal experiences while reading); test-taking strategies; paraphrasing; sound clues; memory and retention strategies; organising information; intensive use of strategies from Tiers 1 and 2.

## Vignette of a Tier 3 Session

In a Tier 3 session, the ELs might have a whole-class period with the ESL specialist. The ESL specialist would work with the learner one-on-one and more intensively.

Consider a third-grade learner who had experienced interrupted learning because his parents follow the seasonal crop harvests. He cannot understand basic oral statements or read a simple sentence, but needs to learn multiplication. First, the ESL specialist would identify his oral comprehension and try to ascertain how much reading and math the learner had acquired. Next, the ESL specialist might work on oral explanations and reviews of enabling math skills to determine what English the learner understood when talking about the math. The ESL specialist might work with him on recognising and understanding the meaning of basic sight words and key mathematic vocabulary. He might teach simple sentence structures. He might explain basic math words and concepts in English and build up to multiplication concepts through intense daily sessions for a longer period of time. Each step would include an assessment of background knowledge and enabling skills, direct instruction and numerous practice activities and tasks. This pattern would continue until the student was ready to learn multiplication concepts, equations and terms or be routed back into the general education class for that instruction. In this case, the general education class may have already moved beyond the concept.

The degree of severity in this knowledge gap is the hardest to overcome, because there are so many concepts mathematically and linguistically that the learner needs in oral and written language in order to be able to understand the classroom instruction. While the student is not in the general education classroom, he is also falling behind his peers.

## Cultural Considerations in RtI

Understanding learners' background cultures impacts testing, placement and instruction. Without an understanding of learners' cultural patterns and expectations, implementation of RtI may not succeed.

We are concerned that if we do not engage in dialogue about how culture mediates learning, RTI Models will simply be like old wine in a new bottle, in other words, another deficit-based approach to sorting children, particularly children from marginalized communities. (National Center for Culturally Responsive Educational Systems [NCCRESt], 2005: 1)

This position statement from the NCCRESt highlights the precise issue of treating ELs in the RtI system, that of cultural interaction with learning and the potential deficit nature of the RtI model.

Let us consider the issue of 'deficit' first. Special educators work predominantly with native-English speakers who have cognitive, learning or behavioural problems. The inherent basis for their work is to remediate the problem to the best degree possible in order to help the learner to reach his/her potential. My beloved nephew, 'Jonas', has a condition along the autism spectrum, which manifests itself differently than other autism cases, and attention deficit hyperactivity disorder (ADHD). He is extremely bright (e.g. IQ of 160 while distracted), highly energetic, affectionate and funny. He has no problem remembering any information he finds interesting. He becomes distracted by his favourite things in school, which include girls' hair, and can become highly emotional if upset. On his IEP, the special educators emphasise focus and patience on academic tasks, accommodations on assessments so that distractions are minimised, and choice of topics of interest to him and high interest subject matter. Jonas has and will always have these clear learning challenges. With modifications, he will be able to learn enough to have a meaningful life, but he may never be able to live independently.

I have also worked with another learner who I will call Tae Un for this discussion. She had a slight cognitive delay, which was not diagnosed during the time I knew her. She was in a university ESL programme and had taken all the classes several times. She was hard working and could speak and listen like a native speaker in social conversation. Her academic oral English was weak, but her writing is where I noticed a challenge. She wrote like a child in kindergarten. Large, irregularly shaped letters formed words that held little meaning to a reader. When the words were comprehensible, the sentences were constructed using basic common words and simple sentence formats with grammatical and lexical issues throughout. Although she had been counselled by her ESL instructors and programme director to be tested by the special education department, she refused as it was a shame upon her and her family within her culture to have a learning challenge.

Whereas an EL, for instance, 'Sophie', a bright, sweet, fifth-grade learner from China with whom I had worked had been in the US for 2 years when I met her. She was fluent and articulate in Chinese as was measured on oral proficiency interviews with a native speaker of Chinese. She also had a great deal of academic knowledge from her schooling in China. She was receiving ESL services because she arrived in the US without ever having experienced English. In her general education classes, she did her best to participate while acquiring her second language. She was *working through two languages simultaneously.* She was making mental connections between concepts and vocabulary in the first and second language while remembering the new academic information. This is a Herculean task for anyone, let alone an elementary school student.

This is why being an EL is not a deficit. ELs have needs, but their needs are temporary and based on acquiring a new language. Eventually, she will be fully bilingual. Acquiring a new language is additive. It is a benefit for the learner long term and studies show that bilinguals consistently outperform monolinguals on a variety of measures (Bialystok, 2011; Bialystok *et al.*, 2009, 2010; Bialystok & Feng, 2009). Approaching the education of Sophie in the same manner that one would Jonas or Tae Un is a disservice to each of these learners.

Cultures have similarities and differences that surface in interesting ways in the classroom. Very young learners who pick up a book and page from back to front are not necessarily preliterate. Instead, they may come from Arabic or Japanese reading traditions. Learners who think there are only five or six world continents may not be struggling, but may be from Peru where children are taught that Antarctica is not a continent. This grey area requires educators to ponder the question of whether it is a difference or a disability prior to implementing interventions. Educators also need to be informed of various cultural patterns throughout the world.

## Cultural Patterns and the Classroom

In the field of foreign languages, there is a useful distinction to describe many aspects of culture, 'Big C' and 'Little c' culture. Big C culture is the perceived 'high culture', such as the arts, monuments and what the culture is known for internationally. Little c culture describes the daily habits, activities and lifestyle of the people. For example, what modes of transportation are used, what foods are eaten in the home and how people communicate. The types of cultural patterns excluded from this distinction involve more global patterns of a people, for example, what values do individuals hold and what are the roles of members of a family. These cultural patterns are somewhat invisible, hard to identify and cause many misunderstandings in the classroom.

There are other helpful cultural patterns that all teachers would benefit from knowing as they impact learners' interaction in the classroom. Here is a selection of important concepts:

(1) *Saving face*: In many cultures it is simply not acceptable to focus attention on an individual that would embarrass the person; whether the person deserves to have an issue addressed or not does not matter. In the cultures that employ this pattern, it is important to go out of your way to avoid addressing individual issues in public. This may mean that a teacher avoids a direct correction that would greatly embarrass a learner. The teacher might also choose to address

*(Continued)*

significant issues in private to save the learner's face in public, or to address the issue in an oblique way as a generalisation not directed at a particular learner. Another strategy is to praise students for the expected behaviour or answer as opposed to highlighting those who have not achieved in these areas.

(2) *Collaborative and independent work*: Some cultures value working collaboratively to solve problems and help each other. Learners raised in academic cultures in which learners support and help each other may also feel that allowing one of their members to fail is a shame on the group and society. Learners may be unwilling to work independently and it may seem as though they are cheating if they talk when they are forbidden to do so. Appropriate strategies are to allow for more group tasks and assessments and figure out ways to assess each individual for his or her contributions. Working with learners to find compromise ground and build towards independent work is necessary for success in many Western cultures.

(3) *Distinguishing oneself*: When learners are asked to distinguish themselves individually for their accomplishments, they may be hesitant to do so. It could be perceived by the group as putting himself/herself in a higher position in relation to his/her peers. Therefore, individual praise would need to be thoughtful and judiciously given.

(4) *Teacher and students' roles in the classroom*: From Confucian teachings, Chinese learners are told that the teacher ranks only after God and one's parents, so that learners owe the teacher a high degree of respect. In many cultures, the teacher's role is to teach and the learners' role is to listen. If a teacher chooses an interactive instructional style and the learners are accustomed only to lecture formats, myriad problems may result along with misunderstandings on both parts. When learners come to the classroom from this perspective they may not choose to talk as it may be perceived as a direct challenge to the teacher's authority. To engage the teacher in an academic debate would be considered an outrage. When learners holding these beliefs witness disrespect, they may interpret the situation as poor teaching among other possibilities.

A related concept about the teacher's role is that parents from some cultures believe that teachers do the teaching, the parents do not. When teachers ask parents to read to their children, be involved in school activities, work with their children on their homework, the perception is that the teacher is not doing his/her job. The deference that parents give to the teacher and his/her role extends to parent–teacher interaction. The parent might not perceive his/her role as being part of the team or see the need or value in interacting with the teacher, so the parent might not ever come to school for parent–teacher conferences, for example.

(5) *Politeness and deference*: Although politeness and deference have already been mentioned, there are other ways that these cultural patterns impact classroom interaction. Learners might not make eye contact with the teacher and appear shy.

*(Continued)*

A good gauge is to observe the student with his/her peers to determine if the student is shy and/or introverted. It may be that the learner is trying to be polite. Forcing children to make eye contact in order to adhere to the dominant cultural pattern of the school is not necessarily culturally congruent or valuable.

(6) *Social hierarchies*: In many places in the world, people are conscious of their social standing and it influences their daily interactions and behaviours. When students arrive in our classes, they bring with them a belief about where they stand in the social hierarchy of the community. Social hierarchies are then replicated in our classes. Among the students, some groups might feel superior to others based on financial status, clothing, cultural heritage or family status. In order to engage students in the risky process of learning, we need to convey that all students are equal and valued. Strategies for dismantling disabling hierarchies include building strong interpersonal rapport and respect through small-group work, group projects and fair treatment of all learners.

(7) *Directness and indirectness*: Oddly enough, American culture is known for its directness when it comes to communicating messages. This is odd, because in many cases, particularly difficult or awkward cases, Americans are extremely indirect. Individuals from some cultures, because they believe in saving face or out of respect, are indirect in their self-expression; they may prefer that the listener or reader intuit their purpose or thrust. This approach leaves a more direct culture confused. On the other hand, sometimes learners will overcompensate. They understand that they are in a more direct culture and they are so direct that they are perceived as offensive. When working with learners, teachers should strive to guide learners in socioculturally appropriate ways to express themselves and their needs through their speaking and writing. This should be modelled in the ways that teachers express themselves, too.

It is not always easy to tell the difference between language learning challenges, cultural differences and special education needs, because learners may have learned in a different educational structure with broadly varying exposure to academic content and patterns of education, or they may be experiencing culture shock (situational) which can appear as being despondent, depressed or tuned out. For instance, the learner who does not orally participate in the classroom activities may be from a culture in which the teacher has absolute authority and does not brook learners' perspectives. Knowing the individual child's background, educational experiences and home cultural patterns helps educators to answer the difference or disability question. One rule of thumb is clear though, if a learner exhibits the same need on both the first and second language assessments, and it is not a different cultural belief or pattern, then there is likely a problem.

As educators, we need to provide ample opportunities to learn.

Opportunity to learn is a complex construct that includes not only *access to key resources* (qualified teachers, funding, relevant and rigorous curriculum), but also factors related to the *nature and implementation of school activities* (e.g., culturally meaningful task criteria, teacher-student shared understandings of the purpose of tasks and activities, culturally inclusive participation frameworks in classroom discourse and school deficit ideologies about low-income racial minority students used in referral and placement practices). (NCCRESt, 2005: 1)

We need to evaluate our own preconceptions and examine our biases about culturally and linguistically diverse learners (de Koven, 2013), learn about our students' home cultures and languages and take action to equal the opportunity for learning, to evaluate the types, nature and duration of interventions and to ensure appropriate referrals.

## Affective Awareness in Second Language Acquisition

Imagine a classroom in which all the information you hear and see all day long is in another language, for instance Thai. You are a native speaker of English. Thai does not share any similarities with your native language. The written form of Thai does not use the Latin alphabet. The teacher looks at you and says something, but you do not recognise a single word. You follow gestures and try to follow along. Increasingly, you worry about making a fool of yourself or being embarrassed. If teachers or students ask you questions, you do not understand so you smile and play along as if you do understand. Other children laugh at you. You are asked to participate in the activities, but are unable to do much. The tension and fear are so high that you cannot even think straight. The affective filter is at work.

The *affective filter* is a foundational principle in the field of SLA posited by Krashen (1979, 1981, 1982, 1985a, 1985b). The affective filter refers to the ways that anxiety, stress, tension, fear and inhibition create a potent barrier to processing and learning second languages. The messages of fear, stress and anxiety in the learner's brain overwhelm his/her ability to comprehend incoming information and consequently to formulate grammatically and phonologically correct words and sentences. The term *filter* refers to the ways that the emotional high alert in an EL's brain reduces the incoming and outgoing messages. When the learner's emotional state is on high alert, ESL specialists say that the affective filter is high, for example.

One important consideration for EL inclusive educators is to construct a classroom environment that is an emotionally safe place for learners. When the learner is a newcomer, teachers should allow the student the freedom of a *silent period* in which she/he is not required to contribute linguistically to classroom interaction, but to participate in other ways. When the learner has some basic language skills it is important that the teacher continues to support the learner by keeping anxiety low and protecting the learner from embarrassing situations. For example, the teacher would use group work to determine if the EL was able to contribute to the class discussion. If the learner was able to contribute, the teacher could forewarn the student that she/he will be called on for a particular answer that the learner has done correctly.

Creating an emotionally safe environment also includes making sure that learners feel comfortable taking risks in the language and their learning. The environment allows for mistakes without other students mocking the learner or the risk of a negative evaluation from the teacher. A strategy for this is 'taking a pass'. When a learner is called upon and is unprepared with an answer, he/she can take a pass. The teacher can then indicate that he/she will revisit the student once the student has had a chance to think about the answer or the teacher can ask the student a different question after a short while.

## Rapport Tips

- Create an atmosphere conducive to safe risk-taking in English and subject matters.
- Employ face-saving strategies/respect the learner and his/her dignity.
- Reduce learners' task and class anxiety by giving positive support, like 'Don't worry. I know you are capable of doing this. You can do this!'
- Facilitate learner-to-learner trust and friendships and avoid allowing cliques to develop.
- Use dialogue journal writing to find out about the learners' individual experiences, thoughts and challenges. Offer suggestions and tools to help.

## Planning Tips

- Conduct hands-on activities and language practice before more abstract activities (and language).
- Do one-on-one work before the whole group.
- Engage students in discussions, activities and materials.
- Make cognitively challenging activities at the appropriate language level (Figure 6.2).

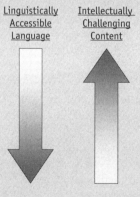

Linguistically Accessible Language

Intellectually Challenging Content

**Figure 6.2** Academic rigor and linguistic accessibility

*(Continued)*

- Analyse/pre-teach enabling skills/knowledge necessary for an activity/task (unwieldy tasks+insecurity=learner passivity leading to learned helplessness or paralysis; Snow & Brinton, 2000).
- Scaffold information and activities in a stepwise manner.

## Lesson Delivery Tips

- Comprehensible input (e.g. slightly modified language used by teacher, modifying/simplifying texts).
- Check learners' comprehension with open-ended comprehension checks.
- Clarify terms/concepts in students' native language, when possible.
- Employ a variety of grouping strategies (i.e. individual, small group, whole group; cross-proficiency, similar proficiency, etc.).
- Give careful correction, constructive feedback.
- Give clear, stepwise explanation of tasks.
- Increase (5–7 seconds) wait time.
- Provide ample practice and interaction.
- Use gestures/non-verbal communication to support your words.
- Use peer teaching.
- Use reciprocal teaching (i.e. the students teach the teacher).

## Materials Tips

- Employ a lot of visuals, graphs, charts, drawings, etc.
- Employ supplemental material to further expand the topic/concept.
- Use your word walls for appropriate and timely information to support the learning.

When the learner is new to the culture and schools, teachers can help the adjustment process and ease the learner's entry into the new environment. The following list has been modified from Law and Eckes (2010) tips for making the classroom environment EL inclusive.

- Sensitise the class, promote respect and empathy. Teach the students how to treat each other and the ELs appropriately. Be a model for all students by showing respect and fairness.
- Introduce the student to the class. Make the student feel welcome. Pronounce the student's name correctly. Do not anglicise it unless the student asks you to do so.
- Learn a few phrases in the student's language and a little about the student's country and culture. Avoid asking the student to represent or provide the perspective of his/her country or culture on every topic. When the teacher contributes his/her knowledge of the learners' culture(s), it affirms them.
- Give the students a 'personal space'. Seat the students so they have access to you and their peers.

- Ask an experienced student to be a buddy for the first few days. Be careful that this relationship does not become one of over-dependency or allow it to continue too long as it might harm both learners. One strategy is to systematically change buddies every two weeks.
- Include the students in activities. Plan interactive activities that help the new student get to know his/her peers. Explain to students how to include the EL in the activity, not to do it for him/her.
- Find out a little about the student's interests and facilitate connections with other students and extracurricular activities.
- Help the student learn school routines, rules and expectations of behaviour. Familiarise the learner with the daily schedule, classroom rules and expectations and demonstrate/model these patterns.
- Connect the home and school cultures by accessing school and community resources (e.g. readers from the library, community speakers and multimedia).
- Provide L1 support where possible. Gathering age-appropriate L1 supplemental readers affirms and supports the learners' L1 and culture.

Affective awareness is a key principle that EL inclusive educators should consider when working with ELs as it has a tremendous impact on many aspects of the learning process for both content and language.

## Assessment Issues of ELs in RtI

One of the most significant challenges for RtI educators working with ELs is assessment. ELs, because they are working in two languages, pose an assessment challenge. First, for valid results, they cannot and should not be assessed monolingually in English similar to their native English-speaking peers. Rinaldi and Samson (2008) justify this,

> When assessing in the child's native language or in English, be aware that (1) many of the tests are not comparable, (b) the tasks may not be fully understood from the child's prior educational experiences, (c) the English language proficiency of each EL is different and may provide a more or less predictive level of learning, and (d) in many cases the assessment does not explicitly test what has been taught in the students' instructional history. (Rinaldi & Samson, 2008: 8)

Second, the number and diversity of L1 assessments for all the subject areas in all first languages just do not exist. Imagine the needs of a large school district with EL learners in grades K-12 who speak over 165 different first languages. All academic tests would need to be developed using sound psychometric evaluation measures and procedures for each of the languages for each of the subjects. The school districts in many areas cannot even find translators for basic school communications let alone those knowledgeable to write test items.

The next challenge for the assessment in RtI is the nature of ongoing assessments. Assessments to measure progress and diagnose needs would need to be developed for classroom use. They also need to be able to be administered by the on-site staff.

Then there is the issue of tests that appropriately embody the processes of SLA. 'A reason for the overrepresentation of bilingual students in special education is that the traditional assessment process cannot adequately distinguish between language acquisition and learning disabilities' (Figueroa *et al.*, 2013: 3).

Lastly, acquiring another language is not simply a journey from point A to point B. The process is a dynamic interplay between languages (Grosjean, 1985) with overgeneralisations, positive and negative transfer, learning, misunderstanding, pruning of interlanguage systems (Selinker, 1972) and variation. Bilingual assessments that allow educators to accurately gauge learners' abilities in both languages and their emerging interlanguage are needed. *Interlanguage* is the interim stage(s) between the first and the developing second language proficiency, which has features of both languages and a great deal of variation in form and performance.

The field of education struggles with assessment issues and more work needs to be done on this topic. One good resource is Scarcella's (1990) chapter on Testing in Culturally Responsive Ways.

## Guidelines for Implementation

When considering implementing RtI for ELs, schools need to identify the number of ELs and their proficiency scores. The learners' proficiency scores on standardised proficiency tests would help school personnel determine the number of ELs who would need to be served at various tiers. In a hypothetical scenario in a high-incidence district, learners would be assessed in their first languages for content knowledge as well as on their social and academic second language proficiency. Newcomers would need to be screened upon arrival. ELs with greater needs, such as novice, beginner/WIDA Levels 1 and 2 of proficiency, could be directed to a Tier 3 EL programme. Intermediate-low to advanced-low proficiency, WIDA Levels 3–5 could be served at Tier 1 with support at Tier 2 provided on an individual basis when needs arise. ELs with special cognitive, learning or behavioural needs could then be evaluated further to create an IEP and identify their placement for special education at the appropriate tier as well. Tier 3 could then be differentiated by need with ELA or special education classes. Figure 6.3 is an illustration of how this might look. Gifted ELs should receive gifted services.

In the literature, attention is given to the issue of testing learners cognitively using IQ measures. Schools would need to be discerning in their choice of assessment measures.

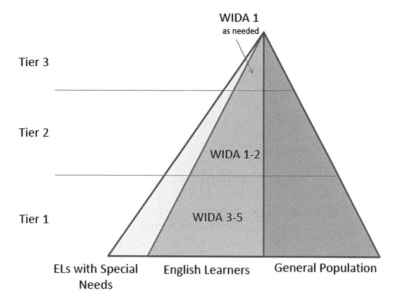

**Figure 6.3** RtI and ESL in high-incidence districts

# Effectiveness of the Model

Due to the wide adoption of RtI throughout the United States, several studies have investigated the effectiveness of RtI with ELLs. One of these studies was by Orosco and Klinger (2010) who used qualitative research techniques to describe teachers' attitudes and implementation of the RtI model with ELLs. Their findings showed that when RtI was employed with ELs, it created a 'negative cycle' resulting in a deficit approach to instruction which perpetuated negative attitudes about the ELs. Furthermore, they state, 'it is too early to know whether RTI will have a systematic effect on the educational opportunities provided to ELLs. Not only must schools adequately interpret the RTI concept, but they then need to decide how to implement this recommended model according to the nature of their student body and the community context' (Orosco & Klinger, 2010: 284).

Another study was conducted by McIntosh *et al.* (2007) who led a descriptive study that evaluated the oral reading fluency of 111 first graders over the course of two academic years using a mixture of the RtI model with sheltered content instruction. Measuring reading fluency gains from first to third grade on the dynamic indicators of basic early literacy skills (DIBELS) indicator, their findings showed that the rate of EL students referred to special education programmes depended on the amount of time the classroom teacher spent with the learners. They suggested that a combination of sheltered content and small-group instruction holds the promise of reducing the numbers of ELs referred for special education services.

Linan-Thompson *et al.* (2006) conducted an experimental study of first- and second-grade ELs' reading to see if RtI would help identify and serve ELs with reading disabilities. First-grade ELs were placed into groups, one group receiving RtI reading interventions in Spanish or English and a control group. Results indicated that RtI was a statistically significant method of effectively identifying and serving ELs with possible reading disabilities. These few studies offer educators some cautious optimism about the use of RtI for ELs, but clearly more research needs to be conducted.

## Strengths of the RtI Model

One strength of RtI is the requirement that all general educators who are subject area specialists endeavour to modify instruction for ELs at Tier 1. ELs, who have greater needs than the general education classroom can provide, can then receive specific skill or linguistic assistance with trained specialists in small groups at Tier 2 or 3, as appropriate.

The instruction at all tiers is focused on teaching learning strategies and skill development through integrated language instruction. Explicit vocabulary instruction is a definite strength. Some analysis of the oral and written features of texts occurs at all tiers as well. During instruction, learners' background knowledge is identified and employed as a basis for instruction, so that connections are made between the learners' experiences and understandings and the academic information in thematic units. Educators are encouraged to utilise a wide variety of strategies and scaffolds and to make informed choices regarding which and when to use them. When direct teaching is employed, it is used briefly to convey manageable chunks of new information.

Another clear strength is the collaboration among all stakeholders and home–school connections. By working collaboratively, teachers and learners have the support they need to meet grade-level expectations. The home–school connections allow learners' home culture to be better included into the school context and assist parents who may be new to the particular academic and cultural context.

Another strong attribute is the screening and ongoing assessment of academics provided in the learners' L1. When ELs are assessed in their L1, educators can get a better sense of their strengths and needs in order to focus their instructional interventions in a targeted manner. SLA needs to be assessed as well, to determine the learners' progress and needs.

The ongoing assessments and ease of movement between tiers in the RtI process is a particularly solid practice for learners so they will not be placed long term into a programme that does not meet their individual needs. Another positive attribute is that the assessments allow learners a range of ways to demonstrate their knowledge.

## Strengths that May Also be Weaknesses

The over-referral of ELs to special education is a common problem (Ford, 2012; Linan-Thompson, 2010). Many EL specialists believe this is a result of general educators' misunderstandings of language learning, their beliefs about ELs and who should teach them and/or their lack of knowledge and abilities to make the necessary curricular, instructional, linguistic and assessment modifications that ELs' need for SLA.

The RtI model itself does not necessarily cause ELs to be placed into special education programmes, which is good. However, an over-representation of ELs in Tiers 2 and 3 continues. Furthermore, if Tier 3 is only special education, how would ELs with greater needs than Tier 2 have their needs met?

The RtI structure is designed so that learners experiencing difficulties are pulled-out for intervention to have their particular needs met through intensive, individual or small-group instruction. However, this situation allows the Tier 1 educators the opportunity to avoid differentiation of instruction in the general education classroom. Another outcome of pull-out is the stigmatisation issue. Learners often feel embarrassed or stigmatised for being removed from the classroom for specialised services. This result is inherent to the RtI design.

## Weaknesses of the RtI Model for ELs

A weakness of the model is that it treats ELs and the SLA theories and pedagogy as no different from other areas of special need. The way that RtI is implemented tends to treat all learners in a 'one-size-fits-all' approach that overlooks the diverse cultures, languages, learning experiences and linguistic and academic needs of the English learning populations (Klingner & Edwards, 2006). Therefore, professional development, teacher educators and general educators are not provided with a clear road map of how to meet the specific needs of ELs in mainstream classrooms. Certainly, RtI was not intended to satisfy all these needs; it was intended as a tool for school districts to use to identify native English-speaking learners' individual needs and meet their needs at the appropriate ability level. Some schools and educators would understand that SLA, cognitive and/or behavioural issues are not necessary synonymous; sadly this is often not the case.

The greatest weakness of the RtI model for ELs is that Tier 1 educators are expected to make modifications for ELs without the basic knowledge of an ESL educator. The RtI model does not embrace knowledge of SLA processes, linguistic structures of English or second language reading processes. Since RtI services may or may not include an ESL specialist on the team, and the model itself does not require these areas of knowledge for educators at the various tiers, ELs' needs tend to be treated as L1 literacy/reading issues. Many of the interventions posited for ELs focus on reading, neglecting oral language, grammar and vocabulary and sociocultural competency. ELs need reading instruction of course, but these interventions are implemented in the same manner as L1 reading interventions, which is not appropriate. They also overlook the interaction between first and second languages when it comes to transfer in reading and the development of second language grammar and vocabulary. Frequently, too, interventions in the ELs' L1 are not part of the RtI intervention sets.

The second area of weakness as it relates to Tier 1 educators' instruction is that they are not prepared to create low-anxiety environments necessary for ELs, content and language objectives for ELs or cognitively challenging and linguistically accessible material or activities. Modifying materials towards linguistic accessibility is not a typical Tier 1 educator skill set. They are also frequently unfamiliar with ELs proficiency levels, laws pertinent to ELs and ELs' cultures, first language(s) and backgrounds.

Finally, the RtI model does little to address the intervention value for linguistic and cultural diversity in the schools, eliminate stereotypes or encourage advocacy for ELs (Table 6.5).

## Optimal Context for Implementation and Suggestions

The optimal context for RtI implementation for ELs is when there are a significant number of ELs who are not achieving in the general education class or who may be struggling. It is crucial though that educators consider how to implement RtI for ELs so that they are not treated as being delayed or having a deficit or deficiency of any kind. Schools should develop an EL path in RtI that provides support for SLA and helps with the ELs' academic needs with the assistance of ESL educators, as opposed to special educators (unless they are needed too).

Another key variable is locating and developing appropriate L1, second language and/or bilingual screening and achievement assessments. Assessments would need to be evaluated for cultural bias too.

If high numbers of ELs are being referred to Tier 2 services, school leaders should evaluate what modifications are occurring to serve them at Tier 1. The types of modifications and strategies needed to facilitate SLA differ in form and function than those for monolingual speakers. All Tier 1 educators should be trained not only in RtI interventions, but also in a model of content-based instruction for ELs in order to serve their needs appropriately and reduce the numbers of referrals (see Chapter 10 about pre-service and in-service teacher preparation).

## Conclusion

The design and speed of the RtI model are valuable characteristics of the model in that it has potential to improve services to ELs. The tiered approach to instructional intervention including the general education classroom as the primary tier of service requires all teachers to modify instruction to the diverse learners in their classrooms through differentiation and supports provided. The intensity and frequency of instructional interventions then increase markedly for each tier after the first. The RtI model ensures quick response to learners' needs and ongoing assessment so that learners are not tracked into dead-end programmes.

The RtI model, when applied to ELs, requires adaptations based on issues that differ considerably from those of learners with special needs. There are significant challenges

**Table 6.5** Evaluative framework for teacher preparation models, approaches and initiatives in EL inclusion

| I. Knowledge | RtI |
|---|---|
| When preparing teachers to include ELs into their content courses and to work with linguistically and culturally diverse groups of ELLs, they should have *knowledge* of the following areas: | |
| • The structures and features of the English language.<br>  • The distinctions between oral and written language.<br>  • The basic units of language, such as parts of speech, types of sentences and the sound system of English.<br>  • The construction of differing discourse units from the sentence level to a variety of social and academic genres and formats.<br>  • The irregularities of English.<br>  • The pragmatic/sociocultural dimensions of language (e.g. voice, audience) and how language varies accordingly.<br>  • An appropriate target for language acquisition/learning is real language use; 'standard' English is a myth. | A weakness |
| • The key principles of second language acquisition (SLA)/learning (Ellis, 2008).<br>  • Instruction needs to include:<br>    • A balance predominantly on meaning but also on forms.<br>    • An understanding of individual differences in learners.<br>    • Environmental modifications to reduce anxiety and affective issues.<br>    • Extensive comprehensible input.<br>    • Interaction with peers and instructors on the academic topics.<br>    • Opportunities for learners develop both 'a rich repertoire of formulaic expressions and a rule-based competence'.<br>    • Opportunities for spontaneous as well as controlled production.<br>    • Output opportunities.<br>    • Social and academic language.<br>    • Transfer of knowledge and skills from the first to the second language. | A weakness |
| • An understanding of ELLs' proficiency levels and their abilities and challenges at those levels. | A weakness |
| • The laws pertinent to ELs' instruction in the particular context. | A weakness |
| • The resources available to learn about ELs' educational backgrounds, first languages and cultures. | A weakness |

*(Continued)*

**Table 6.5** (Continued)

| | |
|---|---|
| • A sociolinguistic consciousness (Lucas and Villegas, 2011) | There is some awareness of these issues. |
|    • Understanding of the relationships between language, culture and identity. | |
|    • Awareness of the sociopolitical context of language use and language education, particularly in the specific context. | |
| • The subject matter; knowledge of one core content area or specialty area. | A strength |
| *II. Performance* | *RtI* |
| When preparing teachers to include ELs into their content courses and to work with linguistically and culturally diverse groups of ELLs, they should have *abilities and skills* in the following areas: | |
| • Curricular and Instructional Planning | |
|    • Planning with assessments as clear targets (e.g. backward design [Wiggins and McTighe, 2005]). | A weakness |
|    • Creating content, language and learning strategy objectives. | A weakness |
|    • Pre-teaching and/or integrating necessary skills, such as process writing, note-taking, etc. into the curriculum. | A strength |
|    • Integrating speaking, listening, reading, writing, grammar, vocabulary and pronunciation instruction and practice into lessons. | A strength |
|    • Developing units with clear connections through a thematic focus. | A strength |
|    • Modifying, developing and locating materials for linguistic accessibility of lessons. | A weakness |
|    • Analysing the linguistic features of oral and written discourse so as to be able to bridge the gap between ELs and a wide variety of genres, subject areas, academic discourse communities and texts. | A strength |
|    • Addressing multiple ESL proficiency levels in the same class by planning for differentiated instruction. | A weakness. Differentiation occurs in pull-out settings. |
|    • Making informed choices (Brown, 2007b) based on solid second language acquisition (SLA) principles and best practices in content and language instruction for the particular context with its unique variables (Kumaravadivelu, 2001). | Teachers are encouraged to make informed choices, but not based on SLA principles. |
| • Instructional Delivery | |
|    • Creating comfortable learning environments and classroom communities with low anxiety. | A weakness |
|    • Identifying learners' background knowledge and building upon it. | A strength |
|    • Making informed choices about instruction and employing a wide variety and frequency of approaches, techniques and resources depending on learners' needs. | A strength |

| | |
|---|---|
| • Explicitly teaching new vocabulary and language needed for oral (speaking and listening) and written (reading and writing) engagement with the academic content using supports and tools for meaning making. | A strength |
| • Creating meaningful, academically focused, engaging, interactive and experiential lessons and tasks that include ELs in activities (Migliacci & Verplaetse, 2008). | Not mentioned |
| • Directly teaching new academic information in small portions or 'chunks' with practice and interaction opportunities. | A strength |
| • Modifying the delivery of speech to heighten learners' comprehension (i.e. making linguistic modifications) or modifying the complexity or quantity of written material to make it more accessible. | A strength |
| • Scaffolding instruction using a variety of supports, such as graphic organisers, visuals, modelling, sentence frames, etc. | A strength |
| • Providing cognitively challenging materials to ELs that are linguistically accessible. | A weakness |
| • Assessment | |
| • Offering learners a variety of ways to demonstrate their knowledge of the content or language. For example, using performance and alternative assessment (see task and product examples above). | A strength |
| • Providing suitable and judiciously chosen accommodations for ELs during academic assessments. Accommodations are state-mandated supports for learners during standardised assessments, such as providing increased time for the test, breaks, dictionaries and/or translators for directions. | A weakness |
| • Measuring learners content knowledge and language ability separately. | A weakness |
| • Providing ongoing feedback on content knowledge and language ability constructively and regularly. | A strength |
| • Assessing learners' progress in language learning according to proficiency indicators. | A weakness. Not mentioned. |
| • Modifying text and teacher-made assessments to support English learners. For example, using visuals and models in directions. | A weakness. Not included. |
| *III. Orientations* | *RtI* |

When preparing teachers to include ELs into their content courses and to work with linguistically and culturally diverse groups of ELLs, they should have *awareness of, value for and appreciation of* the following areas:

(Continued)

**Table 6.5** (Continued)

| | |
|---|---|
| • Value for linguistic and cultural diversity. | A weakness |
| • Inclination to advocate for the linguistic and programmatic needs of ELLs. | A weakness |
| • Willingness to collaborate with language specialists, content teachers, administrators, parents, etc. to provide high-quality instruction for ELs and to create EL-friendly schools and communities. | A strength |
| • Hold high expectations for ELs and all learners. | A strength |
| • Inclination to provide assessments that level the playing field for ELs so that they may demonstrate their knowledge in a variety of ways. | A weakness |
| • Value for reflective instructional processes. | Not mentioned |
| • Willingness to develop positive home/school connections with ELs' parents. | A strength |
| • Willingness to treat cultures respectfully and to eliminate stereotyping of peoples and cultures. | A weakness |

in implementing RtI wholesale with ELs, including the availability of ESL specialists, learners' background knowledge and past learning, and over-referral of ELs to special needs programmes. With thoughtful, culturally congruent, second language research-based adaptations for ELs, the RtI model has the potential to help schools organise their instruction for ELs.

## Note

(1)  An IEP in the K-12 should not to be confused with ESL's IEP.

# Activities and Discussions

(1)  Make a list of learners' needs for three populations: monolingual students, monolingual learners with special education needs (identify which needs) and ELs. What types of needs do they have? How are they different?

| Monolingual students | Monolingual students with special education needs | English learners |
|---|---|---|
| | | |

(2)  Many school districts try to reduce their budgets by reducing the number of specialists they have on staff. Your school does not have an ESL specialist to work with the new ELs. The administration thinks they could be served by the special education specialist. Hold a debate on the topic of whether ELs should be served exclusively by special educators.
(3)  One of the cloudy areas in the RtI model is that many of the modifications and strategies employed at one level are also employed at another. Using the lists provided in the chapter for each tier, evaluate the modifications and strategies with a peer. In your opinion, are there any that really should be implemented at a different tier? Are there any that should be exclusive to one tier? Does the flexibility of modifications and strategies help or hinder the teachers? Use the following graphic organiser to place the modifications and strategies where you think they should belong.

(4)  Based on the research provided in the chapter on the effectiveness of the RtI model for ELs, would you recommend the model to your school district for serving the ELs there?
(5)  Find a teacher-made or textbook test and evaluate it for cultural background or bias issues.

## Chapter Summary

- The RtI model has roots in special education and was designed as a rapid response programme for meeting students' academic and learning needs at tiers that represent levels of intensity.
- Tier 1 is the general education classroom with modifications for all learners. Tier 2 is for students with needs beyond what can be taught in the general education classroom. Tier 3 is for extreme needs. All tiers are fluid so learners move in and out of tiers as they achieve their goals.
- Each tier differs in the size of the instructional group, mastery of content, frequency of progress monitoring, frequency of intervention delivery, instructors' specialisation and focus on content or skills.

- The proportion of ELs who have special needs is the same rate as in the native English-speaking population; although ELs tend to be referred for special education services more than native speakers. The proportion of ELs who are gifted is the same as native English speakers.
- It is frequently difficult to distinguish between special education needs and second language acquisition challenges. There are cultural considerations that also cloud the issue.
- Affective issues have an influence on ELs' participation and success in second language learning/acquisition.
- Assessments of ELs in RtI are a complex enterprise. Educators should endeavour to assess ELs' content knowledge and any potential cognitive or learning issues in their native language. Only their English language skills should be assessed in English.
- Districts implementing RtI should also consider the modifications that general educators are making in their courses, the number of ELs referred in RtI, the specialists' availability and credentials to work with ELs at Tiers 2 and 3 and the inclusion of sheltered content instruction at Tiers 2 and 3.

# 7 Models: Specially Designed Academic Instruction in English Model

| Chapter Aims and Topics |
|---|
| • Present the history and development of the Specially Designed Academic Instruction in English (SDAIE) model. |
| • Express key features of the SDAIE model: content, connections, comprehensibility, interaction. |
| • Discuss the role of first language (L1) literacy and language support. |
| • Consider how to differentiate instruction by proficiency level. |
| • Describe the SDAIE lesson plan format, instructional modifications and materials use. |
| • Analyse how assessments are conducted in the SDAIE model. |
| • Tips for implementing the SDAIE model. |
| • Effectiveness of the SDAIE model for English learners (ELs). |

## Overview

The SDAIE model has a fluid structure that has been honed over time. Unlike other models of content-based instruction with related textbooks, associated scholars and marketing, this model has somewhat lurked in the shadows in states except California. There are some English as a second language (ESL) specialists who are nonetheless strong advocates of SDAIE including Aida Walqui, Carmen Sanchez Sadek and Lynne Díaz-Rico. In the literature, there are many inconsistent perspectives and opinions on what constitutes the SDAIE model. In this chapter, I will attempt to synthesise the disparate information and perspectives presented.

The SDAIE model started to be developed by the Los Angeles Unified School District (LAUSD) in 1993 in order to assist intermediate-proficient language learners to learn English through content and facilitate their transition from bilingual classes to general education classes (Cline & Necochea, 2003) in high-incidence schools. The SDAIE model has been widely implemented throughout California and has influenced the development of other models of content-based instruction (California Department of Education, 1993; Cline & Necochea, 2003; Díaz-Rico, 2004, 2012, 2014; Freeman & Freeman, 1995; Genzuk, 2011; Jimenez, 2005; Tinney, 2007; Walqui, 1991).

**Figure 7.1** Progression of language learners through the programmes

The SDAIE model holds a central position in the instructional programming for ELLs in California. In the Californian context, the SDAIE model is composed of three programme components that build upon one another: English language development (ELD), SDAIE course work and general education. As newcomers, ELs begin their instruction in ELD courses, which are language-oriented courses like ESL. After the learners attain intermediate proficiency in oral and written social and academic language, they would be transferred into SDAIE courses for sheltered content instruction for all or part of their academic day. They would progress to general education classes full-time when they are linguistically ready (Figure 7.1).

## Description of the Model

According to Haynes (2007: 149), the SDAIE model is 'A type of **sheltered English** instruction that allows ELLs to progress in their academic courses as they learn English. The language of instruction is adapted to learners' English level. The two major theories that are used with SDAIE are **comprehensible input** and a supportive learning environment where ELs feel comfortable' (bold in original). Although SDAIE is a type of sheltered content class, some authors use 'sheltered content' as a synonym for SDAIE.

The LAUSD (2013) depicts the SDAIE model with four components (i.e. content, connections, comprehensibility and interaction), which should be modified according to learners' differing linguistic needs. In an SDAIE sheltered content course, rigorous, grade-level *content* is taught. Academic language needed by the learners is extracted from the content discourse. Then the academic language instruction accompanies the content. In contrast to an ESL or an ELD class, content is chosen as a basis for language learning. In other words, the language forms come first and the content topics are chosen as a means to practice the language structures. The *connections* are highlighted between the content and the learners' background and experiences. *Comprehensibility* of material is facilitated in well-planned lessons with instructional and linguistic strategies to make the information accessible. *Interaction* is built into each lesson so that learners can discuss academic content and acquire academic English. Cooperative groupings and active learning emphasise peer-to-peer communication, which allows for the interaction needed in SLA.

The LAUSD's (http://notebook.lausd.net/portal/page?_pageid=33,1170728,33_1181823&_dad=ptl&_schema=PTL_EP) description of the SDAIE model is congruent with Díaz-Rico's (2004, 2012, 2014) methods textbooks and Sadek's (n.d.)

(http://www.educationalquestions.com/qa24.htm, n.d.) representations. Based on a foundation of culturally relevant and responsive pedagogy, the four components (i.e. content, connections, comprehensibility and interaction) serve as the pillars in a building. The other supports in this building for SDAIE are instructional conversation, cooperative and communal learning, academic language development and advancement and graphic organisers used to open doors to content area subjects. Expounding on the content, connections, comprehensibility and interaction tenets of the SDAIE model, Table 7.1 delineates the model further. The remainder of the chapter will address each component.

# SDAIE Content

In the SDAIE model, academic content to be taught is the appropriate grade-level for the learner. The content is as intellectually demanding as it would be for the native speaker. It is not 'watered down' (i.e. simplified) or taught at a slower pace curricularly. These are fundamental differences between the SDAIE model and other models, as other models advance the strategies of simplified content and/or decelerating the speed of the curriculum for ELs. Therefore, the SDAIE classes would use the same academic content standards and similar textbooks as the general education classes and

**Table 7.1** Components of the SDAIE model

*Content*
- Focuses on content-depth and rigor without watering down the curriculum or slowing the pace
- Integrates four language skills across the curriculum
- Emphasises academic language and higher-order thinking skills

*Connections*
- Curricularly:
  - Assesses and taps prior knowledge and schema
  - Builds background knowledge
- Culturally:
  - Affirms learners' culture and multicultural perspectives
  - Utilises culturally congruent instruction
  - Emphasises positive teacher attitudes

*Comprehensibility*
- Clarifies through visuals, non-verbal supports, demonstrations and modelling
- Develops learners' primary language literacy
- Elucidates through primary language supports
- Differentiates instruction by proficiency level

*Interaction*
- Promotes active learning for increased interaction
- Advances collaboration through cooperative grouping

they would be compelled to cover the material at the same rate. ELs would be taught to engage intellectually with the material and employ their higher-order thinking skills.

Like other models, SDAIE teachers are expected to integrate the four language skills (i.e. speaking, listening, reading and writing) across the curriculum. In a civics course, the students would be discussing voting rights and redistricting, listening to radio broadcasts about the pros and cons of redistricting, reading about historical issues of violations of voters' rights and writing opinion papers about the issue of equal access to voting and the impact it has on government, laws and citizens. All the skills would be interwoven into every class in a seamless series of activities and tasks exploring the content from various angles. SDAIE teachers need to be skilled in the development of activities and tasks in the four skills in order to be able to integrate the skills across the curriculum. For examples of many interactive activities and tasks for use across the curriculum, see Sweet Waters School's list at http://mvh. sweetwaterschools.org/files/2012/06/EL-SDAIE-Strategies.pdf.

Academic language is emphasised in the SDAIE model through the integration of the four skills with the grade-level academic content. It may be taught directly through the use of sentence starters/sentence frames that are shared with ELs visually in text-books, on the board or on handouts. It would also be modelled orally by the teacher so that learners understand the syntax, pronunciation and vocabulary involved.

---

Sentence starters for the civics course topic of voting rights and redistricting could be:
- In my opinion, it is fair/unfair, because…
- Redistricting causes…
- Equal access to voting for all US citizens over the age of 18 is…
- Redistricting has had an impact on citizens and laws by…

---

## SDAIE Connections

Making explicit connections is the second tenet of the SDAIE model. SDAIE teachers assess the ELs prior knowledge and schema on new content topics and draw explicit links between what has been previously studied with current studies (Balderama & Díaz-Rico, 2006). For instance, to access learners' schema when discussing voting rights, the teacher might ask learners what they know about voting. Whether they like to vote? When they have voted in classes, clubs or groups in the past? Follow-up questions to assess prior knowledge could include whether someone in their family votes in elections or if they have visited a polling location. The teacher might ask the student to describe the polling station and how voting occurred if someone had participated.

An understanding of ELs' prior knowledge, which may vary considerably from other learners in the general education classroom, is an important trait of educators who are effective at including diverse learners. When working with Mexican children in Arizona, Moll *et al.* (1992: 134) noted the 'ample cultural and cognitive resources' the children had access to in their home communities. For instance, Moll *et al.* (1992)

found that these learners had experiences garnered from apprentice-like opportunities when they worked with adults who taught and modelled for them on areas such as: economics, household management, agriculture and mining, construction/repair, medicine and religion. These learners can draw on these bases of knowledge to inform classroom interaction. An informed teacher could draw upon the learners' knowledge of construction and sewing when teaching measurement skills in math and cooking in chemistry, which would aid learners in forming connections to new learning and assist them in retaining the new information longer. This approach also includes learners in class interactions and affirms their home cultures simultaneously. Referring back to our voting rights example, an SDAIE teacher might draw explicit connections between learners' home community by asking about learners' experience of their families discussing voting in elections or witnessing voting in their town councils.

The affirmation of learners' home cultures is a key component of the SDAIE model, which addresses social inequities inherent in American society. Cline and Necochea (2003) explain,

> Institutional racism often begins with the absence of respect for the learner and the contributions ELs can make to the learning environment. It is a dimension that encompasses the social mirror of how students, their families, cultures and communities are viewed and reflected within the social community. Respecting the learner contributes to elevating the dignity of poor and minority students, improving their social status in schools through contributions, and capitalizing on the strengths of their families. (Cline & Necochea, 2003: 22)

Identifying what and where connections can be drawn to learners' background experiences and local communities affirms learners and creates positive learning environments. It can be challenging for educators unfamiliar with the learners' communities and cultures. An important trait of the inclusive educator is exploring the cultures of the learners in their communities.

In instances where the background knowledge needs to be built, an SDAIE teacher would next provide new information, connected to prior knowledge along with new academic vocabulary clarified through visuals, real objects, demonstrations and other supports to construct learners' knowledge. Returning to our previous example, if the students had not seen a polling station or experienced voting in an election, the teacher might arrange for a visit to a polling station and/or a guest speaker who is a poll volunteer. According to Jimenez (1992: 1), an SDAIE teacher would preview vocabulary '…to identify and teach students essential words and terms before they encounter them in the text or a guest speaker visits. These are often more than the new "key terms" in a content lesson; they are often words that native English speakers at the grade level already know' (see Chapter 6 on vocabulary). She also emphasises the repetition and review of vocabulary.

Remembering that SDAIE is widely utilised in California, this example of voting rights might be a sensitive subject for some learners, because of citizen status. This is an ideal moment to discuss the tenets of the SDAIE model, culturally congruent instruction, multicultural perspectives and cultural sensitivity. An SDAIE instructor would strive to be sensitive to the learners' perspectives at all times. In the voting rights example, if some learners happen to be illegal immigrants, the instructor would desire to approach the subject from various perspectives. The teacher would not identify particular students' citizenship. The teacher could discuss generally with learners their thoughts about living in a country where some people may not be eligible to vote. This might be a particularly gratifying moment for the learners to be able to express their frustration with the system.

Simultaneously, the SDAIE teacher would strive to integrate culturally based patterns of communication and cooperation into the class. For example, Au (1980) discussed the need for Hawaiian children to be able to work cooperatively in groups because it was a common pattern in daily life in their home community; whereas in the classrooms at the time, independent work was the norm. In our voting rights scenario, the cultural and communication patterns of the learners would be welcome in the classroom. If the learners typically overlap in conversation, as many Latinate cultures do, the teacher would strive to facilitate a conversation without raised hands and allow as many speakers to take the floor to express their thoughts on the topic.

For the ELs and the SDAIE instructor, cultural affirmation by the teacher is essential. The SDAIE teacher includes the learners' cultures into the class content in constructive ways and avoids tokenising learners or stereotyping their culture(s). Back to the voting rights scenario, it would also be a good opportunity to discuss various topics related to the issue for the students, such as amnesty, the Dream Act, how voting rights can be violated and how Latinos in Whittier, CA, are fighting for their rights (http://www.scpr.org/blogs/politics/2013/07/11/14217/whittier-latinos-may-use-ca-voting-rights-act-to-s/). Personalising topics, such as how Latinos are fighting for their voting rights and how redistricting has affected their district, is a useful strategy to teach the content in a multicultural manner. If the class had learners of a variety of cultures, the teacher would desire to include readings and listening passages from differing cultural groups present in the class. When the students envision others like them participating in democracy, it empowers them and affirms their culture.

The teachers' attitude towards the learners' culture and home language is a central aspect of the SDAIE model that appears frequently in the literature. The creation of a warm classroom environment, one that is open to various cultures and perspectives, is the product of the teacher who welcomes multicultural learners and possesses a positive attitude towards them. SDAIE teachers are open-minded and interested in their learners. Their dispositions are oriented to fairness, equality and access for all learners. They desire to learn more about their learners' cultures outside of class time (Díaz-Rico, 2014). They avoid asking learners to represent the totality of their home culture. For example, an SDAIE instructor would avoid this question, 'What do Latinos think about voting rights?'. The reason for this is that just like anyone, ELs are unique individuals who may or may not hold the view of the cultural group, and may resent being asked to represent all perspectives held in their culture. A better question might be, 'Has anyone you know been affected by redistricting or experienced a violation of their right to vote?' or 'Among the people you know in the Latino community, have they expressed their thoughts on redistricting? What have you heard about it?'.

## SDAIE Comprehensibility

Similar to the Sheltered Instruction Observation Protocol (SIOP) and the Cognitive Academic Language Learning Approach (CALLA) models, the SDAIE model includes a component addressing comprehensibility. Comprehensibility in SDAIE is about making the oral and written academic content comprehensible and therefore accessible to the ELs.

The theoretical support for this aspect of the SDAIE model is based on linguistics and second language (L2) interaction research.

> Linguists suggest that we all acquire language the same way, by understanding messages. The idea that we acquire language by understanding messages, or comprehensible input, clarifies that the role of the second language classroom should be. We acquire language not when we memorize vocabulary lists or do grammar exercises, but when we understand what people say to us or what we read. (Genzuk, 2011: 7)

The emphasis is on meaningful messages and use of language, not for rote memorisation or isolated grammatical understandings, but for use in communication in learners' lives. Like the SIOP and CALLA models, SDAIE instructors attend to their own use of language to heighten the comprehensibility for learners. Strategies suggested by Genzuk (2011) include increasing wait time, expanding upon learners' contributions as opposed to correcting their linguistic error, modelling the correct form by recasting the sentence, simplifying the teachers' language and avoiding forcing learners to speak. Balderama and Díaz-Rico (2006: 124) add to this list use of the L1 for previewing content and clarification as well as precise articulation, intonation used to stress important concepts, simplified syntax, frequent longer pauses, use of discourse and organisational markers, and repetition. Importantly, SDAIE instructors understand the balance of speaking between teachers and learners that needs to occur in a language-learning environment. They encourage learners to construct knowledge and share their understandings orally and in writing; they do not desire silent students nor to dominate the speaking floor in the classroom (Díaz-Rico, 2004).

LAUSD (2013) offers an excellent list of reflection questions for SDAIE instructors to help them analyse their own language use and improve comprehensibility (paraphrased below). For example, LAUSD encourages teachers to self-reflect on their language use:

- Is my speech clearly enunciated? Can my students hear me distinctly?
- Am I using vocabulary that the students know/are familiar with? Are there any idioms, slang or colloquial expressions that may cause difficulty? Am I explaining any idioms or colloquial expressions I employ or that are employed regularly?

- Am I emphasising key vocabulary, teaching it explicitly, providing multiple opportunities for learners to practice it in context?
- Am I differing the delivery of new information (i.e. deductive and inductive approaches) as well as utilising demonstrations, models and other techniques to help students to understand the new content knowledge and the academic language?
- What visuals, support and other extralinguistic (i.e. outside of language) aids am I using to help my students to understand? Do the resources I opt for elucidate the concept unambiguously?
- Am I checking for comprehension frequently and using a variety of methods?
- Is my feedback timely, appropriate to the cultural patterns, focused on specific language or concepts/skills and graspable to the learner?
  (Reproduced with permission of the Los Angeles Unified Schools District, Language Acquisition Branch).

In order to achieve the goal of meaningful and practical communication, the SDAIE underscores the use of materials such as visuals, graphic organisers, manipulatives, realia (i.e. real objects), anticipation guides, advance organisers, technology and non-verbal techniques to help learners to make meanings. The use of material supports and non-verbal techniques is essential for meaning making, because they allow learners to make cognitive connections directly from the object or gesture to the meaning of the item. For example, if I were to write down the question, 'Do you want a яблоко?', it would be completely unclear to the reader. If I said the question aloud, it would sound approximately like *yableka*. However, if I were to show the image (Figure 7.2) and say the word with the sentence, I would not need to translate яблоко=apple.

The student does not need to translate the new word to the native language for comprehension. If the learners comprehend the meaning of a new word in the target language, they forge mental connections that allow them access to the new information later. If they learn to translate each new word or concept into their native language,

**Figure 7.2** яблоко example
Used with permission from Microsoft

their speed of mental processing will be slowed and they are likely to continue the need to translate the item through their native language.

Jimenez (1992) imparts several key comprehensibility tools:

- Illustrations and visuals including photographs, drawings, artwork, posters, graphs, maps, videos, computer programs, and reproductions of documents…
- Realia (real objects and materials) that reduce abstractions and make new concepts more explicit.
- Graphic organizers including matrices, Venn diagrams, tables, charts, story maps, outlines, study guides, and webs…
- Manipulative materials… (Jimenez, 1992: 1)

Johansen (1997) contributes to this list information about the effectiveness of graphic organisers as tools to aid ELs' comprehension of difficult concepts. Johansen offers four patterns for organising information:

- hierarchical order (i.e. order of importance);

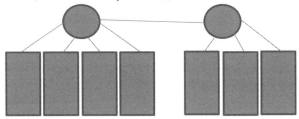

- conceptual or relational (i.e. connections and relationships are highlighted);

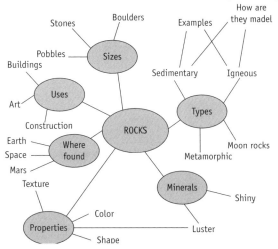

(Used with permission from the National Science Teachers Association)

- sequential (i.e. order of events, cause and effect, continuum);

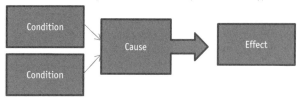

- cyclical (i.e. repeating or looping order).

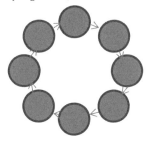

The idea is that we can create graphic organisers in these patterns to enhance learners' comprehension.

Anticipation guides are tools for gauging learners' thoughts, beliefs or knowledge of a topic prior to instruction. It will help prime the learners for what they will read or view. Typical anticipation guides are designed as true/false response types to statements. For example, the anticipation guide shown in Table 7.2 comes from a world geography lesson I conducted for sixth-grade ELs.

Students responded to these statements based on their knowledge and beliefs prior to reading. We discussed them and summarised the class's thoughts in writing on the board. Then we read to see where we were on track. After reading, we revisited these points and corrected our notions where necessary.

For key academic vocabulary, visuals need to be pre-planned as much as possible. If one were teaching geography, one academic term that is important in understanding climate is *elevation*. When I looked up this term in advance of teaching it, I found many

**Table 7.2** Anticipation guide world geography Asia and the Pacific

*Directions: Please make a guess and circle true or false for each of the follow statements*

| | | | |
|---|---|---|---|
| (1) | Asia makes up one-third of the world's land area. | True | False |
| (2) | Europe and Asia share the same land mass. | True | False |
| (3) | Asia is not the world's most densely populated (most people) continent. | True | False |
| (4) | The Yellow River is in Asia. | True | False |
| (5) | Asian countries produce wheat. | True | False |
| (6) | There are deserts in Asia. | True | False |
| (7) | There are volcanoes in Asia. | True | False |

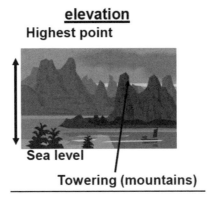

**Figure 7.3** Visual of elevation
Used with permission from Microsoft

images of mountains. Showing only a picture of a mountain will not necessarily help children to understand that elevation is distance that can be measured from sea level to the top of a mountain. Imagine showing a picture of a mountain and pointing from bottom to top to explain elevation. This is still not likely to be clear to all the learners. When faced with this issue, I made the visual shown in Figure 7.3.

Using this visual, I was able to highlight that elevation could be measured between sea level (e.g. 0.5 miles) and the top of a mountain (e.g. 5.3 miles). For this unit, I made connections to all the key academic vocabulary in the general education geography textbook and developed an illustrated glossary that I handed out to the learners, which included visuals like Figure 7.3.

## Total Physical Response Storytelling (TPRS) Illustrated

Enhancing comprehensibility through gestures and movement is another key technique for EL inclusive educators. Total physical response (TPR) and TPRS are two widely employed techniques to connect vocabulary to meaning. TPR (Asher, 1969), described in Chapter 6, helps learners to understand meanings because they do the actions with the teacher. Learners can learn a new verb and connect it to the action by physically doing the action or a noun by interacting with it, touching it, moving it or pointing to it. In practice, TPR resembles 'Simon Says' because the teacher gives commands, but it differs in that the teacher demonstrates the movement for the learner while saying the vocabulary word. Imagine teaching a classroom of students about chemistry equipment. One could hold up a beaker and say the word, then a test tube, Bunsen burner, etc. The teacher would then repeat the words and demonstrate the items a couple of times in a random order while asking the students to hold up the item and say the word chorally. Finally, the teacher would just say the word and see which students understood and can show their comprehension by holding up the proper item. The teacher could then provide the students with a take home list to study (see Figure 7.4).

*(Continued)*

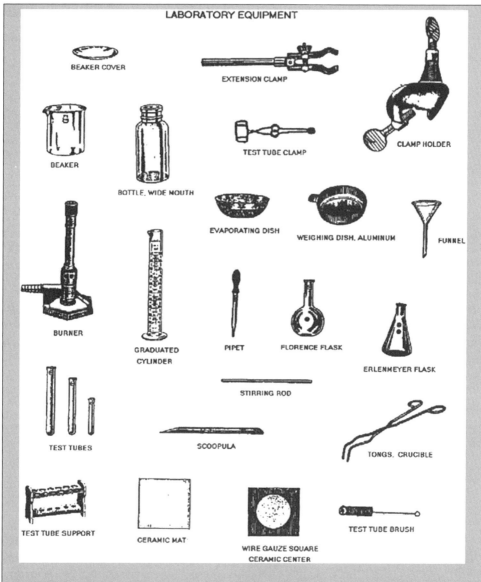

**Figure 7.4** Chemistry equipment visual vocabulary example License free to share and use

*(Continued)*

TPRS is similar in the patterned repetition and actions seen above, but instead of verbs/actions or nouns/concrete items as a basis for the activities, the teacher develops a story with gestures to represent characters, actions and objects. In TPRS, the students would receive a handout with each character and action illustrated, to aid memory. This would be a particularly useful technique for historical or language arts stories.

To illustrate TPRS in a content class, we will use the topic of the Battle of Actium between the Roman general, Marc Antony, and the Egyptian Pharaoh, Cleopatra, on one side against the Roman leader, Octavian, on the other. A teacher would develop gestures to illustrate the characters. First, Marc Antony, who was a burly solider, could be characterised by a gesture of displaying muscles and arching the chest. Next, Cleopatra, a strong, smart, beautiful queen, could be characterised by the action of raising the chin, hands on hips and tossing the hair. Finally, Octavian, a diminutive, cunning man, could be characterised by tapping an index finger on the side of one's temple. The troops on either side could be characterised by a marching action. The ships could be illustrated by a gesture with arms outstretched at the waist and a balancing motion. The ship's rowers could use a rowing motion. Fighting motions could be exemplified by faux sword fighting actions.

The Battle of Actium was a military routing. Both sides engaged in a water battle, Octavian and Marc Antony squaring their ships off against one another. The battle was raging when Cleopatra took her ships, supposedly to reinforce Marc Antony's, and fed the scene (after picking up Marc Antony). Octavian won a colossal victory.

To use TPRS to illustrate this concept, the teacher would teach the characters and the actions through the repetition of the gestures. Then the teacher would tell the story while repeating the actions. The teacher would use the classroom space and position himself/herself to show the sides of the battle. Once the teacher had told the story, he/she would walk the students through the story again with the students mimicking the gestures. Finally, when the students demonstrated a solid degree of understanding, students would re-enact the battle in small groups or pairs, saying the words and making the corresponding gestures.

In terms of non-verbal techniques, an inclusive educator would pre-think which words and concepts link naturally to gestures and how to utilise one's facial expressions and body movements to aid learners' comprehension. I have found that when I conduct read alouds that I can help learners to understand new terms by enacting them as I read. If the character leaps, stares wildly, shivers or cowers, enacting these verbs and asking the learners to act them out with me, helps them to visualise the activities and emotions of the characters while understanding the meanings.

Developing a wide range of meaning making strategies is essential for effective inclusive educators, because teachers need to engage learners in a 'meaning making dance' using an extensive variety and frequency of strategies (Bires *et al.*, 2013).

# Comprehensibility through Demonstration and Modelling

Very similar to making meanings through visual and non-verbal techniques, demonstrations and modelling are vital techniques to aid learners' comprehension in the SDAIE model. Demonstrations are a series of narrated procedures that the learners follow to understand how to do an academic task, for instance, a math problem, a science lab experiment or a read aloud protocol using self-questioning. The teacher would develop the procedures and orally explain to the students what he/she is thinking and doing. A reading of the procedure could follow. The oral explanation is vital for ELs, because they need oral explanation and repetitions of the terms to acquire the academic language in context. If a teacher were to show the students a math problem without the oral explanation, the students would not be able to connect the words to the objects as easily nor would the number of naturalistic repetitions occur.

Modelling is a bit different than demonstrating. Modelling can be described as doing a demonstration with engaging questions to ask students to engage, think and reflect on the process (http://educatech.wordpress.com/2011/02/10/modeling-is-so-much-more-than-demonstrating/). To elaborate, a teacher might conduct a read aloud protocol focusing on self-questioning. The teacher would provide an advance organiser to help the students understand what they will be seeing. In the process of teaching, the teacher would pause and ask himself/herself questions about what he/she is reading to ensure that he/she is understanding the reading correctly. This part is the demonstration. Afterwards, the teacher would ask the learners, 'What was I doing when I became confused? What did you notice about my questions and pauses? Did you notice that I did not understand everything the first time? Is that normal?'. This part is the modelling.

Inclusive educators would want to demonstrate and model all the academic tasks and interpersonal interactions they are teaching their learners. For many students, the only role model for academic language use, knowledge and performance of academic information and procedures is the teacher. It is an atypical home environment that engages learners with academic language in auditory or written form.

One of the best demonstrations I have observed was by a middle school science teacher who created a miniature model of the water cycle. She designed what can only be described as a miniature evaporation tank. The model looked like the coast of an ocean or a lake with land, tiny plants, sand and pebbles on one side and water getting deeper on the other side which represented the ocean. She heated the water (the water side was on a hot plate) until it vaporised to cause evaporation. The vapours were caught by a clear, plastic dome that covered half of the model. In the model, it rained on the land and the ocean once the water particles had become large enough. The water rolled down the land and back to the ocean. She asked the ELs to observe the tank before the water was heated. She then led them through the process of evaporation and condensation while the water was evaporating as steam, accumulating and raining, ultimately returning to the ocean. She asked them engagement questions throughout the process and helped them identify the key vocabulary words for each part of the process. The teacher used these tools to visually demonstrate the process and she orally explained the process while it was happening.

At the students' desks, she had labelled plastic baggies with examples of each type of water formation one could encounter in differing weather conditions (e.g. sleet, rain, snow and hail) made out of styrofoam or liquids. She also had key vocabulary written on word walls and illustrated handouts with key vocabulary defined. Armed with these tools combined with the demonstration and modelling provided as well as the literacy support in textbook readings, ELs would have access to the academic content.

## First Language Literacy and Language Support

A unique feature of the SDAIE model's comprehensibility goal is the development of L1 literacy as well as the use of the primary language for clarification and comprehension. In the previous models, the primary language (i.e. L1) of the learners is a *technique* to be employed only as a 'last resort' in the construction of meaning in classroom discussions. In SDAIE schools, teachers develop the learners' L1 literacy prior to entry into SDAIE content-focused classes (Freeman *et al.*, 2002); later, L1 literacy support is continued in the SDAIE classroom. SDAIE 'teachers recognize that a person's self-concept is involved in his or her own language and that at times students need to use that language' (Díaz-Rico, 2014: 118).

Based on a wide body of literacy research, two principles of L1 literacy have emerged that influence learners' L2 development. First, learners use their oral knowledge of their L1 and their schema (i.e. mental meanings and understandings of words, concepts, etc.) to learn to read in their L1. In this text, we will call this ability *orality* and contrast it to literacy. In a reading passage, native English speakers might be presented with a series of Dolch words, such as girl, boy, dog, cat, tree, park and to walk. The learners would perhaps listen to the teacher read the passage aloud and visually follow along while tracing the words with a finger. At that moment, learners are connecting the oral sounds to the written representations of the words. When the native-English-speaking learners hear 'dog', they know what a dog is from years of prior linguistic interaction. Caretakers have labelled a dog with the word by pointing to the dog and possibly saying, 'That's a dog. Isn't it a cutie?'. They have seen and interacted with dogs; they have heard the word dog connected to the concept of dog so many times that the word is already meaningful to the learner. In the literacy moment, they only need to connect the oral form of dog with the written representation of dog. They do not need to learn the meaning of the word since they already know it.

Second, when learners are literate, able to read and write in their L1, they can transfer their reading and writing skills to L2 reading and writing tasks. For instance, when a student can decode a word such as *arqueologia* in L1 Spanish and connect it to the concept of research in human history, excavation and artefacts, the student can then read the word *archaeology* in L2 English by comparing the word forms and phonemes. The student does not need to *relearn* the meaning of the word, only draw the mental connection. The transfer of literacy skills helps learners by providing a scaffold between the first and second languages.

If a learner is not literate in his/her L1, because the learner did not have reading instruction in his/her L1, it is very challenging for the learner to jump from L1 orality to L2 literacy. For example, if a learner only has orality in his/her native language and sees printed words for the first time in English, he/she would not be able to connect the new printed words to an already developed schema. Furthermore, if the student has not learned the processes involved in reading (e.g. decoding, summarising, questioning, predicting and making connections), the learner would not have skills that he/she could apply to reading. These are two important reasons why SDAIE emphasises the development of primary language literacy. Not only does primary language literacy facilitate the L2 learning process, but it also speeds it up. August and Shanahan (2006) found in their extensive meta-analytical review of L1 and L2 reading studies that ELs who were able to use their native language outperformed those who learned to read in their L2 only.

Primary literacy support can be facilitated by teaching reading initially in learners' native languages, providing pull-out, small-group reading instruction in the native language and encouraging parents to have native language reading materials and read to their children in their native language. In the SDAIE classroom, teachers are encouraged to have content materials present in the learners' native languages, so that learners can read about the content independently and because the presence of native language texts affirms the learners' native language and culture.

Primary language can be supported in the SDAIE classroom by consciously assembling human and physical resources in the primary language or in bilingual form for access and use by the learners. Genzuk (2011) provided a list, which was modified in the table below (Table 7.3).

**Table 7.3** Language resources

| Materials and physical resources | Human resources |
| --- | --- |
| First language/primary language/bilingual textbooks, word banks and glossaries. Reference books. | Bilingual paraprofessionals or aids |
| Audio and video recordings. Audiobooks. DVDs with primary language subtitles. Podcasts. Interactive multimedia. | Parents and volunteers who speak both languages |
| Computer programs and games in the primary and target languages | Peer tutors, buddies, mentors |
| Bilingual dictionaries, illustrated dictionaries, picture dictionaries | University student, teachers/tutors |
| Posters, visuals, maps, globes, charts | Online classes |
| Supplemental readers (below and at grade level) | Community-based resources, community agencies, bilingual schools, etc. |
| Wikis, blogs, listservs and global learning networks (i.e. pen pals, distance education classes) | Grade-level team(s) of teachers |

# Differentiated Instruction

Another key instructional strategy in SDAIE for making information comprehensible is *differentiated instruction*. Differentiated instruction is based upon knowledge of individual learners' strengths and needs. Instructors identify specific learning objectives for an individual student through ongoing formative assessment, so the learner can work on his/her particular needs. The instructor designs learning tasks pertinent to the desired learning outcome in conjunction with clear, focused delivery of new information.

Many pre-service teachers with whom I have worked struggle to visualise differentiation of instruction. When one tries to teach every student individually among 25 learners, it would indeed appear overwhelming. However, when one groups learners with like needs in flexible groupings that change regularly, differentiation is not only easier to visualise, but it is also a great deal more manageable to implement.

In SDAIE, ELs with language proficiency levels of intermediate and higher are integrated into the general education classroom. Teachers would analyse which language and content skills would be most beneficial to the learners. The language and content would be integrated into varied instructional activities to allow groups of students to work productively on a combination of content objectives and the four language skills. Using flexible, small groupings wisely, teachers can differentiate instruction by

- Content: Differentiation by content means that some students would have more complex content or more content details to acquire. Providing only the critical content to the ELs would not be in the spirit of SDAIE; it would be more like SIOP or CALLA.
- Process: Differentiation by process is to assign differing groups tasks that require a range of simple to complex cognitive or physical processing. Think about Bloom's Taxonomy for the cognitive processing. For the physical processing, imagine asking some learners to do more manipulations of the material (e.g. more collaborative writing or peer editing).
- Products: Differentiation by product is to ask some groups to create various products that range in difficulty. For example, one group might have a poster and no presentation, another would have a brochure and presentation and another would have a PowerPoint or Prezi presentation with questions/answers.
- Activity/task expectation: Differentiation by activity or task is to assign assorted tasks for each group to investigate different angles of a problem or concept. For instance, groups might all have different chemicals on which to use their litmus tests. They might then need to write up and compare their results between groups.
- Language skill: Differentiation by language skill is to create stations on a topic for each language skill. For example, a teacher could have a reading station with readings and graphic organisers, a listening station with a podcast, a writing station to

develop opinion paragraphs on the topic and a speaking station to create an 'elevator speech' to tell their caregivers about the issue.
- Supports provided: Differentiation by supports provided means to offer more support for lower levels of proficiency and fewer for more advanced. This strategy does not mean to exclude necessary supports for learners; rather, it means that necessary supports are provided and some learners need more of them. For example, learners at lower-proficiency levels might need a chapter outline, preview, heading/picture walk and key vocabulary pre-teaching, whereas learners at advanced levels might only need the chapter outline and pre-teaching of vocabulary.

All of these approaches to differentiation of objectives and language can be conducted in similar proficiency groupings (with adequate personnel support) or across proficiency levels intermingled with native speakers. Walqui *et al.* (2010) also suggest grouping strategies of 'numbered heads together' and 'think-pair-share' as common SDAIE strategies. As alternative, interactive cooperative groupings (i.e. participant structures) used in SDAIE, Johansen (1997) adds:

- 'Inside/outside circles' (e.g. two circles of students are formed, one circle inside an outer circle. The inner circle of students would face outwards and the outer circle would face inwards. The students would talk with their peer opposite them until they heard a predetermined signal to move to the next student. The outer circle would then rotate one person to the right).
- 'Roundtables' (e.g. sitting in a round formation, students are encouraged to brainstorm, predict or reveal ideas by each writing one thought or idea on a paper, share it out loud and rotate the paper to the next student).

The key implementation strategies are to (1) name the groups so that learners cannot determine a ranking or hierarchy in the groups and (2) change groupings regularly in order to avoid tracking, marginalisation or stigmatisation. When I taught fifth-grade ELs, I used proficiency-level groups that I called by the five senses (i.e. taste, touch, sight, sound and hearing) and for across proficiency groupings I used the names of 'explorers' (i.e. Ballard, Sacagawea, Armstrong, Amundsen and Galileo). Our theme was 'Worlds of Exploration' and we were investigating all the ways that one can explore in life, so the group names connected to the theme.

In a general education class on nutrition that includes ELs at World-Class Instructional Design and Assessment (WIDA) Levels 1–5/the American Council on the Teaching of Foreign Languages (ACTFL) novice to low advanced, a teacher might develop objectives for the lesson that look like those in the following list.

- Undifferentiated Objectives
  - All students will be able to listen to a 10-minute video about the 'Healthy Eating Plate' and categorise which foods go into which category (i.e. meats, vegetables, fruits, carbohydrates, dairy and sweets).

- All students will be able to analyse the parts of a meal with combined ingredients.
- All students will be able to read a story to identify which foods the main character eats that are healthy and unhealthy.
- All students will be able to discuss the main idea of the reading.
- Differentiated Objectives
  - Beginner
    - Students will be able to list orally and in writing the types of food by category/food plate (WIDA 1s/ACTFL novice).
    - Students will be able to write and say a simple sentence about their food likes/dislikes (WIDA 2s/ACTFL beginner) using the sentence frame, 'I like _____. I dislike _____'.
  - Intermediate
    - Students will be able to outline in writing a recipe and/or orally describe making their favourite foods (WIDA 3s/ACTFL high beginner–mid intermediate).
    - Students will be able to describe orally and in writing various common food allergies (WIDA 4s/ACTFL intermediate–mid high).
  - Advanced
    - Students will be able to compare and compute the nutritional value of their favourite foods to describe orally and in writing a healthy/unhealthy meal with evidence (WIDA 5s/ACTFL advanced low).

Appendix C provides an excellent example of differentiated content and language objectives in a unit developed by a student, Maggie, in a content-based instruction course.

## Interaction in SDAIE

Inherent in the use of flexible groupings is another key component of the SDAIE model, which is cooperative learning and collaboration. SDAIE educators desire to make interactive class environments with learners investigating and studying in collaboration. Environments that promote active learning motivate and stimulate learners and aid their retention of new information.

For ELs, active learning and the interaction that is part and parcel of active learning in cooperative groups create linguistic interaction opportunities that are safe and content focused. In the SDAIE model, like the SIOP and CALLA models, interaction is key to L2 acquisition. Academically focused tasks that focus on meaningful communication to accomplish specified objectives will allow learners to practice the academic language they are being taught and shown. Balderama and Díaz-Rico (2006) remind us that interaction in the SDAIE classroom does not only mean student to student and small group interaction, but also includes social and academic language between teachers in team teaching and the teacher to the whole class or to an individual student as well as student to teacher, group to whole class, to content or specific discipline, to self (i.e. reflection and self-evaluation; Genzuk, 2011: 10) and to parents. Some of these interactions may also extend to a wider audience through writing, such as on blogs, to editors, to elected representatives, to school newspapers, etc.

The kinds of interactive activities and tasks employed in a SDAIE lesson are as broad as the teacher's creativity. 'The teacher will facilitate a deep understanding of the core curriculum by incorporating a multitude of strategies and techniques into the lesson design. These strategies and techniques will include, but not be limited to, oral presentations collaborative group projects, graphic illustrations, skits, storytelling, dramatizations, research reports, puppetry, inquiry and discovery, scaffolding, integrated thematic instruction and other instructional practices' (Cline & Necochea, 2003: 21).

## SDAIE Lesson Plan Format

The LAUSD website provides a lesson plan template for SDAIE teachers (http:// notebook.lausd.net/portal/page?_pageid=33,1170728,33_1181823&_dad=ptl&_ schema=PTL_EP), which helps teachers visualise how to develop lessons  activating prior knowledge, content and language objectives, delivery of comprehensible information, guided practice/interactive tasks and ongoing assessments. The LAUSD format has been modified in Figure 7.5.

## Assessment in SDAIE

In SDAIE, assessment is a process interwoven into daily classroom activity. Learners are assessed initially to determine their needs through needs assessments. Then, SDAIE teachers develop objectives for grade-level content with these needs in mind. The teacher would deliver the lesson while observing learners' comprehension and production and gather documents to analyse later. Following the approach of Logan (2007), Sadek (n.d.) explains how SDAIE teachers can confirm if ELs are acquiring the academic language and content.

> To determine if new knowledge has been acquired as the result of a lesson, it is only necessary to check on the acquisition of new academic language. EACH WORD IS A CONCEPT. A student who has acquired and begins to use appropriately new academic language at the end of each lesson is a student who has acquired new knowledge. (Sadek, n.d.; http://www.educationalquestions.com/qa24.htm)

The teacher would gather all evidence of students' learning on an ongoing basis and provide immediate intervention to struggling learners. Teachers would address specific needs in small groups. Students would also have more formal and standardised assessments as determined by the teacher and/or assessment policy. According to Gulack and Silverstein (1997), more formalised assessments are typically more authentic assessments. 'Authentic Assessment is the practice of evaluating a student, not by

## SDAIE Lesson Planner

| Teacher: | Grade(s): |
|---|---|

| Course/Content Area(s): |
|---|

| Learner population: |
|---|

| CONTENT | CONNECTIONS | COMPREHENSIBILITY | INTERACTION |
|---|---|---|---|

| Standard(s): | Enabling skills (needed to achieve the standards): |
|---|---|

| Big idea/Essential question (Why is this important?) |
|---|

| Lesson Goal(s): |
|---|

| CONTENT TOPIC/CONCEPT<br>Students will be able to...<br>1.<br><br>2. | LANGUAGE FOCUS<br>Students will be able to...<br>1.<br><br>2. | LEARNING STRATEGIES/SKILLS<br>Students will be able to...<br>1.<br><br>2. |
|---|---|---|
| Core content terms (10 words max): | Language needed for comprehension (SDAIE vocabulary) (10 words max): | Language forms/processes to be explicitly taught: |

| Materials supports (tools and resources needed to make content comprehensible): |
|---|

**Figure 7.5** Modified SDAIE lesson plan
*Source*: Los Angeles Unified School District, Language Acquisition Branch

basing the judgment on isolated skills, but rather by basing the judgment on a finished project or product which incorporates many skills to ensure its completion' (Gulack & Silverstein, n.d.: 6).

## SDAIE Effectiveness

My literature review found two studies by Callahan *et al.* (2010) and Smith (2009) involving the SDAIE model. Unfortunately, both studies conflated the SDAIE model with other models of sheltered instruction, so the findings were not very useful to differentiate SDAIE from other sheltered content/content-based instructional models or to evaluate the SDAIE model specifically. 'For college preparatory social science course taking, we are unable to disaggregate sheltered or SDAIE and bilingual content-area course placement because of sample size... yet we find a negative statistically significant effect of SDAIE OR bilingual content-area course placement' (Callahan *et al.*, 2010: 18).

Another study by Vuckovic *et al.* (January 2005) investigated the content and language learning progress of ELs in the LAUSD for one academic year using the SDAIE-based textbook series, *High Point*. They found that in classrooms where the teacher had been sufficiently prepared and the text fully implemented, ELs were more likely to perform higher on English language arts and math standardised tests.

In an article comparing the SIOP to the SDAIE model, Echevarria and Short (2010), recognising the value of SDAIE-sanctioned techniques and strategies, noted weaknesses in the research validity of the SDAIE model. First, they emphasise that the SDAIE model is theoretical only, which implies that the model itself lacks a thorough research base. Likewise, it 'has not been operationally defined and therefore cannot be scientifically validated' (Echevarria & Short, 2010: 264). Second, they highlight the lack of consensus on the components and organisation of the SDAIE model, indicating the propensity of SDAIE teachers' random choices of strategies they prefer as opposed to those proven by research to be effective.

In another article by Echevarria (2012), the need for ELs to be literate and possess an intermediate level of English proficiency prior to inclusion into the SDAIE classroom was raised. The SDAIE model has not been promoted for newcomers and lower levels of proficiency by the LAUSD, but has been by others.

Proponents of the SDAIE model, such as Cline and Necochea (2003) stress that SDAIE is an evolving, synthetic methodology that responds to the immediate, local needs of learners and thus serves ELs better than rigid, formalised and inflexible measures. They emphasise, 'The "best" system will be the one that enables "reasonable" flexibility for well-trained general educators to adapt instructional practices to meet the needs of the diverse students in their classes' (Cline & Necochea, 2003: 18).

## Strengths of the SDAIE Model

The strengths of the SDAIE model are extensive, predominantly in curricular and instructional planning, lesson delivery and instructors' orientations/dispositions. In curricular and instructional planning, the SDAIE model is notably strong in pre-teaching, four skills instruction and linguistically accessible materials. In terms of instructional delivery, the SDAIE model is outstandingly strong in creating a safe environment, linking to learners' background knowledge, allowing for variety and frequency in instructional choices, teaching vocabulary explicitly, providing an academic focus and cognitively challenging ELs. Moreover, it is noteworthy for its interactive and experiential tasks and activities, its modification of the teachers' speech and its use of diverse scaffolds and instructional supports.

The model has a strong foundation in L2 acquisition theory and research on comprehensibility, interaction and transfer. The affirmation and incorporation of the learners' home language(s) and culture(s) in the classroom as well as the advancement of culturally congruent practices are unique strengths of the SDAIE model. Finally, the instructors' orientations/dispositions inherent in the SDAIE model that are particularly beneficial are the value for linguistic and cultural diversity, positive home and school connections and high expectations for all learners.

## Strengths that May Also be Weaknesses

A clear strength is its flexibility. General educators are not taught one way to approach the challenges of EL inclusion; rather, they are taught to make modifications in many instruction, planning and assessment areas to better reach the ELs. Making informed choices for the individual learners in the SDAIE class is clearly a strength of the model that other models tend to lack. However, this strength and the freedom of creativity and adaptability for teachers create an 'unstable' model that is impossible to validate empirically. Some of the most potent criticisms come from the SIOP model advocates, because the SIOP is clearly defined and validated. Conversely, a criticism of the SIOP model is its inflexibility. I would also venture the observation that in practice SIOP teachers tend to be flexible and creative and do not tend to follow the SIOP as prescribed.

## Weaknesses of the SDAIE Model

One of the most significant weaknesses of the SDAIE as a model, in my opinion, is the comingling of it with the SIOP model. In Diaz-Rico's text (2014: 118), the author states, 'A popular form of SDAIE employs the Sheltered Instruction Observation Protocol (SIOP) model'. It is clear that SDAIE is the first form of sheltered content, but there are other approaches to sheltered content as well. Clarification of these parameters within the field is advisable.

Interestingly, since the SDAIE model is situated in the California public school system, the LAUSD specifically, the model does not address particular aspects of sociopolitical contexts, laws pertinent to ELs, advocacy and/or collaboration within the system. There are inherent assumptions of these points as shared knowledge within the literature. With the widely differing contexts in which the SDAIE model could be implemented, these issues would need to be considered. If a district wanted to implement the SDAIE model into its system, these areas would need to be explicitly addressed within the context. For instance, in a small central Wisconsin town, the context may be more resistant to the development of SDAIE courses. Teachers would need to advocate for the need for these courses in addition to the funding support. The teachers would need to expend energy and effort to develop allies among teachers and administrators and to find like-minded and prepared collaborating teachers. Knowing the laws pertinent to ELs and their rights helps teachers advocate for appropriate instructional models; although in practice, I have found that on the local level fiscal decisions trump federal educational law.

A weaker area for the SDAIE model is the area of discourse patterns and structures of English. This is one area that could be integrated into the classroom, but would need to be discussed within the tenets of the model. If the SDAIE model were implemented as a truly transitional programme (i.e. a programme designed to help students move from one programme to another as a bridge), then some of the discourse patterns and structures of English may have already been addressed. If the model were being implemented without the ELD component, then addressing discourse patterns and structures of English explicitly along with the content becomes vital. Furthermore, the learners would still need to learn the various discourse patterns of the academic domain (see Chapter 5) in order to be able to analyse it, interpret it and appropriate the patterns in their own academics.

The area of assessment could be strengthened in the SDAIE model by the inclusion of backward design in curricular planning, specifics on content and language assessment and accommodations for ELs in testing. These areas are not mentioned in the model, and may be assumed to be shared understanding within the context. To elaborate, in the LAUSD, accommodations for ELs' standardised testing may be emphasised elsewhere in their system.

A substantial area of flexibility in the SDAIE model is the delivery of new material. Unlike the CALLA model that provides unambiguous examples of delivery of new material, the SDAIE model leaves this to the instructor to decide. Clearer direction on ways to deliver new material in terms of deductive/inductive instruction and the amount of material to be discussed at any given time (e.g. chunking) would strengthen the model, increase consistency of instruction and stabilise the instruction so that it did not vary so widely by instructor. In Walqui *et al.* (2010), one finding about SDAIE was that successful implementation was exceedingly teacher and school dependent. Other areas of instruction that could be strengthened in the SDAIE model are learning strategy instruction and reflective practices (Table 7.4).

## Optimal Context for Implementation and Suggestions

The context for the original implementation of SDAIE was in high-incidence districts with ESL/ELD or bilingual education entry programmes. The SDAIE programme served as a transitional support for intermediate-proficiency learners and above between the language-oriented programmes and the mainstream/general education courses.

**Table 7.4** Evaluative framework for teacher preparation models, approaches and initiatives in EL inclusion

| *I. Knowledge* | *SDAIE model* |
| --- | --- |
| When preparing teachers to include ELs into their content courses and to work with linguistically and culturally diverse groups of ELLs, they should have *knowledge* of the following areas: | |
| • The structures and features of the English language.<br>   • The distinctions between oral and written language.<br>   • The basic units of language, such as parts of speech, types of sentences and the sound system of English.<br>   • The construction of differing discourse units from the sentence level to a variety of social and academic genres and formats.<br>   • The irregularities of English.<br>   • The pragmatic/sociocultural dimensions of language (e.g. voice, audience) and how language varies accordingly.<br>   • An appropriate target for language acquisition/learning is real language use; 'standard' English is a myth. | This is a lower priority for SDAIE. |
| • The key principles of second language acquisition (SLA)/ learning (Ellis, 2008).<br>   • Instruction needs to include:<br>      • A balance predominantly on meaning but also on forms.<br>      • An understanding of individual differences in learners.<br>      • Environmental modifications to reduce anxiety and affective issues.<br>      • Extensive comprehensible input.<br>      • Interaction with peers and instructors on the academic topics.<br>      • Opportunities for learners to develop both 'a rich repertoire of formulaic expressions and a rule-based competence'.<br>      • Opportunities for spontaneous as well as controlled production.<br>      • Output opportunities.<br>      • Social and academic language<br>      • Transfer of knowledge and skills from the first to the second language. | Although some principles are integrated into the model, only comprehensible input, output through interaction opportunities and transfer of skills between L1 and L2 are stressed. |

*(Continued)*

**Table 7.4** (Continued)

| | |
|---|---|
| • An understanding of ELLs' proficiency levels and their abilities and challenges at those levels. | This area is a particular strength of the model as SDAIE instructors are encouraged to differentiate instruction by proficiency level. |
| • The laws pertinent to ELs' instruction in the particular context. | Not mentioned |
| • The resources available to learn about ELs' educational backgrounds, first languages and cultures. | With the focus on learners' home languages and cultures, this is a particular strength of SDAIE. |
| • A sociolinguistic consciousness (Lucas & Villegas, 2011) <br> • Understanding of the relationships between language, culture and identity. <br> • Awareness of the sociopolitical context of language use and language education, particularly in the specific context. | Half of this category is recognised in the SDAIE model. |
| • The subject matter; knowledge of one core content area or specialty area. | It is not clear in the SDAIE model whether teachers are licensed content teachers or ESL/bilingual educators. |

*II. Performance*

When preparing teachers to include ELs into their content courses and to work with linguistically and culturally diverse groups of ELLs, they should have *abilities and skills* in the following areas:

| | |
|---|---|
| • Curricular and Instructional Planning | |
| • Planning with assessments as clear targets (e.g. backward design) (Wiggins & McTighe, 2005). | Not mentioned |
| • Creating content, language and learning strategy objectives. | A strength with the exception of learning strategies. |
| • Pre-teaching and/or integrating necessary skills, such as process writing, note-taking, etc. into the curriculum. | Pre-teaching of vocabulary is a strength; otherwise other areas are not mentioned. |
| • Integrating speaking, listening, reading, writing, grammar, vocabulary and pronunciation instruction and practice into lessons. | The integration of the four skills and vocabulary are foundational in SDAIE; however, grammar and pronunciation are not mentioned. |

| | |
|---|---|
| • Developing units with clear connections through a thematic focus. | Some proponents mention this area, but it does not seem to appear throughout the literature. |
| • Modifying, developing and locating materials for linguistic accessibility of lessons. | A strength |
| • Analysing the linguistic features of oral and written discourse so as to be able to bridge the gap between ELs and a wide variety of genres, subject areas, academic discourse communities and texts. | Not mentioned |
| • Addressing multiple ESL proficiency levels in the same class by planning for differentiated instruction. | A strength. It is interesting to note that only the higher-proficiency levels are included. |
| • Making informed choices (Brown, 2007b) based on solid second language acquisition (SLA) principles and best practices in content and language instruction for the particular context with its unique variables (Kumaravadivelu, 2001). | This category is a particular strength of the model, albeit also a point of criticism. |
| • Instructional Delivery | |
| • Creating comfortable learning environments and classroom communities with low anxiety. | A strength, because the SDAIE model was created as a safe transitional programme between the ELD and general education classes. |
| • Identifying learners' background knowledge and building upon it. | A strength |
| • Making informed choices about instruction and employing a wide variety and frequency of approaches, techniques and resources depending on learners' needs. | A strength, but it is a weakness as well. |
| • Explicitly teaching new vocabulary and language needed for oral (speaking and listening) and written (reading and writing) engagement with the academic content using supports and tools for meaning making. | A strength |
| • Creating meaningful, academically focused, engaging, interactive and experiential lessons and tasks that include ELs in activities (Migliacci & Verplaetse, 2008). | A strength |
| • Directly teaching new academic information in small portions or 'chunks' with practice and interaction opportunities. | Not explicitly mentioned |

*(Continued)*

**Table 7.4** (Continued)

| | |
|---|---|
| • Modifying the delivery of speech to heighten learners' comprehension (i.e. making linguistic modifications) or modifying the complexity or quantity of written material to make it more accessible. | A strength |
| • Scaffolding instruction using a variety of supports, such as graphic organisers, visuals, modelling, sentence frames, etc. | A strength |
| • Providing cognitively challenging materials to ELs that are linguistically accessible. | A strength |
| • Assessment | |
| • Offering learners a variety of ways to demonstrate their knowledge of the content or language. For example, using performance and alternative assessment (see task and product examples above). | A strength |
| • Providing suitable and judiciously chosen accommodations for ELs during academic assessments. Accommodations are state-mandated supports for learners during standardised assessments, such as providing increased time for the test, breaks, dictionaries and/or translators for directions. | Not mentioned |
| • Measuring learners content knowledge and language ability separately. | A strength |
| • Providing ongoing feedback on content knowledge and language ability constructively and regularly. | A strength |
| • Assessing learners' progress in language learning according to proficiency indicators. | A strength |
| • Modifying text and teacher-made assessments to support English learners. For example, using visuals and models in directions. | Not explicitly mentioned for assessment |

*III. Orientations*

When preparing teachers to include ELs into their content courses and to work with linguistically and culturally diverse groups of ELLs, they should have *awareness of, value for and appreciation of* the following areas:

| | |
|---|---|
| • Value for linguistic and cultural diversity. | A strength |
| • Inclination to advocate for the linguistic and programmatic needs of ELLs. | Not mentioned |
| • Willingness to collaborate with language specialists, content teachers, administrators, parents, etc. to provide high-quality instruction for ELs and to create EL-friendly schools and communities. | Not mentioned |
| • Hold high expectations for ELs and all learners. | A strength |

| | |
|---|---|
| • Inclination to provide assessments that level the playing field for ELs so that they may demonstrate their knowledge in a variety of ways. | A strength |
| • Value for reflective instructional processes. | Not explicitly mentioned |
| • Willingness to develop positive home/school connections with ELs' parents. | A strength |
| • Willingness to treat cultures respectfully and to eliminate stereotyping of peoples and cultures. | Not explicitly mentioned |

In the original context, the learners were predominantly Latino, mostly a homogeneous language population. The SDAIE model could be implemented in heterogeneous language classes (i.e. classes with speakers of several different languages), but the L1 literacy and supports might pose a challenge. How would the learners be taught reading their L1 when there are several first languages present? Would the teacher and district have the L1 support materials? These are two of the challenging questions to be faced when implementing the SDAIE model in heterogeneous environments.

For districts with second- or third-generation immigrants whose families speak their native language in the home, the SDAIE model would be a good choice. The reason is that these learners, if their English language exposure was high, would not be typical newcomers without some knowledge of oral, social English. In my home district, the Hmong have lived here for a couple of decades. Many of the children have a range of awareness of oral, social English prior to entering school. They do need some oral, social language development, but more importantly they need a great deal of focused academic English and literacy instruction. The supports provided by the SDAIE teacher and the emphasis on the grade-level curriculum are a perfect fit for this population.

Castellano and Díaz (2002: 125) suggest that the SDAIE model is also a good match for 'high ability/gifted students comprising multiple languages'. They suggest employing a SDAIE course as a special class option so that '...gifted English-language learners would attend a specially designed class that extends or enriches the curriculum in a content area or provides enrichment activities' (Castellano & Díaz, 2002: 125).

## Conclusion

The SDAIE model spans many areas of instructional performance while integrating the key principles of L2 acquisition, interaction and comprehensibility. The model includes explicit links to content and the connections between content and language. Many of the techniques employed in SDAIE, such as graphic organisers and visuals, which are known to increase ELs' comprehension have been adopted by other models as well. The SDAIE model is flexible in its implementation, which allows teachers to respond, through differentiation, to the specific population of learners' knowledge, strengths and academic and linguistic needs. The flexibility of the model also makes it difficult to validate by research and implement consistently from one teacher to the next. It was not designed to be implemented as a stand-alone programme without an ELD programme to accompany it. Assessment is treated congruently with instruction, meaning that performance assessments to evaluate learners' language acquisition are utilised.

## Activities and Discussions

(1) Could the SDAIE model be implemented without the ELD/ESL component? If so, how? If not, why not?
(2) Some advocates mention slowing down the academic curriculum in SDAIE. Others do not as they feel it waters down the curriculum. What is your opinion? Is slowing down the pace of the curriculum in fact watering it down?
(3) Create a series of sentence frames for use in the following environments:
    (a) Discussing outcomes of a science experiment.
    (b) Describing the steps to solve a math problem.
    (c) Arguing a historic point of contention.
    (d) Describing the sequence of events/plot of a story.
(4) Develop a series of probing questions on an academic topic to determine learners' prior knowledge on the topic. As a follow-up question, what strategies would you use to summarise the learners' contributions in the class?
(5) Write three content and language objectives and differentiate them for different proficiency levels by (1) products created, (2) tasks and (3) supports provided.

---

**Chapter Summary**

- The SDAIE model was constructed as a transitional programme to shelter language learners from the linguistic complexity of mainstream courses and to serve as a bridge between ELD and general education courses.

- The model emphasises content, connections, comprehensibility and interaction along with culturally responsive instruction.

- Educators employing the SDAIE model use a wide variety of instructional strategies and resources and are not limited to a particular format or strategy.

- SDAIE educators support language learners through connections to the L1 and the development of L1 literacy.

- Differentiated content and language objectives by proficiency level are essential tools for working in multiple-proficiency, EL-inclusive environments.

- Assessment in SDAIE mirrors the ways that instruction occurs.

# 8 Models: Center for Research on Education, Diversity & Excellence Standards and the Expediting Comprehension for English Language Learners Model

| Chapter Aims and Topics |
| --- |
| • Present the history and development of the Center for Research on Education, Diversity & Excellence (CREDE) standards and the Expediting Comprehension for ELLs (ExC-ELL) model. |
| • Describe the key features of the CREDE standards and the ExC-ELL model. |
| • Express the implementation of the CREDE standards and the ExC-ELL model. |
| • Discuss the Reading Instructional Goals for Older Readers (RIGOR) model of reading. |
| • Describe lesson plan formats, instructional modifications and materials use. |
| • Scrutinise the professional development aspects of the ExC-ELL model. |
| • Tips for implementing the ExC-ELL model. |
| • Analyse the effectiveness of the CREDE standards and the ExC-ELL model. |

## Overview

Much of what educators know today of content-based instruction (CBI) is based on the observations of effective practices, those that yield positive learning outcomes. Research has been increasingly conducted on these CBI practices to determine what is most effective in supporting English learners' (ELs) development of content knowledge and skills while simultaneously building second language communicative competency (i.e. the ability to communicate effectively in a variety of social, academic and professional settings). Over the last roughly 20 years, due to the sharing of research and effective practices among teachers, many foundational concepts have been elaborated upon in practice, which has resulted in the evolution of practices. An early practice was 'developing language skills across the curriculum', now practitioners have developed subject-specific practices, such as not pre-teaching math terms, because the concept and the term need to be treated together in order to comprehend it. Unlike history, sciences and literature, terminology can be pre-taught for clarity when the concept is explained by the teacher or read about in a textbook.

Many individuals have proposed and developed variations of content-based models for their instructional contexts. Some of these variations have developed and spread, others have been discarded in favour of different models. This chapter and Chapter 9 will consider less widely implemented models, such as the foundational work of the CREDE, which influenced the development of the Sheltered Instruction Observation Protocol (SIOP) and the Specially Designed Academic Instruction in English (SDAIE) models, and the ExC-ELL model, which was developed to emphasise literacy. Both models are no longer widely used in the field of EL CBI in general education classrooms.

# CREDE's Standards for Effective Pedagogy

## Description of the standards

A research team working for the CREDE proposed five standards for effective pedagogy that have been employed by some educators and consultants as a basis for content-based programme development, planning and instruction. According to the CREDE, the standards are not a model; rather, the CREDE describes them as guiding principles for instruction, 'the Five Standards for Effective Pedagogy do not endorse a specific curriculum but, rather, establish ideals for best teaching practices that can be used in any classroom environment for any grade level or group of students' (http://www.cal.org/crede/). The CREDE standards were originally published in 1999 and 'emerge[d] from principles of practice that have proven successful with majority and minority at-risk students in a variety of teaching and learning settings over several decades' (Dalton, 1999: 5). However, some educators do employ the CREDE standards as a framework to approach CBI for ELs in inclusion classes.

The five CREDE standards for effective pedagogy are

(1) Teachers and Students Producing Together- Facilitate learning through joint productive activity among teachers and students.
(2) Developing Language and Literacy across the Curriculum- Develop students' competence in the language and literacy of instruction throughout all instructional activities.
(3) Making Lessons Meaningful- Connect curriculum to experience and skills of students' home and community.
(4) Teaching Complex Thinking- Challenge students toward cognitive complexity.
(5) Teaching through Conversation-Engage students through dialogue, especially instructional conversation. (CREDE, 2004)

Many of these principles became a foundation used by the original researchers who went on to develop the SIOP model and others.

Although the work of the CREDE in California is no longer active, the past research and pedagogical suggestions are still employed by CBI educators and are available on the website of the Center for Applied Linguistics (www.cal.org). A CREDE site at the University of Hawai'i at Mānoa (http://manoa.hawaii.edu/coe/credenational/) continues to investigate the five standards and their implementation.

## Guidelines for implementation of CREDE's standards

In order to implement the CREDE standards into a curriculum for EL inclusion, teachers and districts could use the standards in curricular and lesson planning. If educators were to include the CREDE standards and link them to specific learning activities, they would serve as an excellent, non-restrictive guide.

## Effectiveness of the standards

The CREDE standards are distinctive among the models and approaches included in this text, because they are heavily researched. Tharp et al. (2003) summarise the extensive research conducted on the implementation of the CREDE standards as well as the methods and techniques that teachers employ to achieve the standards. One study of the CREDE standards that Tharp et al. (2003) cited was a quasi-experimental study with American Indian middle school children by Hilberg et al. (2000). Tharp et al. (2003: 4) explained Hilberg et al.'s findings, 'Students in the Five Standards condition outperformed controls on tests of conceptual learning at the end of the study and exhibited better retention of unit content two weeks later'.

Research evaluating the implementation of the CREDE standards was also conducted by Lin et al. (2010). Using the CREDE standards as a framework of instruction, 11 teachers were prepared through workshops and subsequent coaching lesson development. Researchers gathered and analysed qualitative and quantitative data including 11 lesson plans and the respective assessments. The 'findings indicate instructional coaching was an effective means to develop teachers' understanding and use of the CREDE model and implement the CREDE Standards to a higher degree' (Lin et al., 2010: 210) of success. However, no data on ELs' learning outcomes were analysed in this study.

In a research study on the outcomes of ELs when learning English literature, Saunders et al. (1999) found four strategies to be effective in producing significant learning outcomes for ELs: (1) building students' background knowledge; (2) drawing on students' personal experiences; (3) promoting extended discourse through writing and discussion; and (4) rereading vital portions of the text. Saunders et al. (1999: 11) described the rereading strategy: 'In preparation for the unit, the teacher "chunks" the book into manageable portions of reading that begin and end at meaningful junctures. In one or more chunks, the content is complex and critical to the larger understanding of the story and its theme(s). Such chunks require more time and intensive discussion and may be further divided into parts. Using background knowledge that students gained during study of the story and through further exploration of students' personal experiences, the teacher guides students through each step of a pivotal portion'.

## Strengths of the CREDE standards

The benefits of this framework include the focus on meaningful learning, the emphasis on complex, higher-order thinking and the use of instructional conversation that allows learners to engage orally in classroom interaction and discourse with support. Perhaps the strongest feature of the CREDE standards is how thoroughly the five standards have been researched. It also has strong theoretical support.

## Weaknesses of the CREDE standards

The most significant drawbacks of this framework are that (1) it is no longer being developed by CREDE in California, (2) it does not include details of second language acquisition (SLA) and language knowledge, (3) it does not offer templates for approaching daily instructional planning or assessment, (4) it has too much ambiguity in the framework and (5) it does not delve into the sociocultural aspects of becoming bicultural or bi-literate.

# ExC-ELL Model

The ExC-ELL model was developed by Margarita Calderón in order to help general educators to effectively teach ELs across the curriculum. Her model is situated firmly in second language literacy emphasising reading, writing and vocabulary development in core content classes. She accentuates key SLA principles of academic language, interaction and four skills instruction. She also encourages differentiated instruction. In much of her writing, she links the ExC-ELL model to the RIGOR model and teachers' professional development. I will attempt to do justice to and clarify the models and programmes.

The ExC-ELL framework has 12 components (Calderón, 2007b) (see Table 8.1). The ExC-ELL model focuses on the activities of educators to improve the inclusion and instruction of ELs in general education classes. The first eight components focus on what EL inclusive educators should do in terms of instruction (i.e. goals, instructional strategies); whereas the last four components emphasise teacher support and implementation. For our purposes, I will divide the ways and means from the professional development in our discussion.

## ExC-ELL instructional goals and strategies

The instructional strategies that Calderón (2007b) advances are meant to be employed across the curriculum in math, science(s), social studies/history and language arts. The emphasis is linking the content and language through a focus on making meaning from content-area readings. The idea is that teachers who specialise in their

**Table 8.1** ExC-ELL framework components

| |
|---|
| (1) Direct instruction in reading and vocabulary strategies. |
| (2) Prioritisation of key text content by teachers using content and objectives. |
| (3) Explicit and extensive teaching of words before, during and after reading. |
| (4) Text-based, collaborative discussions between teachers and learners. |
| (5) Explicit teaching of reading and writing skills (i.e. comprehension strategies, modelling fluency, partner reading and class debriefings after peer reading). |
| (6) Instruction of various writing genres, including emerging technology genres. |
| (7) 'Consolidation of content and skills. Teachers use strategies throughout the lesson to anchor knowledge, check for understanding, and assess individual student learning' (Calderón, 2007b: viii–ix). |
| (8) Employing a variety of item formats for the assessment of literacy and content. |
| (9) Support for teachers with models for developing cohesive lesson plans and implementation. |
| (10) Observations using specific protocols of implementation quality. |
| (11) Ongoing professional development for teachers. |
| (12) Learning communities for teachers to support and assist with implementation challenges. |

content area, become trained as reading teachers and focus on learners' reading of the text(s), explicit learning of new vocabulary and use/development of strategies inherent to the genres present in the subject.

Teachers are encouraged to write content and literacy objectives towards comprehension of grade-level texts. The objectives would unify a specific content objective, such as learning the concept of probability, with a reading in a math textbook on probability. For example, the math textbook might discuss what probability is, where in life we encounter it and how we measure it. In the lesson, the teacher would present the text to the learners and work with them through a series of pre/during and post-reading activities, such as teacher read alouds, silent reading, jigsaw reading and partner reading. The learners would use an explicitly taught strategy, like identifying and highlighting the main ideas. They would do independent and paired readings to practice the strategy and share their understandings with the class. During and after the reading, teachers would check for comprehension and address new words and phrases to build learners' text comprehension.

---

When employing a pre/during/post-reading plan in lessons

- Prereading
  - Teach reading strategies (e.g. skimming, scanning, predicting).
  - Pre-teach important concepts and vocabulary; use visuals.
  - Preview the text through picture walks, anticipation guides, title/subtitle discussion, etc.
  - Brainstorm about the topic in general.

*(Continued)*

- Access or build background knowledge.
- Pre-teach essential vocabulary or have students keep a vocabulary journal or do vocabulary activities like picture/definition match.
- Use K-W-L-H charts (e.g. Know-What to know-What you learned-How you learned it).
- Make personally meaningful connections.
- Speak and listen BEFORE reading and writing.
- Use interest builders (e.g. movies, photos, music, field trips, books and anticipation guides) prior to the reading to develop the learners' schema.

- During Reading
  - Use whole language AND phonics=BALANCED LITERACY!!!
  - Increase interaction with the text.
  - To increase learners' comprehension, employ
    - graphic organisers;
    - intermittent comprehension checks to check students' attention and understanding;
    - gestures, pictures, drawings, stories;
    - mnemonic devices;
    - native language (clarification in first language [L1]);
    - overheads, realia, visuals, maps, charts, bulletin boards, timelines;
    - real-life examples and anecdotes;
    - word associations to make connections.
  - Model and employ self-questioning and reading strategies through think-aloud procedures.
    - Vocabulary strategy to think about words
      (1) Skip word/read on.
      (2) Look at pictures.
      (3) Get your mouth ready to say the word.
      (4) Go back and try again.
      (5) Sound it out.
      (6) Match the word.
      (7) Ask: Would it make sense?
    - Self-questioning
      (1) Do I understand what I am reading?
      (2) Can I summarise what I am reading?
    - Revise prior knowledge and predict
      (1) How am I adding to what I already know?
      (2) What will happen next?

(Continued)

- Revisit the text several times, but in new ways:
  - Silent reading, guided reading, Teacher read aloud, choral reading, jigsaw reading, whisper reading (individual), partner reading. Be careful of round-robin reading as students do not retain the information when they focus on the oral recitation.
  - Practice skills with students such as making inference, taking notes, summarising, evaluating, monitoring their comprehension and clarifying when necessary, using context clues, marking confusing passages, rereading and visualising.
- Post-reading
  - Increase interaction interpersonally and with the text after the reading.
  - Check comprehension of concrete items/understandings and inferences.
  - Reflect (check predictions and understandings, add new knowledge).
  - Do review and extension activities: re-telling, drawing, communicative activities and tasks, etc. such as
    - (re)enacting passages in the text;
    - comparing/contrasting understandings and possible interpretations;
    - organising notes;
    - reflecting and responding;
    - summarising or paraphrasing (provide a title);
    - writing in journal;
    - role playing;
    - illustrating the text;
    - writing the ending or an alternate ending;
    - developing character maps and analysing characters;
    - creating student versions or contemporary versions of texts;
    - researching the theme of the text.

At this juncture, it is important to mention the five steps of the RIGOR model of reading instruction (Calderón, 2007a) (Table 8.2).

Linking the ExC-ELL and RIGOR models provides educators with two frameworks of structured literacy instruction which are not dissimilar.

In the ExC-ELL model, it is recommended that teachers analyse texts for the vocabulary present. The RIGOR model provides an approach to teaching vocabulary (above), whereas the ExC-ELL model offers guidance as to which vocabulary to teach. Calderón (2007b) suggests that teachers emphasise high-frequency vocabulary words first, whether from content vocabulary or other words in the text. She suggests viewing vocabulary in tiers: the first tier is high frequency, the second is moderate and the third is low-frequency words. Some resources to identify high- to low-frequency vocabulary are academic word lists, corpora (e.g. http://www.academicvocabulary.info/compare.asp). Based on the frequency and the need, teachers could present the new vocabulary

**Table 8.2** RIGOR model of reading instruction with explanation

| RIGOR model | Explanation |
| --- | --- |
| 'Step 1: Develop phonemic awareness and phonics skills. | In Step 1, teachers would help learners to make connections between the sounds and the meaning of the words and develop word-decoding strategies using phonics. |
| Step 2: Build vocabulary through seven step instruction and practice sequence. | For Step 2, Calderón has outlined a process of pre-teaching vocabulary that builds in repetition and supports auditory and visual learning of the word. The teacher (1) models the pronunciation of the word while presenting it (i.e. the teacher says *electron*); (2) orally and physically points out the word in context (e.g. 'Let's find the word on page 56 of our science book. The line says...'); (3) offers a definition from a dictionary (interestingly, the students are not encouraged to brainstorm about the meaning of the word as they might become confused); (4) gives an illustration to illuminate its meaning in student-friendly language; (5) guides a choral repetition of the word; (6) engages learners in brief, meaningful activities that allow the learners to use the word orally (e.g. think-pair-shares or providing personal experiences with the word/concept); and (7) highlights essential features of the form word (e.g. affixes, spelling, part of speech, tense, pluralisation and/or other meanings). |
| Step 3: Increase reading comprehension, fluency, and content knowledge. | In Step 3, teachers should plan pre/during/post-readings and discussions of the content text described earlier in this section. |
| Step 4: Use writing to expand and reinforce literacy. | In Step 4, teachers would link the concepts present in the readings to written form by engaging learners in individual, pair or group writing activities. Neither Calderón nor Hoff mention any specific instruction on writing forms or formats in this step. |
| Step 5: Compile assessment data to inform instruction' (Hoff, 2010: 1) | In Step 5, teachers would collect papers, write down observations of challenges or difficulties and identify any other form of data that would provide the teacher with insight into the long-term retention of the words and concepts as well as their reading and writing fluency. Although this step is listed at the end, clearly it would need to be ongoing from the beginning of the process. This step does not describe analysing learners' work, but I think it is implied. Therefore, the teacher would also wish to sit down and study the data to identify patterns of comprehension, lack of understanding or need through miscue analysis among other strategies. This information would inform the next day(s) study. |

as outlined in the RIGOR model, engage learners with the new vocabulary word using a variety of English as a second language (ESL) and academic techniques (i.e. miming, semantic maps, word banks, Frayer model and Beck strategy) and host a class discussion using facilitating questions about their new word knowledge and strategies for making meanings with unknown words they encounter.

Teachers employing ExC-ELL are encouraged to directly instruct learners on reading strategies (i.e. predicting, self/text/author questioning, visualising, activating prior knowledge, making connections to past experiences, confirm understandings, contextualising), comprehension strategies (e.g. main idea, cause and effect, inferences, comparing/contrasting, self-correction, summarising) and vocabulary strategies (i.e. context clues, reread, read ahead, cross-check, word attack strategies). A significant difference with this model from the others is that teachers are to prioritise key text passages by focusing learners' instruction on it through in-class readings, discussions and summaries. They are asked to use a variety of reading instruction strategies to enable students to develop their reading and writing skills for independent learning.

One way to communicate important reading concepts to students is to make text-rich classrooms, which facilitate the retention of important concepts, vocabulary or learning strategies (see Figure 8.1).

Another important instructional component of the ExC-ELL model is the use of text-based, collaborative discussions between teachers and learners. These discussions are essential to this model as they allow for interaction about the text meanings and forms in addition to helping teachers guide learners' understandings on an immediate basis. Included in the concept of collaborative discussions are interactive presentations of new material or strategies, text study and class debriefings after peer reading.

Instruction in ExC-ELL should address various writing formats and genres (Table 8.3), including emerging technology genres (e.g. texts messages, blogs, statuses/comments). Teachers would not only want to study the expository texts, but also the supplementary texts on the same subject or theme. For example, some narratives about probability that could be included in a math literacy lesson are: *Bad Luck Brad* by Gail Herman; *A Very Improbable Story* by Edward Einhorn and Adam Gustavson; *Probably Pistachio* by Stuart Murphy and Marsha Winborne; *It's Probably Penny* by Loreen Leedy; and *Pigs at Odds* by Amy Axelrod and Sharon Nally. Then, the teacher would teach the learners the formats of the different genres and help them analyse, compare and write them. For example, an expository text relates facts and

- Label classroom objects
- Provide reading materials in English and students' native languages
- Decorate your bulletin boards or reading areas
    - Alphabet
    - Word walls (high frequency vocabulary)
    - Spelling words
    - Illustrated vocabulary words
    - Grammar concepts
    - Reading strategies

**Figure 8.1** Items for text-rich classrooms

**Table 8.3** Types of genres

| Fiction texts | Non-fiction texts |
|---|---|
| Narratives | Content-area texts |
| Short stories | Letters/emails |
| Novels | Newspapers |
| Poetry | Magazine articles |
| Drama | Advertisements |
| Plays | Messages |
| Dialogues | Information pamphlets |
| | Instructions/directions |
| | Biographies |
| | Autobiographies |

explains; whereas a narrative tells a story with characters, a plot and a climax. One excellent resource for the analysis and writing of various genres is the *Write Source* series, which ranges grades from k-16.

Finally, the assessment in the ExC-ELL model is twofold. First, it occurs during class instruction as an ongoing, formative assessment of individuals. Second, it includes summative testing and alternative written assessments that employ a variety of item formats to assess both the literacy and content.

## An ExC-ELL lesson format

Based on Calderón's (2007b: 14–15) description, a lesson outline in ExC-ELL may resemble the mock-up shown in Table 8.4.

## Professional development in ExC-ELL

Calderón includes four components of professional development in the ExC-ELL model, which are designed to support general educators' short- and long-term implementation of the instructional strategies in Table 8.4. She emphasises teachers' need for ongoing professional development through *learning communities* in which teachers can collaborate in the development of lessons and their implementation. In learning communities, teachers can bring curricular or lesson ideas for assistance in their development, for sharing and improving. They can also bring the challenges they experience in implementation. With peers in a safe, non-judgemental environment, teachers can grow professionally. *Peer observations* are another means of professional development included in the ExC-ELL model. Rooted in the safety and professionalism of learning communities, and not meant as part of teachers' annual evaluation procedures, observations by peers who provide specific feedback on the ExC-ELL protocols can improve implementation and learners' outcomes. The fascinating use of Logitech digital pens with a computerised ExC-ELL Observation Protocol (EOP) form allows coaches and team mates to provide detailed, summarised and ongoing

**Table 8.4** ExC-ELL Guiding Questions for Lesson Planning

*Lesson Format Questions for Teachers*

**(1)  Standards as a start**
Which standards and objectives link to the curriculum and text(s)?
What learning outcomes do you hope the learners will achieve by the end of the instruction?

**(2)  Analyse the texts**
What are the key content sections in the text? What is the essential content that must be mastered in each section?
Are there any passages that could be simplified by removing any extraneous information?

**(3)  Give the global perspective**
How would you summarise the information in the text(s)? Write an 'elevator speech' (i.e. a brief but meaningful overview of the material) you could share with learners to introduce the unit and each of the lessons. How will you reconnect the learners to the material from the previous day?

**(4)  Background building**
What audio and visual supports do you need to provide a background for the learners new to this material?

**(5)  Links to past learning**
How will you situate this new information in the previously studied information?

**(6)  Develop new vocabulary**
What is the key content vocabulary to be taught? What are the other important/new words that need to be discussed for comprehension of readings? What instructional strategies will you employ to make the new vocabulary meaningful and retained by the learners?

**(7)  Scripting background building**
What questions will you ask learners to elicit from them links to their background knowledge of the topic?

**(8)  Strategic reading**
What reading or comprehension strategy will you explicitly teach? And how?
How will you model this strategy?
What interactive practice activities will you include?
How will you conclude this series of activities in your whole-class debriefing? What will you say to elicit learners' understandings of the strategy and its use?

**(9)  Cross-curricular four skills instruction**
How will you integrate speaking, listening, reading and writing into the content topic? What activities will you include and where in the lesson procedures?

**(10)  Checking for learning**
What data will you collect from your lessons to confirm learners' acquisition of new language and content? How will you monitor individual learners' progress? What tools will you use? How and when will you collect your data? How and when will you analyse the data? What other assessments (i.e. state or district) will inform your instruction?

professional feedback to teachers (for more information about the computerised EOP, see Calderón, 2007b: 131–136).

## Guidelines for implementation of the ExC-ELL model

For the ExC-ELL model to succeed in any school or district, it is vital to have the whole team's commitment from grade-level teacher teams to reading specialists, to instructional coaches and administrators. Each party must be willing to engage in the professional development aspects of the model as well as to have comprehensive and focused training on the model and its implementation. Entities would need to view this process as a long-term commitment to the improvement of instruction for ELs.

## Effectiveness of the ExC-ELL model

Little external, independent research has been conducted on the ExC-ELL model. One report for the organisation, Future of Children, conducted by Calderón *et al.* (2011: 107) purported to summarise the 'programs and effective practices for improving reading and language outcomes for English learners'. The report then outlined the ExC-ELL model, but no research evidence was provided on the entirety of the ExC-ELL model.

## Strengths of the ExC-ELL model

The first advantage of this model is that it stresses literacy development across content areas. General educators, who are already content specialists, develop instructional strategies to build ELs' literacy and language. The ExC-ELL model provides much needed literacy instruction with both guiding principles and applicable strategies and techniques that general educators can employ to support literacy instruction for all learners and the acquisition of language and literacy for ELs. The instruction is focused on explicit pre-teaching of reading strategies and vocabulary in thematic, cross-curricular units. The instruction is differentiated by proficiency level for literacy instruction and employs the most up-to-date literacy instructional principles. The analysis of texts and genres helps inform instruction on the discourse level and helps focus instruction on critical content.

The environment of instruction is comfortable, learner centred and interactive, which is another strength of the model. Cooperative learning during meaningful, academic tasks provides much needed oral and written practice for ELs. Discussions of content, language and learning processes are enhanced by a solid basis in research.

Scaffolding techniques allow for the lessons to be cognitively challenging while linguistically supportive. General educators concerned with academic rigor can hold all students to high academic expectations and provide support for ELs to achieve the expectations.

Another strength of the ExC-ELL model is the focus on the implementation of CBI for general educators. In other words, there is sustained and concerted support for the professional development of the general educators in the implementation of the model, which is constructive, not face threatening and not part of the annual evaluation. That teams of teachers on-site provide guidance, support and feedback for each other is a crucial element of the effectiveness of this part of the model. The teachers are encouraged to engage in the reflective teaching process through these supportive collaborations and feedback. These collaborations are central to the success of the ELs.

## Weaknesses of the ExC-ELL model

The major drawbacks of the ExC-ELL model are that it excludes much of the knowledge needed by teachers (e.g. structures and features of English and key principles of SLA) as well as the orientation/dispositional aspects of advocacy and the value for linguistic and cultural diversity. The ExC-ELL model is very practical and based on up-to-date literacy research, but it is too literacy based, lacking understandings of oral language development or the differences in first language and second language reading processes. It also lacks independent, corroborative research to demonstrate the effectiveness of the model in yielding the target learning outcomes. Some critical skill sets needed by general educators to include ELs productively into their classes are missing from the model, such as comprehensible input and linguistic modifications, ESL techniques (e.g. TPR/TPRS, tasks, communicative activities and jazz chants) referred to but not taught in the model, writing instruction for ELs, structures of English for general educators and instruction in productive skill forms and formats (i.e. giving an oral opinion in class discussion; writing a persuasive essay).

# Optimal Context for Implementation and Suggestions

| CREDE | ExC-ELL |
|---|---|
| The CREDE standards are broad, and therefore they are applicable to any content-based instructional context. Ideally, the CREDE work would continue and the standards could inform various models of CBI. | The ExC-ELL model was originally designed for the predominantly Latino linguistic context of Connecticut (although other New England states have similar populations of ELs with analogous linguistic, literacy and academic needs). The ExC-ELL model is predominantly useful with learners literate in their first language and with those who have some oral, social language experience in English. Moreover, this model would be helpful at the elementary grades with beginning readers, although it is not exclusive to younger learners or newcomers. |

# Conclusion

Two different approaches to the inclusion of ELs into the general education classes were presented: the CREDE standards and the ExC-ELL model. Although both models

**Table 8.5** Evaluative framework for teacher preparation models, approaches and initiatives in EL inclusion

| I. Knowledge | CREDE | ExC-ELL |
|---|---|---|
| When preparing teachers to include ELs into their content courses and to work with linguistically and culturally diverse groups of ELLs, they should have *knowledge* of the following areas: | | |
| • The structures and features of the English language.<br>  • The distinctions between oral and written language.<br>  • The basic units of language, such as parts of speech, types of sentences and the sound system of English.<br>  • The construction of differing discourse units from the sentence level to a variety of social and academic genres and formats.<br>  • The irregularities of English.<br>  • The pragmatic/sociocultural dimensions of language (e.g. voice, audience) and how language varies accordingly.<br>  • An appropriate target for language acquisition/learning is real language use; 'standard' English is a myth. | Not mentioned. | Not mentioned. |
| • The key principles of second language acquisition (SLA)/learning (Ellis, 2008).<br>  • Instruction needs to include:<br>    ■ A balance predominantly on meaning but also on forms.<br>    ■ An understanding of individual differences in learners.<br>    ■ Environmental modifications to reduce anxiety and affective issues.<br>    ■ Extensive comprehensible input.<br>    ■ Interaction with peers and instructors on the academic topics.<br>    ■ Opportunities for learners to develop both 'a rich repertoire of formulaic expressions and a rule-based competence'.<br>    ■ Opportunities for spontaneous as well as controlled production.<br>    ■ Output opportunities.<br>    ■ Social and academic language.<br>    ■ Transfer of knowledge and skills from the first to the second language. | | Some of these elements are included. |

| | | |
|---|---|---|
| • An understanding of ELLs' proficiency levels and their abilities and challenges at those levels. | Not mentioned. | A strength of the ExC-ELL model. |
| • The laws pertinent to ELs' instruction in the particular context. | Not mentioned. | Not mentioned. |
| • The resources available to learn about ELs' educational backgrounds, first languages and cultures. | Not mentioned. | The wide variety of learners' backgrounds, languages and cultures is a key tenet. |
| • A sociolinguistic consciousness (Lucas & Villegas, 2011).<br>  • Understanding of the relationships between language, culture and identity.<br>  • Awareness of the sociopolitical context of language use and language education, particularly in the specific context. | Not mentioned. | Not mentioned. |
| • The subject matter; knowledge of one core content area or specialty area. | Not mentioned. | Teachers are content specialists. |

*II. Performance*

When preparing teachers to include ELs into their content courses and to work with linguistically and culturally diverse groups of ELLs, they should have *abilities and skills* in the following areas:

| | | |
|---|---|---|
| • Curricular and Instructional Planning | | |
|   • Planning with assessments as clear targets (e.g. backward design; Wiggins & McTighe, 2005). | Not mentioned. | Not mentioned. |
|   • Creating content, language and learning strategy objectives. | Not mentioned. | All three areas are mentioned, but not the writing of objectives. |
|   • Pre-teaching and/or integrating necessary skills, such as process writing, note-taking, etc. into the curriculum. | Not mentioned. | A strength. |
|   • Integrating speaking, listening, reading, writing, grammar, vocabulary and pronunciation instruction and practice into lessons. | A strength. | A strength. |
|   • Developing units with clear connections through a thematic focus. | Not mentioned. | A strength. |
|   • Modifying, developing and locating materials for linguistic accessibility of lessons. | A strength. | Implicitly connected. |

*(Continued)*

**Table 8.5** (Continued)

| | | |
|---|---|---|
| • Analysing the linguistic features of oral and written discourse so as to be able to bridge the gap between ELs and a wide variety of genres, subject areas, academic discourse communities and texts. | Not mentioned. | A strength. |
| • Addressing multiple ESL proficiency levels in the same class by planning for differentiated instruction. | Not mentioned. | A strength. |
| • Making informed choices (Brown, 2007b) based on solid second language acquisition (SLA) principles and best practices in content and language instruction for the particular context with its unique variables (Kumaravadivelu, 2001). | This category is an implicit expectation when using the CREDE standards. | Not mentioned. |
| • Instructional Delivery | | |
| • Creating comfortable learning environments and classroom communities with low anxiety. | Not mentioned. | A strength. |
| • Identifying learners' background knowledge and building upon it. | A strength. | A strength. |
| • Making informed choices about instruction and employing a wide variety and frequency of approaches, techniques and resources depending on learners' needs. | A strength. | A strength. |
| • Explicitly teaching new vocabulary and language needed for oral (speaking and listening) and written (reading and writing) engagement with the academic content using supports and tools for meaning making. | The focus for the CREDE standards is meaning making, so vocabulary instruction would be part of that. | A strength. |
| • Creating meaningful, academically focused, engaging, interactive and experiential lessons and tasks that include ELs in activities (Migliacci & Verplaetse, 2008). | A strength. | A strength. |
| • Directly teaching new academic information in small portions or "chunks" with practice and interaction opportunities. | This category is partially addressed in the research on the standards. | A strength. |

| | | |
|---|---|---|
| • Modifying the delivery of speech to heighten learners' comprehension (i.e. making linguistic modifications) or modifying the complexity or quantity of written material to make it more accessible. | A strength. | Not mentioned. |
| • Scaffolding instruction using a variety of supports, such as graphic organisers, visuals, modelling, sentence frames, etc. | This category would be subsumed under the making meaning standard. | A strength. |
| • Providing cognitively challenging materials to ELs that are linguistically accessible. | A strength. | A strength. |
| • Assessment | | |
| • Offering learners a variety of ways to demonstrate their knowledge of the content or language. For example, using performance and alternative assessment (see task and product examples above). | Not mentioned. | A strength. |
| • Providing suitable and judiciously chosen accommodations for ELs during academic assessments. Accommodations are state-mandated supports for learners during standardised assessments, such as providing increased time for the test, breaks, dictionaries and/or translators for directions. | Not mentioned. | Not mentioned. |
| • Measuring learners content knowledge and language ability separately. | Not mentioned. | A strength. |
| • Providing ongoing feedback on content knowledge and language ability constructively and regularly. | Not mentioned. | A strength. |
| • Assessing learners' progress in language learning according to proficiency indicators. | Not mentioned. | Not mentioned. |
| • Modifying text and teacher-made assessments to support English learners. For example, using visuals and models in directions. | Not mentioned. | Not mentioned. |

*III. Orientations*

When preparing teachers to include ELs into their content courses and to work with linguistically and culturally diverse groups of ELLs, they should have *awareness of, value for and appreciation of* the following areas:

| | | |
|---|---|---|
| • Value for linguistic and cultural diversity. | A strength. | A strength. |
| • Inclination to advocate for the linguistic and programmatic needs of ELLs. | Not mentioned. | Not mentioned. |

(Continued)

**Table 8.5**  (Continued)

| | | |
|---|---|---|
| • Willingness to collaborate with language specialists, content teachers, administrators, parents, etc. to provide high-quality instruction for ELs and to create EL-friendly schools and communities. | Not mentioned. | A strength. |
| • Hold high expectations for ELs and all learners. | A strength. | A strength. |
| • Inclination to provide assessments that level the playing field for ELs so that they may demonstrate their knowledge in a variety of ways. | Not mentioned. | A strength. |
| • Value for reflective instructional processes. | Not mentioned. | A strength. |
| • Willingness to develop positive home/school connections with ELs' parents. | Not mentioned. | A strength |
| • Willingness to treat cultures respectfully and to eliminate stereotyping of peoples and cultures. | Not mentioned. | Not mentioned. |

venture to reach out to ELs using effective research-supported practices, they do so from differing perspectives. The focus of the CREDE standards is universal patterns of making the content subject matter comprehensible to ELs through modifications in the ways that teachers communicate with the class and the tools that teachers employ. These patterns have been expanded upon in other models, such as the SIOP, SDAIE and Cognitive Academic Language Learning Approach (CALLA) models.

The ExC-ELL model approaches the inclusion of ELs into the general education class through reading and writing across the disciplines. The focus is on the literacy development of ELs. The underlying assumption is that the specific population of ELs already have strong communicative competency in the oral language, and only lack the literacy skills. Access to content concepts and knowledge do not seem to factor into the ExC-ELL model to the same degree as the other models. Again, it could be argued that the unique population that Calderón developed her model for did not need these sorts of supports.

Like the SIOP model, the ExC-ELL model includes teacher preparation materials and emphases. Some models attempt to articulate what needs to be done to support ELs' learning of content and language while simultaneously offering guidance on the preparation of teachers. Since these dual emphases appear regularly in the field, this text will consider the pre/in-service preparation of teachers for EL inclusion. This analysis can be found in the final chapter.

## Activities and Discussions

(1)  Debate whether the CREDE standards address all the areas that ELs need to develop their additional language and academic abilities simultaneously. Are there any areas missing in the model?

(2) How could general educators use the CREDE standards in their work with ELs? In what ways do the standards help general educators? What would the model need to be more effective?

(3) The ExC-ELL model focuses on the literacy of ELs. Does the model exclude anything due to its focus? Is it a good choice to focus on literacy to this degree?

(4) Outline a reading lesson for ELs using the RIGOR model. How would you adapt the structure provided to meet the needs of your present or future ELs?

(5) Using the ExC-ELL lesson planning guiding questions, write a lesson. How effective were the guiding questions in helping you develop your lesson? Do you think your lesson would be effective? Evaluate a peers' lesson and provide constructive feedback for improvement.

(6) Professional development for educators working with ELs is a significant part of the ExC-ELL model. Design a professional development plan for your school to help it learn about serving ELs in the ExC-ELL model.

## Chapter Summary

- The CREDE standards for effective pedagogy are: teachers and students constructing language and knowledge together; the development of language and literacy across the curriculum; meaningful lessons; promotion of complex thinking; and instruction through conversation.

- The CREDE standards are no longer being developed so lack thoroughness for effective implementation, predominantly in practical daily instructional delivery techniques and assessments.

- The ExC-ELL model emphasises literacy development across the curriculum and foundational reading skill development by providing particulars on the development of reading skills and an emphasis on comprehending various genres of written work.

- The ExC-ELL model is inclusive of strategies for EL inclusion, such as pre/during/post-reading activities to build learners' text comprehension and teacher support and professional development through ongoing collaboration and professional training.

- The ExC-ELL model offers teacher support and professional development through ongoing collaboration and professional training through learning communities and peer observations.

- The implementation of the ExC-ELL model is flexible and teacher dependent as the model is not highly prescriptive.

# 9 Models: Content and Language Integrated Learning and Content-Based Language Learning through Technology

| Chapter Aims and Topics |
|---|
| • Delineate the history and development of the Content and Language Integrated Learning (CLiL) and Content-Based Language Learning Through Technology (CoBaLLT) models. |
| • Illustrate the key features of the CLiL and CoBaLLT models. |
| • Articulate the implementation of the CLiL and CoBaLLT models. |
| • Discuss meaningful learning and active learning approaches. |
| • Portray lesson plan formats, instructional modifications and materials use. |
| • Discuss text analysis and technology inclusion. |
| • Tips for implementing the CLiL and CoBaLLT models. |
| • Analyse the effectiveness of the CLiL and CoBaLLT models. |

## Overview

The models outlined in this chapter relate to how languages considered 'foreign languages' are being taught in conjunction with content area subjects. Although the target language varies (i.e. Spanish, French, Arabic, Chinese, Japanese or Albanian), the models and strategies are similar to the other models previously described. In some contexts, though, English may be the 'foreign language'.

The term *foreign languages* is a touchy one as foreignness implies oddness or distance. Foreign language departments debate how to name themselves. Are they modern languages? They are not if they teach Greek or Latin. Are they world languages? Possibly. But what about the cultural aspects they teach? This text will utilise the term *foreign languages* because it is widely understood and for lack of a better, more comprehensive term.

## Content and Language Integrated Learning Model

The CLiL model and a series of monolingual and bilingual models were developed and implemented widely in Europe for content and language immersion in any additional language. For example, an art history course could be taught in French to Spaniards or European History in German to Poles. 'CLiL is a value-added, as opposed, to a subtractive, approach that seeks to enrich the learning environment' (Mehisto et al., 2008: 27). Meaning, the philosophy is adding an additional language, not replacing a first language.

Since the European Union recognises 24 working languages, the CLiL model is not exclusive to the acquisition of English, although most CLiL programmes teach English as a foreign language (Cenoz et al., 2013). Rather, the CLiL model allows educators to consider the languages of the area for which the learners need proficiency and provides for flexibility in the creation of programmes. For example, if a teacher were teaching Romanian children in a rural community who have limited exposure to the target language (e.g. English) then the teacher would be empowered to create topical materials for use in places they may need or encounter in English. These children may need to employ English to communicate with Bulgarians about a computer problem.

# Description of the Model

## Goals of CLiL

The CLiL Compendium (http://apise.org.ar/apise/index.php?option=com_content&view=article&id=53&Itemid=77) discusses implementation focusing on the integration of two out the five dimensions (i.e. culture, environment, language, content and learning) in CLiL programmes. Against these dimensions, it suggests modifications of materials, topics and content area by learners' ages, sociolinguistic environment and degree of language exposure in CLiL programmes.

The *culture* dimension of the CLiL model emphasises intercultural knowledge and communication skills and the development of a broad world view in conjunction with knowledge of neighbouring countries and minority groups. The *environmental* dimension focuses on local needs for language that will promote internationalisation. The *language* dimension encompasses overall language proficiency, and particularly oral communication skills, in at least one other language. Interestingly, included in this dimension is the development of 'plurilingual interests and attitudes' (http://apise.org.ar/apise/index.php?option=com_content&view=article&id=53&Itemid=77). The *content* dimension envisages the acquisition of new content and content-related vocabulary through another language, which will offer learners new understandings and divergent viewpoints. Lastly, the *learning* dimension unifies the use of diverse instructional practices and techniques that engage and motivate the learners and build upon individuals' learning strategies.

These dimensions provide a framework against which educational entities can develop programmes, but these programmes seem to be predominantly oriented towards the linguistic diversification of nationals within countries. In a Eurydice Report (May 2009) entitled, Integrating Immigrant Children into Schools in Europe, there is no mention of CLiL in the instruction and inclusion of immigrant children into schools.

Whereas in an earlier Eurydice Report (November 2005: 22), 'involvement in CLIL type provision when it is an integral part of mainstream education is open to all pupils. However, some countries have established conditions governing access to CLIL and select the pupils concerned, particularly when the target language is a foreign language. This selection at the point of entry is often based on tests of some kind (written or oral examinations, interviews, etc.) with a view to identifying which pupils have a good general knowledge of curricular subject matter or aspects of the language used for CLIL'. Implementation of CLiL in some European contexts appears predicated on the development of the local language by immigrants. In other words, immigrants must learn the local language in another programme model and then take an additional language. The CLiL model is not how EU countries teach local languages to immigrants new to their communities. This programmatic structure is similar to the English language development (ELD) newcomers' programme prior to entry into the *Specially Designed Academic Instruction in English* (SDAIE) model classroom (although in SDAIE the target language is English throughout). Maljers *et al.* (2007) explain,

> There is no specific language curriculum in CLiL classes…there are preparatory courses in the first two years of the 'bilingual' programme offering extra contact time in L2. After that, foreign language instruction continues with the same number of lessons per week as in any other secondary school in the country. As a result, in CLiL sections the overall number of contact hours with L2 is much higher, so that learners benefit from extended exposure to the target language. (Maljers *et al.*, 2007: 45)

In the CLiL framework the five dimensions (above) are juxtaposed to four Cs: (1) content, (2) communication, (3) cognition, (4) culture and/or citizenship/community (Coyle *et al.*, 2010; http://blocs.xtec.cat/clilpractiques1/files/2008/11/slrcoyle.pdf). The four Cs are offered as a framework against which teachers would design curricula and lessons. *Content*, according to Coyle *et al.* (2010), is the sequential development of additional knowledge, skills and understandings in the specific subjects via thematic units. *Communication* is the focus on daily interaction and communicative competencies in oral and written modes. *Cognition* is the construction of new knowledge through analysis, involving higher-order thinking skills and problem solving. Finally, *culture* is the focus of analysis of the '"self" and "other"' (Coyle *et al.*, 2010: 54), which will develop complex multicultural understandings and perspectives on identity and citizenship.

## Content Subjects Taught in CLiL

A unique feature of the CLiL model is that it is not prescribed to be the same in each differing European context. The proponents of the approach recognise that each country in the EU has dynamic linguistic, cultural and historic connections that are situated in the particular context. Congruent with Kumaravadivelu's (2001) post-method pedagogy, the CLiL model advances instructional practices that are appropriate and compatible with the context. The post-method pedagogy states that instruction should be particular and practical to a context and strive for the possible.

- **Pedagogy of particularity:** a person's holistic understanding of the unique characteristics of a particular situation. *All politics is local; so is all teaching.*
- **Pedagogy of practicality:** practicality in the classroom, but also teacher-generated theories so that theories are practice-related and realistic.
- **Pedagogy of possibility:** empowering students/participants in learning; developing theory and practice that work with what learners bring to the classroom; empowering learners to seek, try and strive within and without to develop personally and further their possibilities (Kumaravadivelu, 2001).

Maljers *et al.* (2007) lists some of the considerations that schools should ponder in the development of CLiL programmes:

- the geo-political situation of the country or region where the school is located;
- the degree of similarity between the foreign language and the learners' mother tongue;
- the subject to be taught through the foreign language;
- the local resources. (Maljers *et al.*, 2007: 42)

In CLiL, countries also choose which content subjects are taught based on local/regional needs. In most EU countries, all K-12 subjects (with the exception of the learners' native language literature and language arts) can be taught via CLiL. However, exceptions are more the pattern than the universal rule, so countries choose which subjects to teach via CLiL from sciences, social sciences, artistic subjects or physical education (Eurydice, 2005).

When it comes to the local implementation of CLiL, many factors influence which subjects are taught using the CLiL model. In the literature, many contributors have noted that teachers are qualified to teach a subject and the language as well as develop the bilingual or multilingual materials that are lacking (US Department of Education, March 2014; Wolfe, November 2007).

## Implementation of CLiL

Based on field-recognised second language theory and pedagogy such as (1) input, (2) content interaction, (3) form-focused activities, (4) output opportunities/social interaction, (5) strategic language use and (6) cognitive engagement, the CLiL model is described by its originators as a means to 'build intercultural knowledge and understanding, develop intercultural communication skills, improve language competence and oral communication skills, provide opportunities to study content through different perspectives, and increase learners' motivation and confidence in both the language and the subject being taught' (http://ec.europa.eu/languages/policy/language-policy/bilingual_education_ro.htm) among other benefits.

In the CLiL model, no specific instructional methodology or framework is prescribed. However, the instructional choices of teachers implementing the CLiL model resemble foreign language study methods and techniques, but differ by employing the course subjects as the basis for the tasks, language activities and worksheets. There is no specific language curriculum because the content subject is the driving force for the language chosen. According to Mehisto *et al.* (2008: 27), 'The CLiL model encourages teachers to keep using their favourite strategies and to apply standard best practices in education. However, it does require an understanding of those strategies that are essential for CLiL, such as having a three-way focus on content, language and learning skills'. Cenoz *et al.* (2013: 1) explain the extensive array of possible implementations, '… the core characteristics of CLIL are understood in different ways with respect to: the balance between language and content instruction, the nature of the target languages involved, instructional goals, defining characteristics of student participants, and pedagogical approaches to integrating language and content instruction'.

CLiL teachers are encouraged to not only be creative in their engagement of the learners with the content and employ motivating and active language-rich activities, but also to develop reliable classroom routines and patterned discourse. Maljers *et al.* (2007) explain,

> CLiL is not related to one specific methodology. However, it requires active methods, cooperative classroom management and emphasis on all types of communication (linguistic, visual and kinesthetic). The change of the spoken medium may cause some anxiety on the part of the learners. Simulation, game-like activities, involving students easily, getting them to talk without any embarrassment or inhibitions, and helping to promote a relaxed atmosphere are broadly used in foreign language teaching. Learners work in pairs or groups and their primary sources of learning are authentic materials. The tools the CLiL Model applies (brainstorming, problem-solving, induction, rule-seeking, guided discovery, etc.) maximise the opportunities for the learners to become proficient, independent and successful. (Maljers *et al.*, 2007: 45)

These instructional choices make the CLiL model closely resemble the other models presented in this text, particularly the SDAIE and Cognitive Academic Language Learning Approach (CALLA) models. They resemble each other because of the flexibility of instructional choices with the SDAIE and the emphasis on content, academic language and thinking strategies with the CALLA.

When employing the CLiL model, teachers strive to balance both language and content instruction while integrating the language cross-curricularly through themes and projects (see Table 9.1 for examples of themes for the secondary and tertiary levels). CLiL teachers promote the natural combinations of subjects and collaborate with instructional peers to help learners develop content and language connections. CLiL teachers help language learners to understand the language learning process and reflect upon it (adapted from Mehisto *et al.*, 2008: 29).

**Table 9.1** Examples of themes

| | |
|---|---|
| • Diversity | • Power |
| • Self-actualisation | • Honesty |
| • Peace and harmony | • Thought |
| • Injustice/justice | • Courage |
| • Change | • Knowledge/wisdom |
| • Truth | • Happiness |
| • Success | • Materialism/consumption |
| • Spirituality | • Dignity |
| • Humanity | • Integrity |
| • Survival | • Compassion |
| • Rights | • Responsibility |

The CLiL classroom environment is low anxiety for language learners so that they may take risks in the process of second language learning. The environment is language-rich, employing both the content information and the key language to heighten learners' awareness of language forms and connections between content and language. Strategies for awareness raising are word walls, learning stations, bilingual/multilingual texts, current multimedia language materials and content resources.

# Meaningful Learning

Meaningful learning is a key principle in the CLiL model. Meaningful learning is offering opportunities in which learners can connect to the material individually or use the language for personal expression. When material is personally meaningful, research has shown that it is retained longer by learners. Furthermore, the interaction to share meaningful information allows for the authentic practice of language skills in which the learners are not exclusively focusing on the forms or structures of the language.

Suggestions for making content more meaningful to learners in CLiL include:

- seizing students' interests, knowledge and skills as access points to the material;
- drawing connections between the content and the learners' personal lives, attitudes and experiences;
- linking to target language speakers in the community (see Figure 9.1);
- reaching out to dissimilar learning styles;
- building accessibility into presentations of new information;
- nurturing creative and critical thinking;
- creating stimulating learning opportunities for students to pursue their academic objectives through the target language;
- providing opportunities for learners to clarify and confirm their understandings. (Adapted from Mehisto *et al.*, 2008: 29–30)

- guest lecturer visits
- interviews with native and non-native speakers of the target language at local businesses
- expat community activities, clubs and meetings
- art exhibits
- conversation clubs
- cultural events

**Figure 9.1** Activities to connect to target language communities in foreign language contexts

## Active Learning

Another focus for CLiL teachers is creating opportunities for active learning. CLiL proponents note the shift of instruction from transmission to active learner participation in the instructional process, which marks an enormous shift in methodology for Europe. When creating these opportunities, teachers swap the roles and responsibilities of the students and themselves. In the CLiL classroom, learners are active participants in setting learning objectives, outcomes and evaluation. Learners also participate in a more verbally active manner through cooperative learning and interactive activities. The CLiL teacher constructs lessons in which they serve as a facilitator and guide, so that the teacher is not dominating the speaking floor (adapted from Mehisto *et al.*, 2008: 29). For an excellent resource of learner-centred activities and tasks, see Deller and Price (2007).

Naves (2009) emphasises active and interactive behaviours for teachers. She suggests that teachers provide clear and comprehensible instructions, descriptions of tasks and convey their expectations of students. When presenting new information, Naves promotes the use of demonstrations, outlines, visuals, repetition, rephrasing, scaffolding and linking to learners' past knowledge as ways to make the input comprehensible to the learners (Naves, 2009: 34).

An implementation consideration mentioned by the Goethe Institute is the amount of time learners are exposed to the target language. 'An important indicator with regard to the extent that CLIL is integrated into a particular school system is the number of teaching hours available for this approach. *Exposure time* is not defined at all in a large number of countries and depends on the individual school...' (http://www.goethe.de/ges/spa/dos/ifs/ceu/en2751287.htm).

One of the strongest motivators for the development of content-based instruction (CBI) in general was the increase in the amount of linguistic exposure, so that learners would have enough input and output to trigger second language acquisition (SLA). When learners spend *only 3 hours weekly immersed in a language,* there *is simply not enough exposure* to develop linguistic communication skills. This is a bigger consideration when the language being taught is a 'foreign language' as opposed to the language typically spoken outside the school.

# Effectiveness of CLiL

Dalton-Puffer (2007: 5) synthesised many research studies on the use of the CLiL model and various realisations of the model and found that learners achieved 'significantly higher levels of L2 than by conventional foreign language classes'. Although she noted that there seemed to be a strong self-selection influence on the learning outcomes because participants opted into the programmes.

In determining the effectiveness of the CLiL model on learners, there are significant obstacles. 'Students' outcomes are not monitored, but many students graduating from Language Schools go on to study abroad or in Bulgarian universities. Of all graduated students, more than 90% become university students, but there is no official data on how many go to study abroad. There is no quality assurance system in schools specific to CLiL' (Maljers et al., 2007: 38). Without a comprehensive assessment plan and quality assurance from a clearly defined model, the CLiL model is open to criticism.

Several other factors have been noted that influence the learner outcomes of CLiL programmes, including the number of qualified teachers, teacher quality and preparation, and type and quantity of materials.

> Some weaknesses should be mentioned: many schools develop CLiL, but there are not enough qualified teachers and not enough materials - and if there are, the books are literally translated and the language is difficult for both students and teachers. Among the threats is the possible transformation of the schools. Finally - and probably this is the main characteristic of Bulgarian CLiL - there are controversies: there have been many years of teaching subjects in a FL/CLIL but no training for teachers, and there are few studies on the subject or they have started only recently. In my opinion, specific future developments concern widening the training system for teachers and improving the quality of teaching and learning, as well as that of materials development. There should be development and application of specific CLiL criteria along with good practice. (Maljers et al., 2007: 38)

These issues affect the European context more acutely than the American context because of the emphasis on multilingualism. It is not to suggest that an English-only policy is good. Simply put, there are more languages involved, thus issues of teacher preparation and material resources are compounded.

# Strengths of the CLiL Model

The strengths of this model include (1) the solid SLA foundation, particularly the emphasis on intercultural communication; (2) the value for bilingualism and multilingualism and the CLiL's flexibility for monolingual and bilingual learners at various grade clusters; and (3) the respect for local contextual needs. Furthermore, the emphasis on active and meaningful learning and low-anxiety, language-rich environments is useful and congruent with current learning research and SLA theory and research.

## Strengths that May Also be Weaknesses

The CLiL is extremely flexible in curricular and instructional implementation and classroom-based assessments. Its flexibility is beneficial for addressing the desires of local context in terms of which languages are taught and the particular learners' academic and vocational needs. However, this flexibility causes the CLiL model to lack some concrete parameters present in other models. As a result, the CLiL model is not consistent in terms of curriculum, instruction or assessment.

## Weaknesses of the CLiL Model

The CLiL's most significant weaknesses are that (1) it is geared more towards the development of additional languages for native speakers, rather than the inclusion of non-native speaking immigrants into the local language while acquiring the content; and (2) it provides only an outline of what to do in the classes as opposed to detailed instructional techniques, lesson plan models and guided instructional support for teachers. The lack of general consensus of language/content professionals on what constitutes CLiL instruction and differentiates CLiL from other types of language programmes (e.g. as opposed to immersion, bilingual education and foreign language instruction) is a defining issue for CLiL educators and researchers (Cenoz et al., 2013). Research to determine CLiL effectiveness cannot be properly conducted until the field develops an operational definition and distinguishes the model from other language programme types (Cenoz et al., 2013). (3) Assessments are also not clearly defined and standardised, although many CLiL programmes do align with the Common European Educational Framework (CEFR) for proficiency levels. (4) Lack of quality materials in the various languages and teacher preparation consistency are also important weaknesses of the model.

## Description of the CoBaLTT Model

CoBaLTT is a model designed to teach foreign languages (in the US context) through academic subjects. Foreign languages or modern languages for the US are typically Arabic, Chinese, French, German, Italian or Spanish. The vast majority of foreign language courses in the US are Spanish. 'Spanish continued to be the most commonly taught language with a significant increase in the number of programs at the elementary level (from 79% in 1997 to 88% in 2008)' (Thompson & Coble, 2013). The guiding idea behind the CoBaLTT model is to extend the common practices of foreign language instruction that start with social language development to more academic language development. In foreign language instruction in the US, most foreign language texts host a variety of topics and a corresponding set of grammar structures and vocabulary words per chapter, such as colours, transportation, clothing, numbers and occupations. Towards the end of the first year of foreign language study, texts begin to enter topical areas that are related to academic subjects, such as environment, social issues or political systems; however, these introductions tend to be highly simplified versions of the subject. CoBaLLT instruction theoretically would take the next step in this learning by continuing deeper into academic subject areas and teaching the academic language in the foreign language.

Originally, the CoBaLTT model was developed by a team of researchers working at the Center for Advanced Research in Language Acquisition (CARLA). Tedick and Cammarata (2010) shared the CoBaLTT model, which is a model for teacher preparation to instruct any content area in world languages in the US. The CoBaLTT model relies on the large body of research on CBI (http://www.carla.umn.edu/cobaltt/CBI.html) connecting this research to 10 CBI instructional strategies to aid world languages teachers (http://www.carla.umn.edu/cobaltt/modules/strategies/index.html) to teach the social and academic language of the target language. In practice, French programmes could include a unit or course on philosophers like Descartes, Voltaire, Derrida and Sartre while integrating French language instruction. In German, it could be a course in engineering with German language development. In Spanish, a realisation may be history and the impact of the Moors in Spain with Spanish linguistic development.

## Curriculum Development in CoBaLLT

The CoBaLTT model prepares world language teachers in CBI in four main areas: curriculum development, instructional strategies, assessment and technology. In curriculum development, world language teachers are taught to analyse texts to identify patterns for instruction. Tedick and Cammarata (2010: 252) explain the inclusion of text analysis in the curriculum development process, 'As teacher educators, we have learned that teachers benefit from going through a detailed process of analysis to "mine" texts for their content and cultural information as well as for their linguistic features. A thorough analysis of a text is often the first step to constructing excellent CBI lesson plans'.

## Text Analysis in CoBaLLT

Texts in the model are not specifically academic textbooks; rather they can be any oral or written example of language, which will become the foundation for linguistic input in the unit. Novels, magazine articles and historical documents are examples of written texts. Oral texts include podcasts, radio, video, recordings of discussions, lectures, etc. Educators are encouraged to include a variety and breadth of second language texts that represent assorted genres in their CBI courses. Texts are chosen thematically to provide insight into the content from varying angles.

Text analysis focuses on content, culture, genre, possible language activities or learning strategies, communicative/academic functions and grammatical structures.

When analysing the content, teachers are encouraged to list the main facts to be taught, important related concepts and generalisations/enduring understandings. Think of enduring understandings as the broad concepts that the teacher hopes learners will remember.

The cultural aspects to be considered are the concepts that will be unfamiliar to the learners or are used in a novel manner for the learners. Based on the National Standards for Foreign Language Education (1999), educators are to identify the cultural products, cultural practices and perspectives that may be present in the texts, which will need to be discussed in the unit.

The genre of the text is to be analysed for purpose, format/structure, discourse features and linguistic aspects inherent to the genre. For example, the purpose of a magazine article may be to persuade readers to floss every night. The format of the article starts with an attention getter about how gross it is to kiss someone who does not take proper care of his/her teeth, moves to how healthy teeth mean a healthy body, an explanation of the types of problems resulting from gum disease, images of healthy versus unhealthy gums and suggestions for ways to identify good floss, overcome resistance to flossing and a challenge to floss every night for two weeks straight. A discourse feature might be how the author wrote a reader-friendly explanation of research studies. Linguistic aspects would include hypothetical language, modals, compare and contrast, statements, imperatives and descriptions. For details on text analysis, see Butler *et al.*'s report (December 2004) (Figure 9.2).

While teachers are analysing the text for the content, culture, genre, the genre's format, style and unique features, they are encouraged to consider the graphic representations of the text information, learning strategies that learners would need to understand the text and the potential instructional activities that would energise and engage learners in the content. Specifically mentioned are pre/during/post-reading activities and tasks that go well with the material.

When teachers analyse the language in the text(s), they would need to consider the essential vocabulary needed for learning the content at the word and phrase level as well as any novel idioms or expressions present in the text. While considering which vocabulary, teachers should ponder how to include the vocabulary in lessons (e.g. pre-teaching, reviewing past vocabulary and creating vocabulary games or explanations).

The communicative and academic functions of the text should be analysed in addition to the grammatical patterns and structures. The grammatical patterns and structures that are new to the learners or challenging would need to be integrated into the instruction of the unit. The functions, for example, are patterns of interaction common to a communication. Some examples of functions are agreeing/disagreeing, giving an opinion, stating a fact, refusing and justifying. The functions that may be new to the learners or essential for understanding the content would be included in the unit. Teachers will also be considering the ways and means of including this information into the unit through presentation of new material, activities, examples and visuals (Figure 9.3).

The following list defines each of the genres. It is adapted from Recommended Literature: Kindergarten through Grade Twelve (http://www.cde.ca.gov/ci/cr/rl/litrlgenres.asp)

**Fiction-**Narrative literary works whose content is produced by the imagination and is not necessarily based on fact.

- **Drama-**Stories composed in verse or prose, usually for theatrical performance, where conflicts and emotion are expressed through dialogue and action.
- **Fable-**Narration demonstrating a useful truth, especially in which animals speak as humans; legendary, supernatural tale.
- **Fairy Tale-**Story about fairies or other magical creatures, usually for children.
- **Fantasy-**Fiction with strange or other worldly settings or characters; fiction which invites suspension of reality.
- **Fiction in Verse-**Full-length novels with plot, subplot(s), theme(s), major and minor characters, in which the narrative is presented in (usually blank) verse form.
- **Folklore-**The songs, stories, myths, and proverbs of a people or "folk" as handed down by word of mouth.
- **Historical Fiction-**Story with fictional characters and events in a historical setting.
- **Horror-**Fiction in which events evoke a feeling of dread in both the characters and the reader.
- **Humor-**Fiction full of fun, fancy, and excitement, meant to entertain; but can be contained in all genres.
- **Legend-**Story, sometimes of a national or folk hero, which has a basis in fact, but also, includes imaginative material.
- **Mystery-**Fiction dealing with the solution of a crime or the unraveling of secrets.
- **Mythology-**Legend or traditional narrative, often based in part on historical events that reveals human behavior and natural phenomena by its symbolism; often pertaining to the actions of the gods.
- **Poetry-**Verse and rhythmic writing with imagery that creates emotional responses.
- **Realistic Fiction-**Story that can actually happen and is true to life.
- **Science Fiction-**Story based on impact of actual, imagined, or potential science, usually set in the future or on other planets.
- **Short Story-**Fiction of such brevity that it supports no subplots.
- **Tall Tale-**Humorous story with blatant exaggerations, swaggering heroes who do the impossible with nonchalance.

**Nonfiction-**Informational text dealing with an actual, real-life subject.

- **Biography/Autobiography-**Narrative of a person's life, a true story about a real person.
- **Diary or Journals-**Personal accounts of daily experiences written by a real person.
- **Essay-**A short literary composition that reflects the author's outlook or point.
- **Letters-**Written letters or emails shared between to real individuals.
- **Magazine, Newspapers or articles-**Written to describe or share real events, news or opinions.
- **Narrative Nonfiction-**Factual information presented in a format which tells a story.
- **Speech-**Public address or discourse.

**Figure 9.2** Literary genres
Reprinted with permission from California Department of Education Communications Division

# Objective Writing

After text analysis, the second key feature of CoBaLLT curriculum development is to build off the text analysis to develop integrated content, cultural and learning strategies and language objectives. CoBaLLT emphasises these four areas for objective development, which is distinct from other models in the inclusion of cultural objectives. For CoBaLLT educators, objectives are linked directly to state standards and the American Council on the Teaching of Foreign Languages (ACTFL) standards (i.e. the five Cs: communication, cultures, comparisons, communities and connections) (http://www.actfl.org/sites/default/files/StandardsforFLLexecsumm_rev.pdf). Linking the four areas of objectives to the five Cs requires an examination of how content, culture(s), language and learning strategies mesh with the five Cs. Content might be part of communities, comparisons, cultures or connections, for instance. One could examine culture(s) against the communities, comparisons and the connections to the content (i.e. Art of the Mayan and the influences of Mayan Art in contemporary Guatemala). Tedick and Cammarata (2010: 253) explain, 'All well-designed CBI lessons have detailed objectives related to content, culture (as applicable), language and skills development/learning strategies. Objectives are written for each lesson of a CBI unit. Content and cultural objectives point to the primary concepts related to the content of the lesson and cultural information or comparisons as they apply to the lesson'.

CoBaLLT educators are encouraged to use a format for their quadripartite objectives. The formula for CoBaLLT objectives suggested by CARLA is:

Students will use _____ *(grammatical structure)* to _____ (communicative function) with _____ (target language words/word groups). (http://www.carla.umn.edu/cobaltt/modules/curriculum/obj_write.html)

This format differs from learning outcome objectives by three small words 'be able to': 'Students will…' versus 'Students will be able to…'. Those three words change the objective from what learners will *do during the lesson* (CoBaLLT's objective format) to what learners will *master and be able to do after the lesson* (learning outcome objectives). CoBaLLT educators would write two or three objectives to cover the four areas and various five Cs standards for one lesson plan.

CoBaLLT educators also distinguish between content-obligatory and content-compatible objectives. Content-obligatory objectives *require* learners to use a grammatical form while speaking, listening, reading or writing to communicate about a content concept. Content-compatible objectives also focus on using a grammatical form while communicating, but do not require a specific content concept to be present. CARLA offers good examples of this narrow distinction:

Content-obligatory language objective:

- Students will use *hay* (there is/are) to identify geographical features with terms like *las montañas, el río, el desierto, el bosque, la costa.*

# Text Analysis Form

Content Area: _____   Grade Level: _____

Title: _____

Publisher and Publication Date: _____

Learner Populations and Proficiency Levels: _____

Chapter/Unit/Pages: _____   Topic: _____

1) **Vocabulary**
   **NOTE** Academic Vocabulary (bold, italics, highlighted words, words in glossary)
   **REVIEW** Categories of vocabulary necessary to understand the chapter/ not necessarily known to ELLs.
   Provide examples of the category

   _____
   _____
   _____
   _____
   _____
   _____

   Vocabulary used in a new way: _____
   Colloquial language, slang, idioms: _____

2) **Grammatical Structures**
   **NOTE TWO** Sentence stems necessary to discuss the concepts:

   _____
   _____

   **NOTE COMMON PATTERNS:**
   New word forms, verb tenses, etc.: _____
   New sentence structures (e.g., compound sentences, cause and effect sentences, relative clauses,
   etc):

   _____
   _____

   Other grammatical concepts: _____

3) **Genre, Format/Organization:**
   Genre: _____
   Paragraph, section, chapter or unit organization that *needs* to be taught:

   _____
   _____

   Graphic organizer to represent the format: _____

4) **Prior Knowledge Expected or Necessary**
   Concepts requiring pre-teaching: _____

1

**Figure 9.3** (*Continued*)

Unfamiliar cultural information: _____
_____

5) **Activities**

   Are there enough practice activities? Yes or No

   Are there hands-on activities? Yes or No

   Are there real-world application activities? Yes or No

   Are there opportunities to speak, listen, read and write about the concepts?

   | | |
   |---|---|
   | Speaking | Yes or No |
   | Listening | Yes or No |
   | Reading | Yes or No |
   | Writing | Yes or No |

   What activities do you need to develop?

   _____
   _____
   _____
   _____

6) **Visuals**

   Are there enough visuals? Yes or No

   What kinds of visuals are there?

   _____
   _____
   _____
   _____

   What visuals do you need to find or make?

   _____
   _____
   _____
   _____

**Figure 9.3** Example text analysis form

Content-compatible language objective:

- *Students will* use the present tense to express likes/dislikes related to geographic preferences with *prefiero, me gusta/n* and *no me gusta/n*; e.g. *No me gustan las montañas; prefiero la costa.*
  (http://www.carla.umn.edu/cobaltt/modules/curriculum/obj_write.html)

# CoBaLLT Instructional Strategies

During the process of thoroughly planning their curriculum, CoBaLLT educators are pondering which content-based instructional strategies are congruent with and supportive of the content, culture, language (i.e. grammar, vocabulary, etc.) and learning strategy topics. There are 10 CBI instructional strategies that comprise the basis of teaching in the CoBaLTT model:

(1) Building background: For CoBaLLT educators, building background will focus both on the content and on the cultural background knowledge. A particular linguistic concept, such as an idiomatic expression, may need background development as well.

(2) Using learning phases: Learning phases in CoBaLLT describe the sequence of lessons, which start with
    (a) a preview phase: providing an overview of the lesson agenda; warming up and energising the learners; activating prior knowledge; building background knowledge; and furnishing learners with a footing in the content, culture and the language they need to succeed in the lesson.
    (b) a focused-learning phase: orienting learners' attention and raising awareness of key content, culture and linguistic forms; supplying modelling and oral and written practice for learners focused precisely on the key information; scaffolding learning; clarifying, correcting and redirecting learners' understandings when necessary.
    (c) an extension and expansion phase: re/connecting learners' new information with past learning, personal experiences or understandings of other world views and differing perspectives; encouraging creative use of the new linguistic information; and offering follow-up activities and tasks for learners to extend their new knowledge while practicing it. (http://www.carla.umn.edu/cobaltt/modules/strategies/ulp.html)
        Lesson phases work in the curriculum, according to Tedick and Cammarata (2010: 256) '...by encouraging teachers to generate activities that welcome students into the curriculum unit, take them through the key concepts and offer them opportunities to go *beyond* [sic] the basic learning to apply their knowledge in new and meaningful ways'.

(3) Integrating modalities: The modalities of speaking, listening, reading and writing are interwoven throughout each lesson.

(4) Using scaffolding: Three types of scaffolding are suggested for CoBaLLT educators: verbal (i.e. linguistic modifications), procedural (i.e. lesson modifications to include cooperative grouping and interactive activities and tasks) and instructional (i.e. graphic organisers, visuals and manipulatives).

(5) Using graphic organisers: The development and use of graphic organisers to help learners understand the global format of concepts and texts.

(6) Contextualising grammar: The presentation of grammatical forms with enough context so learners understand the sociocultural and discourse competencies and uses of the form. This is a significant change in foreign language instruction from isolated, meaningless sample sentences, such as fill-in-the-blank exercises.

(7)  Providing meaningful input: The CoBaLLT teacher's linguistic output is one source of meaningful input for learners since the teacher can modify his/her output to make it more comprehensible to the learners. However, CoBaLLT educators would also wish to employ a wide variety of other oral and written input devices, such as video, podcasts, radio, textbooks, stories, letters, magazine articles and diaries.

(8)  Maximising output: This strategy requires teachers to plan numerous sequential practice activities that allow learners to develop, synthesise and critique their new knowledge of content, culture and language.

(9)  Giving and receiving feedback: CoBaLLT educators would wish to provide constructive, approachable oral and written feedback to learners on their content knowledge, cultural perspectives and understandings and their linguistic progress through recasts, direct feedback, repetition, questions and prompts for self-correction.

(10) Using learning strategies: The explicit teaching and target practice of language learning, memory or learning strategies so learners can use the strategies independently to extend their language learning.

CARLA addresses one of the most challenging of issues in the field of CBI when it discusses the assertion that CBI is just good teaching. '...many instructional strategies to support content based instruction (CBI), and most are simply reflective of good teaching. Yet in CBI, such strategies are not optional--they are absolutely essential to ensure that students will be successful content learners and language users' (http://www.carla.umn.edu/cobaltt/modules/strategies/index.html). CoBaLLT educators would understand that the instructional strategies situated in a thoughtfully designed curriculum are essential to the development of bilingual and bicultural content competency.

## Assessment in CoBaLLT

CoBaLLT educators are encouraged to employ performance assessments and project-based assessments to evaluate learners' acquisition of new content and linguistic knowledge and competencies. Performance assessments differ from traditional testing by requiring students to perform some linguistic task (see Table 9.2). The distinction in Table 9.2 comes from Blaz's (2001) *A Collection of Performance Tasks and Rubrics: Foreign Languages*.

In the CoBaLLT model, teachers are encouraged to link their instruction with performance assessments. Some examples of common performance assessments for foreign language classes are listed in Table 9.3. In the CoBaLLT model, teachers are encouraged to assess all four language skills through performance assessments and communicative tests. Grammar, pronunciation and vocabulary assessments are then integrated into the assessment of the language skill. Interestingly, they are not expected to assess cultural knowledge, with the exception of when content and cultural knowledge overlap.

**Table 9.2** Difference between traditional and performance assessments

| Characteristics:<br>paper/pencil, true/false, matching, multiple choice | Characteristics:<br>not necessarily written, constructed response required |
|---|---|
| Objective | More than one correct answer |
| Hard to write | Time-consuming to set up |
| Easy to grade/machine-scored | Rubric-scored |
| Testing for validity, group norms | Individualized response |
| Isolated application | Contextualized, authentic application ("meaningful") |
| Facts, memorized data and procesures | Metacognitive, complex behaviors such as collaborative skills and intrapersonal skills |
| Items not interconnected, related | Integrated, possibly even cross-disciplinary |
| Lower-level thinking skills | Reasoning, problem solving, collaborative effort |
| Answering options provided (student passive) | Individualized response (student active) |
| Provided by text or teacher-constructed | Student involvement in setting goals and criteria |
| Standards determined/discovered after test to assure confidentiality | Published standards known in advance |
| Single score or grade | Evaluation on multiple competencies possible |
| Individual assessment | Individual or group assessment |

(Blaz, 2001, used with permission from Taylor & Francis)

# Technology in CoBaLLT

CoBaLLT teachers are encouraged to employ a wide variety of technological resources to reach their curricular objectives. Such resources range from language learning software to web-quests, telecollaboration, digital storytelling, listservs, epals, internet resources (e.g. virtual tours, news reports or television shows) and chat rooms. CoBaLLT educators would wish to integrate the technology into their instruction so as to be able to develop learners' understandings of the content, culture and language use. Some useful technology resources are Polyglot Chat for language practice (http://polyglot-chat.com) and Tongue Out! which is a language exchange network (http://tongueout.net).

# Tips for Implementation of CoBaLTT Model

Implementation of CoBaLLT could be at any of the K-16 levels of instruction. It would require teacher preparation at a highly advanced proficiency level in the target language as well as extensive content and cultural knowledge. Otherwise, teams of teachers, one language specialist and one content specialist could co-teach in the CoBaLLT model.

**Table 9.3** Examples of performance assessments and products

| Oral/aural | Writing/reading | Other |
|---|---|---|
| Present a weather forecast | Construct a timeline of events | Draw a map |
| Conduct a mock interview | Design and write a brochure or booklet | Draw a picture illustrating a scene |
| Conduct a mock trial | Keep a journal | Build a model, diorama |
| Retell a story | Make a poster | Create a chart |
| Conduct a survey | Write a critique | Develop an itinerary |
| Hold a debate | Compare and contrast an essay | Design an app |
| Describe a photo | Write a rationale | Make a game or sport |
| Participate in a values clarification discussion | Write (and perform) a role play or skit | Create a club/activity group |
| Explain a process | Create a sales pitch/advertisement | Develop a calendar of events |
| Describe a problem and possible solutions | Write a poem | Design a tool |
| Make predictions like a fortune teller | Develop a class newsletter | Label a photo, site or plan |
| Retell a famous person's life story | Write a blog | Create a flowchart |
| Explain a math story problem | Design a flyer | Create a comic/cartoon |
| Justify a decision | Write a resume from a biography | Design a portfolio |
| Mentor a peer | Write an email or postcard | Organise/categorise items |

To effectively implement this model, the school personnel and administrators and district administrators would need to be supportive of the initiative as it would require changes in schedules, additional physical resources and materials (including technology), as well as support for teachers' professional development. Community support for the instruction of the target language is also a prerequisite.

## Effectiveness of the CoBaLTT Model

The effectiveness of the CoBaLLT model is based on the thorough research foundation of CBI. Unfortunately, there is little or no independent research on the model. Nor are there observation protocols to aid in research on the effectiveness of the model.

## Strengths of the CoBaLLT Model

CoBaLLT is an extremely solid model. The model is research based and comprehensively connects field-endorsed knowledge and performance practices in CBI for world language educators to implement. The curricular planning and instructional strategies and assessment aspects of the CoBaLLT model are particular strengths of the model.

## Weaknesses of the CoBaLLT Model

The research base of CBI is a good starting point, but the CoBaLLT model needs to have independent research conducted on it in order to be able to show the effectiveness of the model.

The next biggest weakness is the lack of discussion of multiple proficiency levels in the same class. The underlying assumption is that the world language learners would all start at the same proficiency level and advance apace together. However, in practice and according to SLA research, that does not happen. The CoBaLLT model could be considerably strengthened by the addition of differentiated instruction by proficiency and training in teaching language to multiple proficiency levels in the same class.

An area that could be a significant problem for CoBaLLT educators is the credentialing for the core subject area(s). The teachers may not have content area training, knowledge or credentials. Other content area specialists might find this challenging, threatening or insulting. The manner in which content is included into the language classes may be 'content-light', including content for topics in language development only or more thorough and deep 'content-rich or content-focused'. Depending on the degree to which the content is the focus of the CoBaLLT classes, educators might want to consider dual licensure, such as bilingual educators and some ESL practitioners are required to hold. If the educators are not licensed content area specialists, they may not do justice to the content area knowledge. Coverage of the grade-level academics may be an issue as well. Would the content areas be fully covered the same ways as in the core content classes?

Minor weaknesses of the CoBaLLT model are excluding backward design in the curriculum development process, making informed choices by the teacher based on the unique instructional context and learner population and ensuring that the units and lessons are cognitively challenging and academically rigorous. The latter might not necessarily be an emphasis for the model originators, but it would enhance the model.

The orientations of CoBaLLT educators are not discussed much in the model and the absence of these discussions creates a distinct weakness in the model. For instance, there is no discussion of advocacy for world language programmes or the need for proficiency in a language. This is a sizeable challenge in the US context with budget constraints and cuts negatively and heavily altering world language instructional offerings. World language educators need to be able to negotiate with communities their interest and need for language instruction; teachers need to determine whether communities welcome the instruction of a particular language. There is no explicit discussion of connections to the target language communities either technologically or in the immediate community, region or country. These weaknesses could isolate the CoBaLLT practitioners and expose them to potential cuts during times of budget tightening (Table 9.4).

**Table 9.4** Evaluative framework for teacher preparation models, approaches and initiatives in EL inclusion

| I. Knowledge | CLiL | CoBaLTT |
|---|---|---|
| When preparing teachers to include ELs into their content courses and to work with linguistically and culturally diverse groups of ELLs, they should have *knowledge* of the following areas: | For the CLiL and CoBaLLT models, replace English with target language. | |
| • The structures and features of the English language.<br>  • The distinctions between oral and written language.<br>  • The basic units of language, such as parts of speech, types of sentences and the sound system of English.<br>  • The construction of differing discourse units from the sentence level to a variety of social and academic genres and formats.<br>  • The irregularities of English.<br>  • The pragmatic/sociocultural dimensions of language (e.g. voice, audience) and how language varies accordingly.<br>  • An appropriate target for language acquisition/learning is real language use; 'standard' English is a myth. | Some development is occurring in these areas at present. | Structures and forms are addressed, such as grammatical forms and functions of language. Otherwise, the areas are not mentioned. |
| • The key principles of second language acquisition (SLA)/learning (Ellis, 2008).<br>  • Instruction needs to include:<br>    • A balance predominantly on meaning but also on forms.<br>    • An understanding of individual differences in learners.<br>    • Environmental modifications to reduce anxiety and affective issues.<br>    • Extensive comprehensible input.<br>    • Interaction with peers and instructors on the academic topics.<br>    • Opportunities for learners to develop both 'a rich repertoire of formulaic expressions and a rule-based competence'. | Most of these key factors are foundational to the CLiL model. | Since the CoBaLLT model builds on the second language acquisition and pedagogy research, these concepts form a tacit foundation for the model. |

| | | |
|---|---|---|
| • Opportunities for spontaneous as well as controlled production.<br>• Output opportunities.<br>• Social and academic language.<br>• Transfer of knowledge and skills from the first to the second language. | | |
| • An understanding of ELLs' proficiency levels and their abilities and challenges at those levels. | Since learners are tested prior to admission to CLiL programmes, they tend to be at similar levels of language. | Not mentioned |
| • The laws pertinent to ELs' instruction in the particular context. | Not applicable | Not applicable |
| • The resources available to learn about ELs' educational backgrounds, first languages and cultures. | These would need to be found by educators for the language(s) and context. | These would need to be found by educators for the language(s) and context. The inclusion of cultural objectives is a strength of this model in this area. |
| • A sociolinguistic consciousness (Lucas & Villegas, 2011).<br>   • Understanding of the relationships between language, culture and identity.<br>   • Awareness of the sociopolitical context of language use and language education, particularly in the specific context. | The CLiL model seems to be informed by these understandings. | Implied, but not explicitly mentioned. This area would depend on the individual instructor's choices. |
| • The subject matter; knowledge of one core content area or specialty area. | An expectation of teachers. | Not mentioned |

*II. Performance*

When preparing teachers to include ELs into their content courses and to work with linguistically and culturally diverse groups of ELLs, they should have *abilities and skills* in the following areas:

| | | |
|---|---|---|
| • Curricular and Instructional Planning | | |
|    • Planning with assessments as clear targets (e.g. backward design; Wiggins & McTighe, 2005). | Not mentioned | Not mentioned<br><br>*(Continued)* |

**Table 9.4** (Continued)

| | | |
|---|---|---|
| • Creating content, language and learning strategy objectives. | All three areas are mentioned, but not the writing of objectives. | A strength |
| • Pre-teaching and/or integrating necessary skills, such as process writing, note-taking, etc. into the curriculum. | Not mentioned | A strength |
| • Integrating speaking, listening, reading, writing, grammar, vocabulary and pronunciation instruction and practice into lessons. | Not mentioned | A strength |
| • Developing units with clear connections through a thematic focus. | Some proponents mention this area, but it does not seem to appear throughout the literature. | A strength |
| • Modifying, developing, locating materials for linguistic accessibility of lessons. | Some proponents mention this area, but it does not seem to appear throughout the literature. | A strength |
| • Analysing the linguistic features of oral and written discourse so as to be able to bridge the gap between ELs and a wide variety of genres, subject areas, academic discourse communities and texts. | Some proponents mention this area, but it does not seem to appear throughout the literature. | A strength |
| • Addressing multiple ESL proficiency levels in the same class by planning for differentiated instruction. | Only the higher-proficiency levels are included. | A weakness |
| • Making informed choices (Brown, 2007b) based on solid second language acquisition (SLA) principles and best practices in content and language instruction for the particular context with its unique variables (Kumaravadivelu, 2001). | This category is a particular strength of the model, albeit also a point of criticism. | Not mentioned |
| • Instructional Delivery | | |
|    • Creating comfortable learning environments and classroom communities with low anxiety. | A strength | Implicit expectation |
|    • Identifying learners' background knowledge and building upon it. | A strength | A strength |

| | | |
|---|---|---|
| • Making informed choices about instruction and employing a wide variety and frequency of approaches, techniques and resources depending on learners' needs. | A strength, but is a weakness as well. | Not mentioned |
| • Explicitly teaching new vocabulary and language needed for oral (speaking and listening) and written (reading and writing) engagement with the academic content using supports and tools for meaning making. | Not mentioned | Implicit expectation |
| • Creating meaningful, academically focused, engaging, interactive and experiential lessons and tasks that include ELs in activities (Migliacci & Verplaetse, 2008). | A strength | A strength |
| • Directly teaching new academic information in small portions or 'chunks' with practice and interaction opportunities. | Practice and interaction opportunities are a strength; the direct teaching is not explicitly mentioned. | Implicit expectation |
| • Modifying the delivery of speech to heighten learners' comprehension (i.e. making linguistic modifications) or modifying the complexity or quantity of written material to make it more accessible. | A strength | A strength |
| • Scaffolding instruction using a variety of supports, such as graphic organisers, visuals, modelling, sentence frames, etc. | Not mentioned | A strength |
| • Providing cognitively challenging materials to ELs that are linguistically accessible. | A strength | Not mentioned |
| • Assessment | | |
| • Offering learners a variety of ways to demonstrate their knowledge of the content or language. For example, using performance and alternative assessment (see task and product examples above). | Not mentioned | A strength |
| • Providing suitable and judiciously chosen accommodations for ELs during academic assessments. Accommodations are state-mandated supports for learners during standardised assessments, such as providing increased time for the test, breaks, dictionaries and/or translators for directions. | Not mentioned | Not mentioned |

*(Continued)*

**Table 9.4** (Continued)

| | | |
|---|---|---|
| • Measuring learners content knowledge and language ability separately. | Not mentioned | Not mentioned |
| • Providing ongoing feedback on content knowledge and language ability constructively and regularly. | Not mentioned | A strength |
| • Assessing learners' progress in language learning according to proficiency indicators. | Not mentioned | A strength |
| *III. Orientations* | | |
| When preparing teachers to include ELs into their content courses and to work with linguistically and culturally diverse groups of ELLs, they should have *awareness of, value for and appreciation of* the following areas: | | |
| • Value for linguistic and cultural diversity. | A strength | A strength |
| • Inclination to advocate for the linguistic and programmatic needs of ELLs. | Not mentioned | Not mentioned |
| • Willingness to collaborate with language specialists, content teachers, administrators, parents, etc. to provide high-quality instruction for ELs and to create EL-friendly schools and communities. | A strength | Not mentioned |
| • Hold high expectations for ELs and all learners. | A strength | Not mentioned |
| • Inclination to provide assessments that level the playing field for ELs so that they may demonstrate their knowledge in a variety of ways. | Not mentioned | Not mentioned |
| • Value for reflective instructional processes. | Not mentioned for teachers, but is for learners. | Not mentioned |
| • Willingness to develop positive home/school connections with ELs' parents. | A strength | Not mentioned |
| • Willingness to treat cultures respectfully and to eliminate stereotyping of peoples and cultures. | A strength | Implicit expectation |

# Optimal Context for Implementation and Suggestions

| CLiL | CoBaLTT |
|------|---------|
| CLiL is uniquely designed for the European context. It seems best suited to grades 6–16, but could be implemented in elementary schools given the proper degree of support. | CoBaLLT is appropriate for the development of any foreign language and has curricular, instructional and assessment tools that allow for more flexibility than the CLiL model. Likewise, it could be implemented realistically in grades 6–16, but the elementary levels in the US would be extremely difficult contexts without strong stakeholder support. |

# Conclusion

The CLiL and CoBaLLT models both integrate content subjects and foreign languages. CLiL focuses on the integration of culture, environment, language, content and learning through modifications appropriate to learners' ages, sociolinguistic environment and degree of language exposure. The CoBaLTT model encourages world language teachers to integrate content and language through modifications in curriculum development, instructional strategies, assessment and technology. The CLiL model is more fluid and less well-defined than some of the instructional parameters provided in the CoBaLLT model.

# Activities and Discussions

(1) Consider the five dimensions of the CLiL model (culture, environment, language, content and learning). How would you balance these differing areas in a curriculum? Are there any dimensions that take precedence over others? Choose a topic with a partner and write one objective for each dimension that you could teach in a unit. Use the learning outcome objective format (e.g. 'Students will be able to….'). Does your opinion on the priority of some dimensions change when you consider the objectives?

(2) Could the CLiL model work to teach the differing languages in another context than in Europe? What would be the advantages and drawbacks of applying this model in another context?

(3) Define intercultural communication. What should we teach our ELs to develop their intercultural communication skills? What does it mean to be interculturally competent?

| Definition of intercultural communication: | |
|---|---|
| Goals for developing ELs intercultural communication skills: | • <br> • <br> • <br> • <br> • <br> • |

(4) Choose a language of instruction with which you are familiar (i.e. Arabic, Chinese, French, German, Italian, Japanese or Spanish) and an academic subject area (i.e. art, philosophy, history, science(s), geography, economics, archaeology) and a unit topic to teach. In the CoBaLLT model, texts are not specifically academic textbooks. What texts would you look for to teach your language, subject and topic? Where would you look? (Be more specific than 'the internet'). Make a list of all the types of texts and resources you would need to teach a unit in your language, subject and topic. Remember you will need the language resources too.

(5) Based on your language, subject and topic in Activity 4, make a list of the academic functions that learners may encounter in the texts. For example, persuasion in philosophy.

(6) Integrating modalities (speaking, listening, reading and writing) while teaching grammar, pronunciation, spelling and vocabulary can be challenging. Make a lesson outline that includes activities for each of these areas that integrates them relatively equally.

## Chapter Summary

- The CLiL model of language instruction is employed in the European Union and is a model of CBI for various world languages. It is not employed for immigrant populations to Europe in order for them to learn the language of the community.

- Culture, environment, language, content and learning are the dimensions that CLiL curricula plan. Interaction and meaningful and active learning are tenets of the instructional design.

- The CLiL model is adaptable and flexible to the needs of the learners and relies heavily on teacher creativity and ability to develop materials.

- The CoBaLLT model was developed to integrate content, a world language and technology instruction into a cohesive package of instruction based on the ACTFL's five Cs: communication, cultures, comparisons, communities and connections.

- Unlike other models of CBI, the CoBaLLT model explicitly teaches culture.

- Instructional strategies advanced in the instruction of world languages through the CoBaLLT model are: background building, utilising learning phases, integrating modalities (i.e. language skills), using scaffolds, learning strategies and graphic organisers, contextualising grammar, providing meaningful input and maximising output while giving and receiving feedback.

- Assessment in the CoBaLLT model relies heavily on learners' performance using the four language skills in order to gauge learners' acquisition of the five Cs.

# 10 The 'Winner': Which Model Should Be Chosen?

| **Chapter Aims and Topics** |
|---|
| • Demographic considerations of English learners (ELs). |
| • Describe K-12 language programmes.<br>   • English language development/English as a second language (ESL) programmes.<br>   • Newcomer intensive preparation programmes.<br>   • Sheltered content programmes.<br>   • Full inclusion (sink or swim; dual licensed/trained content teachers).<br>   • Push-in programmes.<br>   • Pull-out programmes.<br>   • Bilingual education programmes. |
| • Explore connections between teacher preparation, EL population size, language and grades, as well as community's location, size, resources, beliefs and mandates (bilingual, English only, etc., sink or swim, etc.). |
| • Overview federal laws relevant to EL instruction in the US. |
| • Host a comparative discussion of various models and approaches relative to each other. What strengths can we take from each model? |
| • Address how best to include ELLs and meet their linguistic and content needs to show yearly adequate progress. |
| • Infrastructure challenges to EL inclusion: pre-service and in-service teacher preparation. |

## Overview

This chapter will host a comparative discussion of various models and approaches relative to each other and address how best to include ELLs and meet their linguistic and content needs in order to show adequate yearly progress. First though, background concepts related to communities, schools and ELs will be presented to contextually clarify concepts to undergird implementation and decision-making.

## ELs' Arrival and Residence: Factors Influencing Schooling

One significant factor in programme model choice and design is when and how long ELs have resided in a community. Communities with many diverse languages, including English, have long been the standard of community demographics since the birth of the US. Communities have evolved throughout time according to waves of immigrants who then become established in communities. Through generations, non-native speakers of English in some regions may maintain their native languages, becoming bilingual, while in others they acquire English and endure the languishment of their native language. In the US, English emerged historically as the language of schooling, business and politics. Immigrants continue to arrive in the US, although in lower numbers than at the turn of the 20th century.

Today, there are long-established communities of Spanish speakers, among others, who have been born in the US. Among some educators, they are colloquially referred to as 'born heres'. They maintain their native language and have varying degrees of oral English ability ranging from low to high degrees of oral proficiency when they commence schooling. Since they are an established community, the children tend to enter the public schools at kindergarten and do not typically have well-developed literacy abilities, just like their native-speaking peers (Table 10.1).

There are other communities of migrants who come temporarily. Whether their status is legal or illegal is not a consideration in this discussion, because US public schools welcome all children and may not ask about their immigration status. These learners follow their families as they follow the harvests or jobs. They may have been in schools in their home country or other parts of the US. Commonly, these children do not start school in kindergarten, unlike those born here. They arrive at school at various ages with widely varying schooling and learning experiences. Likewise, they have unpredictable oral and written proficiency in their native language(s) and English. Children will range in school ages and enter the K-12 at differing grades, placed initially by age. For example, a district may welcome a family with learners in

**Table 10.1** Comparison of oral and literacy abilities of native and non-native English speakers born in the US entering schools

| | Grade level | Oral language ability | | Literacy skills | |
|---|---|---|---|---|---|
| Native English speakers<br>*English is the first language.* | Kindergarten | L1<br>Yes | L2<br>Not common | L1<br>Dependent upon socioeconomic familial situation | L2<br>Not common |
| Non-native English speakers, long-term residents/born here<br>*Spanish, Somali, Vietnamese, etc. may be the first language.*<br>*English is the second language in this example.* | Kindergarten | L1<br>Yes | L2<br>Varying degrees | L1<br>Dependent upon socioeconomic familial situation | L2<br>Dependent upon socioeconomic familial situation |

Note: L1 = first language; L2 = second language

**Table 10.2** Comparison of oral and literacy abilities of native and migrant or temporary resident, non-native English speakers entering schools

| | Grade level | Oral language ability | | Literacy skills | |
|---|---|---|---|---|---|
| Native English speakers<br>*English is the first language.* | Kindergarten | L1<br>Yes | L2<br>Not common | L1<br>Dependent upon socioeconomic familial situation | L2<br>Not common |
| Non-native English speakers, short-term residents/migrants<br>*Spanish, Quechan, etc. may be the first language. English is the second language in this example.* | Any | L1<br>Yes | L2<br>Typically no language or very low proficiency | L1<br>Dependent upon past schooling | L2<br>Typically no language or very low proficiency |

Note: L1 = first language; L2 = second language

Grades 3, 7 and 11 who enter the schools at any time during the academic year (Table 10.2).

Finally, there are recent immigrants who enter the US as refugees or in large waves of new immigrants. Currently, due to the wars in Iraq and Afghanistan, the public schools are experiencing an increase in native speakers of Arabic and Afghani languages, Pashto and Dari (among other languages). Another new group of immigrants is the Karen from the border of Myanmar and Thailand who are political refugees. Although Somalis have been immigrating for nearly 20 years now, new families continue to arrive in Minnesota, Ohio and Maine.

The families immigrate to the new community together and are sponsored by families and organisations, such as churches. Since families immigrate together, there will be various generations in the family. Because of the difficult circumstances that nuclear families can encounter, extended families are the usual pattern. Children will range in school ages and will enter the K-12 at differing grades, placed initially by age (Table 10.3).

The age of the learner, their background schooling, their first language oral and literacy abilities, their second language (i.e. English) oral and literacy abilities and exposure, as well as their time within the community are significant variables that should strongly influence language programme models and design.

# K-12 Language Support and Delivery Programmes

Over years of trial and practice, educators have developed several different language support and delivery programmes to serve the various EL populations. These programmes are all immersion programmes in that the learners are immersed in English with or without first language support. Some of the programmes, though, are dual

**Table 10.3** Comparison of oral and literacy abilities of recent immigrant or refugee, non-native English speakers entering schools

| | Kindergarten | Oral language ability | | Literacy skills | |
|---|---|---|---|---|---|
| Native English speakers *English is the first language.* | Kindergarten | L1 Yes | L2 Not common | L1 Dependent upon socioeco-nomic familial situation | L2 Not common |
| Non-native English speakers, recent immigrant or refugee *Arabic, Somali, Afghani languages, Karen, etc. may be the first language. English is the second language in this example.* | Any | L1 Yes | L2 Typically no language or very low proficiency | L1 Dependent upon past schooling | L2 Typically no language or very low proficiency |

Note: L1 = first language; L2 = second language

language immersion, so learners are immersed in English and their native language to varying degrees.

The goal of this discussion is to briefly describe the programmes implemented for differing populations so as to compare them with the content-based instructional models previously discussed. It is not to present detailed implementation plans for each of these programmes. One important concept to note is that the term *ESL programme* describes an eclectic array of programmatic variations (Figure 10.1).

## English Language Development (ELD)/ESL programs

English language development programmes are designed for learners in the K-12 who are residents, migrants or recent immigrants to help them develop oral and written language abilities in order to later transition into grade-level academic classes.

- English Language Development/ESL programs
- Newcomer intensive preparation programs
- Sheltered content programs
- Full inclusion (sink or swim; dual licensed/trained content teachers)
- Push-in programs
- Pull-out programs
- Bilingual education programs

**Figure 10.1** English language programme types

These are the courses commonly described as ESL, but not all ESL programmes are only language skills focused. An analogy to exemplify this is that all kangaroos are animals, but not all animals are kangaroos. Focusing only on language, study skills, language learning strategies and some basic language arts, these classes are intended as a short-duration intensive immersion. Learners may or may not have the support of ESL classes for longer than 1–2 years, depending on the state. Little or no grade-level academic content is included in English language development or traditional ESL programmes. For more on these programmes, see Chapter 6 on the Specially Designed Academic Instruction in English (SDAIE) model or the work of Celce-Murcia (2001), Larsen-Freeman (2000) and Brown (2007b).

## Newcomer intensive preparation programmes

English language and development style ESL programmes compare closely to newcomer intensive preparation programmes and/or transitional programmes. Newcomer programmes are commonly found in locations such as Texas with high numbers of newcomers arriving at any time during the academic year at any grade level. Newcomer programmes are intended to provide intensive linguistic (oral and written) skill development for a short duration, less than 1 year, so that students may quickly join general education classes. Once the learners enter the general education courses, other programmes may support their language acquisition. Like the English language development style ESL programmes, very little academic content is taught in these intensive newcomer programmes. For more information on newcomer programmes, see the work of Short and Boyson (2003).

## Sheltered content programmes

Sheltered content programmes, such as those advocated in the Sheltered Instruction Observation Protocol (SIOP) model, also represent differing implementation practices. Sheltered content programmes, for the purposes of this discussion, are programmes for language learners to support both their academic and language development. These programmes do not comingle language learners with native English speakers in general education classes. Mirroring native speaker's academic courses, sheltered content programmes typically offer an assortment of content courses at grade level in core content areas (i.e. math, science, social studies and English language arts) for non-native English speakers only and balance the dual learning objectives of content and language (Figure 10.2).

An ESL teacher with content area licensure or a content-teacher with ESL licensure may teach courses in sheltered content programmes or they may be co-taught. General educators without ESL licensure or preparation would be unprepared to enact a sheltered content course unique to ELs. For more information on sheltered content programmes, see Chapters 4 and 7 and the work of Echevarria (2012) and Echevarria and Graves (2003, 2011).

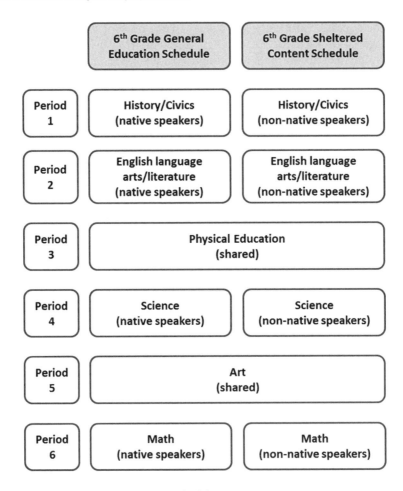

**Figure 10.2** Example of sheltered content schedule

## Full inclusion

The next programme type is full inclusion, which also has various subtypes. Full inclusion is when the EL is in the general education classroom for the majority of the day. The subtypes can be delineated by the amount of support the ELs receive while in the general education class. The first subtype is called 'sink or swim'. This full inclusion type offers no support for the ELs' language acquisition or development and/or academic achievement; no modification of the curriculum, lesson delivery, materials or assessment on the part of the teacher or the paraprofessional/bilingual aide to overcome the language barrier. Additionally, no in-class or outside of class support is provided by an ESL teacher. This type of full inclusion programme is illegal in US public schools according to the *Lau vs. Nichols* (1974) case. Although in some small, rural districts this programme is enacted daily.

The next subtype of full inclusion programmes is EL inclusion. Full EL inclusion is when the learners are placed in general education classes for the majority of the day, but they receive some orchestrated, coordinated form of language learning support. The types of supports that are most effective are when the general education teacher is prepared through formal teacher licensure to make curricular, linguistic, delivery and assessment modifications for ELs or when a general educator and ESL educator co-teach a class so that they can make collaborative curricular, linguistic, delivery and assessment modifications.

Less-effective supports in full inclusion programmes are the support of a bilingual paraprofessional or an ESL teacher who do not co-teach; these supports are less effective than the previous supports, because they are off the cuff, without material supports, simultaneous to the instruction of the teacher and stigmatising for ELs, among other issues. Also, bilingual paraprofessionals and ESL-licensed educators are not synonymous; there is a vast difference in preparation.

## Push-in programme

If this version of full inclusion is implemented so that the ESL teacher follows the ELs into their classes, it is also known as a push-in programme. The ESL teacher is 'pushed into' the general education class to support the EL as opposed to offering a separate ESL or sheltered content course. The push-in programme has its inherent weaknesses, some of which were mentioned earlier, and also many challenges in implementation. Teachers need to be cooperative, mutually respectful and knowledgeable about each other's roles. Depending on the number of ELs in the school, the programme may or may not be suitable. For example, does the ESL teacher need to be in two or more classes at the same time? For information on ESL teachers' perspectives on push-in and pull-out programme formats, see Reynolds *et al.* (2012).

## Pull-out programmes

ESL pull-out programmes are another variation on programme design. The ESL teacher withdraws the EL(s) from a specified course (which course is an area of debate) for one-on-one instruction or tutorial. For example, the learner may be taken out of English language arts/literature for appropriate language development because she/he may not find the content presented for native speakers in the general education class applicable or helpful. The pull-out programme sessions are personalised, but can be enacted with small groups of learners learning the same information as well. Typical subjects are English vocabulary sets, grammar and language skills development (i.e. reading strategies and writing). Pull-out sessions are most effective when the communication and coordination between the general educator and the ESL teacher are clear and timely. The general educator can communicate the learner(s)' area(s) of need and upcoming subject matter and the ESL teacher can assist the learners by providing explanations and practice in areas of need and preview upcoming subject matter vocabulary and concepts. This preview of upcoming subject matter (i.e. *pre-teaching*) is crucial so that learners can understand the new information when it is presented to them; it reduces the amount of information that they miss when the general education class discusses the concept. However, in reality, the communication and coordination between general and ESL educators are not always optimal, so the ESL teacher is not provided with information about the specific learners' linguistic or academic challenges when they come to sessions or about the topic(s) being discussed currently or in the future. Therefore, these sessions frequently develop into tutorial sessions.

Tutorial sessions are a disservice to ELs because (1) they provide instruction the learners missed in the general education class after the students really needed to understand it. They were not able to participate fully in the general education classes without the knowledge, thus they are not prepared linguistically to build on the information being presented. (2) The ELs, learning the information in tutorial fashion, only learn it piecemeal. It is usually based on what is available in the homework and not on all the information presented in the classes. The ESL teacher is not given adequate notice then to prepare a lesson on the topic and therefore respond in a reactive manner to the need. (3) Tutorial sessions tend to only prepare students for the homework and assessments and not cover the concepts in a deeper manner. (4) Tutorial sessions underutilise the knowledge and resources of the ESL teacher.

## Bilingual education programmes

The final type of programme to define is bilingual education. Bilingual education programmes are programmes that seek to teach learners two languages by supporting their orality and advancing their first language literacy while simultaneously developing second language orality and literacy. These programmes are identified in two ways: one-way bilingual programmes serving only non-native speakers of English and two-way bilingual programmes serving native and non-native English speakers.

In one-way bilingual programmes, the non-native English speakers have more instruction in their first language and less in the second language at the beginning. The language of instruction is then shifted over time, so at the end of their programme more instruction is in the second language and less is in the first. Examples of one-way bilingual programmes are:

- native Spanish speakers learning English;
- native Albanian speakers learning English;
- native Chinese speakers learning English.

Native Spanish Speakers                    learning English bilingually

The focus of one-way programmes is to support the first language while acquiring the second.

Two-way bilingual programmes focus on two linguistically distinct groups of learners each acquiring the other language while supporting the first language. Examples of two-way bilingual programmes are:

- native Spanish speakers learning English while native English speakers are learning Spanish;
- native French speakers learning English while native English speakers are learning French.

Native Spanish Speakers    Spanish → ← English    Native English Speakers

Each type of bilingual programme also has to decide whether to maintain the first language orality and literacy. Two decisions can be made, which are called maintenance or transition programmes. Maintenance bilingual programmes have a goal of maintaining the first language orality and literacy, so that learners are fully bilingual in orality and literacy at the end of the programme. This is also considered additive bilingualism because the end goal builds both languages and respects the first language.

**Maintenance**

One-way: Spanish to English

| | English |
|---|---|
| 30 | |
| 70 | Spanish |

**Maintenance**

• Two-way: Spanish to English and Vice Versa

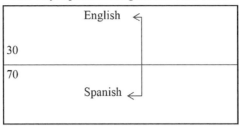

Transitional bilingual programmes emphasise support from the first language during the acquisition of the second language. In other words, using the first language as a support system during the acquisition of the second language; but not necessarily maintaining the first language. This is also considered subtractive bilingualism, because the end goal lessens the first language.

**Transitional**

One-way: Spanish to English

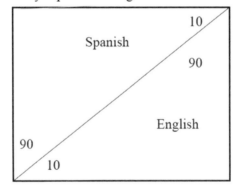

**Transitional**

Two-way: Spanish to English and Vice Versa

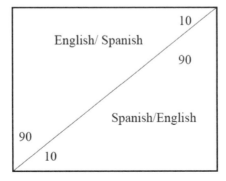

When making decisions about programme design in light of the content-based instructional model, stakeholders need to evaluate which of these programme designs best meet the goals of the school and community, are appropriate for the specific learner population(s) and are feasible based on practical implementation considerations (see the next section for more on practical implementation).

Which programme type is most appropriate for which type of learner? Table 10.4 provides some comparisons between the programme types and learner groupings.

## Differing Variables Result in Differing Models

Each content-based instructional model discussed in Chapters 4–9 presents various approaches to the same challenge: teaching academic content and academic language to a widely differing group of language learners. Context and population have driven many of the models and adaptations. For example, Calderon's ExCELL model

**Table 10.4** Programme types appropriate for various populations

| Programme type | Population | | |
| --- | --- | --- | --- |
|  | Residents/learners born here | Migrants | Refugees/immigrants |
| English language development/ESL instruction | Not particularly appropriate | Appropriate dependent upon learners' needs | Appropriate |
| Newcomer | Not particularly appropriate | Appropriate | Appropriate |
| Sheltered content | Appropriate dependent upon learners' needs | Appropriate dependent upon learners' needs | Appropriate dependent upon learners' needs |
| Full inclusion: sink or swim | Not appropriate under any circumstances | Not appropriate under any circumstances | Not appropriate under any circumstances |
| Full inclusion: co-teaching | Appropriate dependent upon learners' needs | Possibly appropriate dependent upon learners' needs | Not particularly appropriate |
| Push-in | Appropriate dependent upon learners' needs | Possibly appropriate dependent upon learners' needs | Not particularly appropriate |
| Pull-out | Possibly appropriate dependent upon learners' needs | Insufficient support provided; not particularly appropriate | Insufficient support provided; not particularly appropriate |
| Bilingual education: one-way | Appropriate dependent upon learners' needs | Appropriate | Appropriate |
| Bilingual education: two-way | Appropriate dependent upon learners' needs and interests | Appropriate | Appropriate |

takes as its starting point learners who have been in the second language context for many years and who have oral, social language abilities in the second language, meaning they have high oral proficiency in the second language. This population needs academic language and literacy development. This population and context differ from that of the creators of the Center for Research on Education, Diversity & Excellence (CREDE) standards and the SIOP model, which was primarily derived from the context of California. In that context, the learners could be recent immigrants or long-term residents, but they do not have high proficiency in the oral, social language.

Every state has laws pertinent to the delivery of instruction for ELs. These laws originate with the state legislature and departments of public instruction. The departments of public instruction are one oversight entity that ensures some degree of compliance by the local school districts. However, they are not the only body that oversees the quality and equality of school district policies and instructional design/testing. The federal ministries or departments of education, or in the US, the Office of Education and the Office of Civil Rights (OCR), are involved in guideline development and compliance of federal educational laws and policies.

## US Federal Laws Pertinent to ELs

- Civil Rights Act (1964), Title IV pertains to all K-12 learners. It states that a person cannot be discriminated against, omitted from or deprived of any services of any governmentally funded programme based on race, colour or national origin. If a programme, school or otherwise receives any federal funding, they are subject to this law, compliance of which is overseen by the US OCR. The OCR regularly conducts audits of programmes receiving funding, based on public complaints, reported data and/or systematic screening.
- Office of Civil Rights (OCR), Memorandum (1970). The 1970 OCR Memorandum outlined several key guidelines for public schools in regard to the education of ELs.
  - Schools have an obligation to take action to surmount language barriers that hinder students' attainment of an equal education. This guideline holds schools accountable for teaching ELs and providing comprehensible educational information. Often in rural districts, this guideline is simply not known or met.
  - A student with *limited English proficient* (LEP[1]) status is not learning disabled and may not be denied rights to college preparatory classes. It is no longer used in schools, but is present in historical, legal documents. This rule means that educators may not place an EL into a special education programme based simply upon low English proficiency skills. See Chapter 6 on Response to Intervention (RtI) for more information.
  - ELLs must not be kept in a dead-end programme when they are ready for the general education classroom. As recently as the 1990s, ESL programmes failed

*(Continued)*

to serve learners when they did not adequately assess academic and linguistic readiness and appropriately transition learners into the general education classes. The results were that many learners were denied grade-level academic content, which stifled their learning and life possibilities.

- ELs' parents must have the same access to public school information that is available to all parents, if necessary, in their native language. This rule is important as it opens communication between the schools and the ELs' parents. In implementation, it is quite challenging for schools if the parents' English proficiency level is low, they speak a less commonly taught language (i.e. Hmong, Korean, Punjab, Karen, Somali or Albanian) and/or they are not literate in their native language. Schools are responsible for communicating with parents in a manner they can comprehend, so schools frequently must find translators of less commonly taught languages and translate documents. When the parent or guardian is not literate in their first language, which is not as uncommon as may be expected, phone calls from bilingual paraprofessionals to the home are required until a connection is made.

- US Supreme Court ruling in the case of *Lau et al. vs. Nichols et al./Lau vs. San Francisco Unified School District* (1974). This influential court ruling resulted from a lawsuit initiated by Chinese parents in San Francisco who asserted that their child was excluded from an equal education because language barriers were not being overcome by schools and educators. The Supreme Court decision indicated that (1) an identical education does not mean an equal education. An equal education might not be achieved through the use of the same facilities, materials, educators or curriculum if the language barrier is not overcome. (2) Any learner who does not understand the language of instruction (i.e. English) is excluded from any meaningful learning. This ruling holds schools and educators responsible to actively overcome language barriers and adapt information and delivery so that it is comprehensible to ELs.

- The Lau Remedies (1975) (Cardenas, 1976). In response to the *Lau vs. Nichols* Supreme Court ruling, the US Department of Health, Education and Welfare developed guidelines for school districts, which the OCR oversees. Schools must

(a) Identify and evaluate students' English language skills.
(b) Determine appropriate instructional strategies.
(c) Decide when ELs are ready for general education classes.
(d) Determine licensure standards for teachers working with ELs.

In spite of these guidelines, wiggle room remained, which left gaps in the system through which ELs fell. For example, what are appropriate instructional strategies? What about ELs' academic knowledge and language assessment?

*(Continued)*

- Castañada vs. Pickard (1981) and the OCR guidelines. This court ruling offered some practical insight for schools on 'appropriate instructional methodology' by outlining what constitutes an acceptable programme, instruction and outcomes for ELs. The ruling indicated that

(1) Programmes must be undergirded by theory that is sanctioned by field experts to appropriately serve ELs or must be deemed a reasonable and valid experimental programme design. Therefore, programmes must be designed and guided by appropriate theories; they cannot be random ideas of what may seem appropriate. This concept of theoretical underpinnings of programme design has subsequently morphed into research-based instruction and programmatic design; programmes must show empirical evidence of their effectiveness to warrant the design choice.

(2) The instructional practice and materials must be appropriate to serve the EL population. Meaning that the ways that students are taught along with the material employed allow learners to learn the academic concepts. There must be an adequate number of educationally prepared educators and paraprofessionals within the programme. This guideline ensures that the educators working with ELs have appropriate training and there are enough ESL specialists to work with the ELs.

(3) Instructional outcomes on assessments must indicate that language barriers are being overcome. This means that learners' performance on standardised tests of academic knowledge must indicate that they are indeed learning information the same as their native-speaking peers.

- No Child Left Behind Act (2001). This US federal law was the congressional reauthorisation of the Elementary and Secondary Education Act (ESEA) (1965), which provided funding allocations and educational guidelines for all pre-K-12 public schools. No Child Left Behind (NCLB) outlined extensive changes and reforms to public educational policy in all areas of programme design, delivery, assessment and teacher preparation. NCLB reformed allocations of funding and programming for ELs by moving them from the Office of Bilingual Education and Minority Languages Affairs (Title VII) to the of Office of English Language Acquisition (Title III: The English Language Acquisition, Language Enhancement, and Academic Achievement). This change represented a considerable shift in policy direction from teaching bilingual education under the Bilingual Education Act (1968) to teaching English only under NCLB (2001).

  In spite of the shift to an English-only policy, some of the language policies improved and clarified the guidance for programme design and implementation in public schools. NCLB held state and local educational agencies, and all educators including general educators, accountable for

*(Continued)*

> (a) ensuring ELs attain English proficiency *and* the same academic standards that all children are expected to meet;
> (b) increasing the English proficiency *and* core academic content knowledge of ELs by requiring charted adequate yearly progress (AYP) through annual content and language assessment of the language learners on standardised tests.
>
> These requirements have resulted in the development of language proficiency testing that has standardised and regularised the assessments of ELs. One outcome of this requirement was the development of World-Class Instructional Design and Assessment (WIDA) assessments. The requirements also prompted states to develop guidelines for the assessment of ELs' academic content knowledge. For example, when would ELs take the state-required academic achievement tests that all other students take? This is a laden issue because the ELs should be assessed in their native languages for their understandings of academic content, but there are myriad challenges to the development of these tests in all the languages of learners that it becomes unwieldy, exorbitantly costly and unrealistic to do so.
>
> One of the extremely punitive aspects of NCLB was the intention to allot funding based on performances on language proficiency and academic achievement assessments. Meaning that schools would receive higher funding if a school performed well and lower funding if it did not. This is another highly disputed aspect of NCLB. Disputes over NCLB have resulted in the inability of Congress to reauthorise the ESEA since 2001, and *flexibility* requests to the US Office of Education by state educational agencies on specifics of NCLB.

## States' Mandates and Federal Law

Guided by federal education laws, each state has laws pertinent to EL instruction, usually referred to as *mandates*, which dictate the state's direction on the instructional model of second language. Depending on the state's political leanings, mandates are colloquially referred to as bilingual education or English only. Notoriously, California's Proposition 227 changed the state mandate there from bilingual education to English only. That meant that instead of using a model that began with first language literacy and moved to second language orality and literacy development over time (i.e. bilingual education), the state taught second language learners in English immersion without support for their native languages (English only). Currently, California is reconsidering this change in second language instruction to move back to a bilingual model; only time will tell if voters will approve of a change back to the bilingual instructional paradigm. This text is not meant to advocate for bilingual education or English only; rather, the purpose is to highlight the relationship between language policy and implementation.

In spite of a state's mandate, there still may be challenges in implementing and enacting one model over another. A good example of this is the State of Wisconsin, where second language learners are supposed to be taught bilingually (i.e. bilingual mandate state). One of the major challenges to the implementation of bilingual programmes in Wisconsin is that the EL population does not speak one shared native language. Spanish speakers are the largest population, but there are also speakers of Hmong, Russian, Arabic, Somali, Quechan and other languages entering the public schools at all grades. Wisconsin is typical of many states with urban areas that have large numbers of ELs and suburban and rural areas with low numbers of ELs; although there are some exceptions, such as Barron, a rural district with a large number of Somalis. In the urban Madison area in the State of Wisconsin, bilingual programmes are well designed and implemented for its large population of language learners. However, Wisconsin is a state with two large urban centres (i.e. Milwaukee and Madison) and the remainder is composed of rural communities punctuated by small towns.

Creating bilingual education programmes for each grade in all academic subjects for each native language is a challenge. Appropriate bilingual academic resources, including textbooks and assessments, would need to be available at each grade level. Coordinating assessments is vital so that information can be employed in placement and regular formative feedback. Scheduling courses, managing transitions from first to second language so that learners are receiving adequate instruction in both languages consistently is the next arduous obstacle. Along with assessments and scheduling, fiscal and human resources allocations present a logistical challenge. Finding enough trained bilingual educators, who have a high enough level of proficiency in both languages and a licensure in the academic subject and bilingual methods, is a colossal task. There are simply not enough academic subject specialists who are licensed and who are highly proficient bilingual speakers of such diverse languages. When rural districts in bilingual mandate states are presented with small numbers of ELs at a grade level, such as k=2, third grade=1 and seventh grade=1, it is not feasible to enact a full-scale bilingual education programme. Therefore, in bilingual mandate states, some learners still need to learn the second language (i.e. English) in English-only immersion programmes.

This description is not intended to disparage bilingual education programmes. The feasibility of programmes as well as the appropriate and fair allocation of human and fiscal resources is an understandably significant concern for districts.

For the states with an English-only mandate, the numbers of teachers prepared to work effectively with ELs is an important variable in programme design. Issues also arise where there are often too few ESL specialists and resource teachers to serve the needs of learners and/or there is a paucity of adequately prepared general educators to implement EL inclusion.

Often, too, district administrators make difficult decisions about programme models and implementation based more on funding allocation (i.e. reduce ESL staff to reduce the operational budget), rather than appropriate education for ELs. Funding is allocated from states and the federal government (in the US context) to support ELs' language acquisition and academic achievement.

Aside from the state mandate, other variables relate to school district and community resources and preparedness. The size and location of a community are considerations in that if a community is a larger urban centre, they would have enough learners to warrant an entire language programme at all grades because they would have a clear need to justify it. The need is determined by the number of learners, not the needs of the ELs based upon their level of proficiency. The number/need for support is one condition upon which state and federal funds are granted to school districts. For instance, there may be more learners at higher levels of proficiency in one district that would receive more money than another district with fewer ELs at lower-proficiency levels.

Larger urban communities are likely to have already welcomed diverse ELs into their schools, developed a model for instructional delivery and hired ESL educators. (It is another discussion whether the number of ESL educators is appropriate in terms of student/teacher ratios and workload.) If a community is smaller and rural without a neighbouring town with more resources, the community is less likely to have an entire EL programme in place and the requisite ESL staff to handle an influx of ELs. In larger communities and school districts, the staffing for EL instruction is composed of general education teachers with varying degrees of preparedness for working with ELs, ESL specialists and ESL resource teachers. In smaller communities, there may be no ESL specialists or ESL resource teachers on the faculty. The general educators also have varying degrees of preparedness. Often, the teacher who is the most concerned about the academic success of the ELs is the individual who by default becomes an ESL teacher and advocate.

Prior to arriving at a decision about programme design/model, the numbers of ELs by grade, proficiency level(s), competencies and needs should be balanced in light of the number of highly qualified teachers and their teacher preparation. One major concern is that most general educators only have cursory preparation to work with ELs. (See the section 'Infrastructure Challenges' at the end of the chapter).

A school district with ELs would need to consider the variables of the distinctive EL population when considering which content-based instruction (CBI)/EL inclusion model(s) and programme types to adopt or adapt. Many of the variables relate specifically to the particular learners: first language(s), ages, EL population size, grades, background schooling, home school locations, proficiency level(s), age on arrival and time of arrival during the year (Figure 10.3). For example, where are their home schools (e.g. are they mainly in one school or are they spread out in several different schools)? Are there a sufficient number of language learners at a given grade to warrant a full ESL programme? If not, then how will the school meet their needs in order to serve their educational rights and comply with federal laws? Will learners be bussed? Would ESL specialists float between schools?

If there are enough ELs at a given school location, what is the learners' background schooling like generally? What is the native language(s) of the learners? How long have

```
┌─────────────────────────────────────────────────────────────────────────┐
│ District EL Information Questionnaire                                      │
│                                                                           │
│ 1.  How many ELs are in the district?                                     │
│ 2.  How many different L1s are spoken and which languages do ELs speak?    │
│ 3.  How many ELs are there in each school?                                │
│ 4.  What grades are they in?                                              │
│ 5.  What are their English proficiency level(s)?                          │
│ 6.  What is their educational background/prior academic experience? Do they have │
│     interrupted learning?                                                  │
│ 7.  Were the ELs born in this area/when did the learner(s) arrive?         │
└─────────────────────────────────────────────────────────────────────────┘
```

**Figure 10.3** EL information questionnaire for districts

they been in the immersion culture? What is their first language orality and literacy? What is their second language proficiency in orality and literacy? What are their oral and written proficiency levels in social language and academic language? The answers to all of these questions would greatly impact the type of model chosen. Table 10.5 is a questionnaire to help amass information necessary to identify the appropriate CBI/EL inclusion model and programme type.

The answers to these demographic questions would help steer districts to adopt/adapt the best model for their learners needs and to utilise human and fiscal resources the best ways possible. Often, in practice, school districts' decision-making is ad hoc and reactive, not based on planning, data and appropriate programme designs.

## CBI/EL Inclusion Model Comparison

From the deconstruction of each CBI model presented in the previous chapters, there is no obviously perfect model for EL inclusion. Each model has strengths and

**Table 10.5** Questions about the EL population and their skills

| | First language (L1) | | Second language (L2) | |
|---|---|---|---|---|
| What percentage of the English learners have strong educational/academic background in...? | _____ % Yes | _____% No | _____% Yes | _____% No |
| What percentage of the English learners have strong oral language in...? | Social language: _____% Yes _____% No | Academic language: _____ % Yes _____% No | Social language: _____ % Yes _____% No | Academic language: _____% Yes _____% No |
| What percentage of the English learners have strong literacy skills in...? | Social language: _____% Yes _____% No | Academic language: _____% Yes _____% No | Social language: _____% Yes _____% No | Academic language: _____% Yes _____% No |

weaknesses that must be taken into consideration when educators are determining which one is optimal for their unique context. No matter which model a school or district were to choose, the drawbacks of the model should be taken into consideration and remedied as much as possible in its implementation.

Table 10.6 lists each model's major strengths and weaknesses as well as suggestions for optimal context implementation. This is only a guide to aid educators to consider if this CBI model is appropriate for the context.

The 'winner' or best CBI/EL inclusion model is the one that best fits the needs of the learners and the variables of the context. All CBI/EL inclusion models have flaws that must be addressed.

The goals of any programme should be to teach the ELs so that they are growing in English language proficiency (first language literacy depending upon the state) and grade-level academics, which should be revealed in their AYP in accordance with NCLB (2001). All programmatic decisions, including which CBI/EL inclusion model, should be weighed against this goal and the contextual variables noted earlier. Aside from the law and the fundamental moral/ethical concerns for educating all learners, there are community considerations as well. When programmatic decisions are made in favour of preparing ELs well, the community has fewer high school dropouts, for example.

Time and talent are two vital variables in the equation. The learners must have a sufficient amount of time to acquire their second language. First, they need enough years to acquire social and academic language (Cummins, 1979, 1980a, 1980b, 1992, 1996), but they also need enough time in classes. Sufficient contact time must be made available to the learners with educators who are prepared to make content knowledge comprehensible to the learners. This is one of the greatest drawbacks of the pull-out programme type; there is simply not enough time for the learners to be exposed to and learn all they need to acquire the second language. The talent part of the equation refers to the educators who are prepared to make content accessible and comprehensible to the ELs. **Without a sufficient amount of contact time and prepared talent (i.e. educators), no model or programme will be effective.**

Visionary and collaborative leadership is one key to the development, reception and implementation of EL programming. School districts facing a new influx of ELs are positioned to make thoughtful, comprehensive and appropriate programmatic choices. Long-established programmes should engage in regular, systematic programme evaluation to ensure that the needs of ELs are being appropriately met, particularly as changes to the EL population, teacher preparation, other contextual variables and language policies occur.

While this is not the place to discuss all the technical details of programme evaluation, Table 10.7 outlines the steps to initiate a programme evaluation. For more information on programme evaluation, see Patton (2008) and Lynch (1996).

**Table 10.6** Suggestions for CBI/EL inclusion models and programme types according to context

| CBI model | Pros | Cons | Language setting (bilingual education, English-only, foreign language) | Congruent with programme types | Context variables | | | |
|---|---|---|---|---|---|---|---|---|
| | | | | | No. of ELs | No. of languages | Community size and location (urban/ suburban/ rural) | No. of ESL faculty; No. of bilingual paraprofes- sionals; No. of ESL licensed general educators |
| SIOP | Research based; standardised tools useful to teachers unfamiliar with CBI. | Too much time in plan- ning; does not include recent field developments; strategies are too general; knowledge of language needed by gen- eral educators. | English-only | Sheltered content Full inclusion Co-teaching Push-in | High per- centage of population are ELs | Many diverse languages | Urban and/or suburban | General educa- tors with ESL training; ESL faculty to serve as resource teachers; bilingual paras to assist in the general educa- tion classroom. |
| CALLA | Practical, educator- friendly guidelines and tools for implementa- tion; discourse analysis for educators. | Lacks the observa- tion proto- col of SIOP; long lesson preparation; knowledge of language needed by gen- eral educators. | English-only | Sheltered content Full inclusion Co-teaching Push-in | Low–high percentage of popula- tion are ELs | Many diverse lan- guages or bilingual content delivery | Urban, suburban or rural | Co-teaching; ESL specialists. |

The 'Winner': Which Model Should Be Chosen?   259

| | | | | | | | | |
|---|---|---|---|---|---|---|---|---|
| RtI | Adaptations are expected by general educators to meet the linguistic needs of ELs; additional, specialist support provided; rapid response. | Not developed for ELs; places ELs automatically into Tier 2 or 3; tendency to view second language acquisition as a deficit; no language-specific instructional strategies. | English-only | ELD/ESL instruction Full inclusion Co-teaching Pull-out | Low–high percentage of population are ELs | Many diverse languages | Urban, suburban or rural | General educators with ESL training; ESL faculty to serve Tiers 2 and 3; bilingual paras to assist in the general education classroom. |
| SDAIE | Specific and practical instructional strategies; responsive to the needs of the learner population; assessment is a strong component. | Since it is a more flexible design than other models, it is harder to validate; knowledge of language needed by general educators. | English-only or bilingual education | Sheltered content ELD/ESL instruction Newcomer Full inclusion Co-teaching Push-in | Low–high percentage of population are ELs | Many diverse languages | Urban, suburban or rural | General educators with ESL training; ESL specialists; bilingual paras to assist in the general education classroom. |
| CREDE | Solid research base and foundation for other models that developed later. | Too vague and open-ended; not many instructional and practical specifics; knowledge of language needed by general educators. | English-only or bilingual education | All programme types except ELD/ESL instruction and pull-out | Moderate–high percentage of population are ELs | Many diverse languages | Urban or suburban | General educators with ESL training; ESL faculty; bilingual paras to assist in the general education classroom. |

(Continued)

**Table 10.6** (Continued)

| | | | | | | |
|---|---|---|---|---|---|---|
| ExC-ELL | Outstanding integration of literacy instruction for second language learners. | The focus on literacy work is not applicable for all EL populations; knowledge of language needed by general educators. | English-only or bilingual education | All programme types except sheltered content, ELD/ESL instruction and newcomer | Moderate–high percentage of population are ELs | Best with one dominant second language group | Urban | ESL specialists; bilingual paras to assist in the general education classroom. |
| CLiL | Integration of content and language for foreign language instruction. | Too open-ended and not well defined in terms of strategies; knowledge of language needed by general educators. | Foreign language | Possibly bilingual education two-way | Moderate–high percentage of population are target language learners | Many diverse language learners | Urban or suburban | Licensed foreign language specialists. |
| CoBaLLT | Integration of content, language and technology for foreign language instruction. | Multiple proficiency levels are not addressed differently; the content areas may not be adequately or fully covered; knowledge of language needed by general educators. | Foreign language | Possibly bilingual education two-way | Moderate–high percentage of population are target language learners | Many diverse language learners | Urban or suburban | Licensed foreign language specialists. |

**Table 10.7** Steps to evaluate programmes

| Step | Examples |
| --- | --- |
| (1) Developing research questions to guide programme evaluation and inquiry | • How are ELs performing on the content and language learning? <br> • Do ELs have adequate contact time with sufficiently prepared educators? |
| (2) Gathering data on programme effectiveness | • Test scores, surveys of graduates, focus groups with groups of learners, teachers and/or parents, etc. |
| (3) Analysing effectiveness | • Quantitative analysis with statistical measures for certain types of data. <br> • Qualitative analysis for interviews and focus group data. |
| (4) Reporting evaluation outcomes to stakeholders | • Report(s) generated and discussed with all stakeholders (e.g. parents, teachers, administrators, boards of education, etc.). |
| (5) Developing an action plan for programme improvement | • Model and/or programme enhancement, reform or reorganisation. <br> • Continuing with the current model and programme. |

# Infrastructure Challenges: Issues of Pre-Service and In-Service Teacher Preparedness

A long-standing void exists in teacher education programmes of preparation for general educators to understand second language acquisition, learners' background cultures, the influences of culture on the classroom and best practices in EL inclusion (Menz, 2009; Sox, 2011). The outcome of the void is that ESL specialists and general educators have far fewer shared understandings than they should.

> Because of this schism [between general educators and ESL specialists] and the status quo educational structures that continue related to it, many EL students fare less well at school than other student populations. Remedying this schism requires sustained, transformative, professional development that supports the reimagination of how schools should support ELs. This development must help all teachers develop EL-responsive pedagogical knowledge; it must compel educational administrators and teachers to see ELs and former ELs as collective responsibilities; and it must improve program alignment between special language support services and the mainstream that ELs transition into. (Hamann & Reeves, 2013: 82)

Teacher preparation in EL inclusive instruction efforts dates back to the early 1990s' efforts in high-incidence states, such as Florida, California, Massachusetts and Arizona. With the high numbers of ELs in pre-service teachers' future classrooms it became necessary to include some background in ESL instruction.

The requirements ranged by state and the degree of professional engagement with ELs. For example, in Florida educators were mandated by the Florida Consent Decree (1990). Since then, those who teach language arts to ELs must take 300 hours of ESL preparation; whereas non-language arts teachers are required to take 60 hours to prepare them to work with ELs (Harper & Platt, 1998; The School District of Osceola County Florida, 2007). In Massachusetts, educators are required to have 10 hours of preparation to work with ELs and 20–25 hours for literacy teaching for ELs (Adams & Jones, 2006). A formidable need nonetheless subsists for the preparation of new educators in university teacher education programmes (i.e. pre-service educators) and of experienced educators who are already engaged in teaching K-12 (i.e. in-service educators).

## Overview of Pre-Service Preparation and Challenges

The US Federal Department of Education and many US states have high expectations for ELs' academic performance as ELs are included in schools' grades of effectiveness under NCLB (2001). Yet, there is no federal requirement for pre-service preparation for EL inclusion and only 'gateway' states, such as Florida and California, have instituted requirements. Pre-service teacher preparation has been cited as the reason teachers are unprepared to work effectively with ELs in their general education courses. Téllez (2005: 1) describes Tedick and Walker's (1994) stance, '...preservice teacher education is largely to blame for this condition. In their view, teacher education has overlooked the importance of validating home culture and students' first language. This oversight encourages beginning teachers to view language as an object rather than a complex process'.

Since there is no US federal standard for teacher preparation to work with ELs, various US states have approached pre-service teacher preparation for EL inclusion differently. The types of responses were studied by Arens *et al.* (2008), who conducted a comprehensive research study on teacher preparation for EL inclusion by describing 14 university-level, pre-service teacher programmes and the means through which these programmes were equipping general educators to include ELs in their future classes. The researchers focused on the largest teacher education programmes of universities from seven central states: Colorado, Kansas, Missouri, Nebraska, North and South Dakota and Wyoming. Each of these universities had training programmes for elementary and secondary teachers, so 14 programmes from these universities were analysed. They found that all 14 programmes included *embedded* or *infused* (i.e. two terms used to indicate that competencies necessary to the specific field have been added to other courses where congruent) multicultural education and diversity competencies into courses and 7 out of the 14 had an additional three-credit hour course in multicultural education and diversity.

Teaching English to speakers of other languages (TESOL) educators recognise a distinction between multicultural education and diversity training to address dispositional competencies versus the knowledge, performance and dispositional preparation necessary to successfully include ELs into the general education class (Menz, 2009; Sox 2011; Xu, 2011). Tellez and Waxman (2006) noted that most professional teaching associations, and as a consequence schools of education, have avoided adding course-work on EL inclusion. 'Only 20% of traditional teacher education programs have a stand-alone course focused on ELs' (Wilde, 2010: 11). Schools of education have instead attempted to bridge this preparation gap by emphasising teacher preparation to work in culturally diverse classrooms, but not linguistically diverse classrooms.

Next, Arens *et al.* (2008) considered EL-specific preparation in these 14 pro-grammes (see Figure 10.4). Four out of the 14 programmes (at two universities out of the seven) had embedded EL competencies included in their teacher preparation. Expressing the view of many TESOL teacher educators, Arens *et al.* (2008: 6) explain, '...incorporating information on EL-specific approaches into existing courses may not provide sufficient exposure to the necessary information'. Only 1 out of the 14 pro-grammes had a three-credit hour course designated for EL teacher preparation, the elementary programme at Kansas State University.

Of the number of credit hours for licensure at these institutions, 120 is the low-est and 130 is the highest. The hours of coursework designated for EL instruction, 3 hours at only one institution, can be compared to the state averages of teachers working with ELs: Colorado 60%, Kansas 30%, Missouri 28%, Nebraska 33%, North Dakota 22%, South Dakota 18% and Wyoming 28% (Arens *et al.*, 2008). The disparity is astonishing.

In another wide-reaching research study investigating the preparation of pre-service educators in Ohio, Menz (2009) surveyed 272 pre-service educators and interviewed 10 pre-service and 12 in-service educators in 29 teacher education programmes in Ohio to determine the approaches and quality of teacher preparation efforts for EL inclusion. The only approaches to pre-service preparation reported were coursework; 25% of respondents had no coursework and 31% had taken one course. Of the programmes that had coursework, one or two courses were required in multicultural and diversity education, not EL inclusion. The majority of pre-service participants reported that diversity and multicultural courses were unhelpful in their work with ELs; 71% had no second language acquisition, TESOL methodology, immigrant experience or linguistics courses.

Menz (2009) also found that pre-service educators felt starkly unprepared to work effectively with ELs in their general education courses. One participant illumi-nated this perspective, 'At my university, we have a course that is called "Exceptional Learning" which covers everything from students with special needs to ESL/ELL learners. We learned a little bit about the many needs of diverse learners, but I don't feel that we learned a lot about any of them, or at least enough to feel sufficiently prepared' (Menz, 2009: 117).

In low-incidence states, such as Wisconsin, there is no state course requirement or expectation of pre-service teacher preparation to work with ELs; even though there were 52,100 ELs in 2010 (WI Department of Public Instruction, 2011). The numbers of ELs in the State of Wisconsin have continued to increase dramatically

| State | Largest teacher prep program | Level | Number of credit hours required | ELL-specific course(s) required? (yes = √ + number of hours) | ELL information embedded in courses? (yes = √) | MC/diversity course required? | MC/diversity embedded in courses? (yes = √) |
|---|---|---|---|---|---|---|---|
| CO | University of Northern Colorado | Elem | 126 | | √ | | √ |
| | | Sec | 120 | | √ | | √ |
| KS | Kansas State University | Elem | 125 | √ 3 hours | | √ 3 hours | √ |
| | | Sec | 126 | | | | √ |
| MO | University of Missouri Columbia | Elem | 120 | | | | √ |
| | | Sec | 120 | | | | √ |
| NE | University of Nebraska at Lincoln | Elem | 125 | | | √ 3 hours of coursework and 1 hour of student teaching * 3 hours | √ |
| | | Sec | 125 | | | √ 3 hours of coursework and 1 hour of student teaching | √ |
| ND | University of North Dakota | Elem | 125 | | √ | √ 3 hours | √ |
| | | Sec | 125 | | √ | √ 3 hours | √ |
| SD | South Dakota State University | Elem | | | | √ 3 hours | √ |
| | | Sec | | | | | √ |
| WY | University of Wyoming | Elem | 130 | | | √ 3 hours | |
| | | Sec | 120 | | | | |

**Figure 10.4** Teacher preparation programme requirements for general educators in seven central states
*Source*: Arens *et al.*, 2008: 10, reproduced with permission from Mid-continent Research for Education and Learning (McREL)

since the 1980s. Since 2000, the number of ELs has risen from 32,588 to 52,100 in 2010. The number of Wisconsin school districts reporting at least one LEP student enrolled grew to 85% and doubled from 184 in 2000 to 361 in 2010 (WI Department of Public Instruction, 2011) and yet there is no concerted effort at the state level to properly equip general education teachers to work effectively with ELs.

Pre-service educators minimally need concerted preparation in EL inclusion, language analysis, cultural diversity/sensitivity, second language acquisition, content-based ESL instruction and language assessment.

# 'Essential' Content for Inclusive Education

If programmes can find the freedom within the curriculum, then questions arise as to what topics in the field of ESL to include. Because the knowledge, performance and dispositions necessary span separate TESOL courses (e.g. second language acquisition, TESOL methods, assessment), it is not easy to identify just one class to include.

> The question facing decision makers will undoubtedly be what is *absolutely essential* for mainstream teachers to know and be able to do to create instructional conditions in which ELs can productively engage in key practices called for by the common standards. (Bunch, 2013: 329)

Quality-minded faculty who emphasize quality preparation would avoid choosing only one of these courses to substitute for all the knowledge, performance and dispositions needed by general educators. What is essential information for general educators in EL inclusion? This question has resulted in much debate in the field (Cajkler & Hall, 2009; de Jong & Harper, 2005; Dewe, 2011; Lucas & Villegas, 2010, 2011, 2013; McGraner & Saenz, 2009; Milk *et al.*, 1992; Téllez, 2005). For instance, Bunch (2013) lists an essential body of knowledge that general educators need to be prepared to include ELs.

(1) Knowledge of
   - Diversity of the EL population.
   - Educational linguistics.
     - Discourse patterns and language structures.
     - Functional linguistics.
     - Linguistic features of texts.
   - Participant structures.
   - Second language literacy development.

(2) Performance of
   - Genre-based pedagogies.
   - Critical language awareness.
   - Apprenticing ELs into academic practices.
   - Integrating language and context.
   - Developing interactive classrooms.
   - Scaffolding ELs language development and academic success.

To this list, Milk *et al.* (1992) add 'dispositional' competencies:

- Skill to build on learners' funds of knowledge.
- Skill and willingness to develop and include learners in instructional dialogue.
- Acceptance of differing perspectives than those of the teacher.

While Lucas and Villegas' (2011) article, A Framework for Preparing Linguistically Responsive Teachers, added to the orientations and knowledge competencies listed in Milk *et al.*'s work (1992).

Orientations and Knowledge

1. Orientations of Linguistically Responsive Teachers
2. Sociolinguistic consciousness:
    a. Understanding of the connection between language, culture, and identity
    b. Awareness of the sociopolitical dimensions of language use and language education
    c. Value for linguistic diversity
    d. Inclination to advocate for EL students
3. Knowledge and Skills of Linguistically Responsive Teachers
    a. Learning about EL students' language backgrounds, experiences, and proficiencies
    b. Identifying the language demands of classroom tasks
    c. Applying key principles of second language learning
        i. Conversational language proficiency is fundamentally different from academic language proficiency.
        ii. ELLs need comprehensible input just beyond their current level of proficiency.
        iii. Social interaction for authentic communicative purposes fosters EL learning.
        iv. Skills and concepts learned in the first language transfer to the second language.
        v. Anxiety about performing in a second language can interfere with learning.
    d. Scaffolding instruction to promote EL students' learning. (Lucas & Villegas, 2011: 57)

Courses that have been developed to span this range of information tend to include what is perceived as basic, need-to-know second language acquisition theory, such as Cummin's (1979, 1980a, 1980b, 1992, 1996) social language/academic language distinctions, Krashen's (1979, 1981, 1982, 1985a, 1985b) Comprehensible Input Hypothesis, Long's (1981, 1983) Interaction Model and Vygotsky's sociocultural theory and instructional conversation (Vygotsky, 1986; Wertsch, 1985). Most courses gloss over or avoid grappling with the more detailed concepts of interlanguage, communicative competence(ies), memory, optimal social distance, personality or sociocultural variables. Téllez (2005: 1) suggests teachers of ELs minimally need '...a strong understanding of language acquisition and the concept of communicative competence and know how language function forms the basis for EL instruction'.

Coursework tends to focus the instruction on learner-centred, interactive methodology in which the teacher serves as a facilitator for information in courses, providing essential content information in clear, concise and visually supportive chunks and allowing students to practice the language while engaging in content tasks.

As for the assessment piece, this area is the least emphasised when trying to reduce the vast amount of information required of a TESOL specialist licensure into a single quintessential EL inclusion course. General educators are typically taught to modify tests with clear, learner-friendly directions, questions and prompts, provide visuals to support the texts and offer ELs state-sanctioned accommodations. They are often encouraged to gather multiple sources of assessment data from ELs, so learners can demonstrate their understanding in a variety of ways using performance and alternative assessments.

One can see the wide array of knowledge, performance and dispositional competencies needed by general educators. Even the evaluative framework employed through this text could also be honed and adapted to further define essential competencies. This is clearly an area open to debate.

Without a field-sanctioned framework for EL inclusion, texts, such as the SIOP, CALLA and SDAIE texts, are often used to span this range of competencies in order to prepare teachers for EL inclusion. The weakness of employing one text over the other is that it promotes only the CBI/EL inclusion model without addressing its areas of weakness or offering a comparative viewpoint. Cognisant of this fact, the textbooks by Richard-Amato and Snow (2004) and Díaz-Rico (2012) for general educators overview this span of information.

## Why In-Service Teacher Preparation in EL Inclusion?

Study after study report the under-preparation of pre-service teachers needing to be remedied by in-service training (Gándara et al., 2005; Li & Protacio, 2010; Reeves, 2006). For example, in 2002, the National Center for Education Statistics (2002) noted that, '41 percent of teachers in the U.S have taught ELLs, while less than 13 percent of U.S. teachers have received any training or professional development on teaching these students' (as seen in Antunez, 2002). Gándara et al. (2005: 13) echoed this information, 'only half of the new teachers in the sample, those required by law to participate in some EL-focused in-service as part of their induction and progress toward a credential, had done so'. Although educators bemoaned this gap in preparation, this pattern continued to be reported over the years; Arens et al. (2008) indicated a national average of 44% of general educators teach ELs whereas only 14% have had preparation to do so.

Some evidence has been reported that preparation initiatives are having a positive impact on the quantity of teachers prepared to include ELs (Platt et al., 2003; Tellez & Waxman, 2006). Educators such as Harper and de Jong (2009) remain concerned that the quality of the instruction of ELs is still lacking even if the numbers of educators with EL inclusive training has increased.

The awareness of educators' needs for EL inclusion preparation is growing. Continued efforts need to be made to convince opposing and entrenched teacher educators to modify their curriculum. The approaches to modifying the preparation of general educators to better include ELs still have a long way to go. One solution to help all teacher education programmes and personnel is to require coursework or competencies in pre-service preparation at the federal or state level. Finally, more thought and research needs to be given to appropriate EL inclusion. What does effective EL inclusion look like? What are the essential competencies? Without a clear target, many attempts will be mistake-prone.

# Conclusion

No easy answer exists as to which CBI/EL inclusion model to employ when including ELs into general education courses. Each model presented has the potential to meet learners' needs to varying degrees if the time, talent and conscientious implementation are present. Administrative support must also be present to ensure appropriate time, talent and implementation. Nonetheless, ELs are valuable individuals that schools must endeavour to reach and support. Collaboratively, educators must overcome existing obstacles to serve these learners well.

## Note

(1)   A stigmatised term because it implies a deficiency.

# Activities and Discussions

(1)   Rank which law is

  (a)   the most influential=
  (b)   the most detailed for ELs=
  (c)   the most helpful to ELs=

  These answers may differ. Why do you assign these rankings? How do these laws help educators advocate for ELs? What are the laws' weaknesses?

(2)   Discuss the demographics of your school district. Which programme type is presently being employed? (There may be several concurrently.) Which programme type would be the best for the district?

(3)   Based on Question 2, which CBI model for EL inclusion is the best for your district and why?

(4)   What do you wish you had in terms of pre-service preparation for EL inclusion? What is/was missing from your preparation? What do you think the programme did well?

(5)   Write an editorial to your local newspaper justifying a modification to EL programming and EL inclusion. How would you argue for the programme and model?

## Chapter Summary

- Demographics of EL populations such as time of arrival and age on arrival in an English-speaking context, background schooling and abilities in the first and second language were discussed in light of how they influence programme and model decision-making.

- Descriptions were offered of several types of ESL programming currently being employed. These ESL programme types were compared to EL demographics and needs as well as to CBI/EL inclusion models.

- US federal education laws relevant to the instruction of ELs were described. These laws require any educational entity receiving funds from the US government to take appropriate actions to overcome language barriers and teach grade-level academic content.

- A discussion of the best CBI/EL inclusion model was provided. All models have their strengths and weaknesses. It is incumbent upon educators to make the choices relevant to the local context and specific learners' needs.

- It is vital to have adequate administrative support and to implement models and programmes which have been shown to be effective in aiding learners to acquire English and learn grade-level academic information.

- Programme evaluation should occur on a continuous basis to establish to what degree ELs' language and academic needs are being met.

- An overview of the weaknesses of pre-service preparation and suggestions for essential content knowledge were provided. Teacher education programmes must be responsive to the changes in the learner populations in pre-K-12 schools and modify their curricula to meet pre-service (the future in-service) educators' needs.

# Appendix A: Bloom's Taxonomy

**Low to High**

- **Knowledge**
  - List Name Identify Show Define Recognise Recall State Visualise

- **Comprehension**
  - Summarise Explain Interpret Describe Compare Paraphrase Differentiate Demonstrate Classify

- **Application**
  - Solve Illustrate Calculate Use Interpret Relate Manipulate Apply Modify

- **Analysis**
  - Analyse Organise Deduce Contrast Compare Distinguish Discuss Plan Devise

- **Synthesis**
  - Design Hypothesise Support Schematise Write Report Justify

- **Evaluation**
  - Evaluate Choose Estimate Judge Defend Criticise

# Appendix B: Dolch Words

A basic sight vocabulary of 220 words, comprising all words, except nouns, common to the word list of the International Kindergarten Union, the Gates List and the Wheeler–Howell List

## CONJUNCTIONS
and
as
because
but
if
or

## PREPOSITIONS
about
after
at
by
down
for
from
in
into
of
on
over
to
under
*upon
with

## PRONOUNS
he
her
him
his
I

it
*its
me
my
*myself
our
she
that
their
them
these
they
this
*those
us
we
what
*which
who
you
your

## ADVERBS
again
*always
around
away
*before
far
fast
first
here
how

just
much
never
no
not
now
off
once
only
out
so
soon
then
there
today
*together
too
up
very
*well
when
where
why
yes

## ADJECTIVES
a
all
an
any
*best
*better
big

black
blue
both
brown
*clean
cold
*eight
every
*five
four
full
funny
good
green
hat
kiɪd
*light
little
long
many
new
old
one
*own
pretty
red
right
round
*seven
*six
small
some
ten

| the | VERBS | buy | do | fly |
| three | am | call | does | found |
| two | are | came | *done | gave |
| warm | ask | can | don't | get |
| white | ate | carry | draw | give |
| yellow | be | come | drink | go |
| | been | could | eat | *goes |
| | bring | cut | fall | going |
| | | did | find | |

## A BASIC SIGHT VOCABULARY 459

## VERBs-Cont.

| got | laugh | please | show | walk |
| grow | let | pull | sing | want |
| had | like | put | sit | was |
| has | live | rani | sleep | *wash |
| have | look | read | *start | went |
| help | made | ride | stop | were |
| hold | make | run | take | will |
| *hurt | may | said | tell | wish |
| is | must | saw | thank | work |
| jump | open | say | think | would |
| keep | *pick | see | *try | *write |
| know | play | shall | *use | |

*The 27 words marked with asterisks were included in only two of the lists.

# Appendix C: Example of a Unit with Differentiated Objectives for Content and Language

X in the matrix signifies that the learner will meet the standard without modification.

## ES 408: Unit Design Fall 2012

**Grade and proficiency levels:** Fourth grade, mainstream classroom (25 students) multilevel proficiency: five Spanish speakers (variety of levels); two Somali students (Level 1s); child with ADHD; child with dyslexia

**School name:** César Chavez Elementary

**Academic subject and unit theme:** Using Data to Predict/'Survivor: César Chavez Elementary Island'

**Content standards:** *Common Core Mathematics Standards 4th Grade*

**CCSS.Math.Content.4.MD.A.1** Know relative sizes of measurement units within one system of units including km, m, cm, lb, oz, l, ml, hr, min, sec.

**CCSS.Math.Content.4.MD.B.4** Solve problems involving the addition and subtraction of fractions by using information presented in line plots.

**CCSS.Math.Content.4.MD.A.2** Use the four operations to solve word problems involving distances, intervals of time, liquid volumes, masses of objects and money, including problems involving simple fractions or decimals, and problems that require expressing measurements given in a larger unit in terms of a smaller unit.

**CCSS.Math.Content.4.OA.B.4** Find all factor pairs for a whole number in the range 1–100. Recognise that a whole number is a multiple of each of its factors. Determine whether a given whole number in the range 1–100 is a multiple of a given one-digit number. Determine whether a given whole number in the range 1–100 is prime or composite.

# Language Standards:

## TESOL 2006 Standards

**Standard 1**: English language learners communicate for social, intercultural and instructional purposes within the school settings

**Standard 3:** English language learners communicate information, ideas and concepts necessary for academic success in the area of mathematics

## WIDA 2012 Amplified English Language Development Standards

**Standard 1:** Social and instructional language

**Standard 3:** The language of mathematics

**Complementary Strand:** The language of technology and engineering

# Unit Goals:
- To collect and interpret data through experiments and texts (listening and reading).
- To calculate the averages of data use to predict the outcome of similar data.
- To communicate and evaluate these predictions within a peer group.
- To explore different modes of measurement units using proper labels.
- To develop and practice the four modes (speaking, writing, listening, reading)+grammar, pronunciation and vocabulary within the content of mathematics.
- To develop the process of collecting, recording, displaying, synthesising and predicting data.

| Differentiated content standards | WIDA 1–2s | WIDA 3–4 | WIDA 5 | Struggling Readers | Gifted | SPED |
|---|---|---|---|---|---|---|
| *Students will be able to gather and record data in a table through various experiments and group cooperation (CCSS.Math.Content.4.MD.A.1, CCSS.Math.Content.4.MD.A.2, TESOL and WIDA Standard 1)* | X | X | X | X | X | Students will record data with assistance of a peer/aid |
| *Students will be able to generate factor trees to identify factors of a given integer (using visual aids) (CCSS.Math.Content.4.MD.A.2, CCSS.Math.Content.4.OA.B.4, TESOL and WIDA Standard 3)* | Students will divide smaller integers that only have two factors | Students will divide integers using a factor tree with a partner | X | X | Students will find factors of larger integers | Students will divide smaller integers that only have two factors |
| *Students will be able to design line plot graphs to display a data set of measurements using proper labels (CCSS. Math.Content.4.MD.A.1, CCSS. Math.Content.4.MD.B.4)* | Students will be given a pre-made graph to use and add points to graph | X | X | X | X | Students will be given a pre-made graph and must use add points to graph |
| *Students will be able to calculate the average and differentiate between the mean, median and mode (CCSS.Math. Content.4.OA.B.4, TESOL and WIDA Standard 3)* | Students will match the definitions and terms: mean/ median/mode to the calculated average | Student will be able calculate two of the three (mean, median or mode) | Student will be able to calculate all three and define in a graphic organiser | Student will be able to calculate all three and define in a graphic organiser | Students will use an increased data set to find the mean/ median and mode | |

| Standard / Objective | | | | | | |
|---|---|---|---|---|---|---|
| Students will be able to time and measure during peer activities and record data in a table using proper labels (CCSS.Math.Content.4.MD.A.1, TESOL and WIDA Standard 1, TESOL and WIDA Standard 3) | X | X | X | X | X | X |
| Students will be able to draw the line of best fit using a line plot and use this line to predict extensions beyond the data set (CCSS.Math.Content.4.MD.B.4) | Students will be able to draw the line of best fit and physically extend the line beyond the data to show predictions | Students will be able to draw the line of best fit orally describe predictions with a one or two sentence written prediction | Students will be able to draw the line of best fit and describe the predictions in a written format | Students will be able to draw the line of best fit and orally describe predictions with a one or two sentence written prediction | Students will draw lines of best fit on multiple graphs and compare/contrast data | Students will be able to draw the line of best fit and physically extend the line beyond the data and/or orally describe predictions |
| Students will be able to create the line of best fit using a line plot (using computer software) and use this line to predict extensions beyond the data (CCSS.Math.Content.4.MD.B.4, WIDA Complementary Strand) | Students will be able to use the computer to draw the line of best fit and physically extend the line beyond the data to show predictions | Students will be able to use the computer to draw the line of best fit orally describe predictions with a one or two sentence written prediction | Students will be able to use the computer to draw the line of best fit and describe the predictions in a written format | Students will be able to use the computer to draw the line of best fit and orally describe predictions with a one or two sentence written prediction | Students will use the computer to draw lines of best fit on multiple graphs and compare/contrast data | Students will be able to use the computer to draw the line of best fit and physically extend the line beyond the data and/or orally describe predictions |
| Differentiated language standards | | | | | | |
| Students will develop problem-solving techniques through collaboration with peers (TESOL and WIDA Standard 1) | X | X | X | X | X | X |

| Objective | | | | | | |
|---|---|---|---|---|---|---|
| Students will be able to listen to a text and extract key data (CCSS.Math.Content.4.MD.A.2, TESOL and WIDA Standard 1 TESOL and WIDA Standard 3) | Using a recording, students will listen to the text numerous times to highlight (using a highlighter) at least three key data points in with text support | Using a recording, students will listen to the text to write three key data points while reading the text | Students will listen to the text to write at least three key data points | Using a recording, students will listen to the text to write three key data points while reading the text | Students will use a more difficult text and rewrite text in their own words including the key data | Using a recording, students will listen to the text to write three key data points while reading the text |
| Students will be able to communicate patterns of data through speaking and writing using prepositions (TESOL and WIDA Standard 1 TESOL and WIDA Standard 3) | Oral: simple sentence descriptions using the prepositions up/down accompanied by gestures | Oral description and written sentences using the prepositions up/down/towards/beyond/below | Oral description and written sentences using the prepositions up/down/towards/beyond/below | Oral description and simple written sentences using the prepositions up/down/towards/beyond/below | | Oral description and simple written sentences using the prepositions up/down/towards/beyond/below |
| Students will discover patterns and create predictions using 'If clauses' (TESOL and WIDA Standard 1 TESOL and WIDA Standard 3) | Students will write simple 'If sentences': 'If x, then x'. Students will highlight the different parts of the clauses | Students will write simple 'If sentences': 'If x, then x'. Students will highlight the different parts of the clauses | Students will write compound 'If sentences': 'If x, then x' | Students will write simple 'If sentences': 'If x, then x'. Students will highlight the different parts of the clauses | Students will write compound 'If sentences': 'If x, then x'. Students will highlight the different parts of the clauses | Students will write simple 'If sentences': 'If x, then x'. Students will highlight the different parts of the clauses |
| Students will be able to summarise data orally and written (TESOL and WIDA Standard 1 TESOL and WIDA Standard 3) | Students will write two or three simple sentences to describe data | Students will write two or three sentences to describe data | Students will write a paragraph to describe data including predictions | Students will write two or three simple sentences to describe data | Students will write a paragraph to describe data including predictions | Students will write two or three simple sentences to describe data |

| | | | | | | |
|---|---|---|---|---|---|---|
| *Students will be able to differentiate the term 'average' in different contexts (social/academic) (TESOL and WIDA Standard 1 TESOL and WIDA Standard 3)* | While listening to the word used in a sentence, the student will point to the proper definition of average accompanied by graphics | While listening to the word used in a sentence, the student will point to the proper definition of average | The student will create their own sentences using 'average' in four different contexts (also creating graphics) | While listening to the word used in a sentence, the student will point to the proper definition of average | The student will create their own sentences using 'average' in four different contexts (also creating graphics) | The student will create their own sentences using 'average' in four different contexts (also creating graphics) |
| *Students will be able to read a text and extract key data (CCSS.Math.Content.4.MD.A.2, TESOL and WIDA Standard 3)* | Using a modified text, students will be able to extract and highlight (using a highlighter) at least three key data points | X | X | Using a modified text, students will be able to extract and highlight (using a highlighter) at least three key data points | Students will use a more difficult text and rewrite text in their own words including the key data | Using a modified text, students will be able to extract three key data points |
| **Learning strategies** | | | | | | |
| *Students will use the strategy of 'skimming' to find the main idea* | X | X | X | X | X | X |
| *Students will use the strategy of 'note-taking' while reading to highlight key points (CCSS.Math.Content.4.MD.A.2)* | Reading: Using a modified text, students will be able to extract and highlight (using a highlighter) at least three key data points | X | X | Reading: Using a modified text, students will be able to extract and highlight (using a highlighter) at least three key data points | Reading: Students will use a more difficult text and rewrite text in their own words including the key data | Reading: Using a modified text, students will be able to extract three key data points |

| | | | | | | |
|---|---|---|---|---|---|---|
| *Students will use the strategy of 'note-taking' while listening to highlight key points* | Using a recording, students will listen to the text numerous times to highlight (using a highlighter) at least three key data points with text support | Using a recording, students will listen to the text to write three key data points while reading the text | Students will listen to the text to write at least three key data points | Using a recording, students will listen to the text to write three key data points while reading the text | Students will use a more difficult text and rewrite text in their own words including the key data | Using a recording, students will listen to the text to write three key data points while reading the text |
| *Students will use the strategy 'make predictions' based on various data sets* | Students will orally state two or three predictions and include graphic representations of predictions | Students will orally state two or three predictions and write phrases to coordinate with the predictions | Students will orally present and write predictions using complete sentences | Students will orally state two or three predictions and write phrases to coordinate with the predictions | Students will orally present and write predictions using complete sentences | Students will orally state two or three predictions and write phrases to coordinate with the predictions |
| *Students will use the strategy of 'summarising' to describe various data* | Students will write two or three simple sentences to describe data | Students will write two or three sentences to describe data | Students will write a paragraph to describe data including predictions | Students will write two or three simple sentences to describe data | Students will write a paragraph to describe data including predictions | Students will orally state two or three simple sentences to describe data |

(1) Students will design their own (individual or in pairs) 'Survivor Challenge' where their peers will perform the experiment and the students will collect and record data.
(2) They will then construct a line of best fit, find the averages and synthesise the results in a creative format (including a written portion).
(3) Students will present these to their classmates in a 'science fair format'.

# Appendix D: Wisconsin Professional Development Plan Example

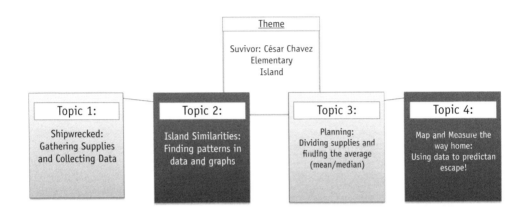

Theme

Suvivor: César Chavez
Elementary
Island

**Topic 1:**

Shipwrecked:
Gathering Supplies
and Collecting Data

**Topic 2:**

Island Similarities:
Finding patterns in
data and graphs

**Topic 3:**

Planning:
Dividing supplies and
finding the average
(mean/median)

**Topic 4:**

Map and Measure the
way home:
Using data to predictan
escape!

# Glossary

**Affective filter**: refers to the ways that anxiety, stress, tension, fear and inhibition create a potent barrier to processing and learning second languages.

**Asynchronous interaction**: communication occurring with time breaks of indeterminate duration, as opposed to synchronous interaction which is in real time. Example: an email exchange.

**Auditory processing**: the ability to mentally process incoming auditory or sound quickly and accurately during listening events.

**Bilingual programme**: programmes that teach academic subjects in two languages. There are two forms of bilingual programmes: one-way and two-way. One-way bilingual programmes are designed to teach a group of language learners who all speak the same first language, academic subjects while incrementally transitioning the learners to the second language. Two-way bilingual programmes are designed to teach two linguistically different groups of learners each other's languages while teaching academic subjects.

**CALLA**: Cognitive Academic Language Learning Approach, a model of content-based instruction for English learners.

**CARLA**: the Center for Advanced Research in Language Acquisition at the University of Minnesota is one of the US Department of Education's National Language Resource Centres, whose purpose is to promote research and effective practice in second language teaching and learning. http://carla.acad.umn.edu/index.html

**Circumlocution**: a language learning strategy used to 'talk around' or describe a word that the speaker either does not know or cannot recall.

**Class-based construction**: a phrase or word that is used only within a social class or differently within a social class. For example, stock can be cattle or it can be an investment in a company.

**CLiL**: Content and Language Integrated Learning model used primarily in Europe to teach second language learners academic subjects through a second or additional language.

**CoBaLLT**: Content-Based Language Learning through Technology is a model designed to teach foreign languages (in the US context) through academic subjects.

**Cognitive Theory**: Cognitive theory is concerned with the mental processes and processing involved in learning new information.

**Colloquial expressions**: expressions or phrases commonly used in informal conversation.

**Colloquial language**: informal language used in casual or familial situations, not necessarily slang.

**Communication strategies**: a variety of means that second language learners employ to overcome areas of weakness in their proficiency, grammatical or lexical knowledge. The use of strategies may aid the learner to avoid communication breakdown.

**Communicative competence**: the ability to use a second or additional language meaningfully to achieve one's communication objectives. Having a high enough level of language proficiency to communicate one's goals.

**Communicative competencies**: specific capabilities, or ability areas, needed to be communicatively competent: linguistic, discourse, sociocultural, strategic and organizational/actional.

**Comprehensible input**: incoming information to the listener or reader that is accessible and understandable; information that may have been modified so that the listener or reader is better able to comprehend it.

**Comprehension check**: questions asked by teachers to gauge learners' understanding of concepts.

**Connected discourse**: when ideas flow logically from one to the next through clear associations in the language used. Ideas are not disjointed or tangential.

**Content or content areas**: a shorthand version of academic content areas used to describe any academic subject that can be taught in schools. Most commonly employed to describe core content areas, such as math, language arts, literature, social studies, history and science(s).

**Content-based instruction**: an approach to the instruction of second languages that integrates academic content concepts and skills with language learning skills by employing materials from academic subjects to achieve on par with grade-level academic expectations and language proficiency development.

**Content objectives**: programme or lesson objectives in academic subject areas that describe what the students are to learn at the end of instruction in terms of grade-level standards for academic subjects (e.g. math, language arts, literature, social studies, history, science(s)). For example, students will be able to describe in writing the events leading up to World War I.

**Contextualised instruction**: providing enough background information in language activities so that students understand the context of the language use. The term is used in opposition to isolated instruction.

**Cooperative learning**: a widely employed technique of grouping students to work together on activities or tasks. For example, think-pair-share.

**CREDE**: Center for Research on Education, Diversity & Excellence is an organisation for research into teaching and learning second/foreign languages.

**Culturally congruent pedagogy**: teaching instruction that works in unison with the cultural pattern(s) of the learner(s) that can be contrasted with enforcing rules and methods that clash with cultural patterns.

**Curricular modification strategies**: the application of building or adapting curriculum and/or lessons to take into account the specific needs of English learners. Strategies include: incorporating explicit vocabulary instruction, sequencing activities differently, alternating deductive and inductive presentations of new material and including more interaction opportunities for learners to use the target language.

**Deductive presentation of new material**: delivering new material by providing the rule or topic and explaining it to the students, then allowing for practice of the rule in exercises.

**Dialect**: a variety of language used by a social or regional group, which is distinct from other versions within the same language family because of the different application of phonological, lexical and grammatical patterns.

**Discourse**: a term used to describe all spoken or written communication. It can include electronic communications as well.

**Discourse analysis**: a research tool used to understand the language patterns in use.

**Discourse markers**: also known as transition words or connectives, these words help readers to understand the connections or relationships between ideas in different sentences. Examples: although, then, next, therefore, however, rather, etc.

**Discursive**: the adjective form of discourse.

**ELL**: the term English learner (EL) or English language learner (ELL) refers to students who are learning English as a second or additional language.

**Enabling skills**: any skill a learner would need to accomplish a given task. For example, to write a passage on Chinese inventions, a student would need to be able to conjugate in the regular and irregular past tense (among many other abilities). The ability to conjugate in the regular and irregular past tense is an enabling skill for writing about the past.

**ESL**: English as a second language (ESL) describes the study of English when the individual speaks another native language or languages.

**Evaluative framework**: a structure underlying an organisation, text or concept used as an outline or guide to evaluate and describe something.

**Extended discourse**: a tract of spoken or written text longer than a sentence or short paragraph.

**Extralinguistic**: outside the boundaries of oral or written language, typically refers to non-verbal communication.

**Inductive presentation of new material**: delivering new material through discovery or inquiry techniques that allow students to discern the rule or pattern of instruction individually or with teams from a sample. The discovery or inquiry activity is then followed by a teacher-facilitated discussion in which students explain the rule or pattern. Teachers then reinforce the rule or pattern and provide practice activities.

**Input**: any incoming information to the listener or reader. Compare to **comprehensible input**.

**Instructional conversation**: individuals (i.e. novices) learn new information when they interact using instructional conversation with an expert; one technique for interacting with learners beyond the IRE/IRF pattern.

**Instructional strategies**: the ways (i.e. approaches, methods and techniques) teachers use to deliver lessons and engage learners. Instructional strategies in lessons include scaffolding information and questioning learners as well as ESL tasks and activities, such as ranking, jazz chants, TPR and values clarification.

**Interactional opportunities**: any type of activity that necessitates communication between two individuals.

**Interlocutors**: individuals involved in a conversation whether spoken or written.

**Isolated instruction**: exercises comprised of unrelated sentences that lack enough background information to make the language use applicable.

**L1**: an abbreviation for first language.

**L2**: an abbreviation for second language.

**Linguistic competence**: the knowledge of a linguistic concept, grammatical rule or pattern, such as the construction of the simple, regular past tense using –ed endings.

**Linguistic modifications**: adjustments in the rate of speech, the choice of vocabulary, pausing and the grammatical complexity of language employed by a speaker so as to make it more accessible to the non-native speaker of English.

**Literary allusions**: a device employed by writers to refer to a culturally shared concept, character, event or symbol in another text, which can be direct or indirect/implicit in nature. For example, 'Her choice of jobs was like choosing between Scylla and Charybdis', a reference to Homer's *Odyssey*.

**Output**: any language generated or produced in spoken or written form. Compare **input**.

**Participant structures**: grouping arrangements in classes. For example, whole class, small group, individual, pair work.

**Pedagogy**: a synonym for teaching or instruction.

**Post-structuralism**: a theory of literary criticism that critics the tenets of structuralism.

**Pre-teaching**: a strategy to present new information (e.g. concepts and vocabulary) to ELs prior to discussing the concepts in general education courses, so that ELs are more likely to understand, retain and build upon the information taught in the general education course. The ELs get to view the information more than once, which aids in comprehension and second language acquisition.

**Relative clause construction**: a clause linked to a main clause of the sentence by a word such as who, whom, which, that or whose. For example: The mail carrier in the truck is the one who used to always complain about the snow.

**RIGOR model**: Reading Instructional Goals for Older Readers (RIGOR) is a programme for literacy develop of non-native speakers who are older.

**RtI model**: Response to Intervention (RtI) model is as a three-tiered model of supports utilising academic and/or behavioural interventions for students with special needs.

**Schema**: the mental organisation of concepts that helps establish, arrange and interpret information.

**SDAIE**: Specially Designed Academic Instruction in English (SDAIE), a content-based instructional model for integrating language and content learning for English learners.

**Sight words**: are common vocabulary needed by emerging English readers to know and comprehend immediately upon recognition (aka Dolch words).

**Silent Period**: a hypothesised time frame during which non-native speakers of English choose to remain silent in order to acquire language and learn patterns prior to volunteering to contribute information.

**Structuralism**: a literary theory whose tenets assert that all literature incorporates patterned structures, such as genres, narratives, etc.

**Superstructuralist**: a theory that advocates a grander, more global structural position than structuralism advances.

**Synchronous interaction**: communication occurring in the same time frame/in real time, as opposed to asynchronous interaction which occurs with time breaks. Example: an in-person conversation.

**Target language**: the new language being acquired or learned by a student. Also known as the second or additional language.

**TPR**: Total Physical Response (TPR) is a technique in which teachers employ repetitions of verbal commands accompanied by corresponding actions to teach vocabulary and some grammar while students mimic the actions of the teacher.

**TPRS**: Total Physical Response Storytelling (TPR) is a technique similar to TPR in which teachers employ repetitions of verbal commands accompanied by corresponding actions while students mimic the actions of the teacher but do so utilising story formats.

**Values clarification**: a type of discussion task in which students share their values, beliefs and opinions on social, political and personal topics.

**Vernacular**: a dialect or language variety spoken by a social group in a particular country or region.

**Wait time**: the time a teacher provides a student to think about and process information to answer the teacher's question(s) or otherwise respond.

**White privilege**: a custom of societal allowances, typically unnoticed by white people, which favour them over people of colour in similar economic, sociocultural, education and political situations.

**Zone of Proximal Development** (ZPD): a concept articulated by Lev Vygotsky (1986) to describe a range of abilities for a particular student with the assistance of a more knowledgeable individual. The range is unique to the individual and is based on where he/she starts (i.e. actual level of development). The ceiling or the individual's personal potential, proximal level of development, is the individual's end point.

# References

Adams, M. and Jones, K.M. (2006) Unmasking the myths of structured English immersion: Why we still need bilingual educators, native language instruction, and incorporation of home culture. *The Radical Teacher* 75, 16–21. See http://www.jstor.org/stable/20710342 (retrieved 13 July 2014).

Adger, C.T., Snow, C.E. and Christian, D. (eds) (2002) *What Teachers Need to Know About Language*. McHenry, IL: Center for Applied Linguistics and Delta Systems.

Antunez, B. (2002) *The Preparation and Professional Development of Teachers of English Language Learners*. Washington, DC: ERIC Clearinghouse on Teaching and Teacher Education. (ERIC No. ED477724).

Arens, S.A., Foster, S.L. and Linder-VanBerschot, J. (2008) *Are Teachers in the Central Region Being Prepared to Teach Linguistically Diverse Students?* Denver, CO: Mid-continent Research for Education and Learning (McREL).

Arroyo, C. (2005) *The Funding Gap*. Washington, DC: The Education Trust.

Asher, J.J. (1969) The Total Physical Response approach to second language learning. *Modern Language Journal* 53 (1), 3–17.

Au, K.H. (1980) Participation structures in a reading lesson with Hawaiian children: Analysis of a culturally appropriate instructional event. *Anthropology & Education Quarterly* 11 (2), 91–115.

Aud, S., Hussar, W., Planty, M., Snyder, T., Bianco, K., Fox, M. and Drake, L. (2010) *The Condition of Education 2010 (NCES 2010-028)*. Washington, DC: National Center for Education Statistics, Institute of Education Sciences, US Department of Education.

August, D. and Hakuta, K. (1997) *Improving Schooling for Language Minority Children: A Research Agenda*. Washington, DC: National Academy Press.

August, D. and Shanahan, T. (2006) Executive summary. In D. August and T. Shanahan (eds) *Developing Literacy in Second-Language Learners: Report of the National Literacy Panel on Language Minority Children and Youth*. Mahwah, NJ: Lawrence Erlbaum.

Balderama, M.V. and Díaz-Rico, L.T. (2006) *Teaching Performance Expectations for Educating English Learners*. Boston, MA: Allyn and Bacon.

Ballantyne, K.G., Sanderman, A.R. and Levy, J. (2008) *Educating English Language Learners: Building Teacher Capacity. Volume III: State Requirements for Pre-Service Teachers of ELs*. Washington, DC: National Clearinghouse for English Language Acquisition. See http://www.ncela.us/files/uploads/3/EducatingELLsBuildingTeacherCapacityVol1.pdf (retrieved 10 July 2012).

Barkley, E.F. (2010) *Student Engagement Techniques: A Handbook for College Faculty*. San Francisco, CA: Jossey-Bass.

Barrett, D.W., Daly III, E.J., Jones, K.M. and Lentz Jr., F.E. (2004) Response to intervention: Empirically based special service decisions from single-case designs of increasing and decreasing intensity. *Journal of Special Education* 38 (2), 66–79.

Bartles, N. (ed.) (2005) *Applied Linguistics and Language Teacher Education*. New York: Springer.

Bateson, G. (1979) *Mind and Nature.* New York: E.P. Dutton.

Batt, E.G. (2008) Teachers' perceptions of ELL education: Potential solutions to overcome the greatest challenges. *Multicultural Education* 5 (3), 39–43.

Bennici, F. and Strang, W.E. (1995) *Special Issues Analysis Center, Annual Report, Year 3, Volume V: An Analysis of Language Minority and Limited English Proficient Students from NELS: 88.* Rockville, MD: Westat, Inc.

Bernier, A. (1997) The challenge of language and history terminology from the student optic. In D.M. Brinton and M.A. Snow (eds) *The Content-based Classroom* (pp. 95–103). White Plains, NY: Longman.

Berube, B. (2000) *Managing ESL Programs in Rural and Small Urban Schools.* Alexandria, VA: Teachers of English to Speakers of Other Languages.

Bialystok, E. (2011) Reshaping the mind: The benefits of bilingualism. *Canadian Journal of Experimental Psychology* 65 (4), 229–235.

Bialystok, E., Craik, F.I.M., Green, D.W. and Gollan, T.H. (2009) Bilingual minds. *Psychological Science in the Public Interest* 10 (3), 89–129.

Bialystok, E. and Feng, X. (2009) Language proficiency and executive control in proactive interference: Evidence from monolingual and bilingual children and adults. *Brain and Language* 109, 93–100.

Bialystok, E., Luk, G., Peets, K.F. and Yang, S. (2010) Receptive vocabulary differences in monolingual and bilingual children. *Bilingualism: Language and Cognition* 13, 525–531.

Bilingual Education Act, Pub. L. No. (90-247), 81 Stat. 816 (1968).

Bires, M., DeStefano, K. and Reynolds, M.K. (March, 2013) Content-based Instructional Strategies Employed by ESL and General Educators. Presentation at the TESOL Graduate Student Forum, 47th Annual Teaching English to Speakers of Other Language Conference, Dallas, TX.

Blaz, D. (2001) *A Collection of Performance Tasks and Rubrics: Foreign Languages.* New York: Eye on Education/Routledge.

Bloom, B.S. (1956) *Taxonomy of Educational Objectives: The Classification of Educational Goals. Handbook 1: Cognitive Domain.* New York: David McKay Company.

Brice, A., Miller, K. and Brice, R. (2006) Language in the English as a second language and general education classrooms: A tutorial. *Communication Disorders Quarterly* 27 (4), 240–247.

Brisk, M.E., Barnhardt, R., Herrera, S. and Rochon, R. (2002) Educators' Preparation for Cultural and Linguistic Diversity: A Call to Action. Washington, DC: American Association of Colleges of Teacher Education.

Brown, H.D. (2004) *Language Assessment.* New York: Pearson.

Brown, H.D. (2007a) *Principles of Language Learning and Teaching* (5th edn). New York: Pearson Education.

Brown, H.D. (2007b) *Teaching by Principles: An Interactive Approach to Language Pedagogy* (3rd edn). White Plains: Pearson ESL.

Buffum, A., Mattos, M. and Weber, C. (2009) *Pyramid Response to Intervention: RTI, Professional Learning Communities, and How to Respond When Students Don't Learn.* Bloomington, IN: Solution Tree.

Butler, F.A., Bailey, A.L., Stevens, R., Huang, B. and Lord, C. (December 2004) Academic English in Fifth-Grade Mathematics, Science and Social Studies Textbooks (CSE Report 642). Center for the Study of Evaluation (CSE), National Center for Research on Evaluation, Standards, and Student Testing (CRESST) Los Angeles, CA: University of California, Los Angeles.

Cajkler, W. and Hall, B. (2009) 'When they first come in what do you do?' English as an additional language and newly qualified teachers. *Language and Education* 23 (2), 153–170.

Calderón, M. (1986) *A Trainer of Trainers Model: Focus on Acquisition of Literacy by Limited English Proficient Students.* Report #GXX8410030. Washington, DC: Teaching English to Speakers of Other Languages.

Calderón, M.E. (2007a) *RIGOR! Reading Instructional Goals for Older Readers: Reading Program for 6th–12th students with Interrupted Formal Education.* New York: Benchmark Education.

Calderón, M.E. (2007b) *Teaching Reading to English Language Learners, Grades 6–12: A Framework for Improving Achievement in Content Areas.* Thousand Oaks, CA: Corwin/Sage.

Calderón, M.E. (2007, Spring) What do we mean by 'quality instruction' for adolescent English-language learners? *Voices in Urban Education* (VUE) 15, 29–36.

Calderón, M.E., Carreón, A., Cantú, J. and Minaya-Rowe, L. (2009, May) Expediting Comprehension for English Language Learners ExC-ELL. Presentation for New Jersey TESOL. See http://ms217goalsettingpd.wikispaces.com/file/view/NJTESOLworkshop_May_09.ppt (retrieved 6 August 2013).

Calderón, M.E., Slavin, R. and Sanchez, M. (2011) Effective instruction for English learners. *The Future of Children* 21 (1), 103–127.

California Department of Education (1993) A Report on Specially Designed Academic Instruction in English (SDAIE). Prepared by the work group of the Commission on Teacher Credentialing and the California Department of Education, Sacramento, CA.

Callahan, R., Wilkinson, L. and Muller, C. (2010) Academic achievement and course taking among language minority youth in U.S. schools: Effects of ESL placement. *Educational Evaluation and Policy Analysis* 32, 84–117.

Canale, M. (1983) From communicative competence to communicative language pedagogy. In J.C. Richards and R.W. Schmidt (eds) *Language and Communication* (pp. 2–27). New York: Longman.

Canale, M. and Swain, M. (1980) Theoretical bases of communicative approaches to second language teaching and testing. *Applied Linguistics* 1, 1-47.

Cardenas, J.A. (1976) *Lau Remedies Outlined.* Washington, DC: ERIC Clearinghouse. See http://www.eric.ed.gov/contentdelivery/servlet/ERICServlet?accno=ED125148 (retrieved 13 January 2014).

Cascio, C. (n.d.) What is foreshadowing in a story? See http://www.ehow.com/info_10027397_foreshadowing-story.html (retrieved June 2012).

Castañada vs. Pickard (1981) No. 79-2253. United States Court of Appeals, Fifth Circuit. Unit A. 648 F.2d 989; 1981 U.S. App. LEXIS 12063.

Castellano, J.A. and Díaz, E.I. (2002) *Reaching New Horizons: Gifted and Talented Education for Culturally and Linguistically Diverse Students.* Boston, MA: Allyn Bacon.

Cazden, C.B. (1988) *Classroom Discourse: The Language of Teaching and Learning.* Portsmouth, NH: Heinemann.

Cazden, C.B. (2001) *Classroom Discourse: The Language of Teaching and Learning* (2nd edn). Portsmouth, NH: Heinemann.

Celce-Murcia, M. (eds) (2001) *Teaching English as a Second or Foreign Language* (3rd edn). Boston, MA: Heinle & Heinle.

Celce-Murcia, M., Dornyei, Z. and Thurrell, S. (1995) Communicative competence: A pedagogically motivated model with content specifications. *Issues in Applied Linguistics* 6 (2), 5–35.

Center for Research on Education, Diversity & Excellence (CREDE) (2004) *Observing the Five Standards in Practice: Development and Application of the Standards Performance Continuum, Research Brief #11.* Washington, DC: Center for Research on Education, Diversity & Excellence (CREDE)/Center for Applied Linguistics (CAL).

Cenoz, J., Genesee, F. and Durk, G. (2013) Critical analysis of CLIL: Taking stock and looking forward. *Applied Linguistics* 1–21. doi:10.1093/applin/amt011

Chamot, A.U. (1995) Implementing the cognitive academic language learning approach: CALLA in Arlington, Virginia. *The Bilingual Research Journal* 19 (3&4), 379–394.

Chamot, A.U. (2007) Accelerating academic achievement of English language learners: A synthesis of five evaluations of the CALLA model. In J. Cummins and C. Davison (eds) *International Handbook of English Language Teaching* (pp. 317-331). New York: Springer.

Chamot, A.U. (2009) *The CALLA Handbook: Implementing the Cognitive Academic Language Learning Approach* (2nd edn). Boston, MA: Longman.

Chamot, A.U. and O'Malley, J.M. (1986) *A Cognitive Academic Language Learning Approach: An ESL Content-Based Curriculum.* Washington, DC: National Clearinghouse for Bilingual Education.

Chamot, A.U. and O'Malley, J.M. (1989) The cognitive academic language learning approach. In P. Rigg and V.G. Allen (eds) *When They Don't All Speak English: Integrating the ESL Students Into the Regular Classroom* (pp. 108–125). Urbana, IL: National Council of Teachers of English.

Chamot, A.U. and O'Malley, J.M. (1994) *The CALLA Handbook: Implementing the Cognitive Academic Language Learning Approach.* White Plains, NY: Addison Wesley Longman.

Chen, G. (2009) Inclusion or exclusion? The ESL education debate. *Public School Review.* See http://www.publicschoolreview.com/articles/95 (retrieved 25 November 2013).

Christie, J. (2012, April 26) More Lay-Offs for Massive California School District. See http://www.reuters.com/article/2012/04/26/us-economy-sandiego-layoffs-idUSBRE83P0IZ20120426 (accessed 6 July 2012).

Civil Rights Act of 1964 § 7, 42 U.S.C. § 2000e et seq (1964).

Cline, Z. and Nocochea, J. (2003) Specially designed academic instruction in English (SDAIE): More than just good instruction. *Multicultural Perspectives* 5 (1), 18–24.

Collier, C. (2010) *RTI for Diverse Learners: More Than 200 Instructional Interventions.* Thousand Oaks, CA: Sage.

Coyle, D., Hood, P. and Marsh, D. (2010) *CLIL: Content and Language Integrated Learning.* Cambridge: Cambridge University Press.

Crawford, J. (2004) *Educating English Learners: Language Diversity in the Classroom* (5th edn). Los Angeles, CA: Bilingual Educational Services.

Cummins, J. (1979) Cognitive academic language proficiency, linguistic interdependence, the optimum age question and some other matters. *Working Papers on Bilingualism* 19, 121–129.

Cummins, J. (1980a) The construct of language proficiency in bilingual education. In J.E. Ablates (ed.) *Current Issues in Bilingual Education* (pp. 81–104). Georgetown University Round Table on Languages and Linguistics, 1980. Washington, DC: Georgetown University Press.

Cummins, J. (1980b) The cross-lingual dimensions of language proficiency: Implications for bilingual education and the optional age issue. *TESOL Quarterly* 14 (2), 175–187.

Cummins, J. (1992) Language proficiency, bilingualism, and academic achievement. In P. Richard-Amato and T.A. Snow (eds) *Academic Success for English Language Learners: Strategies for K-12 Mainstream Teachers* (pp. 224–247). White Plains, NY: Longman.

Cummins, J. (1996) *Negotiating Identities: Education for Empowerment in a Diverse Society.* Ontario, CA: California Association for Bilingual Education.

Cushing Weigle, S. and Jensen, L. (1997) Issues in assessment for content-based instruction. In T.A. Snow and D.T. Brinton (eds) *The Content-Based Classroom: Perspectives on Integrating Language and Content* (pp. 200–212). New York: Longman.

Dahlman, A. and Hoffman, P. (2009) What to do with ELLs? Creating sustainable structures for serving English language learners in schools. *AASA Journal of Scholarship and Practice* 6 (1), 22–27.

Dalton-Puffer, C. (2007) Outcomes and processes in content and language integrated learning (CLIL): Current research from Europe. In W. Delanoy and L. Volkmann (eds) *Future Perspectives for English Language Teaching* (pp. 139–157). Heidelberg: Carl Winter.

de Koven, A. (2013, March) Subconsciously Held Bias: Exposing the Myth of Racial Colorblindness. Presentation at the TESOL International Association Convention in Dallas, TX.

Dewe, J.M. (2011, December) A guide for pre-service teachers in supporting middle school English language learners (ELLs) in general education classrooms. Unpublished MA thesis, State University of New York at Fredonia.

Deller, S. and Price, C. (2007) *Teaching Other Subjects Through English (CLIL).* Oxford: Oxford University Press.

Díaz-Rico, L.T. (2004) *Teaching English Learners: Strategies and Methods.* Boston, MA: Pearson.

Díaz-Rico, L.T. (2012) *A Course for Teaching English Learners* (2nd edn). Boston, MA: Pearson.

Díaz-Rico, L.T. (2014) *The Cross-Cultural, Language, and Academic Development Handbook. A Complete K-12 Reference Guide* (5th edn). Boston, MA: Pearson.

DiPerna, J.C. (2006) Academic enablers and student achievement: Implications for assessment and intervention services in the schools. *Psychology in the Schools* 43, 7–17.

Dolch, E.W. (1936) A basic sight vocabulary. *The Elementary School Journal* 36 (6), 456–460.

Doughty, C. and Pica, T. (1986) 'Information gap' tasks: Do they facilitate second language acquisition? *TESOL Quarterly* 20, 305–325.

Doughty, C. and Williams, J. (eds) (1998) *Focus on Form in Classroom.* New York: Cambridge University Press.

Duke, K. and Mabbott, A. (2001) An alternative model for novice-level elementary ESL education. ERIC Digest. (ERIC Reproduction service No. ED458807).

Echevarria, J. (2012) Sheltered instruction. In J.A. Banks (ed.) *Encyclopedia of Diversity in Education* (p. 1319). Thousand Oaks, CA: Sage Publications.

Echevarria, J. and Hasbrouck, J. (1999, July) *Response to intervention and English learners.* CREATE Brief. Center for Research on the Educational Achievement and Teaching of English Language Learners (CREATE), Washington, DC.

Echevarria, J., Vogt, M.E. and Short, D.J. (2004) *Making Content Comprehensible for English Language Learners: The SIOP Model* (2nd edn). New York: Pearson.

Echevarria, J. and Graves, A. (2005) Curriculum adaptations. In P. Richard-Amato and T.A. Snow (eds) *Academic Success for English Language Learners: Strategies for K-12 Mainstream Teachers* (pp. 224–247). White Plains, NY: Longman.

Echevarria, J., Short, D.J. and Power, K. (2006) School reform and standards-based education: A model for English-language learners. *Journal of Educational Research* 99 (4), 195–210.

Echevarria, J. and Short, D.J. (2010) Effective English literacy instruction for English learners. In California Department of Education (ed.). *Improving Education for English Learners: Research-Based Approaches* (pp. 264–272). Sacramento, CA: California Department of Education.

Echevarria, J. and Graves, A. (2011) *Sheltered Content Instruction: Teaching English Language Learners with Diverse Abilities* (4th edn). Boston, MA: Longman.

Elementary Secondary Education Act of 1965, 20 U.S.C. § 241 (1974).

Elfers, A.M., Stritikus, T., Percy Calaff, K., Von Esch, K.S., Lucero, A., Knapp, M.S. and Plecki, M.L. (2009) *Building Systems of Support for Classroom Teachers Working with Second Language Learners.* Seattle, WA: University of Washington.

Elizalde-Utnick, G. (2008) Using the response to intervention framework with English language learners. *Communique* 37 (3), 18–21.

Ellis, R. (2008, December) Principles of instructed second language acquisition. *CAL Digest.* Washington, DC: Center for Applied Linguistics. See http://www.cal.org/content/download/1553/16478/file/PrinciplesofInstructedSecondLanguageAcquisition.pdf (retrieved 21 May 2013).

Esparza Brown, J. and Sanford, A. (2011, March) *RTI for English Language Learners: Appropriately Using Screening and Progress Monitoring Tools to Improve Instructional Outcomes.* Washington, DC: US Department of Education, Office of Special Education Programs, National Center on Response to Intervention.

Eurydice (2005, November) Content and language integrated learning (CLiL) at school in Europe. Brussels: Eurydice.

Fearon, K. (2008) A team teaching approach to ESL: An evaluative case study. Master thesis. Retrieved from ProQuest Dissertations & Theses. (UMI No. 1456437). See http://gradworks.umi.com/1456437.pdf (retrieved 1 June 2011).

Folse, K.S. (2006) The effect of type of written exercise on L2 vocabulary retention. *TESOL Quarterly* 40 (2), 273–293.

Ford, D.Y. (2012) Culturally different students in special education: Looking backward to move forward. *Exceptional Children* 78 (4), 391–405.

Freeman, D. and Freeman, Y. (1995, January/February) SDAIE and ELD in the whole language. *California Association for Bilingual Education Newsletter* 18, 20–21.

Freeman, Y.S., Freeman, D.E. and Mercuri, S. (2002) *Closing the Achievement Gap: How to Reach Limited-Formal-Schooling and Long-Term English Learners.* Portsmouth, NH: Heinemann.

Fry, R. (2008) *The Role of Schools in the English Language Learner Achievement Gap.* Washington, DC: Pew Hispanic Center.

Fuchs, D. and Fuchs, S.L. (2006) Introduction to Response to Intervention: What, why, and how valid is it? *Reading Research Quarterly* 41 (4), 93–99.

Fuchs, D., Fuchs, L.S. and Vaughn, S. (2008) *Response to Intervention: A Framework for Reading Educators.* Newark, DE: International Reading Association.

Fuchs, L.S. and Fuchs, D. (2007) A model for implementing responsiveness to intervention. *Teaching Exceptional Children* 39 (5), 14–20.

Galland, P.A. (1995) An evaluation of the Cognitive Academic Language Learning Approach (CALLA) in the High Intensity Language Training (HILT) science program in Arlington Public Schools. Unpublished MA research paper, Georgetown University.

Gándara, P., Maxwell-Jolly, J. and Driscoll, A. (2005) *Listening to Teachers of English Learners.* Santa Cruz, CA: Center for the Future of Teaching and Learning.

Gándara, P. and Baca, G. (2008) NCLB and California's English language learners: The perfect storm. *Language Policy* 7, 201–216.

Garet, M.S., Porter, A.C., Desimone, L., Birman, B.F. and Yoon, K.S. (2001) What makes professional development effective? Results from a national sample of teachers. *American Educational Research Journal* 38, 915–945.

Genzuk, M. (2011) Specially designed academic instruction in English (SDAIE) for language minority students. Center for Multilingual, Multicultural Research Digital Papers Series. Center for Multilingual, Multicultural Research, University of Southern California. See http://www.usc.edu/dept/education/CMMR/DigitalPapers/SDAIE_Genzuk.pdf (retrieved 25 May 2013).

Gibbons, P. (2002) *Scaffolding Language, Scaffolding Learning: Teaching Second Language Learners in the Mainstream Classroom.* Portsmouth, NH: Heinemann.

Goldenberg, C. (1992–1993) Instructional conversations: Promoting comprehension through discussion. *The Reading Teacher* 46 (4), 316–326.

Grant, C.A. (1992) Educational research and teacher training for successfully teaching LEP students. In *Proceedings of the Second National Research Symposium on Limited English Proficient Student Issues: Focus on Evaluation and Measurement* (pp. 431–455). Washington, DC: United States Department of Education, Office of Bilingual Education and Minority Languages. Affairs.

Grosjean, F. (1985) Multilingualism and language norming. *Journal of Multilingual and Multicultural Development* 6, 467–477.

Gutiérrez, K., Baquedano-Lopez, P. and Asato, J. (2000) English for the children: The new literacy of the old world order, language policy and educational reform. *Bilingual Research Journal* 24 (1–2), 87–112.

Hamann, E.T. and Reeves, J. (2013) Interrupting the professional schism that allows less successful educational practices with ELLs to persist. *Theory into Practice* 52 (2), 81–88.

Harper, C. and Platt, E. (1998) Full inclusion for secondary school ESOL students: Some concerns from Florida. *TESOL Journal* 7 (5), 30–36.

Harper, C. and de Jong, E. (2004) Misconceptions about teaching English language learners. *Journal of Adolescent & Adult Literacy* 48 (2), 152–162.

Harper, C., Platt, E., Naranjo, C., Boynton, S., Ramanathan, V. and Morgan, B. (2007) Marching in unison: Florida ESL teachers and No Child Left Behind. *TESOL Quarterly* 41 (3), 642–651.

Hatch, E. (ed.) (1978) *Second Language Acquisition: A Book of Readings.* Rowley, MA: Newbury House.

Haynes, J. (2007). Getting started with English language learners: How educators can meet the challenge. Alexandria, VA: Association for Supervision and Curriculum Development.

Hilberg, R.S., Tharp, R.G. and DeGeest, L. (2000) The efficacy of CREDE's standards-based instruction in American Indian mathematics classes. *Equity and Excellence in Education* 33 (2), 32–39.

Hilberg, R.S., Doherty, R.W., Epallose, G. and Tharp, R.G. (2004) The Standards Performance Continuum: A performance-based measure of the standards for effective pedagogy. In H.C. Waxman, R.G. Tharp and R.S. Hilberg (eds) *Observational Research in U.S. Classrooms: New Approaches for Understanding Cultural and Linguistic Diversity* (pp. 48–71). Cambridge: Cambridge University Press.

Hoff, R. (2010, summer) *Reading Instructional Goals for Older Readers (RIGOR).* Academic Interventions for ELLs. Office of English Language Learners: New York Department of Education. See http://schools.nyc.gov/NR/rdonlyres/FC2D4E72-F26E-4101-B092-352570A2F8FB/86116/RIGOR_7_2010_FINAL1.pdf (retrieved on 21 May 2013).

Howard, M. (2009) *RTI From All Sides: What Every Teacher Needs To Know.* Portsmouth, NH: Heinemann.

Hughes, A. (1989) *Testing for Language Teachers.* New York: Cambridge University Press.

Hurtado, S. (2001) Linking diversity and educational purpose: How diversity affects the classroom environment and student development. In G. Orfield (ed.) *Diversity Challenged: Evidence on the Impact of Affirmative Action* (pp. 187–204). Cambridge, MA: Harvard Education Publishing Group.

Jimenez, E. (1992). Raising the achievement of English language learners through SDAIE. See http://setup19.finalweb.net/home/180011622/180011622/docs/raising%20achievement%20level.pdf (accessed on November 12, 2013).

Jimenez, E. (2005) *Raising the Achievement Level of English Language Learners Through SDAIE.* Upper Saddle River, NJ: Pearson Education.

Johansen, E.B. (1997) *SDAIE: A Philosophy, a Pedagogy, a Commitment to Students.* Brea, CA: Ballard & Tighe.

Johnson, E., Mellard, D.F., Fuchs, D. and McKnight, M.A. (2006) *Responsiveness to Intervention (RTI): How To Do It.* Lawrence, KS: National Research Center on Learning Disabilities.

Jurkovič, V. (2010) Effect of explicit language learning strategy instruction on language-test and self-assessment scores. *English Language Teaching* 3 (1), 16–27.

Kasper, G. and Kellerman, E. (1997) *Communication Strategies.* New York: Longman.

Klippel, F. (1998) *Keep Talking.* New York: Cambridge University Press.

Krashen, S. (1979) The Monitor Model for second language acquisition. In R. Gingras (ed.) *Second Language Acquisition and Foreign Language Teaching* (pp. 1–26). Arlington, VA: Center for Applied Linguistics.

Krashen, S. (1981) *Second Language Acquisition and Second Language Learning.* Oxford: Pergamon. See http://www.sdkrashen.com/content/books/sl_acquisition_and_learning.pdf (retrieved 3 October 2013).

Krashen, S. (1982) *Principles and Practice in Second Language Acquisition.* Oxford: Pergamon. See http://www.sdkrashen.com/content/books/principles_and_practice.pdf (retrieved 3 October 2010).

Krashen, S. (1985a) *The Input Hypothesis: Issues and Implications.* New York: Longman.

Krashen, S. (1985b) *Language Acquisition and Language Education.* New York: Longman.

Kumaravadivelu, B. (2001) Toward a postmethod pedagogy. *TESOL Quarterly* 35 (4), 537–560.

Larsen-Freeman, D. (2000) *Techniques and Principles in Language Teaching* (3rd edn). Oxford: Oxford University Press.

Larsen-Freeman, D. (2003) *Teaching Language: From Grammar to Grammaring.* Boston, MA: Thomson/Heinle.

Lau vs. Nichols, 414 U.S. 563 (1974).

Lau vs. San Francisco Unified School District, U.S.D.C., N.D. Cal., No. C 70-627 CW.

Law, B. and Eckes, M. (2010) *The More-Than-Just-Surviving Handbook: ESL for Every Classroom Teacher* (3rd edn). Winnipeg: Portage and Main Press (Peguis Publishers).

Li, G. and Protacio, M.S. (2010) Best practices in professional development for teachers of ELLs. In G. Li and P.A. Edwards (eds) *Best Practices in ELL Instruction* (pp. 353–380). New York: Guilford Press.

Lin, C.J., Wyatt, T.R. and Im, S. (eds) (2010) *Proceedings from the 34th Annual Pacific Circle Consortium Conference*: Assessing Teachers' Use of the CREDE Standards. The Effects of Coaching on Lesson Plans. Ashland, OR: Southern Oregon University.

Linan-Thompson, S. (2006) Response to intervention and EL learners: Questions and some answers. See http://www.ocmboces.org/tfiles/folder898/RTI%20%26%20ELL%20-%20Q%26A.pdf (accessed 18 August 2013).

Linan-Thompson, S. (2010) Response to instruction, English language learners and disproportionate representation: The role of assessment. *Psicothema* 22 (4), 970–974.

Linan-Thompson, S., Vaughn, S., Prater, K. and Cirino, P.T. (2006) The response to intervention of English language learners at risk for reading problems. *Journal of Learning Disabilities* 39 (5), 390–398.

Locke, G. (2005) *Functional English Grammar: An Introduction for Second Language Teachers*. New York: Cambridge.

Logan, R.K. (2007) *The Extended Mind: The Emergence Language, the Human Mind, and Culture*. Toronto: University of Toronto Press.

Long, M. (1981) Input, interaction and second language acquisition. *Annals of the New York Academy of Sciences* 379, 259–278.

Long, M. and Sato, C. (1983) Classroom foreigner talk discourse: Forms and functions of teachers' questions. In H. Selinger and M. Long (eds) *Classroom Oriented Research in Second Language Acquisition* (pp. 268–285). Rowley, MA: Newbury House.

Los Angeles Unified School District (2013) See http://notebook.lausd.net/portal/page?_pageid=33,1170728,33_1181823&_dad=ptl&_schema=PTL_EP (retrieved July 2013).

Lucas, T. (ed.) (2011) *Teacher Preparation for Linguistically Diverse Classrooms: A Resources for Teacher Educators*. New York: Routledge.

Lucas, T. and Villegas, A.M. (2010) The missing piece in teacher education: The preparation of linguistically responsive teachers. *The Yearbook of the National Society for the Study of Education* 109 (2), 297–318.

Lucas, T. and Villegas, A.M. (2011) A framework for preparing linguistically responsive teachers. In T. Lucas (ed.) *Teacher Preparation for Linguistically Diverse Classrooms: A Resources for Teacher Educators* (pp. 55–72). New York: Routledge.

Lucas, T. and Villegas, A.M. (2013) Preparing linguistically responsive teachers: Laying the foundation in preservice teacher education. *Theory into Practice* 52, 98–109.

Lynch, B. (1996) *Language Program Evaluation*. Cambridge: Cambridge University Press.

Madsen, H.S. (1983) *Techniques in Testing*. New York: Oxford University Press.

Maljers, A., Marsh, D. and Wolff, D. (eds) (2007) *Windows on CLiL: Content and Language Integrated Learning in the European Spotlight*. The Hague: European Platform for Dutch Education.

Marzano, R.J. (2007) *The Art and Science of Teaching: A Comprehensive Framework for Effective Instruction*. Alexandria, VA: Association of Supervision and Curriculum Development.

McBride, M. (2007) Effective teacher-directed on-going collaboration (TDOC) to achieve a high level of SIOP instruction: Creating an environment to engage English language learners. Doctoral dissertation. Retrieved from ProQuest Dissertations and Theses database. (Publication No. 3278296).

McClain, D. (2008, Jan. 3) The power of inclusion: Delavan-Darien puts English learners into mainstream. *Milwaukee Journal Sentinel*. See http://www.jsonline.com/news/education/29405674.html (retrieved 27 May 2012).

McGraner, K.L. and Saenz, L. (2009, September) *Preparing Teachers of English Language Learners*. Washington, DC: National Comprehensive Center for Teacher Quality.

McIntosh, A.S., Graves, A. and Gersten, R. (2007) The effects of Response to Intervention on literacy development in multiple-language settings. *Learning Disability Quarterly* 30 (3), 197–212.

Mehisto, P., Frigols, M.J. and Marsh, D. (2008) *Uncovering CLIL*. Oxford: Macmillan.

Menken, K. (2006) Teaching to the test: How No Child Left Behind impacts language policy, curriculum, and instruction for English language learners. *Bilingual Research Journal* 30 (2), 521–546.

Menz, W. (2009) Effectiveness of Ohio teacher education programs for meeting the educational needs of English language learners. Doctoral dissertation, University of Cincinnati.

Migliacci, N. and Verplaetse, L.S. (2008) Inclusive pedagogy in a mandate-driven climate. In L.S. Verplaetse and N. Migliacci (eds) *Inclusive Pedagogy for English Language Learners: A Handbook of Research-Informed Practices* (pp. 317–320). New York: Erlbaum.

Moll, L., Amanti, C., Neff, D. and Gonzalez, N. (1992) Funds of knowledge for teaching: Using a qualitative approach to connect homes to classrooms. *Theory to Practice* 31 (2), 132–141.

Murray, D.E. and Christison, M.A. (2011a) *What English Language Teachers Need to Know (Vol. I), Understanding Learning*. New York: Routledge.

Murray, D.E. and Christison, M.A. (2011b) *What English Language Teachers Need to Know (Vol. II), Facilitating Learning*. New York: Routledge.

National Center for Culturally Responsive Educational Systems (2005, Fall) Cultural considerations and challenges in response-to-intervention models: An NCCRESt position statement. See http://www.nccrest.org/PDFs/rti.pdf?v_document_name=Culturally%20Responsive%20RTI (accessed on 25 May 2012).

National Center for Education Statistics (2004) *The Condition of Education, 2002*. See http://nces.ed.gov/pubsearch/pubsinfo.asp?pubid=2002025 (accessed May 2012).

National Center for Education Statistics (2004) *The Condition of Education, 2004*. See http://nces.ed.gov/programs/coe (accessed 12 May 2012).

National Research Council (2010) *Preparing Teachers: Building Evidence for Sound Policy*. Committee on the Study of Teacher Education Programs in the United States, Center for Education. Division of Behavioral and Social Sciences and Education. Washington, DC: The National Academies Press.

National Standards for Foreign Language Education Project (1999) *Standards for Foreign Language Learning in the 21st Century*. Lawrence, KS: Allen Press, Inc.

Naves, T. (2009) Effective content and language integrated learning (CLiL) programmes. In Y. Ruiz de Zarobe and R.M.J. Catalan (eds) *Content and Language Integrated Learning: Evidence from Research in Europe* (pp. 22–40). Bristol: Multilingual Matters.

New York Immigration Coalition (2008) *Getting It Right: Ensuring a Quality Education for English Language Learners in New York*. NYIC Policy Brief. New York: New York Immigration Coalition.

No Child Left Behind (NCLB) Act of 2001, Pub. L. No. 107-110, § 115, Stat. 1425 (2002).

Nordmeyer, J. (2008) Delicate balance. *Journal of Staff Development* 29 (1), 34–40.

Nordmeyer, J. and Barduhn, S. (eds) (2010) *Integrating Language and Content*. Alexandria, VA: Teaching English to Speakers of Other Languages.

O'Brien, J. (2009) High school social studies teachers' attitudes toward English language learners. *Social Studies Research and Practice* 4 (2), 36–48. See http://www.socstrpr.org/files/Vol 4/Issue 2 - Summer, 2010/Research/4.2.3.pdf (accessed 16 November 2011).

O'Malley, J.M. and Chamot, A.U. (1990) *Learning Strategies in Second Language Acquisition*. New York: Cambridge.

O'Malley, J.M. and Valdez Pierce, L. (1996) *Authentic Assessment for English Language Learners: Practical Approaches for Teachers*. White Plains, NY: Addison-Wesley.

Office of Civil Rights, Memorandum. (1970) *Identification of discrimination and denial of services on the basis of national origin*. See http://www2.ed.gov/about/offices/list/ocr/docs/lau1970.html (accessed 16 June 2014).

Orosco, M.J. and Klinger, J. (2010) One school's implementation of RtI with English language learners: 'Referring into RTI'. *Journal of Learning Disabilities* 43 (3), 269–288.

Owen, W. (2012, April 20) Beaverton school district is facing big layoffs because it delayed cutting staff. *Oregon Live*. See http://www.oregonlive.com/beaverton/index.ssf/2012/04/beaverton_school_district_is_f.html (accessed 25 May 2012).

Oxford, R. (1990) *Language Learning Strategies: What Every Teacher Should Know*. Florence, KY: Heinle.

Patton, M.Q. (2008) *Utilization-Focused Evaluation*. Los Angeles, CA: Sage.

Pica, T. and Doughty, C. (1985a) Input and interaction in the communicative classroom: A comparison of teacher-fronted and group activities. In S. Gass and C. Madden (eds) *Input and Second Language Acquisition* (pp. 115–132). Rowley, MA: Newbury House.

Pica, T. and Doughty, C. (1985b) The role of group work in classroom second language acquisition. *Studies in Second Language Acquisition* 7, 233–248.

Pica, T., Doughty, C. and Young, R. (1986) Making input comprehensible: Do interactional modifications help? *International Review of Applied Linguistics* 72, 1–25.

Pica, T., Young, R. and Doughty, C. (1987) The impact of interaction on comprehension. *TESOL Quarterly* 21 (4), 737–758.

Pica, T., Kanagy, R. and Falodun, J. (1993) Choosing and using communication tasks for second language instruction and research. In G. Crookes and S.M. Gass (eds) *Tasks and Language Learning: Integrating Theory Into Practice* (pp. 9–34). Clevedon: Multilingual Matters.

Pica, T., Lincoln-Porter, F., Paninos, D. and Linnell, J. (1996) Language learners' interaction: How does it address the input, output, and feedback needs of L2 learners? *TESOL Quarterly* 30, 59–84.

Ramirez, E. (2007, November 12) Room to Improve. *U.S. News & World Report* 143 (17), 45–50.

Ray, S.L. (2011) Evaluation of a high school sheltered instruction observation protocol (SIOP) implementation. Doctoral dissertation. See http://digitalcommons.usu.edu/etd/848 (accessed 14 June 2013).

Reeves, J.R. (2006) Secondary teacher attitudes toward including English-language learners in mainstream classrooms. *Journal of Educational Research* 99 (3), 131–142. (ERIC No. EJ744225)

Reimer, J. (2008) Learning strategies and low-literacy Hmong adult students. *MinneWITESOL Journal* 25. See http://minnetesol.org/journal/vol25_html_pages/6_Reimer.htm (accessed 18 January 2014).

Reynolds, K.M. and Gable, D.O. (2007) Getting Good or Getting By: Observations of CBI in Practice. Presentation at the Center for Advanced Research in Language Acquisition (CARLA) Fifth International Language Teacher Educator Conference, Minneapolis, MN.

Reynolds, K.M., Jiao, J., Nolin-Smith, K. and O'Brien, E. (2012) Teachers' perceptions of push-in and pull-out model effectiveness and learning outcomes. See http://tinyurl.com/nsplf8q (accessed 30 August 2012).

Reynolds, K.M., Bires, M. and de Stefano, K. (2014) The Meaning-Making Dance: Variety and Frequency of Instructional Strategies. Presentation at the 48th Annual TESOL International Association Convention, Portland, OR, 28 March 2014.

Richard-Amato, P. and Snow, T.A. (2004) Instructional strategies for K-12 mainstream teachers. In P.A. Richard-Amato and T.A. Snow (eds) *Academic Success for English language Learners: Strategies for K-12 Mainstream Teachers* (pp. 197–223). White Plains, NY: Longman.

Rinaldi, C. and Samson, J. (2008) English language learners and Response to Intervention: Referral considerations. *Teaching Exceptional Children* 40 (5), 6–14.

Rivera, R.L. and Mazak, C. (eds) (2010) Proceedings from Science Education in the 21st Century: Advantages, Pitfalls, and Future Trends. (Is that the name of the conference?) *Science content, language, strategy, and technology learning in a university-level ESL classroom*. Ft. Collins, CO: International Symposium and Alumni Association Meeting sponsored by the Japanese Society for the Promotion of Science (JSPS), co-sponsored by Colorado State University. http://academic.uprm.edu/~sbischoff/science_education/program_abstracts.pdf#page=19.

Rosa-Lugo, L.I., Rivera, E. and Rierson, T.K. (2010) The role of dynamic assessment within the response to intervention model in school-age English language learners. *Perspectives on School-Based Issues* 11, 99–106.

Sadek, C.S. (n.d.) Strategies used in SDAIE. See http://www.educationalquestions.com/qa24.htm (accessed 16 February 16 2013).

Saunders, W., O'Brien, G., Lennon, D. and McLean, J. (1999) *Successful Transition into Mainstream English: Effective Strategies for Studying Literature.* Santa Cruz, CA: Center for Research on Education, Diversity & Excellence, University of California.

Scarcella, R. (1990) *Teaching Language Minority Students in the Multicultural Classroom.* Upper Saddle River, NJ: Prentice Hall Regents.

Schleppegrell, M.J. (2004) *The Language of Schooling: A Functional Linguistics Perspective.* Mahwah, NJ: Lawrence Erlbaum.

Selinker, L. (1972) Interlanguage. *International Review of Applied Linguistics in Language Teaching* 10 (1–4), 209–232.

Shinonhara, R. (2012, May 15) Anchorage school district gives layoff notices to 55 employees. *Anchorage Daily News.* See http://www.adn.com/2012/05/15/2466416/school-district-delivers-layoff.html (accessed 6 July 2012).

Short, D.J. (1993) Assessing integrated language and content instruction. *TESOL Quarterly* 2 (7), 627–656.

Short, D.J. (1994) Expanding middle school horizons: Integrating language, culture, and social studies. *TESOL Quarterly* 28 (3), 581–608.

Short, D.J. (2002) Language learning in sheltered social studies classes. *TESOL Journal* 11 (1), 18–24.

Short, D.J. and Echevarria, J. (1999) *The Sheltered Instruction Observation Protocol: A Tool for Teacher–Researcher Collaboration and Professional Development.* Washington, DC: Center for Research on Education, Diversity & Excellence (CREDE)/Center for Applied Linguistics (CAL).

Short, D.J. and Boyson, B.A. (2003, December) Establishing an effective newcomer program. Center for Applied Linguistics. See http://www.cal.org/content/download/1535/16208/file/EstablishingAnEffectiveNewcomerProgram.pdf (accessed 14 June 2014).

Simons, L.M.B. (2008) Conversations about inclusion: Connecting mainstream and ESL. *MinneWITESOL Journal* 25. See http://minnetesol.org/journal/vol25_html_pages/16_Simons.htm (accessed 23 May 2012).

Smith, G.H. (2009) Learning English through interactive weblogs: Student experiences blogging in the secondary ESL classroom. Unpublished MA thesis, Brigham Young University.

Snow, M.A. and Brinton, D.T. (eds) (1997) *The Content-Based Classroom: Perspectives on Integrating Language and Content.* New York: Longman.

Snow, C. and Biancarosa, G. (2003) *Adolescent Literacy and the Achievement Gap: What Do We Know and Where Do We Go From Here?* New York: Carnegie Corporation of New York.

Sox, A.K. (2011) Teacher preparation for instructing middle school ELL students: A North Carolina Piedmont perspective. Doctoral dissertation, University of Arizona.

Stahl, S.A. (2005) Four problems with teaching word meanings (and what to do to make vocabulary an integral part of instruction). In E.H. Hiebert and M.L. Kamil (eds) *Teaching and Learning Vocabulary: Bringing Research to Practice* (pp. 95–116). Mahwah, NJ: Erlbaum.

Stasz, C. and Stecher, B.M. (2000) Teaching mathematics and language in reduced size and non-reduced size classrooms. *Education Evaluation and Policy Analysis* 22 (4), 313–329.

Stoller, F.L. and Grabe, W. (1997) A six-Ts approach to content-based instruction. In T.A. Snow and D.T. Brinton (eds) *The Content-Based Classroom: Perspectives on Integrating Language and Content* (pp. 78–103). New York: Longman.

Sun, J.W., Nam, J.E. and Vanderwood, M.L. (2010) English language learners (ELL) and response to intervention (RTI): Information for K-6 educators. In A. Canter, L.Z. Paige and S. Shaw (eds) *Helping Children at Home and School III* (p. S8H41). Bethesda, MA: National Association of School Psychologists.

Tagami, T. (2012) Dekalb school district approves layoffs. *Atlanta Journal-Constitution.* See http://www.ajc.com/news/dekalb/dekalb-school-district-approves-1466765.html (accessed 18 June 2012).

Tedick, D.J. and Cammarata, L. (2010) Implementing content-based instruction: The CoBaLLT framework and resource centers. In J.F. Davis (ed.) *World Language Teacher Education: Transitions and Challenges in the Twenty-First Century* (pp. 243–247). Charlotte, NC: Information Age Publisher.

Teemant, A., Bernhardt, E. and Rodríguez-Muños, M. (1997) Collaborating with content-area teachers: What we need to share. In T.A. Snow and D.T. Brinton (eds) *The Content-Based Classroom: Perspectives on Integrating Language and Content* (pp. 311–318). New York: Longman.

Téllez, K. (2005) Effective professional development programs for teachers of English language learners. Spotlight on Student Success, No. 803. The Laboratory for Student Success, the Mid-Atlantic Regional Educational Laboratory, Philadelphia, PA.

Téllez, K. and Waxman, H.C. (eds) (2006) *Preparing Quality Educators for English Language Learners: Research, Policies, and Practices.* Mahwah, NJ: Lawrence Erlbaum.

TESOL/NCATE (2009) *TESOL/NCATE Standards for P-12 Teacher Education Programs.* Alexandria, VA: TESOL.

Tharp, R.G. (2006) Four hundred years of evidence: Culture, pedagogy, and Native America. *Journal of American Indian Education* 45 (2), 6–23.

Tharp, R.G., Estrada, P., Dalton, S.S. and Yamauchi, L.A. (2000) *Teaching Transformed: Achieving Excellence, Fairness, Inclusion, and Harmony.* Boulder, CO: Westview.

Tharp, R.G., Doherty, R.W., Echevarria, J., Estrada, P., Goldenberg, C., Soleste Hilberg, R. and Saunders, W.M. (2003) Research Evidence: Five Standards for Effective Pedagogy and Student Outcomes. Technical Report No. G1, March 2003 (revised March 2004). CREDE, Berkeley, CA. See http://crede.berkeley.edu/research/crede/products/print/occreports/g1.html (accessed 10 November 2014).

Theoharis, G. and Causton-Theoharis, J.N. (2008) Oppressors or emancipators: Critical dispositions for preparing inclusive school leaders. *Equity and Excellence in Education* 41 (2), 230–246.

Thomas, W.P. (1992) County of Arlington (VA) ESEA Title VII Program: The Cognitive Academic Language Learning Approach (CALLA) Project for Mathematics, 1991–1992. Evaluation report submitted to the Office of Bilingual Education, US Department of Education.

Thompson, I. and Coble, S. (2013) *Languages in the U.S. Educational System.* About World Languages. See http://aboutworldlanguages.com/us-schools (accessed 26 May 2014).

Tinney, M.V. (2007) Using specifically designed academic instruction in English (SDAIE) online as a guide for design cross-cultural learning experiences. Doctoral dissertation. Retrieved from ProQuest Dissertations & Theses. (AAT 3279582). See http://gradworks.umi.com/32/79/3279582.html (accessed 9 October 2013).

Turner, J. (1997) Creating content-based language tests: Guidelines for teachers. In T.A. Snow and D.T. Brinton (eds) *The Content-Based Classroom: Perspectives on Integrating Language and Content* (pp. 187–200). New York: Longman.

Ur, P. (1995) *Grammar Practice Activities: A Practical Guide for Teachers.* New York: Cambridge University Press.

Valdez-Pierce, L. (2003) *Assessing English Language Learners.* Washington, DC: National Education Association.

Valli, L. and Buese, D. (2007) The changing roles of teachers in an era of high stakes accountability. *American Education Research Journal* 44 (3), 519–558.

Verplaetse, L.S. (1998) How content teachers interact with English language learners. *TESOL Journal* 7 (5), 24–28.

Vuckovic, G., Hayes, K. and Salazar, J. (January, 2005) *Evaluation of High Point, Year 1 Report.* Los Angeles Unified School District, Program Evaluation and Research Branch. Planning, Assessment and Research Division Publication No. 236. See http://notebook.lausd.net/pls/ptl/docs/page/ca_lausd/fldr_organizations/committee_main/committee_curr_instruct/committee_curr_instruct_agenda/item%201%20(c)22401.pdf (accessed 13 May 2011).

Vygotsky, L. (1986) *Thought and Language.* A. Kozulin (ed., trans.). Cambridge, MA: MIT Press.

Walker, A., Shafer, J. and Iiams, M. (2004) 'Not in my classroom': Teacher attitudes towards English language learners in the mainstream classroom. *NABE Journal of Research and Practice* 2 (1), 130–160.

Walqui, A. (1991) *Sheltered instruction: Doing it right.* MS. San Diego, CA: San Diego County Office of Education.

Walqui, A., Koelsch, N., Hamburger, L., Gaarder, D., Insaurralde, A., Schmida, M. and Weiss, S. (2010) What are we doing to middle school English learners? Findings and recommendations for change from a study of California EL programs (Research Report) San Francisco, WestEd.

Wassell, B.A., Hawrylak, M.F. and LaVan, S.K. (2010) Examining the structures that impact English language learners' agency in urban high schools: Resources and roadblocks in the classroom. *Education and Urban Society* 42 (5), 599–619.

Wertsch, J. (1985) *Vygotsky and the Social Formation of the Mind.* Cambridge, MA: Harvard University Press.

Westbrook, J.T. (2009) Combating the Matthew Effect for English language learners: Making thinking visible in the secondary English classroom. Unpublished dissertation thesis, University of South Africa. See http://hdl.handle.net/10500/2872 (accessed 12 January 2014).

WIDA Consortium (2007) *WIDA ELP Standards and Resource Guide, 2007 Edition, PreKindergarten–Grade 12* (Resource Guide. RG-45). Madison, WI: WIDA.

WIDA Consortium (2012) *2012 Amplification of the ELD Standards, Kindergarten–Grade 12.* Madison, WI: WIDA.

Wiggins, G. and McTighe, J. (2005) *Understanding by Design* (2nd edn). Upper Saddle River, NJ/Alexandria, VA: Pearson/Association for Supervision & Curriculum Development.

Wilcox Peterson, P. (1997) Knowledge, skills, and attitudes in teacher preparation for content-based instruction. In T.A. Snow and D. T. Brinton (eds) *The Content-Based Classroom: Perspectives on Integrating Language and Content* (pp. 158–174). New York: Longman.

Wilde, J. (2010) Guidelines for professional development: An overview. In C.J. Casteel and K.G. Ballantyne (eds) *Professional Development in Action: Improving Teaching for English Learners* (pp. 5–10). Washington, DC: National Clearinghouse for English Language Acquisition. See http://www.ncela.gwu.edu/files/uploads/3/PD_in_Action.pdf (accessed 20 July, 2012).

Wolfe, D. (November, 2007) *Some Educational and Methodological Principles of Content and Language Integrated Learning (CLIL).* Goethe Institute. See http://www.goethe.de/ges/spa/dos/ifs/met/en2747826.htm (accessed 26 May 2014).

Wong-Fillmore, L. and Snow, C.E. (2002) What teachers need to know about language. In A.T. Adger, D.T. Snow and D. Christian (eds) *What Teachers Need to Know About Language* (pp. 7–54). Washington, DC: Center for Applied Linguistics.

Xu, S.H. (2011) Exploring diversity issues in teacher education. *Reading Online* 5(1), 1–17.

Yoon, B. (2008, June) Uninvited guests: The influence of teachers' roles and pedagogies on the positioning of English language learners in the regular classroom. *American Education Research Journal* 45 (2), 495–522.

# Index